❧ REPUBLIC OF LETTERS ❧

REPUBLIC OF LETTERS

🕇

*The American Intellectual
Community, 1776–1865*

Gilman M. Ostrander

Madison House Publishers

Madison, Wisconsin

Ostrander, Gilman M.
Republic of Letters
The American Intellectual Community, 1776–1865

LIBRARY OF CONGRESS CATALOGING-IN-PUBLICATION DATA

Ostrander, Gilman Marston, 1923–1986
Republic of Letters : the American Intellectual Community, 1776–1865
/ by Gilman M. Ostrander.
p. cm.
Includes bibliographical references and index.
ISBN 0-945612-63-x (cloth : alk. paper)
ISBN 0-945612-69-9 (pbk. : alk. paper)
1. American literature—1783–1850—History and criticism.
2. American literature—Revolutionary period, 1775–1783—History
and criticism. 3. United States—History—Revolution, 1775–1783—
Literature and the revolution. 4. American literature—19th century—
History and criticism. 5. United States—Intellectual life—18th century.
6. United States—Intellectual life—1783–1865. I. Title.
PS208.O88 1999
810.9′002—dc21 98-37077

Printed in the United States of America on acid-free paper.

Published by
Madison House Publishers, Inc.
P.O. Box 3100, Madison, Wisconsin 53704
www.madisonhousebooks.com

FIRST EDITION

❧ CONTENTS ❧

⊰ FOREWORD ⊱

WHEN MY FRIEND AND COLLEAGUE Gilman Ostrander died in 1986, *Republic of Letters* was still a manuscript in search of a publisher. Two university presses had turned it down after lengthy review. The book, they said, was literate, urbane, readable, eminently publishable, but perhaps better as a trade book. University presses were meant to be publishers of last resort for academic monographs, and this was certainly no academic monograph. When, as Ostrander's literary executor, I got the same reactions from two more university presses, I took their advice and began approaching trade houses. The trade houses, however, were not interested in a posthumous publication. One trade editor told me, with brutal candor, that a dead author was a non-starter. There were no follow-on contracts, no prospects of more to come, no book-signing tours. They saw no marketing niche for such a book.

Paradoxically, the lack of an easily identifiable niche—the quality more than any other that has made *Republic of Letters* a tough sell to publishers —is one of the very qualities that makes it so worthy of publication, now just as much as when it was written over thirteen years ago.

During the decade or so before Ostrander wrote *Republic of Letters,* the field of American Intellectual History was in ferment. As Ostrander points out in the introductory chapter, American Intellectual History traditionally had to a considerable degree concerned itself with "Minds": The Mind of the South, The New England Mind, and of course The American Mind. There were other words that cropped up in the titles of books and articles, words such as temperament, disposition, political culture, political economy; all similarly meant to denote characteristics that could be traced in collective behavior and in characteristic expressions, including the expressions in the canon of American literature. But the traditional descriptions and methods of American Intellectual History increasingly were coming under attack, often from the perspective of self-described victim cultures and excluded cultures. An emerging women's history, gay history, Native American history, Black history, Chicano history gave the lie to any conception of unified or central "minds." From another quarter, the assault on canons, on Great Books, on 'texts' themselves, often entailed the claim that an intellectual history in the older sense could only be the masqueraded ideology of entrenched social and economic interests.

To read *Republic of Letters* against this backdrop is to experience something of a shock. While asserting from the beginning that an intellectual interpretation of leading episodes in American History might be more persuasive than economic ones, Ostrander never posits any sort of general mind lying behind these intellectual preoccupations. Nor does he engage in the History of Ideas, which is an account of the progress of particular notions and concepts, independent of the minds infected by them. Much less is he interested in the criticism of particular works of literature, or in the relationships, genealogical or other, of texts to one another.

Instead, he explores a question central to the issues raised in the cultural wars, yet rarely directly discussed: how intellectual elites are formed in a particular period of history. Both the masters of the old paradigm and their many critics take the existence of these elites as given. The first group embraces elites as the most sophisticated articulators of the general mind of the age (or nation, or region). The second group, being distinctly anti-elitist in nature, finds elites to be of equal, if different, historical significance. What elites do, according to the revisionists, is to create in their own interest the schools and canons and idealizations and rationalizations of power against which the inarticulate and the excluded must struggle.

What Ostrander demonstrates effectively in this book, without having to say it in so many words, is that the question of the relationship of intellectual elites to the world around them cannot be begged in terms of an ideology, but must be specified from the evidence. Not all elites are born equal, or out of the same material and social opportunities. By tracing the rise of a national intellectual elite, for example, to the conditions presented by the American Revolution, to the nature of eighteenth-century educational institutions, and the reading that was available in those institutions, we have a sense of how and why these elites were constituted, and what their relationship was to the power structures of that world. As in all good history, this sense of distance from ourselves is not achieved merely for antiquarian effect, but amounts to an astute criticism of the drift of our culture.

In spite of the fact that it is not overtly polemical (the tone is so even, the sense of enjoyment in narrative telling so palpable, it is easy to miss the edge and freshness of much of what is being said), I believe *Republic of Letters* will be read, along with the writings of such critics as Christopher Lasch, as an argument for a new order of politics, in which high educational standards and literary and intellectual distinction are reconciled with populist traditions of justice and equality. It is, in short, in an unforced and undogmatic way, a cogently-made case for elites, for canons and hierarchies, and for communities of critics and readers.

Gilman Marston Ostrander was born in California in 1923. His ancestors were merchants and professional men from New England, and he would have been at least part-heir to a San Diego mercantile fortune if it had not more or less evaporated before it reached his generation. His college education, which began at Swarthmore, was interrupted by World War II. He continued his studies at Columbia University after the war, and attended the lectures of, among others, Joseph Wood Krutch. He explained to me once that, from that time on, he had thought that writing and lecturing on American Literature was the grandest thing that a person could do, and the only ambition worth having, but that he knew he was not good enough for that, and so he settled for American History, which seemed not so demanding.

Ostrander took up graduate study in Colonial Economic History at the University of California at Berkeley under Lawrence Harper. Harper was, although a courtly man, notoriously difficult as a thesis advisor. Perhaps because he had once been an accountant, he was simply incapable of letting anything go. Ostrander credited this circumstance with making him a fast typist. His method was to wear Harper down. Each time Harper objected to something in the latest draft, he would dash down to the basement of the building where Harper had his office and type a new one.

Whether his graduate research on the Molasses Act and on the so-called "triangular trade" (which he was one of the first to debunk) was quite the best use of his talents, Ostrander brought to these subjects, as he did to everything he subsequently wrote, his own highly individual, ironical perspective. All his works are marked by a keen eye for the telling detail, for the good story that turns out to be not only funny, or odd, but a key to important insights.

There is such a moment in *America in the First Machine Age,* in the discussion of twenties hemlines and the flapper costume, in which he notices that these were simply the clothes this generation of women had worn as children, the first generation of children to be dressed differently from adults, a perception that turns out to be more revelatory than one would have supposed, and, like much in that book, ahead of its time in stressing the experiences of cohorts in shaping revolutions. Again, in *Republic of Letters* he notices that bachelors were as thick in literary New York as spinsters in New England, and weaves out of this curious fact a serious and shrewd account of difference in artistic communities and urban cultures, the importance of the particular and the local, and the significance of personality.

No doubt had Ostrander written exclusively in one of the many subjects he touched upon, his reputation in the profession would be greater. He also would be more widely known had he adopted the jargons of revisionism in these subjects, and not so often been quietly in front of the profession. *The Rights of Man in America* amounted to an intellectual interpretation of the Revolution well before Bernard Bailyn and his students made it the prevailing interpretation. His *Nevada: The Great Rotten Borough* exemplified a "new" Western History in advance of general changes in writing about the region, and was by a writer not identified as a Western historian. *America in the First Machine Age* says many things about women that were advanced for their time, by a historian who was neither a feminist nor a writer of women's history, and was not seeking particularly to make his mark in these fields.

Ostrander never exploited his literary gift for irony in order to shock, or to demolish a prevailing view. He took up subjects because they interested him, and wrote ironically about them because it was in his nature to do so. He was, in private, a gifted raconteur and ironist. He had an ironic view of his career, of universities, and of the profession, as one might suppose from his account of how he became an historian.

His writing, and most especially *Republic of Letters,* on nearly every page tests our attention and intelligence. A turn of phrase, a choice of slightly off-centered anecdote, and we are expected to get the subtle judgment, the mix of deeply humane seriousness and ironic detachment. Everything Ostrander says about Emerson, for example—whose presence bestrides this book—reflects a conviction that greatness is an ironic blend of genius and moral obtuseness. Ostrander's prose requires a certain readerly grace, a tolerance for sustained irony that is perhaps the least developed of intellectual virtues in America. (Perhaps this explains why his *Concise History of the United States* was never a blockbuster at home, but sold extremely well in Swedish translation.) One of the larger ironies of Ostrander's writing in *Republic of Letters* is the way in which this deeply patriotic man, who could not have been anything other than an American, who spoke no language but English, and had little interest in European travel, writes with such assured detachment about American literary culture, often from the perspective of London, Edinburgh, or Weimar.

His own career he once described to me as a thing he had not had to tend or worry about: one writes a book, one moves to another job, and with the new job comes a promotion. The jobs to which he moved included stints at the History departments of Reed College, Ohio State University, the University of Missouri, Michigan State University, and the University of Missouri at St. Louis. He also spent a year in Japan as a Fulbright Scholar. His last academic tenure, and his longest, was at the University of Waterloo, where I came to know him. By this time, in the late seventies and early eighties, the free-wheeling days of movement in the profession were over, and Ostrander was, in some respects, stranded in Canada. At Waterloo he supervised Ph.D. students, was co-founder of an academic journal, and was a much respected colleague. But he was cut off from the intellectual culture and the professional mobility that had nurtured his talent.

It was in this atmosphere that he undertook the research and writing for *Republic of Letters.* While certainly not intended to be his "last" work, in retrospect it is fitting that it should be so. Having turned away from the study of American literature at Columbia in the 1940s, in *Republic of Letters* Ostrander at last came full circle to make a truly special contribution to that study. Due to the persistence of his family and to the vision of the publishers at Madison House, that contribution is now available both to admirers of Ostrander's other books and to a new generation of readers. No one would appreciate the irony of this publication more than Ostrander himself: it may have taken thirteen years, but his manuscript at last found a publisher that recognized its value.

S. K. Johannesen
University of Waterloo

✌ PREFACE ✌

WHILE MUCH HAS BEEN written about particular intellectual elites in American history from New England Puritans in the seventeenth century to New York Jews in the twentieth, little scholarly attention has been paid to the ongoing history of what Henry Adams called "the literary class of the United States," considered as a distinct community within the national democratic society. Adams, himself, surveyed this literary class in three of the famous introductory chapters to his *History of the United States,* separately considering "The Intellect of New England," "The Intellect of the Middle States," and "The Intellect of the Southern States" at the turn of the nineteenth century. The distinguished example that Adams set in this respect was not to be followed by subsequent intellectual historians however.[1]

As the academic discipline of American Intellectual History evolved along with the interdisciplinary field of American Studies during the 1930s and 1940s, a homogenized conception of the American democratic "Mind" emerged which ruled Adams's separate, elite "literary class" out of consideration. When founders of American Studies at Yale compiled their million-and-a-half-word anthology of *The American Mind* (1937), they stipulated that each selection be "representative of American thought" and also that it be "the best available statement" of that thought. The resulting volume included brief detours among the subliterate, including seven pages of folk songs and ballads to "express the moods and attitudes of otherwise inarticulate groups," but it mainly presented writings of the literary class of the United States which had evidently been vested with the authority to speak the mind of the nation as a whole. No space was allotted to representations of that mass culture which was Americanizing world culture.

Nor did the anthology consider ethnic variations from what was implicitly assumed to be the Anglo-American norm.

In theory, historians of the American Mind aimed to incorporate the national society as a whole into their concept. John Higham indicated the scope of their ambitions in a 1951 *American Historical Review* account of "The Rise of American Intellectual History" when he urged scholars to "explore more thoroughly the incidence and intensity of widespread, popular attitudes through a span of time long enough to show significant transitions" and to examine "such concepts as democracy, nationalism, industrialism, class consciousness, race prejudice, anti-intellectualism, and fundamental beliefs about God and nature," and to account for all of this in the grand synthesis of "the 'American mind.'"[2] In practice, however, literate representations prevailed over subliterary representations, and certain literary sources were rated more equal than others as expressions of the national Mind.

Leading spokesmen for this hypothetical Mind, such as Franklin, Adams, Jefferson, Emerson, Dewey, William James, and Henry Adams were not average Americans at all. As eminent intellectuals they were uncommon men, and to present them as representing the American Mind served falsely to intellectualize the national democratic mentality, while falsely democratizing the intellectual elite of which they were leading members. As intellectuals, they belonged to a select society within the predominantly nonintellectual nation at large, and they remained ever mindful of their membership in this exclusive society. Walt Whitman may have presented himself as Everyman in *Leaves of Grass,* but he distributed copies of his book, not to the man on the street, but to the poets and critics and editors of the literary community. Through these arbiters of literary opinion, Whitman sought to reach that anonymous serious-minded book-reading and book-buying public that existed throughout the nation, influencing literary culture by what it chose to support through its purchases in the literary line. This class of reading men and women has always constituted no more than a small fraction of the American public, judging by the sales of scholarly and literary books and magazines from the eighteenth century through the twentieth. *Republic of Letters* is an account of this "literary class of the United States"—the serious readers and especially writers—from Independence to the Civil War.

The term "literary class" may imply a greater degree of homogeneity than in fact existed in the provincial societies of antebellum America. Henry Adams pointed out that as of 1800, "In intellectual tastes, as in all else, the Union showed well-marked divisions between New England, New York, Pennsylvania, and the Southern States," necessitating those separate considerations of the "intellect" of each region in three separate chapters.[3] Nor did the experience of nationhood perceptibly diminish those provincial differences in the course of the next few generations, as James Russell Lowell indicated in his 1845 essay on Edgar Allan Poe. Lowell observed that American literature had no center; that Boston, New York, and Philadelphia "each has its literature almost more distinct than those of the different dialects of Germany," to which had recently been added Cincinnati in the West, with a literary dialect of its own.[4] Lowell's omission from this list of the Southern literary localities of Baltimore, Richmond, and Charleston in an essay about a Southern writer further illustrated the degree to which the spirit of parochialism remained abroad in mid-nineteenth-century literary America.

These idiosyncratic literary communities did share a common national experience, to be sure, beginning with their commonly shared English cultural heritage. From patriotically remembered common revolutionary origins, the literary class of the nation had together experienced the transition from Federal Republic to Democratic Republic. During this period of political transition, the Republic of Letters had tended to distance itself from the political Republic, philosopher-statesmen such as Franklin, Adams, and Jefferson being supplanted by professional politicians such as Van Buren and Thurlow Weed on the one hand and apolitical literati such as Emerson and Poe on the other. Intellectually, at the same time, the Republic of Letters underwent a transition from the scientifically oriented literary age of Franklin, Adams, and Jefferson to the belletristic age of Emerson and Poe. Throughout the period from the Revolution to the Civil War, meanwhile, the American liberal arts college remained the fundamental institution of the Literary Republic, continuing to educate the literary class of the nation by instilling in it a common fund of humane learning, which constituted the mental furnishing that was deemed appropriate to an enlightened gentleman of the Republic in particular and to a literary class generally.

In *Republic of Letters,* those experiences that the literary class of the United States shared in common are pursued in Chapter 1 on college training, in Chapter 3 on the transition from a scientific to a belletristic orientation in the literary community, and in Chapter 6 on the changing relationship of the literary community to politics in the Democratic Republic. The provincially oriented histories of regional literary communities are discussed in Chapter 2 on Philadelphia, chiefly during the late eighteenth century when it served as the metropolis of the new nation, in Chapter 4 on New York, chiefly from the rise of its literary reputation after the War of 1812 in the times of Irving, Cooper, and Bryant, and Chapter 5 on Boston, chiefly from the era of Emerson and his generation beginning in the 1830s. Chapter 7 concerns itself with the literary communities of the South from the 1820s; while Chapter 8 follows the slavery issue into the Civil War and the reconstruction—Bostonization—of the national literary class. The Epilogue records the founding of the Academy of Arts and Letters in 1904–09 by a literary gerontocracy of men who came of age on the eve of the Civil War, who maintained a genteel cultural continuity with the past through a half century of horrendous change thereafter, and who remained in a position to enshrine themselves in the culturally authoritative Academy at the end of their lives and at the close of the era of republican humanism that they represented.

❧REPUBLIC OF LETTERS☙

⇜ 1 ⇝

THE COLLEGIATE
ARISTOCRACY

ARGUING IN 1787 AGAINST ratification of the Constitution, Anti-Federalists charged the framers with creating a system designed to entrust authority to men of superior attainments and to deny the relatively unlettered and unpropertied common man equal influence. Opposing ratification in New York, Melancton Smith declared "that this government is so constituted that the representatives will generally be composed of the first class in the community, which I shall distinguish by the name of the *natural aristocracy* of the country." This class of gentlemen commanded a superior degree of respect in society, Smith explained, by virtue of their superior capacities. "Birth, education, talents, and wealth" serve to confer "distinctions among men as visible and of as much influence as titles, stars, and garters." Against such men "A substantial yeoman, of sense and discernment, will hardly ever be chosen," resulting in "a government of oppression" so far as the "middling class" was concerned.[1]

In the Massachusetts ratifying convention, Anti-Federalist Amos Singletary charged that "These lawyers, men of learning, and moneyed men, that talk so finely, and gloss over matters so smoothly, to make us poor illiterate people swallow down the pill, expect to get into Congress themselves . . . and then they will swallow up all us little folks like the great Leviathan."[2]

"Federal Farmer," the most successful Anti-Federalist pamphleteer, contributed to this line of argument a remarkably concrete estimate of the size of the superior social class in question. "In my idea of our natural aristocracy in the United States, I include about four or five thousand men; and among these I reckon those who have been placed in the offices of governors, or members of Congress, state senators generally, the principal officers of Congress, of the army and militia, the superior judges, the most eminent professional men, etc., and men of large property," as distinguished from "the natural democracy," including "in general the yeomanry, the subordinate officers, civil and military, the fishermen, mechanics and traders, many of the merchants, and professional people." The qualities that distinguish men of the natural aristocracy from those of the natural democracy, "Federal Farmer" explained, are "a high sense of honor" and the possession of "abilities, ambition, and general knowledge." Members of this elite had "associated together extensively" throughout the nation and were accustomed "to combining great objects."[3]

Many Anti-Federalists went on to oppose the Federalist government and the economic and foreign policies of Alexander Hamilton, but the Constitution itself came to be generally accepted—in time, to be reverenced, together with the natural aristocrats who had framed it. Accordingly, in 1913 Charles A. Beard rudely shocked gentlemanly and patriotic sensibilities by reviving certain of the old Anti-Federalist arguments in *An Economic Interpretation of the Constitution,* recasting them in the context of twentieth-century business civilization.

Leaving aside the eighteenth-century conception of a natural aristocracy of virtue and talent, Beard confined his attention to the material possessions of the fifty-five members of the Constitutional Convention. His famous list of the personalty held by each member demonstrated the evident, that in an age when politics was restricted to property holders, all of the founding fathers possessed property, including real property, and some of them owned large amounts of it. As to the striking educational qualifications and other intellectual attainments of the founders, which had so impressed John Fiske in *The Critical Period in American History* (1888), Beard ignored such data as irrelevant to an economic study. However, the case for an intellectual interpretation of the Constitution remains in some respects more compelling than the case for the economic interpretation.

Had Beard been able to argue a correlation between wealth and influence within the convention, his economic interpretation would have been more impressively sustained, but he did not attempt it. Robert Morris, the most monied man in the convention and the nation, contributed little to the proceedings, for instance; he served on no committees and spoke only twice. On the other hand, the bookish James Madison, who early emerged as the prime manager of the convention, possessed but a modest amount of property and no evident ambition to acquire substantially more. Madison's most effective associate manager, James Wilson, did covet great wealth but was struggling to avoid bankruptcy at the time of the convention. It was as men of highly regarded learnedness that Madison and Wilson acquired influence over an assembly of delegates, who esteemed talents over wealth in matters of state.[4]

The aggregate of higher education among the founding fathers was much more striking than their accumulations of property, for property was far more widely shared than higher education in the national community. Among the general population, approximately one man in a thousand had been to college. Inside Convention Hall, by enormous contrast, thirty-three or perhaps thirty-four of the fifty-five delegates were college men. Nor was intellectual distinction wanting among the remainder of delegates. The minority who had not attended college included the well tutored George Mason of Gunston Hall, mentor to a circle of younger colleagues that included Jefferson, Madison, Monroe, and Edmund Randolph. It included the distinguished classicist Charles Pinckney, of Charleston, whose plans to attend the Inns of Court in London had been upset by the Revolution. It included George Clymer, the founder and first president of the Academy of Fine Arts in Philadelphia; George Washington, LL.D., Harvard, 1776; and Benjamin Franklin, with honorary degrees from Harvard, Yale, Oxford, Cambridge, Edinburgh, Aberdeen, and elsewhere.[5]

Academically distinguished as the men of the Constitutional Convention may have been, they were no more elite a group intellectually than the continuing membership of the Continental Congress from 1774 to 1789. Indeed, a majority of the framers of the Constitution had served previously in the Congress. Intellectuals had led the Revolution from the outset; as constitutionalists in 1787, they intended to consolidate their authority in a somewhat more centralized system. Like Amos Singletary, the framers were concerned about the dangers of a leviathan government that would swallow up the liberties of the people, so they constructed a system of checks and balances designed to prevent excessive concentration of power. They trusted nobody—including themselves—with unchecked power, yet when all is said and done, they were the recognized ruling class of the nation, the natural aristocracy of virtue, talents, wealth, and learning.

Out of a colonial population of 2.5 million in 1776, the total number of college-educated men is estimated to have been 2,500.[6] Viewed in relation to the circumstances of colonial life, the size of this college population is impressive. It entailed the maintenance of eight small colleges, from Harvard in Massachusetts to William and Mary in Virginia, offering in the wilderness academic training that compared favorably with British university standards. It further entailed the expenses and difficulties of educating sons overseas in England and Scotland and on the European continent. Viewed in relation to the colonial population at large, on the other hand, the ratio of one to one thousand is a gaping one. Yet college men made up a majority of the signers of the Declaration of Independence as well as of the Constitution. How extensively the college requirement applied to the revolutionary ruling class as a whole may be gauged by a survey of delegates of the thirteen states to the Continental Congress between 1774 and 1789.

Of 358 delegates to Congress during that period, at least 163 and perhaps more had attended institutions of higher learning, while others had received classical training from private tutors or at private schools such as Francis Alison's in Pennsylvania and Nottingham in England. Overall, those who shared some classical training appear to have been in the majority. For the rest, educational preparation ranged widely, from bare literacy to the famous self-education of Benjamin Franklin.[7]

These men of academic learning were very unevenly distributed among the states, ranging from Massachusetts, with twenty college men out of twenty-four delegates, to Delaware, with but four out of eighteen. Massachusetts and Connecticut (with seventeen out of twenty-three delegates) were well in advance of the others, followed by Virginia (twenty-one of thirty-six), South Carolina (fourteen of twenty-eight), New Jersey (fifteen of thirty-six) and Maryland (seventeen of thirty-seven), to name those states which exceeded the national average of 45.5 percent. Pennsylvania, the world-renowned homeland of the Philadelphia Enlightenment as well as the original seat of the Continental Congress, fell well below the national average, returning but seventeen college men out of forty-six delegates. Even New York, the last capital under the Confederation, with a well-established reputation for money-minded anti-intellectualism, did better than that, returning fifteen college men out of thirty-five delegates. Those that ranked below Pennsylvania on this academic scale were Delaware, Rhode Island (with four out of eleven delegates), and the frontier states of New Hampshire (six of twenty-one), Georgia (six of twenty-two), and North Carolina (seven of twenty-six).

Philadelphia was acknowledged to be the cultural as well as the political center of the new republic, even by the men of Massachusetts, and the paucity of college men among its representatives reflected positive Quaker-inspired ideals of the Philadelphia Enlightenment. These ideals opposed the traditional, aristocratic, Anglo-Catholic conception of culture as academic tradition, inherited from the University of Paris by way of Oxford and Cambridge in England. Pennsylvanian Quakers supported modern learning, especially in the sciences, that might improve the circumstances of human life, but they generally opposed traditional learning as spiritually subversive at worst and as merely ornamental at best. Furthermore, enlightened Philadelphia radicals had fashioned the most democratic of the state constitutions, and the Pennsylvanian delegates as a whole represented this advanced state of Pennsylvanian democracy. Rhode Island and Delaware shared with Pennsylvania large Quaker constituencies, comparatively democratic constitutions, and correspondingly small contingents of college men in the Continental Congress.

Among the Pennsylvanian delegates, Franklin remained the unrivaled exemplar of the self-taught intellectual, but there was also William Henry, who began life as a gunsmith's apprentice and became a wealthy proprietor of his own gunworks, where he maintained a well-equipped laboratory for his scientific investigations. An active member of the American Philosophical Society and patron of Benjamin West and Robert Fulton, Henry appears to have been the first American to experiment extensively with steam power. Timothy Matlock and George Clymer were Philadelphia merchants without college educations who were prominent in Philosophical Society activities. Physicians enjoyed special esteem in Quaker circles, and eleven of the twenty-one practicing physicians to become delegates to the Continental Congress were from Pennsylvania and New Jersey. Some had received extensive higher education, as did Benjamin Rush, who earned a medical degree at Edinburgh following graduation from the College of Philadelphia (Pennsylvania). On the other hand, William Shippen, Sr., honored senior member of the Philadelphia medical fraternity and a founder of both the College of Philadelphia and the College of New Jersey (Princeton), was not himself college trained.

While Pennsylvania promulgated the independence of learnedness from college instruction, the frontier state of Georgia offered impressive examples among its congressmen of both college-bred and self-taught intellectuals. The colony was represented by Abraham Baldwin, the prize divinity student of Yale who had turned down the professorship of divinity at his alma mater to practice law and eventually become U.S. Senator from Georgia. Another Georgia representative was the Swiss gymnasium-trained immigrant John Zubly, whose learning earned him not only two honorary degrees from the College of New Jersey but also the reluctant admiration of John Adams.

Among the autodidacts representing Georgia was Edward Langworthy, the product of a Georgia orphanage school, who became a classics teacher at Baltimore Academy, publisher, newspaper editor, and author of an unpublished history of Georgia; Governor Edward Telfair, a Scottish immigrant who established the Telfair Academy of Arts and Science in Savannah; and Governor George Walton, a self-taught carpenter's apprentice who became founder of Richmond Academy, a trustee of the University of Georgia, and formulator of a program to promote higher education in the state. As a man of means, Walton built a suitable residence which he named College Hill. While the educational achievements of these self-made men advanced them as examples of the enlightened artisan-intellectual that epitomized the Philadelphia Enlightenment, their scholarly aspirations appear to have conformed to the traditional pattern of gentlemanly classicism of Harvard, Yale, and William and Mary.

The most polished and cosmopolitan of the delegates to the Continental Congress were those from the Chesapeake region and from Charleston. These delegates had studied at Eton and Westminster, Oxford and Cambridge, Edinburgh and Aberdeen, the Inns of Court in London, and in the case of Catholic members from Maryland, English House in Portugal and the College de St. Omer in Flanders. A prime example of the completely educated Southern gentleman was Arthur Lee of Virginia. Lee had studied at Eton, earned an M.D. degree at Edinburgh, and read law at two of the Inns of Court. John Adams conceded that "Particular gentlemen here, who have improved upon their education by travel, shine" and "in several particulars they have more wit than we," but that "in general, old Massachusetts outshines her younger sisters"[8] (by which he presumably intended to include the older sister, Virginia, as well). Members of the Southern gentry evidently came in time to share Adams's good opinion of Massachusetts learning, for the coming generations sent their sons north to be educated in increasing numbers. During the antebellum period the largest out-of-state enrollment at Harvard was from South Carolina.

The cosmopolitan educations of Southerners reflected a dearth of institutions for higher education at home—as well as a lack of dedicated interest in establishing them. The only colonial college south of Philadelphia was William and Mary, established in the 1690s, which did not offer a degree or expect four-year attendance. It was possible to receive an excellent education at William and Mary, as the example of its most distinguished product, Thomas Jefferson, indicates, but it was hardly necessary to do so. Proficiency in classical languages was an admissions requirement, and those who were admitted were expected to benefit generally from the experience of collegiate life, if not from classroom exercises, just as was the case with those sent abroad to attend English universities. Among the twenty-one college-educated Virginia delegates, twelve had attended William and Mary; some of these had studied abroad as well. Five had attended one of the Inns of Court in London, five had attended the University of Edinburgh, one had attended Cambridge University, and one—James Madison—had attended the College of New Jersey. Outside of the Virginia delegates, only one congressman, a Maryland representative, had attended the Virginia institution.

In Massachusetts, by contrast, nineteen of the twenty college-trained delegates to Congress had attended Harvard, the twentieth being a Yale man, Theodore Sedgwick. Founded in 1636, Harvard established itself as the seminary of choice for the New England ruling class. No other provincial college, including Yale, enjoyed this distinction. Harvard-trained congressmen hailed from throughout New England, including one from Rhode Island, two from Connecticut, and five from New Hampshire. But none hailed from any state south of New England. Yale demonstrated less dominance provincially but greater influence nationally. Among the sev-

enteen college-trained delegates from Connecticut, two were educated at
Princeton and thirteen at Yale. South of New England there were eight
Yale men among state delegates from New York, New Jersey, Pennsylvania, and Georgia. Yale tended, in particular, to be favored by members of
the New York gentry who disapproved of the Anglicanism of King's College (Columbia).

Judging by geographical breadth of congressional representation, the
College of New Jersey, founded in 1746, led the rest by a substantial margin, with alumni representing nine of the states. Of the fifteen college-
trained congressmen from New Jersey, nine had attended Princeton and
another, the Edinburgh M.A. John Witherspoon, was its president. Three
had attended the College of Philadelphia, and one had attended New
Jersey's second college, Queen's (Rutgers), founded in 1771. The College
of Philadelphia, founded in 1754, educated delegates from six states, including six congressmen from Pennsylvania. King's College, also founded
in 1754, educated the same number of delegates from New York, but none
outside the state. The remaining colonial college, the College of Rhode
Island (Brown), founded in 1764, like Queen's College (Rutgers), could claim
but a single representative to the Continental Congress, and that one had
previously been expelled from Harvard.

⁕ II ⁕

AMONG ALL THE FOUNDING FATHERS, John Adams offers the most conspicu-
ous example of a farm boy who, by attending Harvard, was plucked from
the obscurity that had characterized earlier generations of Adamses. When
Adams entered world history in 1774 as a member of the First Continental
Congress, it was because his father had determined that his son should
matriculate at Harvard, as one uncle had previously done. John himself
would have remained content to pursue the family occupation of farming, but he acceded to his father's wishes and accordingly became a gentleman (the Harvard degree entitled him to add *Esquire* to his name), a scholar,
and a member of the natural aristocracy. Adams's Harvard class of 1755
numbered twenty-four, and they joined the tiny cohort of Harvard men
who provided Massachusetts with its ministers, statesmen, and men of

letters. Adams had intended to train for the ministry, but upon graduation he elected to study law and become a man of affairs. He pursued his legal career with such success that in 1774 he was one of five Harvard men selected to represent Massachusetts as delegates to the Congress in Philadelphia.

As a Harvard-trained mandarin, Adams remained a firm believer in the college requirement for men of affairs, a standard that was not maintained in New York and Pennsylvania as it was in Massachusetts and Connecticut. That Benjamin Franklin and George Washington should have attained their exalted reputations as founders of the Republic despite their irregular educations remained a mystery to Adams, who could never accept them as the equals of Harvard men such as his hero, James Otis, and—for that matter—himself. Adams wrote his former law student William Tudor in 1817 that in the task of nation building, Franklin and Washington

> were often useful instruments in the hands of others; but, to my certain knowledge they were as often terrific embarrassments. They were both not only superficial but ignorant. Franklin's practical cunning united with his theoretic ignorance render him one of the most curious characters in history.[9]

What Franklin and Washington evidently lacked that disqualified them from authentic as opposed to reputed greatness, in Adams's opinion, was the college education that separated the learned from the unlearned. And it was through New England's maintenance of this requirement that the region's gentry manifested superiority over those "educated in the southward," Adams believed.[10]

It was true that the College of William and Mary in the South had not measured up to the standards of Harvard and Yale in New England. Southern colonial gentlemen apparently lacked the commitment of New Englanders to maintaining higher education for the service of their community. But so far as their own sons were concerned, Southern fathers placed the highest importance upon obtaining the best possible educations for them. It was chiefly Southerners who attended Eton, Oxford, Cambridge, and the Inns of Court. And when the English universities acquired an unfavorable reputation among Americans for moral and academic laxity, Virginians were the first to discover the Scottish universities, especially Edinburgh, where a Virginia Club was founded for the stream of students who arrived from the Old Dominion.

When Philip Fithian, College of New Jersey, class of 1772, became a tutor to the family of the baronial Virginia planter Robert Carter of Nomini Hall, he discovered to his surprise that his college degree conferred the status of gentleman upon him in that grand company. He found social rank in Virginia to be related blatantly to wealth, "excepting always," he added,

> the value they put upon posts of honor & mental acquirements—for example, if you should travel through this Colony, with a well-confirmed testimonial of your having finished with credit a course of studies at Nassau-Hall; you would be rated without any more questions asked, either about your family, your estate, your business, or your intention, at 10,000 pounds sterling; and you might come & go converse, & keep company according to this value.[11]

If a college education could turn a farm boy into a gentleman, why did not many more farm boys avail themselves of the opportunity to become men of learning and substance? To begin with, most American boys did not meet college entrance requirements, consisting mainly of proficiency in Latin and some Greek. In addition, college was not normally necessary for the achievement of professional standing in religion, medicine, and law. The basic training in all of these fields was by apprenticeship to an established minister, physician, or lawyer. The college degree remained nonessential except for ministers in certain denominations—notably Anglican, Congregational, and Presbyterian—and lawyers in certain elite jurisdictions. Thus, while college offered appropriate preparation for the professions, it seemed to many an expensive and time-consuming alternative—in a word, impractical.

College offered a possible avenue of advancement to high station in society for boys of relatively common stock, such as John Adams. But college was primarily intended for the sons of gentlefolk, except for young men who intended, as Adams had originally, to train for the ministry. In theory, the natural aristocracy was distinguishable from the social and economic upper class; in practice, the college-educated gentry expected the natural leadership of the nation to emerge from within its gentlemanly circle. Gentlemen of the Revolutionary generation referred to themselves unaffectedly as "the natural aristocracy" of "virtue and talents." And essential to this self-image was the college training, or its equivalent, that distinguished them from the unlearned mass of society and qualified them as a "liberally educated" ruling class.

Eighteenth-century American colleges shepherded students through a curriculum designed to improve their mental processes and to acquaint them with the major elements of civilized knowledge. It presumed to train them for membership in an immortal Republic of Letters that encompassed men of learning in all civilized societies, past and present, since the emergence of the liberal arts in ancient Greece. Just as the Republic of Letters, for some, comprised a definable social caste, so did civilized learning, for them, comprise a similarly definable subject matter. A tangible fund of knowledge, they believed, together with the appropriate division of it into the main branches of learning, had been bequeathed to civilization by the Greeks, the Romans, and the medieval universities. These medieval universities had organized humane learning into two branches of liberal arts, consisting of the trivium, or three roads—dealing with the verbal skills: languages, logic, and rhetoric—together with the quadrivium—dealing with mathematical skills: arithmetic, geometry, music, and astronomy. Advanced students moved on to philosophy and theology.[12]

In the course of time the curriculum broadened to accommodate the accumulating scientific knowledge of the seventeenth century and the increasing attention to literature—belles lettres—in the eighteenth. Colleges held themselves responsible for perpetuating this learning in four-year programs that began with classical studies and proceeded to authoritative Latin texts in the requisite arts and sciences. The student who mastered these subjects qualified for membership in the community of learning that shared this fund of civilized knowledge. However, the accumulations of new subject matter rendered it increasingly difficult for any one scholar to achieve actual mastery of all the arts and sciences. At the same time, the new subjects increasingly challenged scholastic faith in the rationality and unity of the inherited system of knowledge. Although this classically oriented conception of intellectuality suffered continual criticism in America from the eighteenth century on, it remained the guiding principle of most American college curriculums down to the Civil War as well as the main continuing justification for higher education.

Criticism of the classical curriculum did not lack for distinguished and influential proponents from the mid–eighteenth century on, conspicuously including Benjamin Franklin, Thomas Jefferson, and Ralph Waldo Emerson. Franklin and Jefferson created new institutions of higher learning along radically new lines, and the failure of their efforts to contest the reigning classicism attested to its pervasive acceptance among literate Americans generally.

Franklin had picked up a smattering of Latin as a boy in Boston, but he evidently never bothered to study it further, although he took the time and effort to acquire a reading knowledge of French, Spanish, Italian, and German. It was Franklin's opinion that the classics could be studied as profitably in English as in Latin, and late in life he was moved to denounce Greek and Latin as "the quackery of literature." Classical languages, he wrote, had become "the *chapeau bras* of modern literature," comparable to the hats that "the politer people in all the courts and capital cities of Europe" carried uselessly under their arms for form's sake, never wearing them because to do so would disarrange their wigs. Higher education ought to be directed instead toward science and the practical arts, history and the study of society, and English literature and the arts of clear expression.[13]

A leading promoter of the College of Philadelphia and later chairman of its board of trustees, Franklin contributed much to the institution's early development but lost his fight against the ascendency of the classical curriculum there. Franklin critically impaired his ability to shape the development of the academy and the college by recommending the appointment of a young Scottish Aberdeen-trained Anglican minister, William Smith, to its faculty. Smith, who assumed control under the novel title of *Provost*, shared Franklin's interest in broadening the curriculum to include practical subjects, modern languages, and modern history, but he remained steadfast in defense of the priority of the classical curriculum. As a Loyalist during the Revolution, Smith lost control of the college and was forced to leave the state for a number of years. When the college emerged from the Revolution as the University of Pennsylvania, its medical school was able to hold its predominant position in the nation, but the undergraduate part of the university survived as a poorly supported and conservatively oriented college dominated by an overbearing board of merchant-trustees.

By the opening of the nineteenth century, the college had reduced its conventionally classical curriculum to a two-year program, and in 1807 the enrollment reached a low of seventeen students before reviving slowly in the decades that followed.[14]

The new state universities of the young Republic could afford to attempt bold innovations at the outset, and in the case of the University of Virginia, the aged Jefferson was granted the opportunity to experiment lavishly, abolishing the usual classical requirements, omitting theology from the curriculum, and creating separate specialized colleges in which the student would be free to concentrate his studies upon his own chosen field of interest. The student might do all or none of his work in classical studies. He might concentrate upon studies as far removed from traditional learning as business management and agricultural science. However, Jefferson lacked the funds to complete all of his colleges before he died, and thereafter student patronage failed to maintain the system as he had intended it to function. The university succeeded in attracting sizable enrollments from the outset, but students gravitated to the courses in classical studies, and most did not remain at the university long enough to earn degrees in any area. Contrary to Jefferson's intentions, the University of Virginia soon fell into the pattern that the College of William and Mary had established in colonial times: providing a year or more of experience in collegial living for sons of the Virginia gentry.

Emerson, in his 1844 essay titled "New England Reformers," attacked the classical requirement as "a warfare against common-sense." He supposed that "Once (say two centuries ago), Latin and Greek had a strict relation to all the science and culture there was in Europe," and therefore "became stereotyped as *education*," with the result that, two centuries later, in a hundred high schools and colleges

> the pupil is parsing Greek and Latin, and as soon as he leaves the University, as it is ludicrously styled, he shuts these books for the last time. Some thousands of young men are graduated at our colleges in this country every year, and the persons who, at forty years, still read Greek, can all be counted on your hand. I never met with ten. Four or five persons I have seen who read Plato.[15]

Meanwhile Harvard, under the presidency of Josiah Quincy and at the urging of leading faculty members, had departed from the traditional, classically oriented core curriculum in the 1830s and 1840s, eliminating all course requirements after the freshman year. The new system encountered hostility from alumni and members of the Harvard Corporation as well as from veteran faculty members, whose security and status had been threatened by the resulting changes in the teaching routine. Worst of all, enrollments declined. Under Quincy's successors, Harvard returned to the time-honored system of pacing the students through a prescribed curriculum that allotted due weight to classical languages.[16]

Science had traditionally found a place in the college curriculum, and American higher education did respond to changing times by devoting increasing attention to scientific subjects—although not to the point of introducing laboratory instruction in experimental sciences. Indeed, at Yale and Harvard the teaching of science had expanded sufficiently by the mid–nineteenth century to justify its organization into a separate college: the Sheffield School at Yale, the Lawrence School at Harvard. However, the creation of a separate college was evidently intended less to facilitate scientific study than to segregate science courses in the curriculum so that Harvard College and Yale College proper could retain their traditional literary character. Science students were kept separate from liberal arts students in both institutions, ate in separate dining rooms, and received different and less reputable degrees. Edward Waldo Emerson recalled that at the time Louis Aggasiz was strengthening the position of science at Harvard, "the government of the College rather regarded the Scientific and Medical Schools as an impertinence."[17]

One institution established a highly successful partial alternative to the traditional classical curriculum: Union College, under the long tenure of Eliphalet Nott, its president from 1804 to 1866. After a generation of preparation, Union College instituted a "parallel scientific course" leading to the same B.A. degree as the traditional course. Students in the parallel course were required to study Latin and Greek in the freshman year, but they could devote the remaining three years to science, mathematics, social studies, modern languages, and English composition. Under Nott this parallel course proved highly popular. Union rivaled Yale in the size of its graduating classes. Many colleges and universities adopted similar parallel programs, but none enjoyed the success that attended the program at Union under Nott. Columbia, for example, attempted such a parallel program and then abandoned it when enrollment in the program declined to zero.[18]

Many of Nott's students became college presidents themselves, and among them Francis Wayland became an influential spokesman for academic reform. As president of Brown University, Wayland gave influential expression to the assault upon the traditional curriculum in his 1850 "Report to the Brown Corporation." The nation's colleges were failing to sustain themselves, he declared, "because, instead of attempting to furnish scientific and literary instruction to every class of our people, they have furnished it only to a single class and that by far the least numerous."[19] In order to attract students from other classes, Wayland recommended abolishing required courses and adding courses in the agricultural and mechanical arts. Students who wished to pursue one or two years of study at the college ought to be invited to do so; for others, it might be advantageous to remain on for five or six years. In any event, the university should respond to the needs and wishes of all classes in society.

The curriculum Wayland suggested retained the traditional classical courses but supplemented them with a few added subjects. Wayland anticipated the objection that students could choose to study less Latin and Greek under his system than perhaps they ought to. To this he retorted that classical languages have,

> by right, no preeminence over other studies, and it is absurd to claim it for them. But we go further. In our present system, we devote some six or seven years to the compulsory study of the classics. Besides innumerable academies, we have one hundred and twenty colleges, in which, for a large part of the time, classical studies occupy the labors of the student. And what is the fruit? How many of these students read either classical Greek or Latin after they leave college?

In conclusion, Brown University needed $125,000 to survive, and if it did not use the money to broaden its clientele, to include the productive as well as the professional classes, it could not survive anyway.

Wayland's report attracted a good deal of national attention and raised somewhat more than the requested $125,000 and "the New System" went into operation with devastating results. According to an unpublished report of Wayland's successor, Barnas Sears, in 1856, the character and reputation of the university had been "injuriously affected by the low standard of scholarship required" for the A.M. and A.B. degrees.

> Even the personal relations of our professors are humiliating, so that their intercourse with the officers of other colleges is a source of mortification rather than of pleasure. . . . We now are literally receiving the refuse of other colleges. Students who cannot go through a complete course, entitling them to the degree of A.B. in other colleges, look upon this college as a kind of convenient establishment where they can soon build up a broken-down reputation. . . . A liberally educated man who cannot read a sentence of Latin is a solecism in language. Every member of the Faculty is dissatisfied with our present laws in respect to degrees.

Furthermore, the college enrollment was diminishing in numbers as well as quality under the new system, especially with those completing the four-year course. Brown consequently reinstated Greek and Latin requirements in 1857, with immediately beneficial consequences to the university's enrollment.[20]

Yale and Princeton, with nationwide constituencies and missionary interests in expanding higher education, exerted national influence such as the more provincially oriented institutions, including Harvard and University of Virginia, did not aspire to. Accordingly, the Yale University report of 1828 constituted a nationally significant statement of aims in higher education, one that tended to prevail nationally until after the Civil War. Chiefly prepared by Yale University President Jeremiah Day, the report addressed itself to current suggestions "that our colleges must be *newly-modelled*" and responded with a vigorous reaffirmation of the traditional system.

> The two great points to be gained in intellectual culture are the *discipline* and the *furniture* of the mind, [and the liberal arts curriculum was the one approach] best calculated to teach the art of fixing the attention, directing the train of thought, analyzing a subject proposed for investigation; following with accurate discrimination, the course of argument; balancing nicely the evidence presented to the judgement; awakening, elevating, and controlling the imagination; arranging, with skill, the treasures which memory gathers; rousing and building the powers of genius.[21]

As to the furniture of the mind, "Our object is not to teach that which is peculiar to any one of the professions; but to lay the foundation which is common to them all." As to "whether the plan of instruction pursued in Yale College, is sufficiently accommodated to the present state of literature and science; and, especially, whether such a change is demanded as would leave out of this plan the study of the Greek and Roman classics," the report found in favor of traditional practice and the Yale curriculum.[22]

> Whoever . . . without a preparation in classical literature, engages in any literary investigation, or undertakes to discuss any literary topic, or associates with those who in any country of Europe, or in this country, are acknowledged to be men of liberal acquirements, immediately feels a deficiency in his education, and is convinced that he is destitute of an important part of practical learning. If scholars, then, are to be prepared to act in the literary world as it in fact exists, classical literature, from considerations purely practical, should form an important part of their early discipline.

At the time the Yale Report was issued, the ability to converse in Latin and to quote Greek references was actually more important to acceptance in the literary circles of New England than in those of Great Britain. In London or Edinburgh, men who distinguished themselves in one or another branch of the arts and sciences were not obliged to demonstrate college-bred proficiency in all of the others to gain acceptance in cultivated society, as seems to have been the general rule in Boston-Cambridge and Hartford-New Haven. Indeed, by British standards, the Yale Report was in some respects more than a century behind the time in its picture of intellectual society. In England at the turn of the eighteenth century, Joseph Addison had initiated a change in literary thought comparable to the change in moral philosophy associated with John Locke. Addison and Sir Richard Steele had advanced beyond the disputatious tract, the scholastic argumentation, and the ornate erudition of seventeenth-century literary style and set the intellectual fashion for the next century in the clear English prose of the *Spectator Papers*. Addison provided a model that the young Benjamin Franklin emulated, along with other would-be men of letters in England, Scotland, and America.

American college authorities had perhaps never been entirely unmindful of the changing intellectual fashions of London, but they had not permitted themselves to be hurried into new directions by these influences. Josiah Quincy, president of Harvard in the 1830s, observed in his history of the college that "The impulse given to science and literature in England, during the reign of Queen Anne, gradually extended to Massachusetts, . . . but the customs and rules of the College tardily yielded to the influences of the period," chiefly in the form of instruction in belles lettres beginning in 1767. The college in Quincy's own era continued to yield reluctantly to influences of the period, introducing for a time a system of elective courses, only to return later to the old and tried way of comprehensive requirements.[23]

London's metropolitan culture could not, under any circumstances, be transplanted to the provinces. From the moral point of view, the provinces were in many ways considered better off without it. On the other hand, the academic culture historically associated with Cambridge and Oxford in England could readily be reproduced in American colleges, where generations of young scholars could be trained to become civilized gentlemen according to standards that remained established throughout the civilized world. Provincial colleges were intended to perpetuate this ruling class of classically educated gentlemen, and in the nineteenth century even the newer state colleges and universities tended to perpetuate this elitist tradition until the Civil War disrupted the traditional system and the Morrill Land Grant College Act of 1862 prepared the way for comprehensive democratic curricular reforms in higher education.

❧ III ❧

VIEWING AMERICAN HIGHER EDUCATION of the antebellum era from the perspective of the twentieth-century multiversity, modern scholars have been inclined to belittle the small-scale, "old-time" college, where rote instruction was the rule and a traditional curriculum failed to reflect the developing needs of a democratic, rapidly expanding, and industrializing society. But as the argument of the Yale Report indicates, the colleges considered it their business to preserve traditional culture in a changing world. Their constituency in the nation evidently supported them in this view, judging by the prevailingly negative responses to progressive curricular reforms. While anti-intellectual currents of Jacksonian America opposed the elitist classical humanism of the liberal arts college, the college itself evidently remained the very definition of civilized values to the literate community within the national society.

The continued support for traditional liberal arts training on the part of educated Americans manifested itself in ever-increasing enrollments. Between 1800 and 1860 the number of college students increased fourteen-fold, from 1,156 to 16,600, twice the increase in white American males between the ages of fifteen and twenty during that period. In terms of percentages, the number of college-age native white males attending college jumped from 0.59 percent in 1800 to 1.18 percent in the 1859–60 school year.[24] A more rapid expansion might have appeared downright unseemly in a system of higher education that remained consciously devoted, for the most part, to educating a national elite.

Classical learning—Franklin's *"chapeau bras of modern literature"* in the eighteenth century—gradually ceased in the nineteenth to be sufficiently fashionable in most literary circles to be worth caring about. Yet the experience of having studied Latin and Greek survived as a common bond that distinguished college men from the unlettered Republic at large. Beyond disciplining the mind, classical studies drilled into the student the basic liberal arts conception that a tangible body of civilized knowledge serves as the appropriate mental equipment for every educated gentleman.

This putative core of civilized knowledge was not thought to be limited to Latin and Greek, nor was all of it to be acquired through the dull routine of memorization. Beyond the classical requirements, students pursued studies in science, mathematics, history, philosophy, and rhetoric, culminating in the overarching fourth-year course in moral philosophy. Given stimulating texts and teachers, these studies could stir enthusiastic responses in students. And where the classroom failed them, students could resort to their own literary societies, which flourished on most campuses. In either case, a liberal arts college education provided students with widely accepted notions of the universe, society, and a gentleman's proper conduct in both.

The original philosophical framework of instruction for young gentlemen at seventeenth-century Harvard and at Yale had been that of the sixteenth-century French philosopher Petrus Ramus, for whom everything in the world represented an idea in the mind of God and all ideas were reducible to 1,267 propositions. Yale President Ezra Stiles, told how his father, who had attended the college during its early years, studied from texts at least a century old and full of "The old Logic, Philosophy, and Metaphysics he read but never understood, because unintelligible." By the time Stiles himself attended Yale in the mid–eighteenth century, Newtonian science had altered the subject matter of courses in logic, philosophy, and metaphysics without changing the general arrangement of the curriculum or the method by which it was taught.[25]

In the course of the eighteenth and early nineteenth centuries, American colleges modified the scholasticism they had inherited from sixteenth-century Cambridge University in the light of the new science and along lines suggested by more innovative educational institutions in Great Britain, including the dissenting academies in England and especially the reorganized universities in Scotland. Students in the college literary societies kept abreast of current intellectual trends, which were generally in advance of the changes that new texts and new instructors introduced into classrooms. And as Scottish textbooks increasingly predominated in course work, so did Scottish literary quarterlies offer students the latest word on current books and ideas.

By the turn of the nineteenth century, Edinburgh had largely replaced London as the academic heart of Great Britain, radiating new ideas to the American provinces. Liberally supplied by Scottish textbooks, American colleges reformulated the curriculum into a new scholasticism appropriate to a modern, moral, republican, Protestant society functioning within the framework of a divinely planned, orderly, and essentially changeless universe. This world picture came to be challenged by the evolutionary natural sciences and developing industrial society of the nineteenth century, but it continued to dominate academic thought until after the Civil War.[26]

The main change in the new college programs was the deemphasizing of scholastic logic and metaphysics and the introduction of a wide range of new subjects in their places, including civil and natural history, rhetoric, and *belles lettres*. Central to this curricular reform was the course in moral philosophy as taught in the form that Francis Hutcheson had initiated in Scotland in the eighteenth century and that Lord Kames, David

Hume, Adam Smith, Adam Ferguson, Thomas Reid, and others had elaborated upon. This development initiated academic disciplines that in the nineteenth century became the social sciences. This systematized body of new academic learning enabled the American liberal arts college to reconcile the medieval-classical approach to higher learning with the circumstances of American Protestant democratic life.

Harvard and Yale had been established under the old scholastic order, and Harvard remained comparatively isolated from the new Scottish learning until the closing decade of the eighteenth century. South of New England, however, Scottish influences dominated from the outset, even at Anglican William and Mary, where the curriculum had been organized by a Scot, James Blair, along Scottish lines from the outset and where Jefferson later gained his "first views of the expansion of science and of the system of things in which we are placed," according to his autobiographical account, from the instruction of the Scot Professor William Small.[27]

In the middle colonies the Edinburgh-trained Scotch-Irish minister William Tennent created the Log College, which proved to be the forerunner of the seminary at Princeton, both originally devoting themselves primarily to training ministers. Nearly half of the first generation of students at the College of New Jersey at Princeton entered the ministry. However, between 1768 and 1794, the administration of the Scotsman John Witherspoon, less than a quarter did. Under Witherspoon, Princeton became the main American academic outpost of the Scottish Enlightenment, conservatively interpreted.[28]

The nonsectarian College of Philadelphia took shape under the direction of two Scot educators, the Anglican provost William Smith, trained at Aberdeen, and the Presbyterian vice-provost Francis Alison, trained at Glasgow. Irreconcilably at odds with one another on sectarian grounds, Smith and Alison shared the Scottish approach to higher education, which retained the classical basis of the curriculum while expanding offerings in science and *belles lettres*. When Smith secured Anglican control of the College of Philadelphia, Benjamin Rush persuaded another Scottish minister to found Dickinson College on explicitly Presbyterian as well as generally Scottish principles. In New York, King's College, guided by Anglican ministers, looked to Oxford as its model. However, its medical school was organized in 1767 by an Edinburgh-trained physician, Samuel Bard. The medical school in Philadelphia was founded at the same time by Edinburgh physicians, and it continued to be staffed by them almost exclusively for several generations thereafter.[29]

The Protestant scholasticism that supplemented classical studies drew upon a wide variety of sources, but Scottish texts abounded, and a Scottish influence prevailed overall. In moral philosophy Lord Kames's *Essays on the Principles of Morality and Natural Religion* (1751) was among the earliest texts on the subject and the one from which Jefferson early derived the Scottish "moral sense" interpretation of the nature of man that he argued in the Declaration of Independence.[30]

The works of John Locke continued in use in college classrooms of the nineteenth century, and an English text that prominently rivaled those from Scotland was *The Principles of Moral and Political Philosophy* (1785) by the utilitarian clergyman William Paley. Paley's manual of instruction enjoyed immediate popularity in America. James Wilson cited it at the Constitutional Convention, and James Kent drew upon it in his Columbia law lectures several years later. The manual remained widely used until the Jacksonian era, when its aristocratic bias became too obviously anachronistic. However, Paley never dominated the American academic field as some historians have claimed.[31]

The Scottish interpretation that came to prevail in America was the common sense school of Thomas Reid's *Inquiry into the Human Mind on the Principles of Common Sense* (1764). Even more widely used than Reid's texts were those of his followers, including James Beattie, who wrote popularized texts for the classroom, and Dugald Stewart, whose *Outlines of Moral Philosophy* (1793) became the most popular American text in its field. Other Scottish writings that became standard texts were Adam Smith's *Wealth of Nations* (1776), on economics, and Adam Ferguson's *Essay on the History of Civil Society* (1767), on what came to be called sociology. William Smellie, the first editor of the *Encyclopedia Brittanica*, wrote a natural science text that was widely used in American colleges, while writings of Francis Hutcheson, Robertson, Hume, Kames, and Adam Ferguson remained current, as did those of James Beattie and, to an extent, Thomas Brawn. These were followed by William Hamilton and still others discussed by Princeton President James McCosh in *The Scottish Philosophy* (1875).

The introduction of *belles lettres* to college studies in the late eighteenth century followed the example of the Scottish universities, and the field of aesthetics in America was virtually preempted by three Scottish texts: Lord Kames's *Elements of Criticism* (1761), which served as the handbook of the Connecticut Wits; Hugh Blair's *Lectures on Rhetoric and Belles Lettres* (1783), the most widely read of the three; and Archibold Alison's *Essays on the Nature and Principles of Taste* (1790), which offered a degree of romantic license not permitted in the rule books of his predecessors.[32]

Scottish influence of a livelier sort was disseminated in America by the literary reviews, beginning with *Edinburgh Review* in 1802. In the pages of the *Edinburgh* was formulated a new style of literary intellectualism, the review essay. Where formerly reviews of books had served the homely purpose of describing the contents, style, and purpose of the works under question, the Scottish reviewers made the books under review the basis for often wide-ranging and personal essays. Frequently books were "tomahawked" in "slashing" reviews that might reflect upon an entire genre of writings or upon an entire national culture, such as the American. The *Edinburgh Review* was the progenitor of modern literary journalism. Three additional Scottish reviews appeared during the next generation: the *Quarterly Review*, Blackwood's *Edinburgh Magazine*, and Campbell's *New Monthly Magazine*, the latter published in London but edited by a Scot. All four magazines sold widely in America, and each of the four served as the model for one or more American literary magazines. While the Scottish periodicals did not serve as texts for college courses, college literary societies subscribed to them, and they were texts for campus discussions as well as discussions elsewhere in American literary society.[33]

This foreign domination of American academic thought did not arouse xenophobic hostility; in fact, it hardly seemed worth notice. In this respect it contrasted with the introduction of French Enlightenment thought to American college campuses in the late eighteenth century and the subsequent furious and successful campaign on the part of Yale's Timothy Dwight and others to root out all vestiges of French "infidelity." It contrasted also with the attention paid to German culture and the German universities from the end of the War of 1812 onward. Scottish learning remained the standard fare of American colleges, and professors and students associated this learning with academic culture rather than with Scottish culture.

To an extent, Scottish learning was culturally invisible by design. The Scottish *philosophes* wrote in English as though it were their second language—which to an extent it was. Hume, reputed to be the most accomplished stylist among them, compiled a list of Scotticisms that he feared he might otherwise inadvertently commit to writing. The Scottish writers were modestly aware that Edinburgh was no London or Paris. They faced the alternatives of writing for a universal audience or for a provincial one, and they self-consciously composed their essays for intelligent mankind. Jefferson could combine a sense of personal intellectual debt to his Scot professor William Small (as well as to Lord Kames, Adam Ferguson, Adam Smith, and Dugald Stewart) with a pronounced personal prejudice against Scottish culture, based on his contacts with Scottish merchants and Scotch-Irish Presbyterian ministers, the former as a planter and the latter as an educational reformer. The Virginian saw no inconsistency in this, partly because the Scottish writers had consciously divested themselves of any characteristics that might be considered distinguishably Scottish or Presbyterian. They aimed to be entirely *neoclassical*, as that term came to be used.

The power of Scottish scholarship to stimulate American intellectuals found a striking example in the response of Yale undergraduates in the early 1770s to Lord Kames's *Elements of Criticism*. They discovered in the work assurance that literary aspirants in New Haven and Hartford shared the same aesthetic "internal sense" that guided London's literati. Kames taught them that, as with ethics and the universally operative moral sense in human nature, so

> upon a sense common to the species, is erected a standard of taste . . . for ascertaining in all the fine arts, what is beautiful or ugly, high or low, proper or improper, proportioned or disproportioned. And here, as in morals, we justly condemn every taste that swerves from what is thus ascertained by the common standard.[34]

More than a philosophical exposition, *Elements of Criticism* is a how-to book. A chapter on wit, replete with illustrative examples, explains what wit is, the various ways it is created, and the various errors that the would-be wit should avoid. A chapter on dramatic and epic verse similarly defines its subject and prescribes appropriate literary methods. Timothy Dwight,

Jonathan Trumbull, David Humphreys, Joel Barlow, and others studied *Elements of Criticism*, wrote theses on it, introduced it into the college curriculum, and composed volumes of verse according to its rules. Guided by Kames, they gained renown as the Connecticut Wits, demonstrating that native Americans following classical rules of taste could "soar as high as European bards," as John Quincy Adams wrote of them admiringly during a 1785 visit to Hartford.[35]

Evidently the first Harvard students to be introduced systematically to Scottish philosophy were those who attended the course of David Tappan, Hollis Professor of Divinity from 1782 to 1803. There they were exposed to the writings of Francis Hutcheson and Adam Ferguson. William Ellery Channing, a student of Tappan's in the 1790s converted in the course of his studies under Tappan to the doctrines of Hutcheson, Ferguson, and the Welsh Unitarian David Price. From Hutcheson, Channing derived a philosophical basis for liberal Boston's belief in man's natural capacity for holiness; from Ferguson he derived a philosophical argument for Boston's belief in the gradual regeneration of man and of society through the agencies of human reason and moral sentiment rather than divine intervention.[36] Upon being introduced into the Harvard curriculum, Scottish moral philosophy influenced the character of the Harvard program as a whole, providing a new scholastic orientation for the courses in divinity, moral philosophy, rhetoric and oratory, and to some extent natural history, where William Smellie's text was, for a time at least, the required one.

If graduates of the old liberal arts college left their Greek and Latin behind them, as Emerson said, they probably left behind their Scottish moral philosophy texts as well. Yet the college experience likely formed the basis for their worldview thereafter, much as it was intended to. Emerson himself is a case in point. As a Harvard student Emerson immersed himself in Scottish philosophy. He studied Scottish aesthetics and rhetoric under Edward Tyrell Channing, and during his junior and senior years he studied Scottish moral philosophy in two parallel two-year courses taught by Levi Hedge and Levi Frisbie. Hedge and Frisbie assigned him works by Thomas Reid, Thomas Brown, William Hamilton, and especially Dugald Stewart, on whom Emerson wrote one of his major papers. Meanwhile Emerson on his own studied Stewart's *Outlines of Philosophy*.[37]

At the time he graduated from college in 1821, Emerson was a convinced follower of Stewart's moral philosophy, including Stewart's concept of moral sense as an intuitive and reliable guide, inherent in human nature and beyond improvement through education or experience. Stewart therefore took Emerson a good distance toward that transcendentalist conception of reason that Emerson later gleaned from Coleridge, Carlyle, and widely scattered readings. After graduation Emerson departed from the Scottish philosophers of his college years. But even in his most German phase, the Scottish conception of intuitive moral sense as highest reason persisted in his thinking, though Emerson by that time thought of himself as having left the pedantry of Harvard far behind.

Emerson majored in social philosophy and classical studies at Harvard, and so did all students who attended American liberal arts colleges to study the nature of man and society and the universe as propounded in both ancient and modern texts. Had the colleges served as vocational schools, all graduates would have become philosophers, classicists, and literary men by trade, as Emerson did. As a practical matter, there was hardly a living to be made by anybody in this trade, but higher education continued to turn out annually a few thousand latent philosophers as well as certifiably civilized men to leaven the lump of American culture.

ᴈ IV ᴇ

ENROLLMENTS IN ALL COLLEGES remained small. Between 1830 and 1860, the combined enrollments of the nation's seven most successful colleges increased from a combined total of 1,172 to 2,708, keeping pace more or less with the burgeoning population of white, college-age males. Four of these seven colleges had attained enrollments of more than two hundred students by 1830: Yale leading with 324, Harvard, Union, and Amherst following with 211 each. By 1860 four colleges had grown to more than 400: Yale still leading with 502, North Carolina, Virginia, and Harvard following with 409 students.[38]

Curricular matters aside, these colleges remained intimate communities of the nation's selected elite, for whom up to four years of collegial life was expected to be, and inevitably was, an education in itself. Students in this system were expected to exercise their minds by preparing themselves for class recitations. But their free time was their own, to do with as they wished within the limits of rules and regulations. Students laid down their own rules and regulations, a key one of which customarily prohibited fraternizing with instructors. Free time was more abundant than curricular time, and it was through their engagement in extracurricular activities that students, as peers, were most apt to acquire a sense of themselves as the emerging intellectual elite of the province or the nation.[39]

College undergraduates rebelled regularly and often violently against college authorities and disciplinary regulations but not against the academic synthesis, which student literary societies enlivened in debating contests and updated and augmented in their student-owned-and-operated society libraries. Authorized but generally unassisted by college authorities, these literary societies amounted to parallel student systems of education that were intellectually far more enterprising, book-learned, and periodical-current than the required courses of the curriculum.

College was the rite of passage for young men, who normally entered at the age of sixteen or younger into a semi-autonomous society of their peers. After years of submission to the pain and humiliation of ear tweakings and birchings by schoolmasters, college undergraduates found themselves in a position to turn the tables on their teachers, which they did, often with a vengeance. Presumably they were young gentlemen or they would not be attending college, and they could be expected to behave accordingly. Conscious of their incipient status as gentlemen and left to their own resources outside of scheduled hours, teenagers were bound to get into mischief or worse. Campus life was a continual contest between students and faculty in which the faculty, whether they were called tutors or professors, found themselves always at a disadvantage. Bully-ragging the instructor was a customary pastime, and not even such lofty professors as Longfellow and Lowell were exempt from it.

Students made life miserable for unpopular professors and their families, hooting and jeering at them on the street and sometimes smashing the windows of their houses and stirring up rumpuses under cover of night. In southern and western colleges, where students might go about armed, the problem was often indeed serious. According to the College of William and Mary faculty minutes, for instance, a professor came upon three students throwing things at the president's house but found himself help-less to intervene when one of them "snapped a pistol at him" and ran into the main college building, where he was heard "breaking the windows and furniture of one of the lecture rooms" and where he defiled the fac-ulty record books "with human odure and filth." In 1856 five militia com-panies were called in to subdue a riot at South Carolina College.[40]

Riots were endemic in American colleges from the late colonial pe-riod to the Civil War. They were the eruptions of high-spirited youth with time on their hands and regulations to bend. And these youths tended to be accepted as such, even while participants were disciplined or "rusticated" —put off campus to study and mend their ways for a period—or suspended or expelled. As a result of the Great Rebellion of 1823 at Harvard, a major-ity of the senior class was expelled, some receiving their degrees many years later, some posthumously, and some never. One expelled student was the son of Secretary of State John Quincy Adams, and the indignant father protested unavailingly to President Kirkland that, while Harvard had previously "been subject to occasional collisions between the lawful authority of the Government, and the passions or indiscretions of its pu-pils," it had never before responded by degrading a class of students as a whole. (Young John Adams eventually received his degree in 1873).[41]

There appears to have been nothing ideological about these riots, al-though they date from the Revolutionary era. They were manifestations of animal spirits directed against grievances such as arbitrary rules on campus or unpalatable food in the dining hall. In the case of the Harvard outbreak of 1823, the cause had been an unpopular student and the supposed favorit-ism of the administration toward him. Students and faculty were expected to keep their distance from each other, and student opinion enforced this separation. Since contact with professors or tutors tended to be limited to class recitations and curricular and extracurricular discipline, intellectually ambitious students were left to educate themselves in the library or educate each other in their own debating clubs and literary societies.

Student societies of various kinds emerged from the mid–eighteenth century on, beginning with the Flat Hat Club at William and Mary and the Critonian at Yale in 1750. The Linoian Club and the competing Broth-ers Club appeared at Yale in 1753, establishing the pattern of opposing lit-erary societies on each campus. At Harvard a group of students formed the secret Speaking Club in 1770, and a year later Fisher Ames and some of his classmates organized the Mercurian Club, which contested with the Speaking Club once a week. Each club member orated twice a month and faced the criticism of his peers. Students at the College of Philadelphia organized a society that met for mutual improvement in 1771 and continued on to become part of the Philadelphia Medical Society in the 1790s. Phi Beta Kappa started up at William and Mary in 1776 and was introduced into Harvard in 1781.[42]

At Columbia College, clubs included friends and graduates working in the city. In 1784 students along with nonstudents organized a "Society for the purpose of improving themselves in Polite Literature." A number of such societies followed at Columbia, including the Society for Progress in Letters, which produced an offspring among Columbia graduates, mostly lawyers, called the Uranian Club, led by DeWitt Clinton and his brother, George, in the late 1780s and 1790s. The Uranian Club met on Tuesday evenings to debate for "literary" purposes, although political topics predominated, followed by moral, religious, and philosophic subjects. In 1802 students organized the first permanent literary society for Columbia undergraduates, the Philolexian Society.[43]

Sidney Willard, Harvard class of 1798, recalled that a number of coffee clubs had started up or continued during his undergraduate years in the 1790s, some "partly for social intercourse and partly for enjoying refreshments" and others more serious, including a society for religious improvement to which he belonged and the secret society for mutual improvement in elocution and oratory, which Fisher Ames had joined early on. Willard recalled that the Pig Club, or Porcellian Club, had been founded by members of the senior class after 1790 and had included students who became prominent scholars and distinguished men in later life.[44] In the course of a checkered but robust career, the Pig Club became Harvard's most aristocratic society, dedicated to physical pleasures rather than to literary pursuits. William H. Prescott, who joined it in 1812, suffered permanent impairment of one eye in a food-throwing melee.

Student-organized literary and debating societies became vital to student life in the newer colleges of the nineteenth century, in most cases consisting of two opposing debating societies, as originally developed at Yale. In later life J. B. D. DeBow recalled with relish those "rare times . . .

when 'Greek met Greek'" in "fierce reconoitre" during rhetorical exhibitions in the Cliosophic Literary Society at the College of South Carolina.[45] These literary societies acquired libraries of their own that offered more stimulating reading than the college libraries and indeed often actually included larger holdings. The six-thousand-volume collection of the literary societies of the University of North Carolina comprised the best library in the entire state.

For many college graduates the college years would remain their only concerted experience in intellectual sociability, one that would last them for a lifetime. Elements of literary society were everywhere present in mid-nineteenth-century America, existing in isolated situations on plantations and in small towns. The stereotypical participants in small-town intellectual life included the doctor, lawyer, and minister; the newspaper editor, the school principal, and a well-read member or two of a prominent family; to which might be marginally added a village atheist, a poet, a librarian, and assorted bluestockings. Such as it was, this typically American fragment of nineteenth-century intellectual society might gain some measure of coherence from the commonly shared and fondly remembered college experiences of several of its participants.

The conception of college as an introduction to intellectual sociability remained especially characteristic of Southern colleges, where sons of planters customarily took up residence for one or two years to share in the collegial experience with no intention of staying on for a degree but sometimes with the intention of pursuing intellectual interests in the privacy of their plantation libraries in later life. For such scholars the collegial experience might provide a tangible connection with the community of letters at large and with world civilization beyond that. If the south continued to produce superior classicists, as southerners claimed, this continued conversance with Latin and Greek may be explained in part by the absence of English-speaking intellectual company to distract the scholar from traditional studies.

Nowhere in the nation does the conception of intellectuality appear to have been more conservatively equated with academic training than in the Old South. George Tucker of William and Mary College wrote in 1822 of the nation as a whole that "One of the most obvious causes of the humble state of our literature is the small number of persons among us whose minds have been disciplined by academical instruction." He appeared to believe that the effective way to improve the national literature was to increase enrollments in "our seminaries of the first class" in order to augment the national supply of men of letters.[46]

⊰ V ⊱

BEYOND FUNCTIONING AS self-contained communities of learning, colleges served, potentially at least, as centers of intellectual activity for the community at large. This potential was most fully realized in the northeast, where colleges were located in centers of population, and it was least realized in the South, where they mainly were not. Aside from the fact that few centers of population existed in the South, a high-minded reason for situating colleges in small villages had been to protect the morals of the students from the temptations of urban life. One result, however, was to deprive existing urban centers of such intellectual influence as these colleges might have exerted upon them, had they been located in Richmond, Charleston, and Savannah. Instead, Southern colleges created scattered pockets of learning in the rural communities of Columbia, South Carolina; Charlottesville, Virginia; Chapel Hill, North Carolina; and Athens, Georgia, in addition to the existing isolated college community at Williamsburg.

In South Carolina, the small, nonsectarian Charleston College, founded in 1790, did contribute to such organized intellectual life as Charleston offered. But the University of South Carolina under the dynamic and prestigious presidency of Thomas Cooper would have assumed a more influential role had it not been sequestered in Columbia. In Virginia, Richmond emerged as the nearest approach to the cultural, as well as the political, capital of the state. As such, it drew upon the cultural resources of Williamsburg, Charlottesville, and the nearest sizable city, Baltimore. But the cultural vitality of Richmond suffered from this dispersion of the region's cultural institutions. And throughout the rest of the south, with its widely scattered population of liberally educated gentlemen, no other urban center emerged to rival the literary-intellectual leadership, such as it was, that Richmond and Charleston offered.

The state of academic life and town-gown relationships in the south-west were told by the vigorously authoritative commentator Philip Lindsley, graduate of the College of New Jersey, who declined the presidency of Princeton and various other institutions of higher learning to head up the University of Nashville in 1824. Lindsley attributed "the excessive multiplication and dwarfish dimensions of Western colleges" to the fact that "Almost every sect will have its college, and generally one at least in each State." Claiming "to be equal at least to old Harvard and Yale," these sectarian institutions then proceeded "to welcome pupils of all ages, and of every and no degree of literary qualification—with capacious preparatory departments for A, B, C,—*darians* and Hic, Haec, Hoc-*ers*—promising to work cheap." Public colleges and universities suffered in this competitive struggle from the neutral role they were obliged to assume in a vigorously sectarian and contentiously political society, where nearly all of "the preachers, teachers, editors, demagogues, and other friends of the people are hostile to us."[47]

In Lindsley's opinion the university had not done much to elevate the tone of life in the community at large. "We have not what may be called a literary society in Tennessee," Lindsley told the university commencement audience in 1837. "Nothing like it. . . . We meet together to eat, drink, sing, play, and dance; and never to converse as intelligent and intellectual men and women." While he claimed to be "no particular admirer of pedants or *blue-stockings*," Lindsley believed that Nashville could benefit by emulating the cultures of the eastern, or even European, cities. He pointed out that

> A Parisian or Genevese, or Italian *coterie* or *soirée*, or *conversazione*—where the scholar, the artist, the author, the wit, the ethereal spirits of both sexes, the *beaux esprits* of every *clique* and profession, partake of the "feast of reason and the flow of soul," free from the conventional formalities and courtly etiquette—never costs much to the host, and generally proves exhilarating and delightful to the guest.

Yet Tennesseans seemed to be unwilling to give it a try, though the university stood ready to assist in it.[48]

In the Northwest, universities at Ann Arbor, Madison, Urbana, and elsewhere shared the relative isolation from population centers that characterized Southern institutions of higher learning. But in the Northeast, the University of Pennsylvania had been located in Philadelphia and Columbia in New York City, where interaction between college and urban community had been assumed from the beginning. Unfortunately for the development of these town-gown relationships, as well as for the success of the institutions themselves, the Philadelphia and New York colleges came to face the same kind of community hostility that Lindsley complained of in Nashville. In this respect Princeton appears to have remained more favorably situated to draw support and exert influence upon both Philadelphia and New York at a safe distance from the two cities. However, it was Yale at New Haven and especially Harvard at Cambridge that most successfully resolved the town-gown relationship advantageously for the universities themselves and the provincial communities they served.

Yale and Harvard shared the advantage of being situated at the apex of a broadly based public school system, the like of which had existed nowhere else in colonial America, and they were supported by churches that remained established well into the national period and that enjoyed grassroots support at the township level as well as among the ruling gentry. To be sure, sectarian divisiveness remained a factor in New England, as elsewhere, assuming in Massachusetts the distinctive form of Congregationalist-Unitarian struggles that disrupted congregations down to the Civil War, while other sects vied with the more favorably situated Congregationalists and Unitarians. In 1808 conservative Congregationalists founded Andover Theological Seminary after losing all hope of recapturing Harvard from the Unitarians.[49]

The eighteenth-century population of thickly settled Connecticut was distributed among a number of towns, headed by New Haven and Hartford, neither of which constituted a provincial metropolis comparable to Boston. Unlike the Corporation of Harvard College, which came to represent the Unitarian merchant gentry of eastern Massachusetts, the Corporation of Yale represented the Congregational clergy of the province, no layman being admitted to membership until the system was liberalized after the Revolution. Under the guardianship of this ministerial corporation and the Connecticut General Assembly, Yale avoided the idiosyncratic liberalism that came to characterize Harvard. Orthodoxy at Yale was never altogether above suspicion, however; nor did Yale pursue a consistently more conservative course than Harvard in academic matters.[50]

Under the presidencies of Ezra Stiles (1778–95), Timothy Dwight (1795–1817), and Jeremiah Day (1817–46), Yale attracted the largest classes of American college students, including more out-of-state students than Harvard. An important reason for this larger enrollment was the administration's keen sense of Yale's dependence upon the income derived from tuition. Harvard remained better off financially than Yale, maintaining a larger faculty at higher salaries than Yale could afford. In general, the town-gown relationships did not reinforce each other as fruitfully in New Haven-Hartford as in Cambridge-Boston. The promising literary community that Timothy Dwight had fostered in New Haven and Hartford as a tutor at Yale persisted vestigially throughout the nineteenth century without ever recovering its initial vitality, even though Hartford came to number Mark Twain and Harriet Beecher Stowe among its residents for a time. And even during the heyday of the Connecticut Wits in the post-Revolutionary era, Yale men who harbored serious literary ambitions tended to leave the Nutmeg State for New York City and beyond.

Geographically Harvard enjoyed the advantage of a village environment for the students together with a supportive nearby urban center of Boston. Students had been substantially denied access to Boston during the eighteenth century by the intervening Charles River. But in 1793 construction of the West Boston Bridge across the Charles shortened the distance from Cambridge to Boston to three miles. Boston's first public theater was constructed shortly thereafter, raising again the old question of whether Harvard should be relocated to a more distant community to protect the morals of the students from city's temptations. To raise the question, however, was by this time to dispose of it once and for all, given the close associations that had developed between Harvard professors and an informal aggregation of Boston ministers, merchants, and other gentlemen, who together had come to comprise, in the phrase of Harvard's Sidney Willard, a trans-Charles River "intercommunity of the learned."[51]

This intercommunity was notably fostered under the presidencies of Joseph Willard (1781–1804), the affable Unitarian clergyman; John Thornton Kirkland (1810–28), who superintended expansion of the university to the brink of financial ruin; and the layman Josiah Quincy, who continued its expansion, introduced fiscal responsibility, and effected the transition from ministerial to merchant dominion over the institution. Reverence for learning remained an attribute that Harvard fostered among its students. But the outstanding purpose of the college was less to educate its students to the fullest extent than it was to develop them into Boston's version of civilized persons. "Harvard College," recalled Henry Adams, class of 1858, in his *Education*,

> was probably less hurtful than any other university then in existence. It taught little, and that ill, but it left the mind open, free from bias, ignorant of facts, but docile. The graduate had few strong prejudices. He knew little, but his mind remained supple, ready to receive knowledge.[52]

Privately, however, Adams believed that his Harvard training had indoctrinated him for life. As he wrote Henry James in 1903,

> The painful truth is that all of my New England generation, counting the half century, 1820–1870, were in actual fact only one mind and nature; the individual was a facet of Boston. . . . There was hardly a difference in depth, for Harvard College and Unitarianism kept us all shallow.

This Boston-Cambridge mind that held Adams and his peers in thrall was the preeminent provincial mind of America. Possessing a social character all its own, Brahmin Boston's intercommunity of learning bore comparison in some people's minds with Edinburgh in Scotland and Weimar in Germany but with no other literary community in America.[53]

This intercommunity was supplied annually by a thin stream of Harvard students that gradually and unsteadily expanded from the twenty-four in John Adams's class of 1755 to a hundred or so in classes graduating a century later. From this select number Massachusetts continued to supply itself with most of its Congregational and Unitarian ministers, most of its leading political figures, and most of the Brahmins that distinguished literary Boston from the rest of the nation.

To be a Harvard graduate in Massachusetts was something akin to being an army officer in contemporary Prussia, where respect for rank was assumed but where a fraternal bond united those who wore the blue coat as against the rest of society. The patrician agitator Wendell Phillips,

Harvard class of 1831, was famous for his eloquent rendering of billingsgate against his opponents, including most of the leading Harvard men of the Commonwealth's social, economic, and political elite. Yet Phillips could lightheartedly respond to a questionnaire from the secretary of his class by remarking on his surprise "that a quiet moderate halfway sort of sim sam fellow like myself should have somehow the reputation of a fanatic" and assuring the class secretary that "my heart beats high with joy whenever I meet a classmate. Three cheers for the class of 1831."[54] When Phillips met a classmate, the two men would at least recognize each other; for Harvard classes were small, the graduating class of 1860 being the first in history to reach one hundred students, including a number who were from out-of-state.

In his novel *Elsie Venner* Oliver Wendell Holmes coined the term *Brahmin caste* of New England to identify

> an aristocracy, if you choose to call it so . . . by the repetition of the same influences, generation after generation, it has acquired a distinct organization and physiognomy [by comparison to] the common country-boy, whose race has been bred to bodily labor. . . . [Some country-boys] have force of will and character and become distinguished in practical life; but very few of them ever become great scholars. A scholar is, in a large proportion of cases, the son of scholars or scholarly persons, [a member] of the *Brahmin caste of New England*.

Each generation might produce distinction under new names, Holmes added, "but you inquire a little and you find it is the blood of the Edwardses or the Chaunceys or the Ellerys, or some of the old historic scholars, disguised under the altered name of a female descendant."[55]

Not all Harvard men were Brahmins. Some distinguished themselves only in practical life, and some not at all. On the other hand, almost all Brahmins *were* Harvard men, degrees from Yale or Princeton or Oxford or Edinburgh not normally being negotiable as alternatives.

The Harvard requirement is evident in the membership list of the definitive Brahmin in-group, the Saturday Club. Formed in the mid-1850s by the cultural elect of Boston-Cambridge and perpetuated by them into the twentieth century, it numbered sixteen members by 1857. Of these, fourteen were Harvard graduates or professors. The two remaining members were not college men: the lawyer Horatio Woodman had helped

Ralph Waldo Emerson found the club, and E. P. Whipple, the literary critic. During the next seven years, fifteen additional members were admitted, afterward the list was closed for several years. Among these new members, eleven were Harvard men, while one, Hawthorne, was a Bowdoin graduate. The remaining four were without college educations: Samuel W. Rowse, the artist; Whittier, the poet; James T. Fields, the founder of literary publishing in Boston; and John Murray Forbes, a merchant who had attended the elite Round Hill School, where according to the historian of the Saturday Club, Edward Waldo Emerson, he had been "really better educated than many college graduates."[56]

Nor was this Brahmin exclusiveness characteristic only of the Boston-Cambridge establishment. It was hardly less true of the transcendental rebels in Concord. Of twenty-one transcendentalists included in Perry Miller's authoritative anthology, five were Boston women who lacked Harvard degrees because of their sex but nevertheless belonged to the Brahmin community. Among the sixteen men, fourteen were Harvard graduates. The remaining two, who had no college educations, were Bronson Alcott and Orestes Brownson.[57]

The literary circles of Transcendentalism and the Saturday Club did not include professional politicians among their members, but Massachusetts set standards for Harvard-trained scholar-statesmen that it maintained in the teeth of mid-nineteenth-century Jacksonian egalitarianism. Massachusetts continued to elevate the likes of James Bowdoin, John Quincy Adams, Edward Everett, Robert Winthrop, and Charles Sumner to high office. Educational standards for high office remained preponderantly high, especially from the older eastern states. But no other states, including Virginia and South Carolina, maintained such high scholarly standards in political leadership as Massachusetts.

⇝ VI ⇜

A FAVORITE BEGINNING to the history of collegiate education for women in America is December 22, 1783, in the Yale College Library, when President Ezra Stiles examined twelve-year-old Lucinda Foot "in the learned languages, the Latin and Greek," judged her to have given the "true meaning of passages in the *Aeneid* of Virgil, the *Select Orations* of Cicero and in the Greek Testament," and accordingly awarded her a document declaring her to be "fully qualified, except in regard to sex, to be received as a pupil of the Freshman class of Yale University."[58] This engaging episode demonstrated that girls were capable of competing mentally with boys and that enlightened gentlemen of the new republic, such as Stiles and his friend the Reverend John Foot of Cheshire appreciated the fact. It further demonstrated that the effort to compete served no practical purpose, since girls were excluded without exception from the colleges of the day, just as they were excluded from the learned professions of divinity, medicine, and law for which colleges provided learned preparation.

Lucinda Foot's demonstration that girls could compete with boys at the college level posed no challenge to the relationship of the sexes in America at the close of the eighteenth century or later. Girls of Lucinda's age were at that time competing successfully with boys in some of the best private academies in the nation, indicating that they would be able to do so in college as well were that allowed. Some believed an argument against higher education for women could be made on the grounds that their physical systems could not stand it. Thus Reverend John Todd warned that "in forcing the intellect of women beyond what her physical organization will possibly bear," she would be rendered "through the process of education, enervated, feeble, without courage or vigor, elasticity or strength."[59] But whatever might be asserted concerning the female nervous system, the generally accepted argument against educating women at the college level was not concerned with supposed weakness in female health or intelligence. Rather, it was argued that such an education was unsuited to the domestic role that women were expected, almost universally, to assume.[60]

The issue of higher education for women turned on woman's normal role in society, which despite evidence to the contrary was assumed to be a domestic role in the married state. Catharine Beecher never married, yet her educational theory assumed that all girls would become wives and mothers when they grew up. Catharine Sedgwick never married, yet marriage remained the main purpose in life for her heroines. Margaret Fuller had seemingly settled for the single life at age 35, when her *Woman in the Nineteenth Century* (1845) appeared; yet in that work she did not consider the possibility of woman functioning apart from the married state. Many women chose to remain single, especially in the college-educated classes of society, but the higher education of intelligent spinsters did not receive special consideration, even from the spinsters themselves. Ezra Stiles raised five daughters and attended conscientiously to their education on the assumption that they would all become wives and mothers, though in fact three of them spurned offers of marriage from Yale graduates to remain single women in the Stiles household. Had Stiles anticipated such a situation, he might have raised these daughters to be classical scholars like Lucinda Foot. But the idea that women—especially intellectually inclined women—might choose never to marry seemed unthinkable, although commonplace.

Parents felt it their duty to educate daughters to become capable as wives and mothers of educated gentlemen. This sentiment received patriotic republican attention during the Revolutionary era when an influential familial defense of learned women was presented by Benjamin Rush in his "Thoughts on Female Education," an address delivered to the Young Ladies' Academy in Philadelphia in 1787. In opposition to British models of fashionable womanhood, Rush declared, American girls should be taught to be "stewards and guardians" of the household, informed instructors of children, and "an agreeable companion for a sensible man," just as was the case in his own household.[61]

"At the table where I now set," Rush wrote John Adams in 1789, "I have had the pleasure of seeing my dear Mrs. Rush engaged in reading Millot's 'Account of the Manners and Laws of the Ancient Egyptians,' my elder son plodding over Rollin's 'History of Cyprus,' my second just beginning Goldsmith's 'History of England.'" Had he "married a fool," Rush told his wife, "I never should have disturbed a single sleeping prejudice upon any subject."[62] Rush was aware that his description would evoke similar hearthside scenes in the mind of John Adams, whose son, John Quincy, had by then graduated from Harvard and was about to enter law practice. When the "Familiar Letters" of John and Abigail Adams were eventually published by their grandson, in 1848, Abigail was posthumously launched upon an illustrious literary career as a writer of literate, lively, humane, and loving domestic correspondence. More recently—chiefly on the basis of her passing admonition to John in 1776 to "Remember the

Ladies" in framing the nation's "new code of Laws"—she has been enlisted in the woman's rights movement by twentieth-century feminists. However, her letters reveal her to have been a model of the enlightened republican domesticity that Dr. Rush prescribed and a tart critic of women who behaved otherwise.[63]

While the human rights of "the ladies" were not remembered by Revolutionary lawmakers, women did benefit from the humanitarian spirit of the age in the debate over the education of their sex that Benjamin Rush helped initiate and that continued unresolved into the nineteenth century. Some argued for equal education of girls and boys, including instruction in Latin, Greek, and the sciences for any who could master these subjects. Others continued to oppose any instruction for girls beyond the practical requirements of housewifery. "I had rather my daughters would go to school and sit down and do nothing," declared an editorial writer in the *Connecticut Courant* in 1829, "then to study philosophy, etc. These branches fill young Misses with *vanity* to the degree that they are above attending to the more useful parts of an education."[64]

Liberalized attitudes toward the education of women were reflected in the appearance of academies for young women, in the admission of girls to boys' schools, and in the growing ranks of women teachers. At the time of the Revolution, literacy among women in New England is estimated to have been half that of men. By 1850, according to federal census figures, the literacy rate among women in the Northeast was nearly equal to that of men.[65] At the level of higher education, Emma Willard founded Troy Female Seminary in 1821, Mary Lyon founded Mount Holyoke in 1837, and Oberlin College from its beginnings in 1833 admitted students without distinction as to race or sex, dedicating itself to "the elevation of the female character, bringing within the reach of the misjudged and neglected sex all the instructive privileges which hitherto unreasonably distinguished the leading sex from theirs."[66]

Oberlin initially confined coeds to a shortened, "literary" course, designed to prepare them for the domestic sphere. But the college naturally attracted feminist-minded women, such as Lucy Stone and Antoinette Brown, who pressured reluctant college authorities to open the full course to women. Beyond Oberlin, widespread participation in higher education for women awaited the post–Civil War years, when women were increasingly admitted into state universities and well-endowed private women's colleges were founded. Of 633 women listed in Appleton's *Cyclopedia of American Biography* in 1886, only nineteen were identified as college women.[67]

Many a girl besides Lucinda Foot was trained by an ambitious father to excel academically along with the boys, even though it might serve no practical purpose. The most famous such example was Timothy Fuller's daughter. When Margaret Fuller was three, her father set up a lesson plan designed to develop her into a precocious Latin scholar. Margaret read Virgil and Cicero at age six to please a father who promised to "love her if she is a good girl and learns to read."[68] Beyond that, Margaret grew up in the neighborhood of Cambridge, where she came as close to experiencing a Harvard education as was possible for one of her sex, in the company of Harvard boys whose own force-fed early educations in many cases matched her own. Even in this circle, however, Margaret's intellectual assertiveness, against accepted precepts of womanhood, singled her out for the notoriety that she inspired throughout her life and ever since. Failing to achieve recognition as a major writer, Fuller nevertheless "went further than any other women of her time," as Paula Blanchard has put it, "in forcing an unwilling public to accept the idea of a woman as a major intellectual figure."[69] Of key importance in achieving this recognition was her upbringing in the orbit of Harvard, including her return to Cambridge in 1826 as a contemporary of Oliver Wendell Holmes's "famous" class of 1829, which included, besides Holmes, Charles Sumner and Fuller's good friend James Freeman Clarke. In sum, Margaret Fuller launched her career as a major intellectual figure within the sphere of that critical collegial experience for which she was technically ineligible by reason of sex.

ᴥ VII ᴔ

WOMEN WERE BARRED from European as well as from American universities, and they continued to be barred from Oxford and Cambridge Universities after American women had gained admittance to state universities and to Ivy League sister colleges in the late nineteenth century. Virginia Woolf complained in twentieth-century England that she was denied the use of library facilities at "Oxbridge" on grounds of sex. However, Oxford and Cambridge did not dominate intellectual life in eighteenth- and nineteenth-century London as Harvard dominated Boston's. A university education was not the virtually mandatory requirement for entrance into Dr. Johnson's circle of literati that it was for membership in the Anthology Society of Boston, which in other ways had modeled itself admiringly upon Johnson's circle. Johnson's associates came from the theater district and from Grub Street journalism with no particular concern for academic credentials. They were drawn from various regions of London, which offered, Johnson observed, everything that life afforded; to be tired of the city was tantamount to being tired of life.

Bostonians of Margaret Fuller's day did not similarly claim that men and women tired of Boston must be tired of life. Compared to London, Boston remained a small, simple provincial community in which almost all cultural activity would be expected to involve Harvard and Harvard graduates. To be sure, New York City was developing into a commercial center and metropolis in some ways comparable to London, and certainly New York depended no more on Columbia College for its cultural life than London did upon Oxford and Cambridge. But New York in the mid–nineteenth century was not the cultural hub of America in the sense that London was of Great Britain (and of the rest of the English-speaking world, including in good measure the United States). Culturally, America at midcentury remained a confederation of provincial societies, each with its provincial capital.

In this parochial confederation only one cultural institution attracted national support from literate America, possessed the moral authority to set intellectual standards nationally, and gave cultural coherence to the nation as a whole; that institution was the liberal arts college. This distinctively American institution, of which there were 120 throughout the country in 1850, according to Francis Wayland's count, had evolved amid continuing national debate on questions of curricular reform to maintain itself as the cultural consensus of educated Americans.[70]

The old-time liberal arts college served as the bulwark of traditional values. It was the university of the twentieth century that either abandoned this responsibility or proved incapable of fulfilling it. The transition from the age of the college to the age of the university represented a transition from a system of educating gentlemen as generalists to various systems of educating ever broader segments of the population to acquire skills necessary to the development and maintenance of an increasingly complex technological society. The liberal arts college described and defended in Jeremiah Day's Yale report of 1828 would have been incapable of coping with the demands of twentieth-century technological society. But to consider the liberal arts college in this later context is to lose sight of the extraordinary role that a few small institutions played in the training of a governing class during the Revolutionary and early national periods especially and in the training of a literary class through the nineteenth century and into the twentieth.[71]

❧ 2 ❧

THE PHILADELPHIA
ENLIGHTENMENT

THE PRIMACY OF PHILADELPHIA among the cities of Revolutionary America, in cultural institutions as well as in population and trade, was a civic
boast of its citizens that visitors might find irksome but beyond disputa-
tion. "The almost universal topic of conversation among them is the superiority of Philadelphia over every other spot of the globe," complained
the Reverend Jonathan Boucher. "All their geese are swans."[1] A metropolitan population of about forty thousand ranked Philadelphia in 1775 with
Edinburgh, Dublin, and Bristol as one of the most populous provincial
cities of the British Empire, and among these cities it enjoyed by far the
best international reputation as William Penn's famously enlightened
"City of Brotherly Love." In America, New York City ranked second to
Philadelphia in trade as well as population, which stood at about twenty-
five thousand in 1775; however, New York City affected no pretentions
whatever to cultural distinction.[2] Boston, twice the age of Philadelphia,
was less than half as populous.

John Adams was thirty-nine in 1774 when he ventured forth from
New England for the first time to represent the desperate cause of his
"beloved Boston" at a Continental Congress that would be meeting in the
fat, flourishing, and reputedly conservative city of Philadelphia. Together
with his fellow delegates from Massachusetts—all Harvard-trained, as he
was—Adams was eager to acquaint himself with the societies then uniting against British tyranny, and he set about taking their measure by Boston standards and recording his findings in his diary. Adams was especially
concerned to observe the facilities of higher education that these societies supported and to match his findings with his preconceptions.

As recorded in his diary, Adams's trip through Connecticut proved an unmixed pleasure, his party being treated with great "ceremony and assiduity" throughout the province, especially from Hartford to New Haven, where they were taken on a tour of Yale College by Timothy Dwight and another tutor, who waited upon them with "great civility." Connecticut and Yale were highly commendable and at the same time rather unremarkable to the visiting Bostonians. New York would be another matter. The first town the Massachusetts delegates came to after crossing the New York border proved to be without a minister for its Congregational Society, and while the town supported "a school for writing and cyphering," it did not maintain a proper grammar school, there being "no law of this province that requires a minister or school master."[3]

Adams noted in advance that New York City would "be a subject of much speculation to me," and the sight of it initially impressed—not to say dazzled—him. The streets "are vastly more regular and elegant than those in Boston and the houses are more grand as well as neat." At the homes of John Morin Scott and other affluent patriots, he was introduced to elegant living such as he had never encountered in Massachusetts. "A more elegant breakfast, I never saw—rich plate—a very large silver coffee pot, a very large silver tea pot—napkins of the very finest materials, and toast and bread and butter in great perfections," and in other homes "rich furniture again." And yet, "With all the opulence and splendor of this city, there is very little good breeding to be found. . . . [T]here is no conversation that is agreeable." He later met William Smith, "a sensible and learned man," who "received us very politely" and left a favorable individual impression that did not, however, redeem the reputation of a society where elegant appointments were not matched by elegant manners. Nobody, Adams wrote, appeared interested in showing the men from Massachusetts what they would have chosen to see: the college, the churches, print shops, and book stores. And when they did gain the opportunity to visit King's College, Adams found that "There is but one building at this college and that is very far from full of scholars. They never have had 40 scholars at a time."[4] Passing through New Jersey, Adams was much more favorably impressed by the college at Princeton, especially the "most beautiful machine, an orrery or planetarium constructed by Mr. Writtenhouse of Philadelphia." He admired President John Witherspoon as a "clear, sensible, preacher."

And so to the new American metropolis of Philadelphia. Arriving in town, "dirty, dusty, and fatigued as we were, we could not resist the importunity, to go to the tavern, the most genteel one in America," where "a supper appeared as elegant as ever was laid upon a table." Walking about the town, Adams visited the market, the State House, Carpenters Hall, and the hospital and admired all of these as well as the "regularity and elegance" of the city as a whole.[5] He later visited Charles Willson Peale's studio, where he was charmed by Francis Hopkinson and impressed by his breadth of accomplishment. In addition to its accomplished gentlemen, Philadelphia boasted "societies, the Philosophical Society particularly, which excites a scientific emulation and propogates their fame."[6] Much impressed by the institutions that were distinctively Philadelphian, including the hospital and the Philosophical Society, Adams makes no mention in his diary of the College of Philadelphia with its ideologically suspect provost, Reverend William Smith, which presumably would have impressed Adams no more favorably than King's College in New York did.

Adams met cosmopolitan gentlemen in Philadelphia, especially those from the Chesapeake and from Charleston, who demonstrated to Adams's discomfiture the relative provincialism of Boston. But admiration for these polished southern gentlemen soon gave way to scorn for their pretensions. "There is no greater mortification than to sit with half a dozen wits, deliberating upon a petition, address, or memorial," who "are so fond of showing their parts and powers as to make their consultations very tedious." Most exasperating of all was the future governor of South Carolina, Edward Rutledge, educated at Middle Temple, whom Adams described in his diary as "a perfect bob o'lincoln— . . . excessively vain, excessively weak, and excessively variable and unsteady—jejune, inane, and puerile."[7]

It embarrassed Adams that "Our New England people are awkward and bashful; yet . . . pert, ostentatious, and vain; a mixture which excites ridicule and gives disgust;" for "In solid abilities and real virtues they vastly excel, in general, any people upon this continent." For Adams, greater experience in the larger world would remedy this provincialism. Meanwhile, "Philadelphia with all its trade and wealth and regularity is not Boston. . . . We exceed them in every thing but in a market and charitable public foundations."[8] Forgotten for the moment was the Philosophi-

cal Society and Philadelphia's cosmopolitan breadth of cultivation, which
he had remarked upon previously.

Less readily put out of mind was that enormous Philadelphia market,
a huge colonnaded shed extending for two city blocks down the center of
High Street and giving impressive indication of Philadelphia's rich hinter-
land and extensive markets. Commercially, Philadelphia served as an en-
trepôt for the Chesapeake region of Maryland and Virginia, the Delaware
River region of Delaware and New Jersey, and the fertile Pennsylvania
backcountry around the Susquehanna, west to what would become Har-
risburg. Culturally, Philadelphia's book dealers and publishers, its Philosophical Society, its hospital and medical school extended the city's influence throughout this region as far as New York City. And as the age of
Revolution and Constitution developed, Philadelphia developed as well.
As the Federal capital from 1790 to 1800, the city served as a cosmopolitan
center for émigrés from revolutionary France, including Constantin de
Volney and Talleyrand; enlightened refugees from British reaction, including Joseph Priestley and Thomas Cooper; together with refugees
from black revolution in Santo Domingo, including Moreau de St. Mery,
who operated the leading French book store in Philadelphia.[9]

Nobody had asked the Philadelphia gentry whether they wished their
city to serve as the organizing center of the Revolution, temporary capital of the new Republic and haven for refugee partisans from revolutions
and failed revolutions elsewhere in the world. Genteel Philadelphians
made it evident that they did not wish to see their city appropriated in this
manner. With their wholehearted acquiescence, the federal government
in 1800 removed to a comparatively unpopulated section of territory acquired from Maryland and Virginia and designated the District of Columbia. A year previously, political pressures from western districts had
forced the removal of the Pennsylvania state capital from Philadelphia to
Lancaster. Thus divested of both state and national political authority,
Philadelphia at the century's end substantially surrendered its role as the
center for enlightened thought in America, amid the ideological controversies that accompanied emerging party conflicts of the new Republic
superimposed upon French revolutionary conflicts abroad. Never again
did Philadelphia vie with New York and Boston as the center of cultural
leadership within the nation.[10]

Philadelphia had meanwhile lost the commanding primacy among American cities in population, wealth, and commerce that it had enjoyed at the outset of the Revolution. By 1800 New York City was approaching Philadelphia in size, with sixty to seventy thousand inhabitants. New York's burgeoning population was making comparable strides toward commercial leadership in the nation as well. Yet Chestnut Street by no means capitulated to Wall Street in the years after 1800; in the 1830s Nicholas Biddle launched the second Bank of the United States not in lower Manhattan but on Chestnut Street. Nor did New York City achieve leadership in the fields of publishing and literary journalism until the third and fourth decades of the century. Nevertheless, the momentum of commerce favored New York, while the center of literary and artistic activity shifted early in the century to a section of Manhattan that soon would be known to the world as Broadway.

The enfeebled Philadelphia Enlightenment had ended almost officially in 1790 with the happily timed death of Benjamin Franklin and the overthrow by Pennsylvania conservatives and moderates of the radical Revolutionary state constitution of 1776 that Franklin had helped to draft. Politically, Franklin's Pennsylvania had been dominated in the mid–eighteenth century by the Quaker Party. Representing much of the Quaker gentry, the party was supported by Scotch-Irish Presbyterians and assented to by Swiss-German Pietists against the Anglican Proprietary Party. What happened after midcentury was bitterly summarized by Benjamin Rush years later in a letter to John Adams. For more than sixty years before the Revolution, Rush explained, the city's two aristocracies, Quaker and proprietary,

> were enemies to each other, but the Revolution united them. They are now all-powerful in all our monied institutions except one, in our library, Hospital and University. . . . In the city of London or Constantinople I could not feel myself more a foreigner than I do in the city of Philadelphia.[11]

Rush himself had opposed the democratic state constitution of 1776, which had served to divide radical and moderate Patriots while reinforcing the Revolution-born unity of the unrevolutionary Quaker and Anglican gentries. Of Franklin's world-famous, plain, dynamic, tolerant, open-

ended, Quakerish, enlightened Philadelphia, the leading institutions remained in the nineteenth century: the Philosophical Society, the Library
Company, the hospital, the college, and the medical school along with a
number of humanitarian institutions. But these institutions had in most
cases become the heirlooms of the genteel elite that dominated the city.

⊰ II ⊱

A QUAKER MERCHANT GENTRY dominated Philadelphia during the first half
of its existence, presiding over the plain, practical, industrious, law-abiding,
but conscientiously libertarian society that formed the basis for the Philadelphia Enlightenment as it came to be personified by Benjamin Franklin.
Quakers did not forswear the accumulation of wealth, and substantial
fortunes were amassed by the Logans, Norrises, Mifflins, Whartons, Pem-
bertons, and others. However, Quakers did condemn ostentatious show
of wealth, and the practice of plain living by affluent Quakers encouraged the spirit of egalitarianism that distinguished Philadelphia's city life,
despite political domination of the city by an exclusive few.[12]

Quakers had reason to abhor the agencies of their persecution in England, including the Church of England, the legal profession, and the universities of Oxford and Cambridge. Accordingly, they tended to withhold
support from efforts to promote higher education in the colony and to
disapprove of the impractical classicism of such higher education. On the
other hand they extended cordial support to higher training in subjects of
a practical scientific nature, where such training might benefit mankind,
as was especially the case with the science of medicine. Since the Society
of Friends maintained no clergy and since the colony functioned without
lawyers until well into the eighteenth century, the physician was the only
professional man the Quaker community recognized, the title of *doctor*
remaining the one honorific title in common Quaker usage.[13] Physicians
enjoyed high social status among the Quaker gentry, and medical education at the Scottish universities was encouraged, especially at Edinburgh,
where such education could be had without the classical-medieval trap-
pings of the liberal arts.

Quakers extended to the manual arts the esteem they withheld from the liberal arts. In contemporary English usage the mechanic arts were defined "as such Arts wherein the Hand and Body are more concerned than the Mind," the terms *mechanic* and *mechanical* being derogatory because the "mechanick Arts or Handicrafts are more mean and inferior than the Liberal Sciences." In America craftsmen generally enjoyed a status higher than in England, and they further enjoyed ample opportunities for upward mobility into the merchant gentry. Among the Quakers in Pennsylvania and Rhode Island especially, craftsmen enjoyed the highest status and produced the finest workmanship.[14] This Quaker respect for craftsmanship and for practically beneficial sciences encouraged the development of farmer-artisan intellectuals such as the farmer-botanist John Bartram, the glazier-mathematician Thomas Godfrey, and the clock and instrument makers Owen Biddle and David Rittenhouse. Through such men, pragmatic versatility became a hallmark of the Philadelphia Enlightenment.

Unrivaled Quaker dominance of Pennsylvania and Philadelphia ended when the proprietorship of the colony passed to William Penn's Anglican sons in 1727. The succession opened the way for the ascendency of an Anglican gentry that included the Graemes, Willings, Hopkinsons, and Binghams, who were supported by an Anglican clergy, notably including William Smith, Richard Peters, and Jacob Duché. Allied with this Anglican gentry were liberal "old side" Presbyterians, including the Allens, Shippens, and the Reverends Francis Alison and John Ewing. This Anglican gentry did not condemn the ostentatious show of wealth or learning as Quakers did, and it consequently came to overshadow the quieter Quaker gentry and even to corrupt some of the Quaker membership. During a generation of rising prosperity such as characterized Philadelphia during the third quarter of the eighteenth century, conversions from the plain religion to the fancier one occurred, especially where intermarriage weakened Quaker control.

Nor could the Quakers make hard and fast distinctions even regarding classical training. William Penn had been a classical scholar, and so was the Scotch-Irish Quaker James Logan, whom the Penn family appointed as its legal agent and who became the leading merchant and political figure and patron of arts and sciences in Pennsylvania during the early eighteenth century. The Quaker consensus opposed the study of classics for their ornamental as opposed to utilitarian value, but the practical need for Latin in scientific investigation could not be gainsaid. The line between ornamentation and utility became more difficult to draw as classical studies gained influence in Quaker schools. Sound education was very much a Quaker concern, and Quaker schools gained the respect and patronage of non-Quakers. The Anglican minister Jacob Duché observed that Philadelphia Quakers "now think it no more a crime to send their children to school to learn Greek and Latin, mathematics and natural philosophy, than to put them to merchants and mechanics."[15] Quakers mainly withheld support from the College of Philadelphia. But when the college added a medical school on the eve of the Revolution, the school benefited from strong Quaker support as well as from its connection with the general hospital, which Quakers had founded and continued to control.

Wealth was concentrated in relatively few hands in Philadelphia, as elsewhere. According to the 1774 tax list, the upper 10 percent of taxpaying households—about five hundred men—owned 89 percent of the taxable property. Artisans and shopkeepers nevertheless remained the representative members of Philadelphia society and were its most remarkable aspect. Economically, Philadelphia presented an extreme of individualism, where the average man worked for himself. A storekeeper might keep a helper, and a craftsman would normally take on an apprentice; but helpers and apprentices could look forward to establishing their own shops in a few years' time. No regulations limited their opportunities, as craft guilds were unable to impose controls upon so dynamic an economy. Carpenters and cordwainers succeeded in controlling the price of their product, but they failed in their efforts to control membership in their trades. A man could enter any line of activity, or any combination of them. Those who succeeded and amassed wealth would not greatly change their daily routine or their appearance as a consequence.[16]

The Benjamin Franklin encountered in the *Autobiography* represented the typical mid-eighteenth-century Philadelphian: an artisan whose printing trade led him to newspaper publishing, then to book printing and selling; an advocate of self-improvement whose observations and studies led him to original scientific discoveries; and a public-spirited citizen who organized useful municipal institutions such as a fire company and a library company and engaged equally effectively in colonial and state politics, in international diplomacy, and in the founding of the federal system of government. The unique status of "B Franklin, Printer" lay in his ability to transform without any apparent disconnection from printer's apprentice to polymath to world statesman. Franklin was not only recognized as the archetypal American; he was probably the most world-famous individual person of his day.

Franklin was twenty-one when he organized his Junto of fellow artisans with inquiring minds. The Junto perfectly reflected Franklin's genius in its combination of homely modesty (as Franklin instituted it) with absolutely grandiose possibilities (as Franklin envisioned them). Club life was a prominent characteristic of Philadelphia society, and Franklin's club was in various ways similar to any number of such groups, including three Masonic lodges that must have influenced Franklin's conception.[17] Among the most striking features of the Junto was the leather-apron status of its original members; among them were four printer's helpers, a joiner, a shoemaker, a glazier, a surveyor, a copier of deeds, and a merchant's clerk. These were very much the sort of characters Shakespeare assembled in *A Midsummer Night's Dream*. Under the leadership of Bottom, uncrowned King of the Mechanicals, Shakespeare's plebians present farcical demonstrations of their ludicrous pretensions to art and learning. In Shakespearian England the effort earned Bottom an ass's head; in eighteenth-century Pennsylvania the effort led Franklin into activities that earned him international renown as a leading *philosophe*.

Franklin's Junto continued to function for decades as a secret society of twelve who met weekly and responded to rather elaborate sets of questions concerning what they had read, done, witnessed, and heard about during the week. Their colloquies ranged from matters of universal import to local business developments and gossip. The Junto combined a mutual benefit society, a merchants' association, a political caucus, a philosophical club, and a library society. For a time Franklin experimented with several methods of extending the benefits of the Junto to others in the community, without enlarging its own membership. His first plan was to form a chain of such clubs by urging each member to organize a similar club on his own. Five or six of these were actually founded, by which time Franklin, who had become a Mason, was thinking of universalizing the Junto into a United Party for Virtue.

Less pretentiously, meanwhile, Franklin initiated the organization of an American Philosophical Society in 1743 around a nucleus of Junto members, drawing in men of learning from Philadelphia and elsewhere. This philosophical society disappointed Franklin, who served as its secretary. Its members were "very idle gentlemen," he wrote Cadwallader Colden in New York. "They will take no pains."[18] Meetings were irregular, and nothing was published. Thus the Junto continued to function as Franklin's main intellectual resource. It was the Junto, for instance, that between 1746 and 1752 carried out the electrical experiments which won Franklin his chief acclaim as a *philosophe*.

The American Philosophical Society having failed to take hold, Franklin turned his organizing talent towards the formation of an institution of higher learning in Philadelphia. To effect this enterprise he joined forces with his political opponent in the colony, Chief Justice William Allen. A Scotch-Irish Presbyterian merchant who had accumulated a large fortune in commerce and land speculation, Allen succeeded the Scotch-Irish Quaker James Logan as the foremost merchant, political leader, and patron of culture in the colony. Allen assumed leadership of the Proprietary, or Gentlemen's, Party and faced the opposition of Benjamin Franklin, who organized the Country Party coalition of Quakers, Lutherans, Pietists, Presbyterians, and others who opposed the policies and interests of the Proprietors. Allen had been a patron of Franklin in earlier days, as had James Logan, and he and Franklin were capable of cooperating in worthy enterprises while opposing each other politically.

The College of Philadelphia traced its legal origins to a board of trustees formed in 1740 in the midst of the George Whitefield religious revival to establish a charity school for the city. A group of four trustees for the land and building comprised two carpenters, a brickmaker, and a weaver. A second group of "Trustees for Uses" consisted of gentlemen merchants and included Whitefield himself. Nothing came of the project for nine years. Then Benjamin Franklin emerged as a leading participant, with a plan for founding the school as an academy and eventually, perhaps, as a college. The trustees, who elected Franklin as president in 1749, were "the principal gentlemen of the province," according to Franklin. No artisans were among their number except the silversmith and Junto member Philip Syng and the printer Franklin. Among the trustees the most substantial contributor of funds to the Academy was Chief Justice Allen, who was additionally responsible for attracting the Presbyterian minister Francis Alison to the academy and college from Alison's own widely esteemed academy in New London, Pennsylvania.[19]

Educated at the Middle Temple and a pensioner of Clare Hall, Cambridge, Allen was more like the other trustees in background than Franklin. From the outset Franklin found it necessary to compromise with his fellow trustees, notably in accepting the inclusion of classical languages in the curriculum. Meanwhile, Provost William Smith entered politics in the province on the side of the Proprietary Party against Franklin's party. Smith's primary purpose, it appeared, was to advance the interests of the Anglican Church. It soon turned out that Smith harbored ambitions to become the first Anglican bishop of America, and while he was disappointed in this ambition, he largely succeeded in transforming the College of Philadelphia from an explicitly nondenominational institution to a covertly Anglican one.[20]

A suspected Loyalist during the Revolution, Smith lost control of the college and was forced to leave Pennsylvania for a number of years. When the college emerged from the Revolution as the University of Pennsylvania, its medical school was able to hold its predominant position in the nation, but the undergraduate college continued to suffer from the alienation of non-Anglican supporters, notably the Presbyterians, many of whom had transferred their loyalties to the College of New Jersey at Princeton. In 1783 Presbyterians additionally founded Dickinson College, while Franklin College was started in 1787 to train young men from the German communities of the western counties and assume responsibility for the German studies Benjamin Franklin had planned for the College of Philadelphia.[21]

The Edinburgh-trained physician Benjamin Rush, a founder of Dickinson College, resented the slide of enlightened Philadelphia and its college into genteel classicism just as Franklin did. Rush later used the death of David Rittenhouse in 1796 to make his point. The creative genius of the one-time clockmaker, Rush explained in his eulogy of Rittenhouse, had been facilitated by his freedom from the encumbrance of "what is called a liberal education." Unhindered by "the pernicious influence of monkish learning," Rush went on, Rittenhouse had been able to observe nature freshly and directly. This sally provoked the expected response. Rittenhouse's nephews, the university-educated Bartons, complained that Rush had impugned their uncle's education, which had not been as rudimentary as Rush implied. William Smith, returned to Philadelphia after the Revolution, became not unreasonably convinced that Rush was actually attacking him indirectly since as Provost of the College of Philadelphia he had earlier encouraged Rittenhouse and awarded him an honorary degree. Faculty members at the University of Pennsylvania similarly interpreted the eulogy as an indirect attack. Inevitably the issue became political when Rush's eulogy received the strong endorsement of leading Jeffersonians.[22]

Altogether, the response tended to demonstrate that the age of the artisan-intellectual, the distinctively representative man of the Philadelphia Enlightenment, was at an end, even in Philadelphia. When the Franklin Institute was founded in the 1820s, it was dominated by merchant-industrialists and scientific technologists, with whom the artisans and mechanics of the day found themselves increasingly in class conflict. The institute reflected the persistence in Philadelphia of Franklin's scientific and mechanical interests represented by his inventions—including smokeless street lamps, the lightning rod, and bifocal glasses—and his scientific contributions—including original observations concerning heat conduction, winds, whirlwinds, lightning, the origin of the Gulf Stream, and as the crowning achievement of his career, original research in the field of electricity. At the same time the institute unintentionally memorialized a vision of democratic enlightenment that had failed to survive Franklin himself in his adopted city.

❧ III ☙

IN ENLIGHTENED PHILADELPHIA the medical profession attained a moral-intellectual status in some ways comparable to that of the clergy in Boston. David Ramsay observed in his eulogy of Benjamin Rush in 1813 that

> Since the first institution of the medical school in Pennsylvania, its capital, Philadelphia, has been the very atmosphere of medicine. . . . A

portion of knowledge floated about that hallowed spot, which was inbibed by every student without his being conscious of it, and had an influence in giving his mind a medical texture.[23]

Medicine was virtually worshiped as the highest form of humanitarianism. Benjamin Smith Barton wrote that

The man who discovers one valuable new medicine is a more important benefactor to his species than Alexander, Caesar or a hundred other conquerors. I will venture to go farther. All of the splendid discoveries of Newton are not of so much real utility to the world as the discovery of Peruvian bark, or of the powers of opium and mercury in the cure of certain diseases.[24]

Elsewhere in America the physician enjoyed a less lofty position. In New York the medical profession gained strength from the proximity of Philadelphia and in some ways rivaled it. In Virginia more gentlemen received medical training at Edinburgh in the late colonial period than attended Pennsylvania and New York together. In South Carolina Scottish physicians, together with the Edinburgh-trained governor of the colony, formed a brilliant scientific circle, but one that received scant support from the law-trained Charleston gentry. A Scot, William Douglass, was the first university-trained physician to practice in Massachusetts, and in mid-eighteenth century Boston he was recognized to be the leader of his profession. That secured him little intellectual credit outside of the mainly ill-trained local medical fraternity, however. During the Revolutionary era Boston lagged far behind cities to the south in the educational qualifications of its leading physicians. This changed with the introduction of medical education to Harvard in 1782. But the improvement in medical learning did not noticeably enhance the status of physicians in Boston's literary community.[25]

The absorbing intellectual concern with medicine and science that characterized literary society in Philadelphia derived most evidently from Quaker humanism. Functioning as a religion without ministers, the Society of Friends conferred upon physicians a status reserved for clergymen in other denominations. The Pennsylvania Hospital, unrivaled elsewhere in the British colonies, received the ardent support of Quakers. That is not to say that medicine in Philadelphia was a predominantly Quaker profession. An Anglican physician, John Kearsley, mainly organized medicine there as a learned profession in the 1720s; the wealthy Presbyterian philanthropist William Allen sponsored medical students abroad; and the nonsectarian Benjamin Franklin, as colonial agent for Pennsylvania in London, guided Americans to the University of Edinburgh for medical training.[26]

From the 1720s promising medical students were sent abroad from Pennsylvania for training, beginning with Thomas Cadwallader at University of Reims, Thomas Bond in Paris, and his younger brother, Phineas, in London, Leyden, Paris, and Edinburgh. Charles Moore earned a medical degree at Edinburgh in 1752, and thereafter the Scottish university established itself as the leading center for medical training for Americans from New York to South Carolina. Between 1758 and 1788 sixty-three Americans received medical diplomas from Edinburgh, and many more attended lectures there.[27] The Philadelphia medical profession was dominated by Edinburgh men in the Revolutionary era and early national period. As Edinburgh men they were trained to be philosophers of medical science as well as practicing physicians.

In addition to a course of medical training that was of dubious practical value in some respects, the moral philosophy of the Scottish Enlightenment was absorbed by medical students at Edinburgh and reinforced in its influence upon the Philadelphia Enlightenment. Benjamin Franklin was the chief agent in this transfer of medical and moral culture from Edinburgh to Philadelphia. In 1759 Franklin visited Scotland to accept an honorary doctorate from St. Andrews University. While in Scotland he stayed at the homes of David Hume and Lord Kames, among others. Franklin became a friend of the historian and principal of the University of Edinburgh William Robertson, and upon his return to London, Franklin became an unofficial agent for Robertson's university. He persuaded John Morgan to attend Edinburgh rather than Leyden, and he sponsored William Shippen Jr., Benjamin Rush, and other American students there.[28]

Edinburgh did not offer clinical training, which American students were expected to pursue during the summers, between terms, in London hospitals. Instead, Edinburgh fostered medicine as a science in lecture courses taught by world-famous authorities, the most influential of whom was William Cullen. Cullen sought to found medicine upon a unifying law comparable in scope to Newton's law of gravity. To this end he formulated a system based upon the hypotheses that life processes depend upon the nervous system's response to stimuli and that disease results from disorders of the nervous system, manifesting in fevers. Treatment for disease under this system ranged from meat and medications, for restoring a debilitated nervous system, to bleeding and purging for repairing an over-stimulated system.[29]

Cullen's theory of medicine, which included an elaborate classification of diseases, did not go so far as to reduce medical practice to the single approach of adjusting systemic responses to stimuli. But some of Cullen's students simplified the system along those lines, and one who did was Cullen's most influential American student, Benjamin Rush. Rush organized a comprehensive system of medical treatments based upon the single factor of nervous excitability. This system of "heroic medicine" prevailed in Philadelphia, and therefore in American medical practice, through the first half of the nineteenth century. Rush's more original and constructive investigations into the relation between mental and physical disorders were not similarly influential.[30]

As the Pennsylvanian medical student George Logan observed, the lectures of leading Edinburgh professors were better suited to the training of philosophers than practitioners, and they accordingly served to elevate medicine as a branch of learning, enhancing the doctor's prestige if not always his skills as a healer. From this point of view, clinical training lacked elegance, and surgery was seen as a barbarous act, unsuited to gentlemen. Indeed, John Morgan sought to separate "the low drudgery of surgery" into a subordinate occupation together with the operation of apothecary shops. Among the founders of the medical school at Philadelphia, the Paris-trained surgeon Thomas Bond taught the course of greatest practical value, a series of clinical lectures delivered in the Pennsylvania Hospital. Students disliked the course, however, and when they attempted unsuccessfully to eliminate it as a requirement, they gained some faculty support since it departed from Edinburgh precedent. Bond continued the course until his death in 1782, after which it was dropped.[31]

Planned by Morgan and Shippen while they were medical students at Edinburgh, the Philadelphia medical school opened in 1766, staffed by

Shippen, Morgan, Bond, Edinburgh-trained Adam Kuhn, and upon completion of his Edinburgh degree three years later, Benjamin Rush. Morgan's attempt to relegate Shippen to an inferior position in the school precipitated an internecine wrangling among the Philadelphia medical fraternity that continued into the nineteenth century. In 1766 Morgan organized the Philadelphia Medical Society and did not invite the Shippens, father and son, to join. In response Thomas and Phineas Bond reconstituted Franklin's defunct American Philosophical Society, of which Thomas Bond had been a charter member in 1743, and invited the Shippens and disgruntled older physicians to become members. Meanwhile, a second learned association, the American Society, came into being, also tracing its origins to Franklin's original society, and included Morgan among its members. In 1768 Morgan and the Bonds came to terms, and after a good deal of altercation, the two organizations, by then expanded to include most of the leading men of the community, united to revive together the American Philosophical Society.[32]

The melding of two rival medical-scholarly associations into the American Philosophical Society in 1769 happened to coincide with the transit of the planet Venus across the sun, an event that would not recur for 105 years. This opportunity for measurements of the solar system mobilized the Philosophical Society together with Professor John Winthrop of Harvard and amateur astronomers throughout the colonies. The results, laboriously compiled and published in the initial volume of *American Philosophical Society Transactions* (1771), were enthusiastically received by scholars and learned societies in Europe. A correspondent from England reported that the *Transactions* were "much sought after by the literati of London." In Sweden the transit observations were said to have given "infinite satisfaction to our astronomers; as well as the rest of your *Transactions* to the literary world."[33] This impressive intercolonial scientific achievement remained an indication of America's unrealized potential in the world of science, as nothing followed it. The second volume of the society's *Transactions* did not appear until 1786, and then only after the rival Academy of Arts and Sciences had organized in Boston and published a volume of its papers that attracted favorable responses in Europe. The second volume of the *Philosophical Society Transactions* sadly failed to meet the expectations aroused by the first.

Meanwhile, the achievement of the rival Philadelphia medical societies in uniting to form the Philosophical Society did not unify the faculty of the medical school at Philadelphia. When the Revolution broke out, two medical school professors, Rush and Shippen, entered the army, and presently Rush brought charges against Shippen of peculations in army hospital supplies. Rush resigned his commission and busied himself gathering evidence against Shippen, with Morgan's support. In the end, despite substantial evidence from disinterested witnesses, Shippen was acquitted. When further efforts by Morgan to pursue the case proved unavailing, Morgan resigned his position on the staff of the Pennsylvania Hospital and thereafter gradually withdrew from professional life. Rush filled the resulting vacancy on the hospital staff and continued as professor of chemistry in the medical school, training a long line of distinguished students. He continued to teach until his death in 1813, by which time two of his best students, Caspar Wistar, president of the American Philosophical Society, and John Redman Coxe, were colleagues on the faculty.[34]

By then, however, the medical profession had lost much of its intellectual distinction in Pennsylvania and the region south of New England generally. Rush himself proved to be the principal contributor to this intellectual decline. The physician could reasonably present himself as a man of letters only so long as he possessed the best education in the community—and also only while science, including medical science, offered subject matter of general interest to educated laymen. Thus Dr. David Hosack, in his introductory lecture at the New York College of Physicians and Surgeons in 1811, could equate medicine with letters in observing that the city of New York "has not hitherto sustained that high literary character that had distinguished the metropolis of Pennsylvania" and vowing that "this otherwise flourishing city will be rendered the literary, as it is now the commercial emporium of our country" at that future time when "the city of New York shall become no less distinguished for its medical schools, than it is for its commerce."[35]

However, the academic standards of American medical schools declined, even as the schools increased in number. By the time Rush died, in 1813, seven medical colleges had been chartered, among which the college at Philadelphia retained the greatest national influence and number of students. Nevertheless, Jefferson, who examined the state of American medical education in the course of organizing the University of Virginia, did not believe that the Philadelphia college was living up to its reputation in the 1820s. It had "lost its character of primacy," Jefferson wrote, "by indulging motives of favoritism and nepotism and by conferring the appointments as if the professorships were entrusted to them as provisions for their friends."[36]

More fundamentally, academic standards declined there and elsewhere with the introduction of the simplified system of heroic medicine propounded by Rush. Heroic medicine treated disease using a method that, although uniform and comprehensive, required neither demanding study nor breadth of learning. No Greek or even Latin was needed beyond the ability to understand medical nomenclature—one reason why Rush had discouraged the pursuit of classical studies in college. How relatively unlearned medicine had become by comparison with the professions of law and divinity is indicated by the fact that, while 80 percent of theological students and 65 percent of law students in the United States were college graduates in 1850, only 26 percent of medical students held bachelor's degrees.[37] Individual Americans, including such leaders of the profession as John W. Francis, Valentine Mott, and Jacob Bigelow Jr., continued to study medicine in Europe and to pursue intellectually distinguished careers in America. But the profession they headed had as a whole substantially abandoned earlier ambitions to learnedness.

⇥ IV ⇤

THE PHILADELPHIA ENLIGHTENMENT personified by Benjamin Franklin was a man's world almost entirely: the Junto, the Library Company and Fire Company, the Philosophical Society and the Academy and College were all male forums—not to mention the manly arenas of politics, warfare, and diplomacy. After Franklin married Deborah Read Rogers in 1730, she proved, according to his *Autobiography*,

> a good and faithful helpmate. . . . It was lucky for me that I had one as much disposed to industry and frugality as myself. She assisted me

cheerfully in my business, folding and stitching pamphlets, tending shop, purchasing old linen rags for the papermakers, etc., etc.[38]

Franklin certainly gives no hint here of intellectual companionship like Benjamin Rush's loving appreciation for his "dear Mrs. Rush engaged in reading Millot's 'Account of the Manners and Laws of the Ancient Egyptians.'" Nor did Franklin seek feminine intellectual companionship outside the household.

The same Franklin who later attracted the affections of alluring and intellectual younger women in Europe appears to have made no close friendships with Philadelphia women. While passing through Rhode Island in 1855, at age 49, Franklin struck up a friendship with Catherine Ray and later corresponded with her. Ray became the first in a succession of intelligent and attractive younger women in Franklin's life.[39] Mixed intellectual company was also available in eighteenth-century Philadelphia for those who sought it, sometimes in social gatherings modeled upon the salons of London and Paris. However, Franklin seemingly never found the occasion, or perhaps had not reached the age, when he could take pleasure in the company of intellectual women.

Where mixed social intercourse of a literary nature was concerned, Americans were virtuously and patriotically inclined to be wary of European examples. Conscious of the relative purity as well as the provinciality of their society, Americans did not seek to replicate what they perceived as the decadent societies of London and Paris. Nevertheless, to facilitate social intercourse of a literary nature where women were involved, Americans, led by certain strong-minded women, did draw upon and domesticate two models of such mixed intellectual company, one French and the other English.[40]

The social institution of the salon was native to France, where it was identified with women of great personal attraction as well as great force of intellect, women who exerted intriguing rather than domineering authority in mixed literary company. For Americans at the beginning of the Republic, the best-known mistress of such a salon was Madame de Staël, who was herself especially attracted to America and during Jefferson's administration actually intended to move there. The model of the French salon especially influenced drawing room society in America during the early years of the Republic, when French ideas and fashions enjoyed their greatest vogue. French influence declined thereafter, but American ideas of French manners and fashions survived the subsequent American reaction against French morality and politics—perhaps especially among women.

Intellectual women in eighteenth-century England organized gatherings that borrowed the intellectual sociability of the French salon without what they considered to be the nonsense that went with it. Solid learning rather than facile wit was offered as the basis for good conversation. A generation before Mme. de Staël, Lady Montagu, already noted for her literary breakfasts, became the leading member of a coterie that included Hannah Moore and Fanny Burney and that evolved into the Bluestocking Club in the 1760s. Samuel Johnson, David Garrick, Edmund Burke, and Horace Walpole were among the frequent visitors to the Bluestocking salon. The name of the club attracted attention at once, and *bluestocking* entered the English language as a term denoting a woman with serious intellectual or literary interests.

In America intellectually motivated women consciously emulated these two European models of sociability: the ever fashionable French model of mistress of the salon, drawing upon feminine social adroitness in arranging meetings of minds, chiefly male, and the ever unfashionable English bluestocking model of no-nonsense, cultivated discourse, chiefly among women. Outside literary salons and clubs, society at large was mixed by nature, as were the families that constituted it. And whether or not men of letters chose to include *femmes savants* in the Literary Republic, literary women shared such sociability as society at large afforded. This varied widely in America from one locality to another.

Eighteenth-century Philadelphia was not lacking in cultivated Quaker, Presbyterian, or Anglican women. Friends' schools offered what was essentially college preparatory training, including optional programs in Latin and Greek, and Quaker girls received educations more nearly equal to those of boys than elsewhere in America. Affluent Quaker families such as the Drinkers, Callenders, and Wistars trained their daughters at home and in Friends' schools to be bluestockings from social conviction. Elizabeth Drinker was such a Quaker bluestocking, drawing widely on the resources of the Philadelphia Library, including works of Rabelais, which she expected to be "very sensible and clever—but on looking over ye books, found them filled with such obscene dirty matter that I was ashamed I had sent for them."[41] While Quaker women might be encouraged to improve their minds, they were no more expected to make an ostentatious show of their learning than were Quaker men. Authorized by their church to express themselves on public matters as women of other denominations were not, they were at the same time obliged to devote themselves to worthy and benevolent causes. Some Quaker women became especially interested in the abolition of slavery and in women's rights, as were Lucretia Mott and Sarah and Angelina Grimké.

Organized interest in *belles lettres* among women and men in Philadelphia was chiefly nurtured by cultivated Anglican clergymen: Richard Peters, Jacob Duché, and Provost William Smith of the College of Philadelphia. As provost, Smith early gathered about him a brilliant circle of young men, including the painter Benjamin West, the playwright Thomas Godfrey, the poet Nathaniel Evans, and the artist-poet, Francis Hopkinson. But the circle dissolved as these men pursued their varied careers, while Smith and the college were increasingly distracted from aesthetic pursuits by the politics of revolution.[42]

Philadelphia society was introduced to the bluestocking salon by the daughter of a prominent Anglican physician and jurist. Elizabeth Graeme, having been jilted by Benjamin Franklin's son, William, was sent to England in the party of the Reverend Peters, who was well connected in London. According to Benjamin Rush, "She sought, and was sought for, by the most celebrated literary gentlemen" in England. Returning to Philadelphia, she became mistress of her father's estate, Graeme Park, in the summer and of his Philadelphia town house in the winter. At the town house Graeme presided over Saturday "evenings" that at one time or another attracted most of Philadelphia's literary society. According to Rush, Graeme's evenings were,

> properly speaking, of the Attic kind. The genius of Miss Graeme evolved the heat and light that animated them. . . . [S]he charmed by a profusion of useful ideas . . . combined with exquisite taste and judgement into an endless variety of elegant and delightful forms. Upon these occasions her body seemed to vanish, and she appeared to be all mind.[43]

It was no easy thing to be an accomplished intellectual woman in America, either then or later.

Graeme's successor as mistress of Philadelphia's leading salon was Anna Willing Bingham. As the daughter of Thomas Willing, president of the Bank of North America, and wife of Senator William Bingham, the nation's richest merchant, Anna came from the top drawer of the city's Anglican establishment. In Paris the Binghams were presented to the court of Louis XVI; in London and Bath they circulated among aristocrats; and upon returning to America, Anna Bingham became the acknowledged queen of the "Republican Court" in Philadelphia. An intelligent and witty as well as rich and beautiful woman, she attracted the American minister in France, Thomas Jefferson, who wrote her upon her return to America that she was to tell him "truly and honestly, whether you do not find the tranquil pleasures of America preferable to the empty bustle of Paris," when "the society of your husband, the fond cares for the children, the arrangements of the house, the improvements of the grounds, fill every moment with a healthy and useful activity."[44]

However she may have replied to Jefferson's rhetorical question, Anna Bingham did not permit domestic activities to fill her life. Instead she gave parties for the elite of the nation, who gathered in the federal capital. Her racy vocabulary and the extravagance of her parties shocked the puritanical French visitor Brissot de Warville, but she impressed New Englanders, including John and Abigail Adams. Abigail observed that "Mrs. Bingham has certainly given laws to the ladies here, in fashion and elegance," while John was surprised to be able to carry on "something of a political conversation with her" at the dinner table, receiving "more ideas on the subject and a correcter judgment" than he had expected from a lovely lady of fashion.[45] Anna Bingham died in 1801, and the Republican Court died with her, the Federal government having relocated itself to the District of Columbia. Subsequent efforts of Philadelphia hostesses to organize their own salons failed to come up to Bingham's parties or Graeme's evenings. On the contrary, Philadelphia's literary society from the turn of the century onward was increasingly characterized by the separation of women from the serious intellectual life of the community.

Other Philadelphia hostesses might pride themselves on their conversational adroitness in the drawing room and at the dinner table without necessarily thinking of themselves as mistresses of salons. What most evidently distinguished the Binghams following their return from Europe in 1796—and before them the even richer Robert Morrises, before Morris went to financial ruin—was their enthusiasm for entertaining out-of-towners. Visitors from abroad and members of the federal government and their wives were less welcome in other Philadelphia households. The Revolution-racked Philadelphia gentry had reestablished itself and consolidated its position by the time the federal government took up residence in 1790. Philadelphians had their own circles of acquaintances and did not necessarily feel honored or obligated to invite outsiders to their social events.[46]

Visitors with favorable social connections in Philadelphia tended to admire the city and enjoy themselves there. Virginians, who possessed no comparable metropolis of their own other than Norfolk, sometimes had good things to say of it. Robert Hunter Jr. thought Philadelphia the most beautiful city he had ever seen, next to London, and predicted it would become "the first city in the world." Jefferson wrote that London, though handsomer than Paris, was "not so handsome as Philadelphia."[47] Jefferson remained very much at home among his scientific and political friends in Philadelphia, where he was elected vice president of the American Philosophical Society and then elevated to president following the death of David Rittenhouse in 1796. President Washington was well appreciated in social circles as the first gentleman of the Republic and as an addition to any gathering he might choose to grace with his presence. On the other hand, John and Abigail Adams, as president and first lady, were snubbed by some of the same party-givers who had sought the Washingtons' company.

Most of the Philadelphia gentry continued to socialize among themselves as they had mainly done even during the Washington administrations.[48] The duc de Liancourt found Philadelphia to be the least hospitable of all American cities, and Noah Webster observed that this was the deserved reputation of the city generally. In 1798 Harrison Gray Otis, a more sociable and sociably eligible Bostonian than President Adams, wrote his wife in Boston that the Philadelphia elite were "all an unsocial formal crew" who "do not choose to notice me or others out of their own circle." Philadelphia was frequently compared unfavorably to New York in this respect. An English merchant, Isaac Weld, visiting Philadelphia at the turn of the century, was amazed at the "pride, haughtiness and ostentation of the city's leading families," who seemed to wish to belong to an order of nobility. Two generations later the English novelist Thomas Hamilton wrote, "There is no American city in which the system of *exclusion* is so rigidly observed as in Philadelphia. . . . There is a sort of holy alliance between its members to forbid all unauthorized approach."[49] High culture in nineteenth-century Philadelphia remained the very exclusive preserve of these established families.

The 1790s were horrendous years for Philadelphia. The most catastrophic year of the decade was 1793, when the Jacobins established a reign of terror in France and Jacobinic Democratic-Republican societies formed themselves in Philadelphia and elsewhere throughout the United States. These societies exacerbated ideological and economic divisions that were defining organized and furiously warring political parties of Federalists and Republicans. Thousands of émigrés, fleeing the Reign of Terror, crossed the ocean and took up residence in Philadelphia. There they grew into a socially and politically disturbing presence, an alien, French-language culture that shocked Anglo-Americans by flaunting the scandalously revealing women's fashions of revolutionary France.[50] Several thousand additional French refugees fled to Philadelphia from a slave rebellion in Santo Domingo in 1793, bringing with them a contagion more virulent than French fashion.

Yellow fever was endemic in eighteenth-century Philadelphia, as in other American cities. But in the summer of 1793, yellow fever deaths rose from three to five to a dozen or more each day, increasing to an estimated total of five thousand—one for every ten residents—before the November frosts ended the epidemic. Through it all heroic Benjamin Rush remained in the city, attending patients when other doctors fled the area, applying his heroic medicine of purgatives and bleedings that hastened the victims to their deaths.[51] Recurrence of the plague in subsequent summers, with another severe epidemic in 1798, kept the city in a seasonal state of alarm throughout the federal period, which ended for Philadelphia when President Adams departed the city in 1800 to take up residence in the muddy, swampy District of Columbia. Philadelphia was left in the undisputed possession of its leading families.

≼ V ≽

WASHINGTON, D.C., IN 1800 held little appeal for Adams, but it was home territory to his successor, Thomas Jefferson of nearby Monticello. Jefferson had personally chosen the site and arranged for its establishment as the new national capital. While serving as president of the United States, Jefferson continued to hold the office of president of the American Philosophical Society, and when he moved from Philadelphia to Washington, the Philadelphia Enlightenment in effect moved with him.

To some politicians Washington in the early days was a "desert city," an "abomination of desolation."[52] One leaky wing of the Capitol was nearing completion amid mud and construction rubble at the time Jefferson took office. In the executive mansion, the stairs on the second floor were not completed until Jefferson's last year as president, and the main reception room was not plastered until after John Quincy Adams arrived in 1825. Clustered around each of the main public buildings were boardinghouses where legislators, judges, and government workers put themselves up. Legislators' wives, who had formerly taken up residence in Philadelphia during the legislative and social season, tended not to accompany their husbands to Washington.

From the beginning the diplomatic corps contributed a cosmopolitan air to the community, however, and presently the village grew to a town of twenty thousand when Jackson entered the White House and to 40,000 at midcentury. The British diplomat Augustus Foster considered Jeffersonian Washington to be "the most agreeable town to reside in for any length of time which I have seen in the United States," in spite of "its inconveniences and its desolate appearance." Administration leaders were "generally very hospitable and agreeable persons, some of them having even been in Europe, while the *corps diplomatique* are a great resource and would alone suffice to place society on a good footing." It was true that most congressmen "keep to their lodgings, but still there are a sufficient number of them who are sociable or whose families come to the city for a season, and there is no want of handsome ladies for the balls" from the surrounding towns, though "the literary education of these ladies is far from being worthy of the Age of Knowledge, and conversation is apt to flag."[53]

For Jefferson, Washington was an inviting corner of his native province. "This may be considered as a pleasant country residence," he wrote Joel Barlow from Washington, "with a number of neat little villages scattered around within the distance of a mile and a half, and furnishing a plain and substantially good society." To another friend he wrote that Washington afforded "a charming society and not too much of it, all living on affectionate and unceremonious terms."[54]

Of the capital's permanent population, a large number were beggars and welfare cases who had arrived under the mistaken impression that easy money would be available. As to Jefferson's plain and substantially good society, it was chiefly limited to the diplomatic corps and the 201 persons who made up the federal government, including some of the young republic's most distinguished intellectuals. Within his cabinet Jefferson enjoyed the scholarly companionship of James Madison, Albert Gallatin, and Levi Lincoln. Congress was liberally supplied with such men of intellectual distinction as Harvard professor of rhetoric and oratory John Quincy Adams; Columbia professor of medicine and the sciences Samuel Latham Mitchill; geologist William Maclure; and economist Adam Seybert.

Jefferson was generally recognized throughout Europe and America to be the outstanding American philosopher of his generation, just as Franklin had been of the preceding generation. Even those Federalist enemies who slandered him recklessly regarding his religious, moral, and political character often acknowledged the amazing intellectual attainments of the man they attacked as "the American Condorcet." Jefferson the lawyer, political philosopher, agricultural scientist, inventor, natural historian, architect, classical scholar, man of letters, and musician impressed his contemporaries as much as he has subsequent generations. Jefferson's second administration ended badly with the diplomatically ineffective and politically and economically disastrous Embargo Act, but the first seven years of his presidency were successful socially and intellectually as well as politically. Jefferson retained firm control of Congress throughout his presidency, and among his most effective means of maintaining this control were nightly dinners at the executive mansion, which also constituted a continuous intellectual event without parallel elsewhere in the nation or ever afterward in the White House.

Ten or twelve persons were invited to dine with the President nightly at a round table, designed to circumvent social precedence and inhibit private conversations. Wine and food appeared in the room in a dumbwaiter—a Jeffersonian invention—and were served to the guests by the President himself to dispense with the presence of servants. The widower Jefferson had brought a French chef home from Europe, and the meals were extraordinarily lavish as well as delicious. Excellent French wines flowed freely, and Federalist legislators, who were coolly reserved upon their arrival at the executive mansion, habitually found themselves lingering on into the evening, enjoying the wine and the conversation. Jefferson did not mix Federalists with Republicans at his dinners, and politics was ruled out as a subject of conversation, though not as Jefferson's basis for planning his guest list.[55]

Jefferson the conversationalist is best known from Pennsylvania Senator William Maclay's sympathetic description.

> He sits in a lounging manner, on one hip commonly, and with one of his shoulders elevated above the other. His face has a sunny aspect. His whole figure has a loose, shackling air. He had a rambling, vacant look, and nothing of that firm collected deportment . . . I looked for gravity, but a laxity of manner seemed to shed about him. He spoke almost without ceasing; but, even his discourse partook of his personal demeanour. It was loose and rambling; and yet he scattered information wherever he went, and some even brilliant sentiments sparkled from him.[56]

Senator John Quincy Adams periodically attended Jefferson's dinners, as did all of the legislators. Quincy Adams enjoyed the dinners but came in time to detest his host, criticizing the sage of Monticello for telling tall stories and setting himself up somewhat pontifically as a connosieur of fine wines. Nevertheless, Adams conceded that Jefferson had a good mind and much learning and that the table talk in his dining room could be most agreeable. During the years of Jefferson's administration, the political society of the small capital town conformed as well as could ever be expected to Jefferson's notions of a natural aristocracy of virtue and talents. When Jefferson left office in 1809, he moved his intellectual feast home with him to Monticello, a hundred miles away. Afterward the federal capital lost the intellectual sociability he had brought to it, despite the formidable intellect of his successor, James Madison, and the sociability of Madison's wife, Dolley.

Had the federal capital remained in or around Philadelphia or New York and had a national university been created in connection with it—as Benjamin Rush, George Washington, and other founding fathers urged— the result would have been an American political-commercial-cultural metropolis on the model of London or Paris. But American patriots did not intend to replicate the sprawling squalor and decadence of Europe's great urban centres, if that could be avoided. Furthermore, provincial jealousies opposed establishing the national capital permanently in any of the existing cities, since such a move would establish that city in a commanding position over the other cities of the nation. What Americans opted for instead, at the urging of Jefferson and other Virginians in 1791, was the founding of a capital village at more or less the nation's midpoint, the Virginia-Maryland border. Although Washington, D.C., was planned on a scale befitting a great republic, what came into being was the appropriately modest capital village of a decidedly provincial nation.[57] That the first citizen of this capital village from 1801 to 1809 was simultaneously president of the United States and of the American Philosophical Society might have given American politics an appearance of unity to those outside the Republic. Any such impression would have been misleading. As a political leader Jefferson was fiercely opposed by his enemies and widely reviled, especially by New England intellectuals. For instance, Fisher Ames, Boston's leading man of letters, wrote of Jefferson's presidency in 1801:

> Our days are made heavy with the pressure of anxiety, and our nights restless with the visions of horror. We listen to the clank of chains, and overhear the whispers of assassins. We mark the barbarous dissonance of mingled rage and triumph in the yell of an infatuated mob.[58]

The political-literary talent that Ames employed against the Jeffersonians won him in 1804 the offer of president of Harvard; he declined on grounds of ill health.

Despite the fulminations of Ames and other bitter Federalists, Jefferson managed to accumulate substantial political support in New England during the years that followed. Certainly his political writ ran more authoritatively throughout the nation than did his intellectual mandate as president of the American Philosophical Society. By the turn of the century, the society seemed less truly national than when Jefferson joined it, for during the post-Revolutionary years other regions of the nation organized their own competing societies.

◈ VI ◈

DURING THE REVOLUTION the Patriot minister-historian Jeremy Belknap of Boston corresponded with fellow historians such as David Ramsay in South Carolina and Ebenezer Hazard in Philadelphia to advance their common objective of weaving their separate provincial histories into a coherent American national history, tracing their common struggles for liberty from the first settlements to the founding of the nation. In the course of this exchange, Belknap wrote Hazard to suggest that the sort of communications they were engaged in might fruitfully be expanded and systematized on a national basis by the creation of "inferior societies or boards of correspondents in the several states, connected with the principal one at Philadelphia, and united in the same views." Indeed, Belknap went on,

> Why may not a *Republic of Letters* be realized in America as well as Republican Government? Why may there not be subordinate philosophical bodies connected with a principal one, as well as separate legislatures, acting in concert by a common assembly? I am so far an enthusiast in the cause of America as to wish she may shine Mistress of the Sciences, as well as the Asylum of Liberty.[59]

Belknap's fellow Bostonian John Adams could have told him why there might not be such a system of subordinate philosophical bodies connected with the principal one at Philadelphia. Several years earlier, when John Adams learned about the American Philosophical Society at first hand in Philadelphia, he wrote Abigail, "They have societies, the Philosophical Society particularly, which excites scientific emulation, and propagates their fame," and he thought it fitting for Boston to have its own society, "if I have wit and address enough to accomplish it, sometime or other."[60] Following a diplomatic mission to Paris, Adams was charged in 1780 with formulating a constitution for Massachusetts; he simultaneously busied himself founding the American Academy of Arts and Sciences. Belknap became an enthusiastic charter member. The American Academy was emphatically independent of the American Philosophical Society, not the subordinate organization Belknap envisioned in his patriotic effusion to Hazard.

But Belknap himself did not act upon his nationalistic impulse, so far as writing history was concerned. His bold correspondence with Hazard and other like-minded scholars led nowhere. Instead, Belknap narrowed his focus and convinced four Boston associates to join him in forming the Massachusetts Historical Society in 1794, the first of its kind in the nation. Scholars elsewhere became determined that similar historical societies should be founded in their states, and before long state historical societies existed nationwide. A national historical association did not superimpose itself upon state institutions until the age of the university and the academic historian, a century later.

Independence inspired all sorts of learned and professional societies to proliferate at the local and state level. New medical, agricultural, horticultural, and natural history societies sprang up, augmented by overlapping memberships and subdivided by local cliquish antagonisms. To the Philosophical Society and the Medical Society, Philadelphians added the Agricultural Society, the Medical Lyceum, the Academy of Natural Sciences, and the Linnaean Society. Similarly, New York boasted the County Medical Society, the Philo-Medical Society, the Society for the Promotion of the Useful Arts, the New York Linnaean Society, the New York Lyceum of National History, the New York Horticultural Society, and the County Agricultural Society, as well as the Literary and Philosophical Society, the New York Academy of Fine Arts, and the New-York Historical Society.[61]

As the American Academy of Arts and Sciences was Boston's response to the American Philosophical Society at Philadelphia, so was the Connecticut Academy of Arts and Sciences New Haven's response to Boston's claim to represent the New England intellect. These and other societies aimed to enroll distinguished members, nationally and internationally. Conversely, multiple memberships in learned societies added to an intellectual's distinction, and consequently there was much overlapping of memberships in these societies.

In New York the physician-scientist-linguist-historian-senator Samuel Latham Mitchill belonged to at least fifty learned societies at home and abroad, a record that his colleague Dr. David Hosack did his best to break. Hosack served as president of the New-York Historical Society, as vice president under DeWitt Clinton of the Literary and Philosophical Society, and as member and patron of numerous other associations, including the American Philosophical Society in Philadelphia, the American Academy of Arts and Sciences in Boston, the Academy of Arts and Sciences in New Haven, and the Linnaean Society in London. To top all of this off, in 1818 Hosack managed to finagle membership as a fellow of the Royal Society of London. Hosack's membership in the Royal Society was elaborately planned by him and successfully carried out by his junior partner in medical practice, John W. Francis, while Francis was on a visit to London. Afterward, replying to a letter of congratulation, Hosack wrote that

> Our friend Mitchill is teased at every corner, that he has been omitted. . . . [B]elieve me I feel very modest upon this occasion. . . . [I]t will excite expectations that cannot be realized. . . . I am not a little gratified— for let me add it was altogether unexpected and unsolicited by me.[62]

A national Republic of Letters such as Belknap proposed may perhaps be said to have emerged in the membership lists of these learned societies. Yet the societies themselves remained parochial in character, however cosmopolitan their membership lists might be. Nor were these societies scrupulous about maintaining robust standards of scholarship, as Hugh Henry Brackenridge indicated in his send-up of the American Philosophical Society in *Modern Chivalry.* Regarding "a society of Philosophers" in "a certain great city," Brackenridge conceded that unquestionably "there were in this body some very great men, whose investigations of the arcana of nature deserve attention"; yet it was also the case that others were admitted "who were no philosophers at all." It had been necessary for them as candidates

> to procure some token of a philosophical turn of mind; such as the skin of a dead cat, or some odd kind of mouse-trap, or the like; or to

have some phrases in their mouths about minerals or petrifactions, so as just to support some idea of natural knowledge, and pass muster. [However,] these exuviae or spoils of the animal kingdom were but the tokens and apologies for admission.[63]

In addition to exemplifying the inveterate parochialism of early American national culture, these learned societies reflected a basically utilitarian, unbelletristic conception of prose shared by men of the American Enlightenment. As a boy in Boston, Benjamin Franklin copied Joseph Addison in developing a literary style of his own. As the compiler of his *Poor Richard's Almanac*, he ransacked writings of such literary masters as Pope, Swift, La Rochefoucauld, and Rabelais. As printer he published Samuel Richardson's *Pamela* (1744), the first novel printed in America. As bookseller he handled such literary works as were in demand. Yet he never developed any evident interest in literature for its own sake, nor did he publish much of a literary nature after the one novel. As a London resident beginning in 1757, his circle of friends included William Strahan, the printer of Samuel Johnson's dictionary, but not Johnson or other members of Johnson's circle. Franklin and his friend James Pringle, the medical scientist, did dine once with James Boswell, according to Boswell's journal. But no mention of the occasion is to be found in Franklin's writings.[64]

Franklin was the prosaic sort of literary man who composed pamphlets on practical matters such as political science, education, demography, and economics. It was literary men of this ilk that Jeremy Belknap had in mind when he suggested "a national *Republic of Letters*." He envisioned it as a confederation of scholarly bodies subordinate to the American Philosophical Society and sharing the same views. The community of scholars enrolled in this confederation would devote themselves to "promoting useful knowledge" through the pursuit of natural history, emphasizing the agricultural, mechanical, and medical sciences, together with the pursuit of civil history, observing the working out of natural law in human societies and drawing useful morals from the past experiences of mankind. Belknap himself qualified perfectly for such a literary society. His major work, the scholarly and still valuable *History of New Hampshire* (3 vols., 1784–92), comprises a natural history of upper New England together with a civil history of New Hampshire to 1789.

Jefferson's *Notes on the State of Virginia* similarly combines a natural history of Old Dominion with an examination of its civil history, political structure, and society. Written in Jefferson's lucid style, the exposition serves throughout to elucidate Jefferson's social philosophy. Jefferson wrote Charles Thomson from Paris in 1785, "In literature nothing new; for I do not consider as having added any thing to that field by my own Notes of which I have had a few copies printed."[65] Jefferson greeted the appearance of William Bartram's *Travels* (1790), describing the plants, animals, and native peoples of the American southeast, as a literary event. Together with George Washington and John Adams, Jefferson was among those who purchased subscriptions to pay publication costs for Bartram's work.

The affinity between intellectual Philadelphians and natural history oriented toward medical science had a parallel in Boston, where intellectuals gravitated to civil history. When John Adams, Belknap, and others founded the American Academy of Arts and Sciences in Boston in 1780, they elected an amateur historian, Governor James Bowdoin, as president, and Bowdoin inaugurated the proceedings of the academy with a discussion of historical development as revealed in the rise and fall of four ancient empires. Among Bowdoin's qualifications to be a historian, political experience was of the first importance. Active participation in public affairs had been considered appropriate if not essential to the training of the civil historian since Thucydides participated in the Peloponnesian War and recorded its history as well. American men in public life had been conscious of filling significant historical roles since the times of America's founding historians, Captain John Smith of Virginia, Governor William Bradford of Plymouth, and Governor John Winthrop of Massachusetts.

In the years preceding the Revolution, the careers of William Smith of New York and Governor Thomas Hutchinson of Massachusetts united historical scholarship with statesmanship, as did the careers of David Ramsay of South Carolina, John Marshall of Virginia, and Governors Bowdoin and James Sullivan of Massachusetts after Independence. As a clergyman Belknap sought no political office, but the Massachusetts ratifying convention of 1787 met in his Federal Street Church with Belknap serving as recording secretary. John Adams made substantial contributions to civil history: *A Dissertation on the Canon and Feudal Law*, initially published as four newspaper articles in 1765; *Defence of the Constitutions of the United States of America against the Attack of M. Turgot*, published in three volumes in 1787; and *Discourse on Davila*, published in 1791.

Belles lettres and aesthetics were no part of the Harvard curriculum at the time John Adams attended that institution, and while belles lettres was introduced to William and Mary by Jefferson's favorite professor, William Small, Jefferson himself does not appear to have appreciated literature's intrinsic beauty any more than Adams or Belknap did. The academic emergence of belles lettres as an aspect of American letters got its most auspicious start at the College of Philadelphia, where Provost William Smith's circle of undergraduate literati included the painter Benjamin West, the artist-poet Francis Hopkinson, the poet Nathaniel Evans, and the playwright Thomas Godfrey. In 1767 Godfrey's *The Prince of Parthia* became the first play by an American to be produced by a professional troupe when it was staged by Lewis Hallam's English company in Philadelphia. Several years later Yale undergraduates and instructors, including Timothy Dwight and later Joel Barlow and Noah Webster, formed themselves into the patriotically American circle of poets who became known as the Connecticut Wits. At President John Witherspoon's College of New Jersey, Hugh Henry Brackenridge and Philip Freneau coauthored a commencement poem for the graduating class of 1771 on "The Rising Glory of America," envisioning a "seat of empire" where "fair freedom shall forever reign" and where science, literature, and the arts would flourish.

Might there have been a place for these belletrists and artists in Belknap's proposed Republic of Letters? When John Adams met his fellow Continental Congressman Francis Hopkinson in Charles Willson Peale's studio in 1776, he hardly knew what to make of the "curious gentleman" who was a painter, poet, playwright, and musician as well as lawyer and public man. John wrote Abigail that Hopkinson proved to be "genteel and well bred, and is very social," adding that he wished he himself "had leisure and tranquility of mind to amuse myself with those elegant and ingenious arts of painting, sculpture, statuary, architecture, and music. But I have not. A taste for all of them is an agreeable accomplishment." On the other hand, a taste for such arts could be supported only at a risk to civic virtue. Adams admonished the aristocratic painter John Trumbull to

> Remember that the burin and the pencil, the chisel and the trowel, have in all ages and countries of which we have any information, been enlisted on the side of despotism and superstition. . . . [A]rchitecture, sculpture, painting, and poetry have conspired against the rights of mankind.[66]

Jefferson had a taste for the elegant and ingenious arts, particularly architecture and music, and as a young man he professed a taste for belles lettres as well. The list of recommended books that Jefferson drew up in 1771 for Robert Skipworth included an extensive list of novels, plays, and verse under the heading Fine Arts. Jefferson defended their inclusion with the argument that "the entertainments of fiction are useful as well as pleasant" and that "Considering history as a moral exercise, her lessons would be too infrequent if confined to real life." Later in life, however, Jefferson came to condemn the novel as offering effeminate reading for men while serving "to debauch the morals of the fair sex." Rather than providing a moral exercise, Jefferson now concluded, the novel "infects the mind, destroys its tone," and insinuates "disgust toward all the real business of life."[67]

In his earlier letter to Skipworth, Jefferson disparaged "the learned lumber of Greek and Roman reading" and the hypothetical "reverend sage" who might suppose that no other reading was useful. Four decades later, on the other hand, he wrote John Adams that he had "given up newspapers in exchange for Tacitus and Thucydides, for Newton and Euclid; and I find myself much the happier." To this Adams replied that he had "read Thucydides and Tacitus, so often, and at such distant Periods of my Life, that elegant, profound and enchanting as is their style, I am weary of them." During their correspondence over the next fourteen years, Adams and Jefferson returned repeatedly to classical writings but left all of English belles lettres out of account except for a reference to Milton's angels here and a quotation from Pope's translation of the *Iliad* there. The letters contain no mention whatever of English novelists and none of Shakespeare.[68]

Had Jefferson valued belles lettres as he valued natural history and classical literature, he would have given leadership to the little band of young literary nationalists that included such ardent Jeffersonians as Freneau, Brackenridge, Peale, Dunlap, and Barlow. But Jefferson remained intellectually a man of his own generation rather than theirs. He was generous in his praise of Freneau as a journalist but evidently oblivious to Freneau's achievements as a lyric poet. When Joel Barlow presented Jefferson with a copy of his own "patriotic legacy to my country" in verse, *The Columbiad* (1807), Jefferson wrote to thank him for the book, mentioning that he had not had an opportunity to read the verse itself but expressing his admiration for the beauty of the book's binding.[69]

Samuel Latham Mitchill was an extraordinarily accomplished man of letters of the old school who outlived the Enlightenment era only to be treated by irreverently belletristic literati of the younger generation as a figure of fun. Mitchill, who graduated from Edinburgh in 1786, became known to his contemporaries as "the Doctor": professor of natural history at Columbia, Jeffersonian congressman and senator from New York, and representative of a vanishing breed of enlightened universal man in an age when fields of scientific knowledge were rapidly expanding beyond the capacity of any individual to comprehend them all. The breadth of Mitchill's learning was phenomenal, even by the standards of Jefferson, who fondly referred to the Doctor as "the Congressional Dictionary." Learned in chemistry, geology, icthyology, botany, anthropology, and history, Mitchill was also a linguist who produced translations from Spanish, German, Latin, and Dutch and who was versed in American Indian languages as well as in classical Greek. If any one scholar could be said to have remained conversant with the proliferating scientific information of the day, it was Mitchill. "No one in our scientific ranks," declared Henry Rowe Schoolcraft, "is more alive to the progress of discovery in all its physical branches."[70] From 1797 to 1813 Mitchill edited the nation's leading scientific periodical, *Medical Repository*, which reflected the wide-ranging nature of his intellectual interests.

There was something almost absurd about the incredible content of Mitchill's knowledge. President Benjamin Moore of Columbia referred to his star professor as a chaos of knowledge, and Moore's successor believed that Mitchill's learning was less valuable to him than it was to the many others who used him as a living encyclopedia. He served as a favorite butt of ridicule for the fiercely anti-Jeffersonian literary aesthete Joseph Dennie in Dennie's *Port Folio*. Young literary wits of New York with no political axes to grind also enjoyed making light of him. Indeed, Washington Irving's *Knickerbocker History of New York* started out as a parody of Mitchill's somewhat fulsome as well as remarkably recondite guide to Manhattan, *Picture of New-York* (1807). As it turned out the pedantic introductory chapter Irving intended to write in Mitchell's manner developed into the history as told by Irving's own different creation, Dietrich Knickerbocker. A generation later Mitchill reappeared, lampooned for perhaps the last time as the "Fellow of forty-nine societies," in *The Croakers*, a highly popular satirical verse by Fitz-Greene Halleck and Joseph Rodman Drake that appeared off and on during the 1820s in the New York *Post*.[71]

Literary levity at the expense of the encyclopedically learned doctor may with some justice be taken as a burlesque of the culture of the American Enlightenment as a whole by a younger post-Enlightenment generation. Nineteenth-century literati came to doubt the rationally mechanistic conception of progress to be laboriously but assuredly achieved through the correct classification of greater and greater quantities of knowledge and the useful application of this knowledge to human problems. Literary levity was itself a breach of decorum by Enlightenment standards, which were as morally earnest as Victorian standards ever came to be. It has been aptly said of Benjamin Franklin that humor was "his chief gift, his hallmark, and saving grace."[72] Yet Franklin's *Autobiography*, the classic confession of the American Enlightenment, is a moral tale in which the author presents himself as role model to future generations of young men. Basically that was no laughing matter. Not unnaturally the younger generation of educated Americans who grew up after the establishment of the Republic tended to question the moral authority of the parental generation which had grown up under colonial circumstances which continued to shape their thinking in the drastically altered circumstances of the Federal Republic.

ᴈ 3 ᴈ

REPUBLIC OF
BELLES LETTRES

In November 1807 Senator John Quincy Adams recorded in his diary a dinner at President Jefferson's where there was "much amusing conversation" between the President and Samuel Latham Mitchill. During the course of the evening, Mitchill's

> conversation was very various, of chemistry, of geography, and of natural philosophy; of oils, grasses, beasts, birds, petrifactions, and incrustations; Pike and Humboldt, Lewis and Barlow, and a long train of et cetera—for the Doctor knows a little of everything, and is communicative of what he knows—which makes me delight in his company. . . . On the whole, it was one of the most agreeable dinners I have had at Mr. Jefferson's.

Twenty-four years later, in November 1831, former President John Quincy Adams recorded in his diary an evening spent with former Chancellor James Kent of New York, "talking of his Commentaries, of Blackstone and Wooddeson, Mansfield, Pothier, Emerigon, and Valin, common law and civil law, Littleton's Tenures, and Justinian." Adams read Kent some verse he had written, which Kent "approved, but which reminded him too much of both Gray's *Elegy* and Goldsmith's *Deserted Village*." The conversation turned to Shakespeare's women:

> I observed to him how much of the charm and interest of the tragedy of *Romeo and Juliet* depended upon the age of Juliet—a child in her fourteenth year; how emphatically the poet had marked that age; and how stupidly the stage-men had changed the age from fourteen to nineteen. I said I took little interest in the character of Desdemona, whose sensual passions I thought over-ardent, so as to reconcile her to a passion for a black man; and although faithful to him, I thought the poet had painted

her as a lady of rather easy virtue—very different from the innocence
of Miranda or the rosy pudency of Imogen.[1]

Born in 1767, the year Harvard introduced a course in "English Rhetoric, and other parts of Belles Lettres" to the curriculum,[2] John Quincy
Adams grew up to be equally at home in the enlightened world of his
father and the world of literary sensibility that succeeded it. John and
Abigail Adams carefully raised their eldest son not only to become president but also to be the most broadly cultivated gentleman ever to attain
that office. Whereas John Adams himself had seen nothing of the world
before attending the first Continental Congress in Philadelphia at the age
of thirty-nine, John Quincy was eleven when his father took him to Paris
in 1778, and he had by then already acquired his lifelong daily discipline of
journal writing. John Quincy attended Latin school in Amsterdam, studied at Leyden University, and graduated from Harvard in 1787. He studied
law with Theophilus Parsons, went to the Netherlands on a diplomatic
assignment from President Washington, and spent the four years of his
father's presidency as American minister in Berlin. Returning to Boston
he entered the United States Senate in 1803 and three years later received a
concurrent appointment as professor of rhetoric and oratory at Harvard.

Versed in the classics, the sciences, and the law, much as Jefferson and
John Adams were, John Quincy was also conversant with belles lettres,
which they were not. To be sure, John Adams and Jefferson never questioned the respect that was universally accorded Shakespeare by educated
gentlemen of their generation. However, unlike John Quincy (or his
mother Abigail) they demonstrated no understanding or appreciation of
the bard as the author of plays that remained worth seeing as well as reading. For them, Shakespeare served as a literary moralist whose aphorisms
retained a value quite independent of their sources.[3]

John Quincy Adams overcame inhibitions that had prevented his
father from indulging those aesthetic tastes which John Adams associated
historically with decadence and tyranny. Like Jefferson, John Quincy
schooled himself to be a gourmet and a judge of fine wines, and during
that otherwise agreeable evening at Jefferson's in 1807, he found the
president's "usual" dinnertime "dissertation upon wines" to be "not very
edifying." The Whig political boss, Thurlow Weed, recalled a lavish din-

ner in New York where John Quincy astonished the other guests by identifying eleven of fourteen varieties of Madeira served him by his host. The gentlemanly New York diarist Philip Hone wrote of John Quincy Adams that

> With all his eccentricities, prejudices, and want of tact, we have not his equal in this country for the most minute information on all subjects, technical, statistical, historical and diplomatical. No man knows so much, nor so accurately. He has probed deeply into the arcana of all the sciences, understands and can explain all subjects from the solar system down to the construction of a toothpick. He has the Holy Scriptures at his fingers' ends, knows every line of Shakespeare, can recite Homer in the original Greek; could name, if he had a mind to do it, the author of "Junius," and knows all about Jack the Giant Killer.[4]

Knowledgable as John Quincy Adams might have wished to be in the arcana of all the sciences, he could not hope to keep up with current developments as Mitchill had attempted to do. Mitchill, the encyclopedically learned physician, was among the last of his kind. Mitchill's *Medical Repository* ceased publication in 1813. It was followed in 1818 as the nation's leading scientific periodical by *The American Journal of Science and Arts*, known for two generations thereafter as *Silliman's Journal*. Unlike Mitchill, Benjamin Silliman was not a physician but a scholar who had educated himself in the sciences the better to raise standards of scientific instruction at Yale University. *Silliman's Journal* contained wide-ranging subject matter, much as *Medical Repository* had, and similarly aimed at a generally educated readership. Nevertheless, it reflected a developing professionalism that resisted what the next generation referred to as the "popularization" of science.

Scholarly gentlemen who considered themselves to be versed in the sciences as well as the arts were apt to resent the elitism and seeming obscurity that was coming to characterize scientific discussions. Robert Hare of the University of Pennsylvania wrote Silliman in 1819 of being "told in New York that many said they could not understand my memoir, who considered their standing such as to feel as if this were an imputation against me rather than themselves." It would not have been possible, Hare pointed out, to address the subject to such laymen "without making

it too prolix and commonplace for adepts." In short, "we cannot write anything for the scientific few which will be agreeable to the ignorant many."[5]
"Adepts" and serious amateurs continued to get along with each other after
a fashion, cooperating in 1848 in organizing the American Association for
the Advancement of Sciences (AAAS) to maintain the integrity of scientific
learning against "quackery," a favorite epithet of the professionals. The
AAAS provided a national orientation for the sciences, but its membership
included many who did not meet the rigorously professional, research-
oriented standards of their professional colleagues. The professional members preferred to function more privately among themselves.

In 1832 Joseph Henry arrived at Princeton, bringing him in the vicin-
ity of science-oriented Philadelphia and of Professor Alexander Dallas
Bache of the University of Pennsylvania and Girard College. As Henry
wrote Bache some years later,

> I almost always return from New York dispirited in the way of science.
> I am there thrown among, it appears to me, all the Quacks and Jim-
> crackers of the land. I am disgusted with their pretensions and annoyed
> with their communications. How different is my feeling on a return
> from the [city] of Brotherly Love!! There is there a jealousy and rivalry,
> but also science and intelligence, and trade and money not the only
> things which occupy the mind.

Together Bache and Henry served for more than three decades as the zeal-
ous guardians of professional science, beginning in 1832 with the organization of "the Club," which was limited to men with full-time commitments
to science and dedicated to "promoting research and especially for scruti-
nizing the labor of its members."[6] When Bache and Henry went abroad,
the club ceased to be active, but several remaining members who belonged
to a Philadelphia archery club continued to meet to discuss professional
matters. Bache and Henry later joined with other prominent professionals,
including Louis Agassiz of Harvard, in organizing the informal but influential Order of the Scientific Lazzaroni (named after the poorest class of
Neapolitan beggars) to oversee scientific culture in a nation that, according
to Henry, was overrun with charlatanism and quackery, where "every man
who can burn phosphorous in oxygen and exhibit a few experiments to a
class of young ladies is called a man of science."[7]

The growing division of educated American society into two separate cultures, one scientific and the other humanistic, did not affect some men of learning. Until his death, in 1873, Louis Agassiz participated with gusto and aplomb in both the literary Saturday Club in Boston and the Lawrence Scientific School and the Natural History Museum in Cambridge. On the other hand, a self-consciously belletristic culture came abruptly into being a century or so earlier with the pre-Revolutionary introduction of belles lettres into American college curriculums, followed by the rise of literary lawyers. In Philadelphia at the turn of the nineteenth century, lawyers led by Joseph Dennie advanced a positively antiscientific conception of letters in the columns of Dennie's *Port Folio* magazine, a view that was echoed by literary ministers and lawyers in Boston from 1803 to 1811 in their *Monthly Anthology and Boston Review.*

An ultra-Federalist antagonist of the Jeffersonian Republicans, Dennie retreated from the political contest waged against Jefferson personally when a libel suit persuaded him to moderate his editorial attacks against the president. But Dennie was on the winning side in the literary battle he waged against "the American Condorcet" over possession of the Republic of Letters. Around the turn of the nineteenth century, writers of polite literature supplanted practitioners of utilitarian prose in the Literary Republic. Henceforth, men and women who shared a common interest in belles lettres and allied arts maintained their status as literati whether or not they took an interest in natural history or any other science or useful study.

⇜ II ⇝

BELLES LETTRES EMERGED conspicuously on three college campuses in eighteenth-century America; at Provost William Smith's College of Philadelphia in the 1750s and 1760s, John Witherspoon's College of New Jersey around 1770, and Naphtali "Tunker" Daggett's Yale College, also around 1770. In each institution students responded favorably to the stimulating academic innovation, which had been imported by Smith from Aberdeen and by Witherspoon from Edinburgh. Smith's success with his sponsorship of belles lettres was qualified by the narrowly Anglican orientation of his program, which entailed student trips to London where possible, and by the untimely deaths of two of his protégés, the poet-playwright

Thomas Godfrey, at the age of twenty-seven, and the poet Nathanial Evans, at twenty-four. Witherspoon's program at Princeton imbued Hugh Henry Brackenridge and Philip Freneau with the ambition to pioneer an American national literature. At Yale, under the ineffective presidency of Daggett, tutors and undergraduates, drawing instruction from Kames's textbook *Elements of Criticism*, created their own literary movement. As the "Connecticut Wits," Timothy Dwight, John Trumbull, David Humphreys, and Joel Barlow became the core of the most creative literary circle to emerge in eighteenth-century America. Several other Yale men worked at the movement's periphery, including the editor, textbook writer, and lexicographer Noah Webster and Elihu Hubbard Smith, organizer of the Friendly Society in New York City.

Smith inspired his students by the catholicity and novelty of his ambitions for them and by his infectious confidence in their ability to create a cultural London in Philadelphia as painters, musicians, playwrights, and poets. In 1757 Smith brought out *The American or Monthly Chronicle for the British Colonies*, the fourth magazine to be published in the colonies. For thirteen monthly issues the periodical served as a vehicle for writings by Hopkinson, Godfrey, and other members of Smith's circle. Such serious musical events as occurred in Philadelphia took place at the college, and in 1759 Smith's circle made history when Thomas Godfrey's *The Prince of Parthia* became the first play by an American to be produced by a professional troupe.

Only one professional troupe of actors existed in pre-Revolutionary America. Originally called The London Company of Comedians, the troupe was renamed The American Company of Comedians upon arriving in Virginia in 1752. As such they performed throughout the colonies wherever the law allowed, under the direction of David Douglass and members of the Hallam family. Quaker Philadelphia abhorred the theater, but the Anglican proprietor of the colony was an enthusiastic theatergoer, and plays were produced at the Southwark Theater just outside the Philadelphia city limits. In 1767 the American Company slated for production *The Disappointment*, an original farce lampooning certain Philadelphia citizens. Threatened hostility to the performance persuaded Douglass to cancel it, and in its place Godfrey's properly classical *Prince of Parthia* was posthumously performed.[8]

Among Smith's protégés Francis Hopkinson fulfilled his promise abundantly, writing verse encomiums to other members of Smith's circle and commemorations of passing events, all the while training himself to be an accomplished artist, musician, and composer. Hopkinson learned to play the harpsichord and studied the Italianate music then in fashion in Europe, also serving as organist at St. Peter's Church in Philadelphia. Taking up the law, Hopkinson became a delegate to the Continental Congress and afterward served as judge of the Court of Admiralty in Pennsylvania. Chiefly remembered for his ballad *The Battle of the Kegs*, he was, according to Moses Coit Tyler,

> a mathematician, a chemist, a physicist, a mechanician, an inventor, a musician and a composer of music, a man of literary knowledge and practice, a writer of airy and dainty songs, a clever artist with pencil and brush and a humorist of unmistakeable power.[9]

With David Rittenhouse he was the only one of Smith's college circle to survive the Revolution and achieve honor and distinction in the new Republic. However, Benjamin West, who counted Smith among his patrons, received honor and distinction in England exceeding that of any contemporary Philadelphian but Franklin.

A country Quaker, West was permitted by the Friends community to exercise his talents in this morally dubious occupation because, early on, they were so patently superior as to appear God-given. Arriving in Philadelphia in 1756 at age eighteen to set up as a portrait painter, West attracted the attention of Smith, who created a special program for him at the college. West soon won the admiration of the wealthy patron Chief Justice William Allen as well. Financed by Allen and other patrons of art in Philadelphia and New York, West in 1760 sailed for Italy, where he was welcomed as the first American to be seen there and as an exceptionally talented painter. After three years in Italy, West journeyed to London, where he won immediate recognition. King George III became his patron, and in 1772 he was appointed historical painter to the king. In 1792 he was elected president of the Royal Academy, an office he held until his death in 1820.

In 1764 West accepted Matthew Pratt as his first American art student, and for more than a half century thereafter West remained teacher and guide to an unending stream of American painters. Charles Willson Peale, a debt-ridden ex-saddlemaker from Maryland, went to London in 1767 with the financial backing of a member of the Maryland gentry and a letter from William Allen. West told Peale "that if he had not brought any recommendation, as an American he would have given him all the assistance in his power, but that the recommendation from Mr. Allen, was the most powerful he could have brought."[10] John Singleton Copley arrived in 1775 to take up an immediately successful career as portraitist. Another of West's students, Gilbert Stuart, arrived the same year; Ralph Earl followed several years later.

In 1780 John Trumbull, carrying a letter of introduction to West from Benjamin Franklin, was admitted to England despite having served in the Continental Army, on condition that he stay free from any further involvement in the Revolution while in England. Patience Lovell Wright, a widow from New Jersey whose wax figures won high acclaim in London, openly supported the Revolution and may have spied for it as well. West warned her that her sex would not protect her if she were convicted of treason, but she survived the war to die in 1786 as the result of a fall following a visit with the American minister and his wife, John and Abigail Adams. Following the Revolution William Dunlap and Robert Fulton arrived from America to study with West, and they were followed by others in the decades ahead. In 1810–11, West took on a new generation of students: Charles Bird King, Washington Allston, Thomas Sully, Samuel F. B. Morse, and Charles Robert Leslie. Until his death he remained the central figure of this American colony in London, extending hospitality to literary visitors from America as well as to diplomats who lacked the ready access to high places that West enjoyed.

Peale returned to Maryland in 1769 and moved permanently to Philadelphia, having by then established his reputation as the foremost painter in British America. During the Revolution Peale served as a member of the Philadelphia Committee of Public Safety, helped to raise a militia company, and fought in the battles of Trenton, Princeton, and Germantown, busily painting—mainly miniatures—all the while. In the new Republic his status as Revolutionary hero as well as preeminent American portraitist did not prove sufficient to maintain him and his growing family of painters in a state of solvency, however. He was still obliged to seek out customers, travel widely to paint them, and press some of them repeatedly for payment. When these exertions proved insufficient, he adapted his art to his republican situation by producing what he called "moving pictures": transparent scenes from nature and history that could be manipulated and lighted before a theater audience to produce the illusion of reality. From moving pictures Peale turned to popular natural history, creating Peale's Museum of Natural History Objects and Portraits as a major public, paying attraction in Philadelphia. A dauntless republican patriot, Peale had turned his back on the aristocratic English world of patronage in the arts to devote his life to establishing art upon a popular foundation. He demonstrated that the American artist who wished to do well for himself should be a business-minded jack-of-all-trades and master of as many of them as possible.[11]

Art appreciation—but not its practice—was included in John Witherspoon's curricular innovations at the College of New Jersey following his appointment as president in 1768. Witherspoon thought of his college as a training ground for future patrons, not practitioners, of the arts. But the gentlemen he had in mind ought to be proficient in belles lettres as befit civilized gentlemen. And Witherspoon's views proved to be of national significance. The Scottish-influenced academic orientation he introduced in New Jersey foreshadowed the Scottish-influenced reorientation of American colleges generally, culminating in the conversion of Harvard to the Scottish philosophy at the end of the eighteenth century. Witherspoon put the College of New Jersey at the head of higher education in America, where it remained at least until the revitalization of Yale under Timothy Dwight at the end of the eighteenth century and the renaissance of Harvard early in the nineteenth.

Witherspoon effectively reconciled his Scottish system with the prevalent curricula, modeled on Cambridge and Oxford, by adopting and emphasizing English nomenclature. He explained that "The regular course of instruction is in four classes exactly after the manner, and bearing the names of the classes in the English universities: Freshman, Sophomore, Junior and, Senior," and he listed the course offerings for each year with descriptors borrowed from the conventional English liberal arts program. However, in substance his curriculum followed the newer pattern of the Scottish universities, as exemplified by King's College and Marischal in Aberdeen, where the curriculums had been comprehensively reconstructed in 1753.[12]

A Presbyterian minister, Witherspoon was associated in Scotland with the moderate wing of the Evangelical Party, which had aligned itself against the Moderate Party. Witherspoon proved to be a master at firmly taking a moderate position and browbeating the opposition on either side of him into submission. Associating himself with a stout "common sense" defense against Berkeley and Hume, Witherspoon felt free to write that, although Hume was "an infidel in opinion," he was also "of great reach and accuracy of judgement in matters of criticism."[13] Witherspoon pursued the modern and eclectic approach to moral philosophy that came to characterize this crowning senior course as it would be taught by college presidents in other American colleges. His approach to rhetoric and belles lettres was similarly eclectic, citing the ancient authors as models while paying equal attention to English writers from Shakespeare and Milton to Swift, Johnson, and Hume.

Witherspoon's most distinguished student was James Madison, who arrived at the College of New Jersey in 1769, graduated two years later, and remained for an additional year of study under Witherspoon. During his first year Madison organized the Whig Society, enlisting William Bradford, a future U.S. Attorney General, Philip Freneau, the foremost poet of the Republic to come, and Hugh Henry Brackenridge, author of the American classic *Modern Chivalry*. The Whig Society engaged in debates with its Tory counterpart, and upon graduation, Freneau and Brackenridge coauthored a commencement poem for the class of 1771 on the *Rising Glory of America*, envisioning a "seat of empire" where "fair freedom shall forever reign" and where science, literature, and the arts would flourish "not less in fame than Greece and Rome." The poem was received with "great applause," and both authors looked forward to the possibility of rewarding careers as literary professionals.[14]

When the Revolution came, Brackenridge turned out a stream of patriotic, propagandist literature, including two plays as well as poems and prose pieces. As the Revolution progressed Brackenridge joined Peale and others in anticipating an epic postrevolutionary efflorescence of science, arts, and letters in the land of liberty. Once the American people had cast off the imperial chains that restricted cultural as well as commercial enterprise, their national genius would express itself freely. "America," Brackenridge declared in 1779, "will produce poets, orators, critics, and historians, equal to the most celebrated of the ancient commonwealths of Greece and Italy." Others pursued this theme in the postwar Republic. "The world," Francis Hopkinson wrote more than a decade later, "looks toward us as a country that may become a grand nursery of arts and sciences." Samuel Cooper of Boston believed that science could truly flourish only in America, where liberty "unfetters and expands the human mind."[15]

By the time of Hopkinson's statement, Brackenridge had drastically modified his expectations and was beginning to publish the rollicking, episodic accounts of America's makeshift republican culture that appeared together as the novel *Modern Chivalry*. Brackenridge had tried his hand at literary journalism briefly, editing the *United States Magazine* in 1779. That experience had dispelled his dreams of a Periclean or Augustan age in America. He informed readers in his final issue of the magazine that most of their fellow citizens "inhabit the region of stupidity, and cannot bear to have the tranquility of their repose disturbed" and that he would henceforth allow them to *"sleep on and take your rest."*[16]

Philip Freneau pursued two literary careers, as lyric poet and partisan Jeffersonian newspaper editor. Fifty years later William Cullen Bryant managed to combine these seemingly incompatible vocations successfully, but Freneau was born too soon to carry it off. Failing to make ends meet as a poet-journalist, he earned his livelihood chiefly as a ship's captain and farmer. In later life Freneau remained on terms of warm friendship with his classmates, Brackenridge and especially Madison, but he evidently came to doubt the value of academic training to the creative artist. In 1788 Freneau wrote an essay of "Advice to Authors" in which he warned them to

> Be particularly careful to avoid all connexion with doctors of law and divinity, masters of arts, professors of colleges, and in general all those that wear square black caps. A mere scholar and an original author are two animals as different from each other as a fresh and salt water sailor.[17]

Unlike the literary activities associated with Provost Smith's college in Philadelphia and President Witherspoon's in Princeton, the emergence of the Connecticut Wits—the first coherent literary movement of the new nation—occurred as a student enterprise that a conservative but weak college administration could not effectively oppose. In 1765 Thomas Clap was forced to resign as president of Yale when discipline among the students collapsed and a statement signed by almost all of the students called for his dismissal. Naphtali Daggett was named president pro tempore and remained in that equivocal position for thirteen years, until a new president, Ezra Stiles, was appointed in 1778. In contrast to the rigidly dogmatic Clap, Daggett pursued an amiable but ineffectual course as administrator. During his incumbency, the tutors, most of whom were recent Yale graduates, were more than willing to assume authority on their own. Belles lettres entered the curriculum after two former students, John Trumbull and Timothy Dwight, became tutors in 1771.[18]

Trumbull had entered Yale in 1763 and Dwight in 1765, each at thirteen years of age and each having completed in advance the required course of study for the first two years of college. They were serious students, prepared for a more intellectually challenging course of study than the college under Clap and "Tunker" Daggett provided. Searching the college library they came up with Lord Kames's four-volume *Elements of Criticism*, which showed them how to write all acceptable forms of verse and introduced them to the moral philosophy of the Scottish Enlightenment. Trumbull's master's essay was taken bodily from Kames, and Dwight's epic verse. *Conquest of Canaan* followed Kames's rules to the letter. David Humphreys's *The Progress of Dulness*, Part 1, comprised a rhymed statement of Kames's approach to the study of literature.

Originally published in 1762, Kames's *Elements* came out in a cheap American edition in 1770. Dwight adopted it as the text for a course in belles lettres that he introduced to the curriculum, and younger students, including Joel Barlow and Noah Webster, both of the class of 1778, were schooled in Kames by their tutors.[19]

These self-instructed poets and critics of Yale gained the name of Connecticut Wits—initially Hartford Wits—when a number of them who settled in Hartford—Trumbull, Humphreys, Barlow, and Lemuel Hopkins—cooperated in the production of a series of satiric papers, supposedly concerned with an ancient American literary work but in fact serving as an attack against radical, paper-money politics and other controversies of the day. Meanwhile, Timothy Dwight, off teaching school at

Greenfield Hill, contributed the satiric *Triumph of Infidelity* and the pastoral "Greenfield Hill," reminiscent of Goldsmith's "Deserted Village," to the accumulating store of Connecticut verse. In 1787 Barlow published *The Vision of Columbus*.

Noah Webster, working in Hartford, produced from 1783 to 1785 his three-volume *Grammatical Institute of the English Language*, consisting of a speller, a grammar, and a reader. *The Blue-Backed Speller*, which went on the market in 1783, was soon selling 200,000 copies a year and was up to a million a year at the time of Webster's death in 1843.[20] Before finishing the speller, Webster persuaded the legislatures of Connecticut and New York to pass copyright laws guaranteeing him exclusive publishing and marketing rights, and he went on to win similar laws in the other states of the northeast. Some years later he sold his ownership of the *Grammatical Institute* to his publisher and lived to regret it. Meanwhile, in addition to a continuous outpouring of contentious writings on various subjects, Webster worked on his *American Dictionary of the English Language*. The first edition appeared in 1825, and Webster had completed a revision of it shortly before his death. Webster did not live long enough to benefit financially from his dictionary, but his heirs made fortunes on it. He had initiated a series of copyright laws that made it possible for authors to profit from their writings, and he demonstrated that there was good money to be made in writing, that writing as a profession was a possibility in the United States. The Connecticut Wits were mainly gentlemen for whom writing was a cultivated avocation, but Barlow, who had helped his friend Webster to promote the *Grammatical Institute*, marketed his *Vision of Columbus* effectively and realized a handsome profit.[21] For literary patriots like Barlow and Webster—and Freneau and Brackenridge—belief that American writers would be supported by American readers was an article of faith at the outset and, in most cases, the eventual basis for sad disillusionment.

Hartford-New Haven lacked the capacity of Boston-Cambridge to secure the loyalties of its literati. By the end of the 1780s, Barlow and Humphreys were off to Europe, while Webster had left Hartford to edit a magazine in New York City. In 1791 a younger set of wits appeared in Hartford with their own forum for satire, *The Echo*. The younger wits included two of Timothy Dwight's younger brothers, Theodore and

Nathaniel, and a young physician, Elihu Hubbard Smith. In New York City ambitious Connecticut Yankees found opportunities lacking in their own state, and in 1793 Smith moved to New York. When Smith died six years later of yellow fever, he was only twenty-eight years of age, but in those six years he had attracted and sustained the most creative, variegated, and productive literary circle to come out of the Republic to that time.

Introduced by Noah Webster to members of the city's literary society, Smith organized his new acquaintances into the Friendly Club shortly after his arrival. Membership was limited to ten and included two other physicians, Samuel Latham Mitchill and Edward Miller, the artist-playwright William Dunlap, the jurist James Kent, the clergyman-historian Samuel Miller, the novelist and magazine editor Charles Brockden Brown, and perhaps Noah Webster.[22]

The Friendlies met every Tuesday evening at each others' homes to discuss an author selected by the host. In addition, they supported one another in a variety of literary enterprises. Smith assisted Edward Miller and Mitchill in starting the *Medical Repository*, which Mitchill continued to edit for fifteen years. In addition to assisting with the *Medical Repository*, Smith wrote the libretto *Edwin and Angelina* (set by Victor Pelissier) and published the first anthology of American verse. Smith seems also to have been the one who persuaded Brown to start *The Monthly Magazine and American Review* in 1799. Brown achieved startlingly sudden literary success with the publication of four Gothic novels, *Wieland*, *Ormand*, *Arthur Mervyn*, and *Edgar Huntley* in a period of eleven months in 1798–99, while at the same time launching his magazine and publishing a treatise, *Alcuin*, on women's suffrage. All four novels received glowing reviews at home and abroad without, however, bringing substantial financial returns to their author.

It was during his membership in the Friendly Club that James Kent delivered his first Columbia law lectures. Later Kent expanded the lectures into *Commentaries on the American Law*, published 1826–30, one of the first influential expositions of the subject. Samuel Miller's groundbreaking intellectual history, *Brief Retrospect of the Eighteenth Century*, was published in 1803, several years after the Friendly Club was dissolved.

A quality that distinguished the Friendlies from other literary clubs of the age was their spirit of professionalism. Brown especially devoted his life to becoming a professional writer who made a living at his craft. Dunlap pursued a career as theater manager as well as playwright, producing thirty-one plays and translating and producing at least twenty-seven more. Since this prolific career could not be made to support him, Dunlap, who had studied painting in London under Benjamin West, earned his bread and butter painting miniatures and portraits, while continuing throughout his career to foster professional status for New York artists.[23]

Following Smith's death, in 1799, the Friendly Club disintegrated. The members had differed politically, and although politics seems to have been ruled out as a subject for club discussion, the heat of the Adams-Jefferson-Aaron Burr imbroglio of 1800 apparently soured the fellowship. Brown returned to Philadelphia, where he wrote two more novels, contributed articles to *Port Folio*, and in 1803 started another literary journal. He was at work on a two-volume general geography text when he died in 1810 at the age of thirty-nine.

⊰ III ⊱

NOAH WEBSTER WON LITTLE appreciation from fellow writers for his efforts to put the literary profession on a paying basis. First, few men of letters of his day considered literature to be a profession; second, Webster's copyright laws largely failed to secure substantial remuneration for the few who did. Literary-minded men who contributed to belles lettres in the early Republic tended to be ministers, physicians, lawyers, and the like. For them, belles lettres remained a gentlemanly avocation, the writer being sufficiently rewarded by the attendant pleasures of intellectual stimulation, creativity, and literary fellowship. Among the learned professions medicine had contributed substantially to letters in the Philadelphia Enlightenment. In New England the ministry had been a literary vocation from the beginning and remained so in the nineteenth century. Nationwide, however, law was the profession most frequently associated with literature. The rise of polite letters in America is closely associated with the rise of the legal profession to a position of power and respectability in national life.

It was only a generation or so before the Revolution that the legal profession came into its own in the colonies. Law had been practiced by lawyers before then, but also by ministers, physicians, merchants, and farmers, all of whom had also served as magistrates in the courts. The law, in short, had been anybody's business. During the second half of the eighteenth century, however, lawyers established their special calling as interpreters of the law. They went on to lead the colonies into Revolution, create a federal system of government, and then manage the government they had created. Nothing in the history of colonial lawyers, wrote Charles Warren, "is more striking than their uniformly low position and the slight part they played in the development of the country until nearly the middle of the Eighteenth Century."[24] Yet twenty-five of fifty-six signers of the Declaration of Independence and thirty-one of fifty-five members of the Constitutional Convention had trained in the law. With no hereditary aristocracy to serve, lawyers themselves became America's ruling class and, at least to their own way of thinking, the nation's civilized class as well.

The high esteem in which lawyers held themselves was not shared by less privileged citizens of the new Republic who suffered from the ravages of litigation. Those same high-sounding authorities on liberty and great constitutional questions of the age were also experts on farm foreclosures and the detection of flaws in land titles, and their expertise in these lesser arts was at the service of those who could afford their fees. Popular resentment against the "pettifoggers" and their "law craft" spread throughout the states following the Revolution, a time of widespread indebtedness, and in Massachusetts it culminated in Shays' Rebellion. In most states the fledgling legal profession had by then been decimated by the Loyalist emigration. The more reputable lawyers were too engaged in the new government to maintain an active private practice. Huge backlogs of court cases accumulated. The era of fiercest animosity toward the legal profession was also a time of extraordinary opportunity for new lawyers. Bright young men were attracted to law in increasing numbers, and public animosity alarmed and united most of them in conservative resistance to the attacks upon their profession.

These attacks went beyond hostility toward lawyers to challenge the validity of the legal system itself. Many patriots thought they ought to have won their liberation from English common law along with their independence from Crown, Parliament, and the rest of the English system. Judges ruled otherwise, but that did not in itself authorize a body of existing law suitable to fit American circumstances. During more than a half century after the Revolution, this American system of law emerged from court decisions together with compilations of law reports, institutes, and commentaries, culminating in James Kent's *Commentaries on American Law* (1826–30) and Joseph Story's volumes of commentaries, published during the 1830s.

Viewing America in 1831 at the close of this primitive period in its legal history, Alexis de Tocqueville observed that the legal profession in America had assumed the role played by nobility and aristocracy in Europe, being "the only aristocratic element that can be amalgamated without violence with the natural elements of democracy." The aristocratic character of American law was the more pronounced for being patterned after English law, which is based upon precedents, rather than Continental law, which is based upon principles. While Continental European legal codes might be difficult to comprehend, Tocqueville wrote, they were intended to be comprehensible to anyone, whereas English and American legal codes were not. "The French lawyer is simply a man extensively acquainted with the statues of his country; but the English or American lawyer resembles the hierophants of Egypt, for like them he is the sole interpreter of an occult science."[25]

The English aristocracy, "which has taken care to attract to its sphere whatever is at all analogous to itself," Tocqueville continued, conferred an authority and importance upon the legal profession that was second to its own but nonetheless sufficient to content the lawyers, who "consequently mingle the aristocratic tastes and ideas of the circles in which they move with the aristocratic interests of their profession." By contrast, "In America there are no nobles or literary men, and the people are apt to mistrust the wealthy; lawyers consequently form the highest political class and the most cultivated portion of society."

Preparation for this cultivated profession had ranged from matriculation at one of the Inns of Court in London in the eighteenth century or at Harvard Law School in the nineteenth to rudimentary programs of self-study involving perhaps a reading of Blackstone's *Commentaries* and attendance at circuit court sessions. However, the basic method of training for the law remained the apprenticeship system. Indeed, the Philadelphia bar prevented the University of Pennsylvania from adding a law school until 1850 out of a desire to conserve the existing apprenticeship system.[26] Consequently the role of letters in legal training depended much on the literary taste of the lawyer to whom the candidate was apprenticed.

Among the few books available for law students in colonial America, the impenetrable *Coke on Littleton* was favored by mentors and dreaded by their students. John Adams read law with Jeremiah Gridley, perhaps the foremost lawyer of New England and possessor of one of its best law libraries. Adams read a multitude of law books—mastered but few— "Wood's *Institutes of Common Law* I never read but once and my Lord Coke's *Commentaries on Littleton* I never read but once. These two authors I must get and read over and over again. And I will get them too and break through, as Mr. Gridley expressed it, all obstructions." A generation later, John Quincy Adams wrote that he had gotten through *Coke on Littleton*, "which has been hanging heavily upon me these ten weeks . . . a vast mass of law learning, but heaped up in such an incoherent mass that I have derived very little benefit from it." Joseph Story's heart sank as he entered "into the intricate, crabbed, and obsolete learning of *Coke on Littleton*." Daniel Webster "was put to study in the old way, that is, the hardest books first, and lost much time. I read Coke-Littleton through without understanding a quarter of it."

William Blackstone's gracefully written *Commentaries* became available to American law students in the 1770s; they remained the basic text, especially for self-taught lawyers, down to the Civil War. Blackstone himself was neither a distinguished moral philosopher nor a learned legal scholar, and his *Commentaries* were flawed by inconsistencies, distortions, and omissions. Blackstone considered English law to be a type of natural law, like the law of gravity, and the *Commentaries* comprised an undeviating rationalization for the existing order of things. At the same time Blackstone presented a comprehensive account of the law, and of substantive principles underlying the law, and the *Commentaries* remained the only such account available.

Jefferson recalled that when he was a law student, *Coke Littleton* was the universal elementary book of law students and a sounder Whig never

wrote nor profounder learning in the orthodox doctrines of British liberties. Our lawyers were then all Whigs. But when his black letter text
and uncouth, but cunning learning got out of fashion, and the honeyed
Mansfieldism of *Blackstone* became the student's horn book, from that
moment, that profession (the nursery of our Congress) began to slide
into Toryism.

James Kent, the deeply conservative authority on American jurisprudence, implicitly confirmed Jefferson when he averred that he owed his
reputation to one book: Blackstone's *Commentaries* had been his only text
when studying law during the Revolutionary War, but that one text he
mastered. Later Kent was put through a full course of readings, including
substantial assignments in history, as became customary for law students
in the early national period. John Quincy Adams, studying under Theophilus Parsons, read Coke, Blackstone, and other law texts but also Robertson's
History of Charles V, Gibbon's *Decline and Fall of the Roman Empire*, and
Hume's *History of England*. John Randolph, reading law with Edmund
Randolph, began with Hume's *A Treatise of Human Nature* and after he
returning the book, he received *Shakespeare*, to read, then the Scot James
Beattie's *An Essay on the Nature and Immutability of Truth*, Lord Kame's
Elements of Criticism and Gillie's *History of Greece*. Of this course John
Randolph exclaimed, "What an admirable system of study!"[27] The proper
study of law had become philosophy, history, and literature.

The Scot-Pennsylvanian lawyer James Wilson became the first to formulate a general exposition of American law with a series of lectures in
1790. The text for his subject was natural law, and in the absence of any
native legal system to expound, the argument was drawn from moral philosophers of the Scottish Enlightenment. During the decades that followed, court cases generated large quantities of precedents. Joseph Story,
addressing the Boston bar in 1821, could point to the compilaton of over
150 volumes of law reports and observe that "our happy danger now is
not that we shall want but be overwhelmed" by native product. At the
same time story upbraided the profession for vulgar tendencies within it,
ignorance of general principles, and looseness of declarations.[28]

Throughout America well-recognized hierarchies of distinction and
authority developed within the legal fraternities. Lawyers who argued
cases before the Supreme Court or in other ways distinguished them-

selves gained the recognition of their peers as outstanding ornaments of their profession. The best of America's lawyers were seen to be delving through the civilizations of Greece, Rome, and medieval and modern Europe as well as England in the service of legal wisdom. *DeBow's Review* explained that "Our own system, sometimes erroneously supposed to have been dug out of our peculiar form of institutions, is but ancient ore, dug in other countries, and passed through the furnace of men's minds for centuries." And Silas Jones in his *Introduction to Legal Sciences* observed that the law is eminently historical and requires of us such researches as "possess all the interest that the traveller feels in lingering about the ruins of ancient cities, monuments of exquisite taste and skill in the arts." The art and science of law drew upon literary as well as historical sources; Shakespeare might be effectively cited along with Coke. The law, Story declared, "demands the energies of the most powerful minds, and exhausts all the stores of learning."[29]

The conception of the law as the general repository of civilized experience achieved its most authoritative written expression in the commentaries of Story and Kent, and even Story conceded that "the technical doctrines of a jurisprudence . . . must have a tendency to dull that enthusiasm, . . . to obscure those finer forms of thought, which give to literature its lovelier, I may say, its inexpressible graces." By the mid–nineteenth century, with the accumulation of law reports and the increasing division of law into specialized fields, the view of the law as a repository of general historical and literary wisdom lost credibility within the legal profession. A writer in the *United States Monthly Magazine* in 1850 complained that lawyers were no longer sought to attain "a comprehension of the great principles, the wide, extending analogies, which are everywhere pervading and everywhere giving a reason and consistency to the law." Others were beginning to affirm that the law was neither a particularly learned nor literary profession but rather a practical vocation.[30]

Oratory was a lawyerly skill that boasted a tradition as venerable as the law itself, extending from Demosthenes to Daniel Webster. From medieval universities to nineteenth-century liberal arts colleges, orations remained an essential part of higher education, and forensic eloquence remained the mark of a cultivated man. Patrick Henry rose to the head of the Virginia bar chiefly on the basis of his forensic ability, being admittedly unqualified for practice so far as his technical knowledge of the law was concerned. The Olympian prestige and appeal of oratory in the ages of Patrick Henry and Daniel Webster is hard to appreciate in our present age of mass media, but in mid–nineteenth century America, Emerson observed that "The highest bribes of society are all at the feet of the successful orator. . . . All other fame must hush before his. He is the true potentate."[31]

Oratory in the age of Webster, Clay, and Calhoun was widely appreciated as the highest expression of the human creative faculties. It called upon a vast fund of knowledge, the mastery of which enabled great orators like Webster to expatiate by the hour, quoting literally and at length from literary and historical sources extemporaneously or with the aid of but a few notes. Oratory drew upon the dramatic arts in the grand style, and implied a large experience in life and in public affairs on the part of the speaker.

The signal esteem in which Edward Everett was held as an orator led to his unanimous selection in 1863 by seventeen northern governors to deliver the major address at Gettysburg. A half century earlier Everett had begun his public speaking career as pastor of Brattle Street Church in Boston. Everett had been a student of John Quincy Adams during the brief period when Adams served as Harvard's first Boylston Professor of Rhetoric and Oratory. Adams later took personal pride in the achievements of his prize student, writing in his diary:

> Of the thousands and tens of thousands of these orations, which teem in every part of this country, there are, perhaps, not one hundred that will be remembered . . . and of them, at least half have been, or will be, furnished by E. E. He has largely contributed to raise the standards of this class of composition.[32]

Adams was right about the tens of thousands of orations but wrong about E. E. As it turns out, none of Everett's orations have been well remembered except for the extended Gettysburg oration that has served as an invidious contrast to Lincoln's brief address on that occasion. Unfortunately, as contemporaries were themselves well aware, oratory is a perishable form of expression. "Literary characters may leave their works behind them," St. George Tucker wrote William Wirt in 1813, but orators sink into immediate oblivion. I very much doubt if a single speech of Richard H. Lee's can be produced at this day. Nevertheless, he was the most mellifluous orator that ever I listened to. . . . The truth is that Socrates himself would pass unnoticed and forgotten in Virginia, if he were not a public character, and some of his speeches preserved in a newspaper; the latter might keep his memory alive for a year or two, but not much longer.[33]

Harrison Gray Otis, who "astonished and delighted" Emerson with the most "prodigious display of eloquence" Emerson had ever heard, rarely associated with literary people in Boston, and his speeches do not survive as part of Boston's literary remains, although they were part of its literary life.[34] Even where speeches remain in print, either they go unread, like Everett's, or they survive as essays, like Emerson's. In fact, Emerson's writings convey little of his compelling platform presence. Among Bostonian orators only Daniel Webster survives beyond his age in apothegms that later generations of school children, lawyers, and politicians have committed to memory, along with Patrick Henry's defiant dictum on liberty and death.

◄ IV ►

A GENERATION OF YOUNG LAWYERS, literary and elitist by training, found their literary master of ceremonies in Joseph Dennie, founder of *Port Folio* and its editor from 1801 to 1811. The son of Boston Loyalists, Dennie cherished his parents' Tory sentiments throughout his life, ever regretting the ill fortune that located him provincial Boston rather than metropolitan London, where he might have proved a worthy successor to Dr. Johnson. Making the best of his situation, Dennie became host to an American "Confederacy of Men of Letters," as he called it. These companions in belles lettres enjoyed his engaging personality at the same time they valued his abilities as editor and literary critic. Dennie wrote in 1806 that he had "been most ably seconded by the lawyers of the country; men who are unquestionably the best patrons which literature can hope to find in America."[35] Dennie did not require that these patrons of belles lettres share his reactionary political sentiments, and contributors to *Port*

Folio included Jeffersonian Republicans as well as monarchists. However, Dennie's snobbish confederacy radiated a self-conscious air of superiority absent in Jeremy Belknap's enlightened conception of a Republic of Letters. This literary elitism must have appealed widely to the contributors and subscribers to *Port Folio*, who made it the most successful literary periodical published in America to that time.

Dennie attended Harvard, studied law, and moved to New Hampshire along with other bright young lawyers—including Royall Tyler, Thomas Green Fessenden, and Jeremiah Mason—who, like Dennie, were readily attracted to literary journalism conducted in agreeable company. Dennie assumed editorship of the *Farmers' Museum* in Walpole, New Hampshire, and turned it into the liveliest show in town, converting Crofts Tavern and his own house into "the resort of a *coterie* of . . . wits, and literati from all the surrounding country." According to a local historian, the tavern became "a literary *pandemonium*" in the course of "wine drinking, late suppers, card playing, joke cracking, and the like."[36] Joseph T. Buckingham, later editor of the important *New-England Magazine* and other periodicals, began his journalistic career working as Dennie's printer's devil in Walpole, and he recorded vivid impressions of this sybaritic dandy in generally sober-minded rural New England. He recalled a morning when Dennie "came into the office dressed in a peagreen coat, white vest, nankin small-clothes, white silk stockings, and shoes or *pumps*, fastened with silver buckles," his hair pomaded and powdered and "augmented by the addition of a large queue" that reached halfway down his back. Dennie customarily stayed up late and rose late. On occasion he might choose to scribble his copy at the tavern, where the printer's devil would fetch it piecemeal to take to the print shop.[37] Dennie's closest associate on the *Museum* was Royall Tyler, author of the delightful patriotic comedy *The Contrast*, which had played in Philadelphia to a distinguished audience, including George Washington, in 1789. Tyler and Dennie developed a literary routine under the signature of Colon and Spondee that was later resumed by them in *Port Folio*.

Dennie moved to Philadelphia in 1799 to take advantage of several editorial offers and the post of private secretary to Secretary of State Timothy Pickering. Pickering was dismissed by President Adams, however, and the national capital presently moved to Washington, D.C., leaving Dennie to reconsider his situation. Accordingly, in January 1801 Dennie launched "A new weekly paper to be called, THE PORT FOLIO By Oliver Oldschool, Esq." In it he revived editorial departments developed in the *Farmers' Museum* such as "Drama," "Original and Selected Poetry," "Literary Intelligence," "Musical Intelligence," "Fine Arts," "Festoon of Fashion," "Amusement," "Morals," "Law Intelligence," and "Political Synopses," and "Miscellany," under which were printed the "Lay Preacher" and "Farrago" essays that contained Dennie's most serious criticism. A major feature of *Port Folio* at the outset was a "Journal of a Tour through Silesea" by former minister to Berlin John Quincy Adams, which ran serially through most of the first year.

Except for Adams's contribution, most of *Port Folio* in the early years appears to have been the work of the editor. Dennie organized contributors and supporters of *Port Folio* into the Tuesday Club, which met variously at a tavern, bookstore, or member's home. Active members included William Meredith, Joseph Hopkinson, Horace Binney, Nathaniel Chapman, Samuel Ewing, and Charles Brockden Brown, as well as Jeffersonian Republicans like Charles Jared Ingersoll and Richard Rush. Later recruits included Nicholas Biddle, a brilliant young lawyer who became Dennie's chief assistant during a lengthy period of declining health for the editor and who assumed the editorship for several years following Dennie's death in 1811. A high point in the activities of the Tuesday Club occurred in the summer of 1804 when the Irish poet Thomas Moore visited Philadelphia. Afterward Moore wrote a long poem reviling America and Jefferson but praising Dennie and noting that

> In the society of Mr. Dennie and his friends, at Philadelphia, I passed the few agreeable moments which my tour through the states afforded me. Mr. Dennie has succeeded in diffusing through his cultivated little circle that love of good literature and sound politics which he feels so zealously himself, and which is so rarely the characteristic of his countrymen.[38]

Politics interested Dennie far less than literature, but he delighted in attacking Jefferson and all his works. *Port Folio* began several months before Jefferson took office as President, and from the outset Dennie vented his spleen against the "cool-headed philosopher, a disciple of Condorcet," who with "some of the most profligate, unprincipled men in the nation, for his counsellors and co-adjutors," was pursuing a "career of universal revolution in property, in men, and measures." Jefferson's Declaration of Independence was "a rotten prop," according to Dennie, viciously employing hatred against the Mother Country to unite the colonies. Jefferson's first inaugural address was a rhetorical disaster. Dennie had "met with few instances, in writers of reputation, where so many high-sounding expressions were used with so bad effect."[39]

Representatives of the Jefferson administration indicted Dennie for seditious libel after publication of an essay attacking democracy. Dennie was defended by Charles Jared Ingersoll and Joseph Hopkinson and acquitted two years later. After the suit, Dennie tempered his political commentary, though not his expression of "the profound contempt I entertain for the herd of society." His contempt for Jefferson remained implicit in his literary criticism. Dennie took exception to the entire "enlightened" conception of letters as comprising the morally and practically useful sciences of natural and civil history rather than the more highly cultivated realm of belles lettres. Whereas the three men of letters to whom Jefferson paid highest homage were Francis Bacon, Isaac Newton, and John Locke, the three men most honored by Dennie were Joseph Addison, Oliver Goldsmith, and Samuel Johnson. For Dennie, useful knowledge was uncouth knowledge, and the sciences as a whole largely remained beneath the notice of *Port Folio*.

When it came to poetry, Dennie proved capable of rising above politics to make perceptive and sympathetic judgments. He was among the earliest to praise Wordsworth and Coleridge's *Lyrical Ballads*, a volume better received in America than in England. Dennie likewise praised Washington Irving and James Kirke Paulding's satirical essays collected in *Salmagundi*, despite the author's "Columbian" and "Jacobinical" shortcomings. Joel Barlow's patriotic *The Columbiad* won only faint praise from Dennie, but *Port Folio* ran a series of appreciative essays on the poetry of the Jeffersonian Philip Freneau.

> For the *politicks* of the authour, [Dennie wrote] it is pretty well known that we have no peculiar partiality, but of the *poetry* of this versatile bard we must say that, by the impartial, it will be, at length considered as entitled to no ordinary place in a judicious estimate of American genius.[40]

Under Biddle's editorship, *Port Folio* eschewed politics altogether, and under later editors it became a forum for literary nationalism. A succession of owners and editors changed *Port Folio* from a weekly to a monthly to a quarterly before suspending its publication in 1827.

Dennie's success in Philadelphia was approved and even actively supported by some Bostonians who shared his literary and political views. Although literary activity had remained at a comparatively low ebb in Boston since the Revolution, *Massachusetts Magazine* survived there as a general-interest monthly from 1789 to 1796, publishing much belles lettres and literary criticism, including a series of essays by Dennie written under the pseudonym Socialis.

In 1803 a young Boston schoolmaster started up a new magazine, *Monthly Anthology and Boston Review*, which languished from the outset for lack of both subscriptions and editorial contributions. William Emerson, pastor of First Church of Boston, heeding appeals from the magazine's supporters, agreed to edit it. He proceeded to organize an Anthology Society of friends to supply it with articles. Members included the staunchly Tory pastor of Trinity Church, John Sylvester Gardiner, as well as the young Unitarian minister Joseph Stevens Buckminster, lawyer-merchants William Smith Shaw and William Tudor Jr., Professor Andrews Norton of Harvard and the Reverend John Kirkland, who became president of Harvard in 1810.[41]

The Anthology Society conducted its business at bibulous suppers that became ends in themselves. One entry in the society's journal notes that "After supper wit and burgundy came in abundance, but our duties were not forgotten." Another entry candidly admits that "At this meeting no business, except eating, drinking, and smoking was attended to."[42] Like Dennie and his circle in Philadelphia, the Anthologists took Samuel Johnson as their model and Johnsonian sociability as their ideal. Ministers among them aimed to be broadly liberal, worldly, not puritan and provincial. As their president the Anthologists selected Gardiner, an English-educated High Church Anglican who lamented America's parochial and materialistic culture: "Everything smells of the shop. . . . We seldom meet here with . . . the scholar and the gentleman united."[43] Gardiner proved too high-toned for other members. His contempt for American provincialism clashed with the patriotism of other, younger members, including Buckminster and Tudor. Gardiner's dismissal of Thomas Gray as a serious poet led to an altercation with Buckminster and to a pervasive unpleasantness that defeated the society's social purpose.

The end to the society and the *Monthly Anthology* came in 1811 with this discord and the realization that the group could not succeed in defining the vocation of the man of letters or establishing critical standards. One permanent legacy of the society was its library, developed under the direction of William Smith Shaw, into the Boston Athenaeum.

Four years after the Anthology Society disbanded, William Tudor started a literary quarterly, which in the War of 1812's patriotic aftermath he named the *North American Review*. Organized in closer association with Harvard than the *Anthology* had been, with less ministerial involvement, and without a supporting club of contributors, the resulting enterprise became impressive for its longevity, if not always its vitality. Thoreau dismissed it several decades later as a "venerable cobweb . . . which has hitherto escaped the broom."[44] Yet the *Review* survived in Boston until 1878 and continued on thereafter in New York City until past the middle of the twentieth century.

≈≼ V ≽≈

THE GENERATION OF AMERICANS born during and after the Revolution differed in outlook from the Revolutionist generation. The colonial rebels, who had grown up in an empire where King George was the first gentleman in a realm ruled by gentlemen, inevitably remained a part of the system they overthrew. Americans born during the Revolution, by contrast, were republicans by birth, and they came of age in a society centered around simple equality, not a hierarchy of deference. Consequently, the Federalist and Jeffersonian eras were inevitably marked by generational conflicts that began within ordinary family life, quite aside from their expression in national discourse. These generational divisions, heightened by the French Revolution and its consequences, worked themselves out in the growth and decline of the first two-party system.

In politics generational conflict asserted itself most vehemently within the Federalist Party following its defeat in 1800. Jeffersonian Republicans presented themselves as the party of all the people and of progress, in line with Jefferson's proposition that "The earth belongs always to the living generation."[45] The Federalist Party remained, by comparison, the bearers of a no longer viable ideology, marked by respect for traditional practices and for deferential arrangements in society. That it remained the party of the past, at odds with the living generation, was no less evident to Federalists of the post-Revolutionary generation than it was to Republicans. The historian David Hackett Fischer delineated the trials of the younger Federalists—including Robert Goodloe Harper of South Carolina, Harrison Gray Otis of Massachusetts, and James A. Bayard of Delaware—as they contended against old-school Federalists afflicted, as New Hampshire's William Plumer complained, with "that uprightness which cannot accommodate itself to events—which cannot flatter the people—that stiff, ungracious patriotism, which professes to save the people from their worst enemies, themselves."[46]

Less open to public scrutiny were the conflicts within such families as the Sedgwicks of western Massachusetts and the Ingersolls of Philadelphia. Jared Ingersoll had broken with his Tory father to become a Federalist patriot. He had raised his son Charles Jared to be a Federalist in his own image with evident success, only to witness the son's apostasy upon entering politics in his twenties. After coming out as a conventionally Federalist scourge of Jacobin mobocracy in his youth, Charles Jared changed into a radical Republican, asserting that "majority bespeaks popularity, and popularity involves right. I have great faith in the instincts of the people. I prefer those instincts to the reasoning faculties of honorable gentlemen."

Even where party differences did not divide father and son, bitter divisions might arise within families as provincial colonials came only reluctantly to embrace their offsprings' national loyalties. Benjamin Rush was a sterling Revolutionary patriot, but before that he had been a Pennsylvanian. His son Richard, born in 1780, was an American by birth who viewed the nation from that perspective. Benjamin Rush had wanted the national capital to remain in Philadelphia; when it moved to the District of Columbia it departed from Benjamin's native turf. Richard was to spend an extensive career in Washington from 1812, when he was appointed comptroller of the treasury, through 1829, when he served as vice-president under John Quincy Adams. This career was launched at the expense of bitterly disrupted family relations. Benjamin Rush considered Richard's departure from his natal city as the desertion of his family for a position that was, under any circumstances, a "degradation" to "a man of literary and professional talents." As for himself, Benjamin wrote his son, "Philadelphia I like; to Pennsylvania I belong and trust always shall."[47]

Theodore Sedgwick, who retired to his Berkshire estate when he became convinced that "the people would make an experiment of democracy," suffered a democratic insurrection of his entire family. A wealthy, Yale-educated, self-made lawyer, Sedgwick had assumed the honors of his station, demanding and being seemingly accorded due deference from the lesser orders of his community. A dogmatic Hamiltonian Federalist, he viewed Jefferson as "the greatest rascal and traitor in the United States." The visiting duc de la Rochefoucauld-Liancourt wrote of Sedgwick that "In all the private relations of society he is an excellent man" but that "in his politics he is somewhat warm, and not a little intolerant."[48] After serving in the Confederation Congress, the United States Senate, and the House of Representatives, where he was elected speaker, Sedgwick retreated to the state judiciary following the election of Jefferson as president.

Sedgwick fathered ten children, of whom seven survived: four sons and three daughters, including the novelist Catharine Sedgwick. All four brothers grew up to be active Jacksonian Democrats, led by Theodore Jr., who wrote extensively on the political economy of egalitarianism and ran perennially and unsuccessfully for governor or senator on the Democratic ticket in Massachusetts. Catharine Sedgwick concerned herself little with politics or economics, but she accepted her brothers' opinions over her father's in these matters.

Two of her brothers, Henry and Robert, went into law together in New York. It was they who persuaded William Cullen Bryant—another Jacksonian son of a staunchly Federalist father—to leave Massachusetts and take up an editorial career in New York. Among the Sedgwicks' frequent visitors, James Fenimore Cooper was another Jacksonian son of a conservative Federalist county squire, the self-made William Cooper. Founder of Cooperstown, William had settled a population of forty thousand homesteaders on 750,000 acres of virgin land and governed them by "the art of hook and snivery" until his death in 1809 in a barroom brawl at the hands of a Republican.[49] A Jacksonian Democrat (as Jefferson's party had become known), James Fenimore Cooper was no less contentious than his father, and no less a believer in aristocratic perogatives. Nevertheless, his membership in the Democratic Party placed him in the mainstream of the nation that he represented as its most popularly successful literary artist.

Brahmin Boston also nurtured some Jeffersonians and Jacksonians among the post-Revolutionary generation. Among these, George Bancroft became ideologically influential through his ten-volume *History of the United States*. Boston's greater impact on the Republic in that era of stultified Massachusetts Federalism resulted from the turn of some of Harvard's brightest students away from politics to religion. From the 1750s, when John Adams and other Harvard men shifted their field from divinity to law, the legal profession attracted the brightest undergraduates. In the late 1790s, however, when a president from Massachusetts remained viciously embroiled with a Massachusetts-based "Essex Junto" of Hamiltonian Federalists, the best and brightest at Harvard rediscovered the religious vocation. Joseph Stevens Buckminster, William Ellery Channing, Charles Lowell, and Horace Holley found in religion the freedom to pursue intellectual inquiry and the liberal reforms that remained anathema to Massachusetts Federalists. The religious vocation brought these Harvard alumni a further advantage: as men of the cloth they were vested with intellectual and moral authority by the community at remarkably early ages. Buckminster was nineteen years old in 1804 when he became pastor of the Brattle Street Church, "the politest congregation in Massachusetts" according to John Adams.[50] Edward Everett was nineteen when he succeeded Buckminster to the same pastorate ten years later. Each of these teenagers became recognized as an outstanding moral and literary-intellectual leader of Boston by virtue of his appointment.

An even more remarkable example of precocity among the post-Revolutionary literati was that of Nicholas Biddle. Admitted to the University of Pennsylvania at the age of ten, Biddle was transferred to Princeton, losing two years' academic credit in the process but nevertheless becoming class valedictorian in 1801 and at age fifteen the youngest student ever to have graduated from that institution. Following three years of legal study in Philadelphia, where he became a member of Dennie's *Port Folio* circle, Biddle was appointed secretary to the American minister in Paris and later to the minister in London, James Monroe.[51]

Raised a Federalist and pressed into diplomatic service by Jeffersonian Republicans, Biddle found little attraction in either politics or diplomacy. Returning to Philadelphia he developed a lucrative legal practice and resumed his literary activities in Dennie's circle. As Dennie's drinking increased and health declined, Biddle assumed more and more editorial control over *Port Folio*, and he additionally assumed the task of editing the journals of the Lewis and Clark expedition. Following Dennie's death in 1812, Biddle assumed full responsibility for editing *Port Folio* until family problems in 1814 forced him to give it up.

As he became increasingly occupied with editorial work, Biddle considered giving up law altogether for literature. But in 1810 he was persuaded to run for the state legislature in the interests of educational reform, to eliminate "the most odious of all distinctions, the practical inequality between the educated and the ignorant."[52] When the charter of the first Bank of the United States expired in 1814, Biddle prepared a defense for it that established his reputation in the field; five years later President Monroe appointed him to the board of the second Bank of the United States, starting him out on what proved to be his major vocation in life.

Meanwhile, as editor of *Port Folio* Biddle had expanded and improved its commentary on art, eliminating political discussion altogether. Normally he remained a Federalist, despite his association with the Jeffersonians; contributors to his magazine ranged across the political spectrum, however, from Ingersoll on the left to Horace Binney, leader of the Philadelphia bar, on the right. (Binney classified himself as an adherent of republicanism but added that there was a smaller interval between a monarchy and a republic as he conceived of it than there was between a republic and a democracy.)[53]

In 1809, following the repeal of the embargo, Biddle wrote a friend an account of the times. In it he captured the malaise of those among the younger literati who, like himself, held aloof from the bitter partisanship of the older generation without being able to formulate an effective alternative to the problems confronting the nation.

We have had during the winter a sort of civil war here [Biddle wrote] which has fortunately ended in nothing worse than the disgrace of Penna. . . . Our political atmosphere is very gloomy and unpromising, but we endeavor to indemnify ourselves by professional occupations & the enjoyment of society.[54]

It was during these distressingly agitated and nationally aimless times that Charles Jared Ingersoll made his literary reputation and initiated the second period of American literary nationalism with his *Inchiquin, the Jesuit's Letters* (1810), subtitled *A Favorable View . . . of the United States, and a Refutation of Many of the Aspersions Cast Upon the Country by Former Residents and Tourists.*

⧼ VI ⧽

In *Inchiquin, the Jesuit's Letters* Ingersoll was concerned to counter hostile accounts by Loyalists and a few English travel books, including the one in verse by the Irish poet Thomas Moore that praised Dennie and his circle but disparaged the rest of American society. The *Inchiquin* essays sought to present an urbane, balanced, thoughtful, and informed survey of American society such as was not available to English or American readers at the time. Ingersoll accomplished his purpose with a gracefully written work that still repays reading. Then America went to war with Britain, and the unseemly battle of the quarterlies ensued.

Angered by a U.S. congressional committee report alleging British wartime atrocities against Americans, the British poet and critic Robert Southey led off in 1814 in *Quarterly Review* with what purported to be a review of *Inchiquin's Favorable Views of the United States* but consisted instead of extravagant slanders culled from travel books and perhaps from the author's inventive imagination. Despite its patent absurdity, American literati took it seriously, Timothy Dwight and James Kirke Paulding each replying with pamphlets that refuted Southey's aspersions one by one. As earnest expressions of wounded American feelings, Dwight's and Paulding's responses were perversely calculated to tickle the risibles of British reviewers. Having gotten such a rise out of the Americans with that first article, *Quarterly Review* returned with several even more savage essays and was joined in the attack by *Blackwood's Magazine, British Review*, and *Edinburgh Review*.[55]

Sydney Smith took up the sport with an initial essay in *Edinburgh* on "Travellers in America" in 1818, followed two years later with what became the classic essay of its kind. Ostensibly reviewing Adam Seybert's *Statistical Annals of the United States*, Smith briefly described its contents and moved onto the attack.

> Such is the land of Jonathan, and thus has it been governed. In his honest endeavors to better his condition and in his manly purpose of resisting injury and insult we most cordially sympathize. Thus far we are friends and admirers of Jonathan. But he must not grow vain and ambitious, or allow himself to be dazzled by that galaxy of epithets by which his orators and newspaper scribblers endeavor to persuade their supporters that they are the greatest, the most refined, the most enlightened, and the most moral people upon earth. The effect of this is unspeakably ludicrous on this side of the Atlantic.[56]

A decade later *North American Review* was still complaining that "The *Quarterly* reviles us, the *Edinburgh* sneers at us, *Blackwood* bullies us. . . . In short we are daily, weekly, monthly, and quarterly, from one year's end to the other, accused before these self-created courts of sundry high crimes and misdemeanors."[57] Actually, it was not really as bad as that. Amid occasional digs at Brother Jonathan, the British magazines had monitored the American branch of English literature more or less conscientiously and often appreciatively. Indeed, beginning at the close of 1824, *Blackwood's* hired the American novelist John Neal, posing as a recent English visitor to the United States, to prepare an essay in defense of American culture followed by a series of essays that, taken together, comprised the first published history of American literature.

Neal gave much offense in his articles, however, by loosing personal as well as professional sallies upon his literary enemies in America, employing the free-swinging style that had delighted *Blackwood's* editor and persuaded him to engage this American. The rawly indecorous Downeaster Neal did not meet accepted standards of gentlemanliness anywhere in the American Republic of Letters, though Poe, Whittier, Longfellow, and especially Hawthorne, as literary neophytes, were inspired and instructed by Neal's frenetic American novels of the 1820s. When the authorship of the *Blackwood's* articles became known, respectable American critics considered the source and discounted them. Neal's main critical judgments have nonetheless remained sound to twentieth-century critics.[58]

More substantial causes for American complaint than sporadic attacks in British reviews were English travelers' accounts of America. During the generation after the War of 1812, more than forty such accounts appeared, most of them superficial, ill-informed, pretentious, and condescending, and some of them hostile. Their publication peaked during the early 1830s, when twenty-five volumes appeared within five years; thereafter their numbers declined.[59] It was by paying serious critical attention to these often patently unreliable travelers' accounts that British literary magazines slandered American society most unfairly.

Genteel American defenders against British calumny could be as unkind to American society as the English accounts that offended them. Edward Everett, writing in *North American* in 1821, assured English readers that "the judicious public in our country" were as aware as the English critics of the worthlessness of Joel Barlow's *Columbiad*; that "The persecution of Americanisms at large has nowhere in Great Britain been pursued with such keenness as in America"; and that "As for specimens of pretended American dialect found in the books of travellers, we pity the Englishman who cannot see that they are fabrications compiled from local observations made in the porter-houses and oyster-cellars of Boston, New York, and Philadelphia."[60]

In Sydney Smith's 1820 essay, the famous question, which lingered in American minds for decades, had been: "In the four quarters of the globe, who reads an American book?" A year later, when Everett penned his equivocal apology for America, there was a ready answer to this question. Literary Englishmen were at that moment reading three American books: Washington Irving's *Sketch Book* (1819–20), and Fenimore Cooper's *Precaution* (1820) and *The Spy* (1821). Soon they were reading more: Irving's *Bracebridge Hall* was published in 1822, followed by Fenimore Cooper's *The Pioneers* in 1823. John Neal published four novels in 1822–23 and was arranging for their publication in England at the time of his contentious survey of American literature in *Blackwood's*. Catharine Sedgwick's *A New England Tale* appeared in 1822, followed by *Redwood* in 1824.

James Gates Percival's reputation as a lyric poet had by then risen in England as well as in America and was itself in the process of being overtaken by that of William Cullen Bryant. A Republic of Belles Lettres was actually coming into being in the United States at the very time that Sydney Smith raised the question. And the center of its activities was neither Philadelphia, the erstwhile capital of the American Enlightenment, nor Boston-Cambridge, the nation's preeminent "intercommunity of learning." Rather it centered its activities in the booming, culturally unpretentious commercial metropolis of Manhattan.

KNICKERBOCKER
NEW YORK

WHILE BOSTON HAD BEEN FOUNDED as a Puritan "city upon a hill" and Philadelphia as a Quaker "city of brotherly love," Manhattan Island had been settled because its port made an excellent facility for the Dutch West India Company and later for the Duke of York, who took it from the Dutch. Manhattan remained valuable real estate for the Anglo-Dutch landed gentry and city merchants who gained title to pieces of it, and New Yorkers acquired a reputation in the eighteenth century which they retained in the nineteenth for an all-absorbing money-mindedness that blinded them to higher civilized values. The saying had it that the Bostonian would ask you what books you had read; the Philadelphian, what family you belonged to; and the New Yorker, how much you were worth.

New York boasted powerful native Anglo-Dutch families—Livingstons, Clintons, Van Rensselaers, Beekmans, Courtlands, and others—who were hardly less haughtily pretentious than their counterparts in Philadelphia and Boston, though by reputation they were more hospitable to outsiders. There were patricians aplenty who considered it their responsibility as well as privilege to serve as trustees of Columbia College, the American Academy of Fine Arts, and other cultural institutions of the city. As stewards of culture they were not notably conscientious, enterprising, or open-handed, however. Patronage of contemporary artists was enthusiastically assumed by men of new money, notably Luman Reed, rather than by those of more seasoned wealth. And the huge bequests that established New York's major cultural institutions in the course of the nineteenth century were mainly made after the Civil War and from fortunes that had been mainly accumulated within the century.[1]

William Dean Howells, born and bred in Ohio, paid his first visit to

New York on literary business in 1860 and in 1891 moved there from Boston to be near his publishers. To Howells's way of thinking, from the retrospect of 1900, Boston constituted the only true literary center that had ever existed in America. What Boston possessed for Howells that other cities lacked was "distinctly a literary atmosphere which more or less pervaded society." By comparison, New York had never been a literary center worthy of the name, always granting the grubby fact that New York "is a literary centre on the business side, as London is."[2]

Cultivated New Yorkers tended to accept this materialistic stereotype of their city, whether in anger and sorrow—as with William Smith Jr. and William Livingston in the eighteenth century—or in fun—as with Washington Irving and the Knickerbocker writers in the nineteenth. From the Knickerbocker point of view, New Yorkers' penchant for business at least lent some recognizable character to a city with no ideological tradition save a manifest ethic of unfettered commercial interest among its competing and very mixed breed of citizens. Intellectually an outpost of the Philadelphia Enlightenment until the Revolution, New York City was left to draw upon its own cultural resources when the City of Brotherly Love retrenched and was simultaneously outstripped by its northern neighbor in wealth and population. New York's dramatic urban growth dimmed Philadelphia's prestige without enhancing its own cultural status. More than ever, New Yorkers were reputed to be culturally *nouveau riche*.

Yet New York possessed the virtues of its defects in abundance, as Elihu Hubbard Smith's remarkable Friendly Club early demonstrated. As a city of newcomers, New York provided opportunities to aspiring literati and artists from throughout the nation that patrician Philadelphia and Boston did not. And if the spirit of commercialism pervaded Manhattan, it served to inspire artists and writers with the spirit of professionalism. In other eastern cities and in the plantation south, the model for the man of letters remained the gentleman amateur. In New York, too, artists and writers aspired to be gentlemen. But over successive generations, newcomers competing for a foothold in New York evolved professional standards that relegated amateur standards to the provinces left behind. New York was no community of readers by comparison to Boston, New Haven-Hartford, or even Philadelphia. But by the 1820s it had established itself as a magnet for artists and writers whose ambitions were more than provincial.

Colonial and Revolutionary New York had indeed been remarkable for its freedom from any serious pretentions to culture. When John Adams singled out William Smith Jr. as the one "sensible and learned man" among all of the gentlemen he encountered in New York on his way to the Continental Congress, he hazarded an opinion with which Smith himself substantially agreed (excepting his close friends and fellow Yale graduates William Livingston and John Morin Scott). "This *Province* above any other," Smith complained in the *New-York Weekly Journal* in 1749, "has felt the miseries of ignorance, and they still remain our sorest afflictions. A sordid thirst after money, sways the lives of our people." For his part, William Livingston wrote a friend that "[our] gentry are nothing better than wealthy, distinguished, illustrious & exalted block heads."[3]

By 1750 at least forty members of that gentry had benefited from college educations at Yale, at Harvard, or abroad, but they did not band together in common cause as learned men did in Philadelphia and Boston. Cadwallader Colden, who emigrated to America in 1708, was probably the most ambitiously learned New Yorker of the mid–eighteenth century. A university-trained physician (Edinburgh, 1705) and in later life a leading New York political figure, Colden wrote extensive treatises on a wide variety of learned subjects and was published in Europe as well as North America. Though he became well known in England as an American man of letters, he was not similarly recognized by his fellow New Yorkers. Colden wrote a fellow philosopher in London in 1742 of his pleasure in being able "to communicate some thoughts in natural philosophy which have remained many years with me undigested, for we scarcely have a man in this country that takes any pleasure in such kinds of speculations."[4] A year later Colden met Benjamin Franklin by chance, and Franklin became the sometimes bemused recipient of letters outlining Colden's scientific speculations.

Franklin, who acquired an interest in a New York newspaper in 1742 and organized his philosophical society in Philadelphia a year later, sought to interest Colden and others in starting a similar society in New York. A New York society did meet for a time, and it was followed by others, including a "Society for improving themselves in useful knowledge" to which William Livingston and William Smith Jr. belonged. Meanwhile Livingston was engaged in a campaign to found a college in New York that would serve to increase the pitifully few men of letters in the province to "a glorious multitude of statesmen and heroes, philosophers and orators."[5]

Also interested in a New York college were a number of Anglican ministers from New York's four downriver counties. These ministers, together with prominent Anglican laymen, were roused to action in 1746 by the founding of a Presbyterian college in Princeton. The day after the College of New Jersey was chartered, the New York assembly began work on a bill to found King's College in New York. Livingston, a Presbyterian, became a member of the trustees in charge of the project, but Anglicans formed a majority of the board and were seemingly determined that King's should be an Anglican college. Anglicans were in fact a minority in the colony among Presbyterians, Lutherans, and members of the Dutch Reformed Church. However, the governor and his council were Anglicans, and the Anglicans won support from leading Dutch Reformed citizens who shared their antipathy to the evangelism of George Whitefield and the Great Awakening.[6]

Following years of public controversy, King's College opened in 1754 under the presidency of a scholarly Anglican minister from New Haven, Samuel Johnson, and under the control of a predominantly Anglican board of trustees. While it retained the loyal support of some Dutch Reformed members, others of the Dutch Reformed Church reacted by founding Queen's College (Rutgers) in New Jersey in 1771. Thereafter sons of the New York gentry might attend the college of their religious choice in New Haven, Princeton, New Brunswick, or New York. King's College failed to win the broad patronage of the provincial gentry that Harvard and Yale commanded, but it did not suffer from the domineering interference of trustees that stifled the University of Pennsylvania during the early years of the Republic. Under a succession of capable presidents, who were given a comparatively free reign, Columbia (as King's was renamed in 1784) survived as the select and necessarily modest college of the Episcopalian establishment and its friends. A medical school was added to the college on the eve of the Revolution at the same time that the medical school was founded in Philadelphia and proved similarly successful. Columbia did establish itself as the local center of academic learning, and it maintained this position thereafter. In 1830 the far more ambitiously conceived University of the

City of New York was founded under nationally distinguished scholarly auspices and with the enthusiastic focal support of Columbia's old enemies. The panic of 1837 reduced this major experiment in American higher education to a struggling college, however, returning Columbia to its leading position in the community.

Columbia's cultural position in New York was challenged less by rival colleges than by what Maria Lowell disdainfully referred to as "the meridian of Broadway": institutions of commercial culture that were gravitating to New York in the national period. The city's commercial culture provided theaters with a moral climate more tolerant than elsewhere and gave its artist community a degree of freedom from patronage unknown to painters and sculptors of nineteenth-century Philadelphia and Boston. Most influentially, this culture included men and women of the fourth estate: printers, engravers, publishers, editors, reporters, poets, critics, and "magazinists." Together with artists and thespians, these members of the public press gained ready entry into New York's ever-changing intellectual society where college education and family background did not define one's status as strictly as in other, older urban seaboard communities of the Republic, from Boston to Charleston. Genteel New Yorkers who desired to determine cultural standards in their community lacked the moral authority to do so in a city that was becoming the cultural as well as commercial crossroads of the nation. Consequently, while Manhattan could not be compared with London as a cultural metropolis, "Broadway" early became the nearest approximation in America to Dr. Johnson's London, which was culturally as close to Grub Street and Drury Lane as it was to Oxford and Cambridge.

⊸ II ⊱

IT WAS WASHINGTON IRVING'S achievement to make cultural capital of New York's lack of civic character. Together with his brother William and his brother-in-law, James Kirke Paulding, Irving wrote a series of Addisonian papers, *Salmagundi; or, The Whim-Whams* (1807–8), that delighted New York society by making light of it. Then Irving turned New York City into a huge joke, and a ribald one at that, with *A History of New York from the Beginning of the World to the End of the Dutch Dynasty, by "Diedrich Knickerbocker"* (2 vols., 1809). Because the history lampooned only Dutch New York, Dutch-Americans, including the literary man Gulian Verplanck, resented it. But Anglo-New Yorkers were delighted, and across the Atlantic the British received it with acclaim. Thus was launched the Knickerbocker school of light-hearted literati, who set the tone of New York culture for the next two generations.

Three Irving brothers, Peter, William, and Washington, were up-starts in the cozy literary world of New York, and they attracted enemies as well as admirers with their literary antics. Raised to help their father in his hardware business, the brothers lacked the classical education that certified the man of letters. Washington Irving studied law half-heartedly and was admitted to the bar, but he did not pursue the profession. The Irvings' showed themselves to be able students in their command of English literature, especially from the times of Addison and Steele. Literary devices of *Salmagundi* were lifted from Addison and Goldsmith, and the individual pieces were strewn with borrowings from eighteenth-century English novels. *Salmagundi* collected sixty-five pieces that had originally appeared irregularly at weekly to monthly intervals, a scheme that allowed the authors to respond to comments on earlier pieces as the series progressed. Following the success of *Salmagundi*, Peter and Washington planned a parody of Samuel Latham Mitchill's *Picture of New-York*, but Peter was sent to Europe on family business, and Washington abandoned the original plan for his *Knickerbocker History*. In its stead he shamelessly ransacked English literature for characters and episodes and indulged in a raunchy, Rabelaisian humor that he toned down when revising the work.[7]

Irving never returned to the earthy writing of *Knickerbocker History*. After an unhappy stint as editor of *Analectic* magazine in New York, he followed his brother Peter to England in 1815 to help with the family hardware business. He hoped that the change of scene from provincial New York City would revive his flagging literary creativity, and it did. The genteel charm of *The Sketch Book of Geoffrey Crayon, Gent.* (1820) won enthusiastic praise from British critics, some of whom found it difficult to credit its American authorship. It was followed two years later by *Bracebridge Hall*, a loving treatment of English country life that further enhanced Irving's reputation. Francis Jeffrey wrote in *Edinburgh Review* that "The

great charm and peculiarity of his work consists now, as on former occasions, in the singular sweetness of the composition."[8]

In the cause of American letters, Irving was an ambivalent hero at
best. A whole-souled Anglophile, he equated England with civilization
and America with provincialism. He rebuked a younger American friend
in England, William B. Preston of South Carolina, for "Americanizing"
when Preston responded with extroverted good humor to English reti-
cence. Such American behavior "ought to be suppressed in a gentleman,"
Irving admonished Preston, and one of the objects of travel was to rid
oneself of such provincialisms. Irving's acceptance in England effectively
secured his reputation among American readers who continued to defer
to the mother country in matters of taste, while literary patriots abused
the Anglophile as "a toad-eater, a sycophant, a courtier."[9] Philip Freneau,
who had continued to publish verse and bring out collections of them—
the last one in 1815—had been able to retire rather precariously to the life
of a gentleman farmer while remaining in touch with such New York literary friends as Samuel Latham Mitchill and John W. Francis. In 1820, at a
time when Freneau was having trouble arranging for the publication of
his collected poetry, the English success of Irving's *Sketch Book* aroused
him to fighting verse:

> See, IRVING, gone to Britain's court
> To people of *another sort*
> . . . Why pause? Like IRVING, haste away;
> To England your addresses pay;
> . . . In England what you write and print,
> Republished here in shop and stall
> Will perfectly entrance us all.[10]

Reservations concerning Irving's authenticity as an American writer
persisted and were not entirely put to rest by his later biographies of Columbus, Washington, and Captain Bonneville. After the War of 1812, a rising American cultural nationalism dissuaded American literary aspirants
from following Irving in seeking their literary fortunes in London. Irving,
meanwhile, remained in Europe for seventeen years before returning to
New York in 1832, the year of Freneau's death. He returned to a hero's
welcome. A committee of the Corporation of New York met him at the

harbor and escorted him on a civic walk to Blackwell's Island, to Bellevue, and thence to a select dinner at Philip Hone's. But much more was in store. The citizens of New York were invited to a public dinner in honor of their distinguished son. The week after Irving's arrival, "the spacious saloon of the City Hall was opened to its three hundred guests," who took their places at three lines of tables "covered with all the substantials and delicacies of the season."[11] A year later *Knickerbocker Magazine* launched upon a long and highly successful career in the spirit of Irving's earlier American writings, aided by contributions from Irving, for which he was very generously paid. Irving took up permanent residence thereafter as a gentleman of modest fortune, hard earned by literary labor, at his estate, Sunnyside, on the Hudson.

However Irving may be ranked as a writer of literature, his extraordinary influence upon the American Republic of Letters remains unique. Subsequent generations of writers responded both to the writings of his youth, which were the most American, and to those of his maturity, which consciously eliminated Americanisms from their lexicon. Irving's literary skill and its international reception gave great encouragement to other Americans with literary ambitions, including such future New England luminaries as Longfellow, Prescott, Emerson, and Hawthorne. When *The Blithedale Romance* appeared in 1852, Hawthorne sent Irving a copy with a note declaring that

> your friendly and approving word was one of the highest gratifications that I could possibly have received, from any literary source. Ever since I began to write, I have kept it among my cherished hopes to obtain such a word; nor did I ever publish a book without debating within myself whether to offer it to your notice [as the one American writer with the qualities to awaken such] intellectual and heart-felt recognition.[12]

The belles lettres that Joseph Dennie advanced found the literary distinction he sought in Irving's *Sketch Book*, which served as an inspiration to other American writers, whatever Irving's opinions might have been concerning the validity of an American literature.

The more concrete and enduring influence derived from the New York writings of Irving's youth. Irving taught New York how to efface the portentiously metropolitan character it was inadvertently assuming. "In

New York they make a man jocose in spite of himself," a writer in the Philadelphia *Literary Gazette* observed in 1821; "[A]t least, . . . ever since they have had to boast of 'Salmagundi' and 'Knickerbocker,' as indigenous productions . . . they have laughed at their own charicature in every variety of shape." Others laughed along with them. "We all remember the success of Salmagundi," Edward Everett wrote in *North American Review*, "with what rapidity and to what extent it circulated through America, how familiar it made us with the local pleasantry, and the personal humors of New York, and what an abiding influence it has had in that city."[13]

Indeed, Irving continued to set the tone of the city's literary culture in absentia during the seventeen years that he remained abroad. The chief vehicle of Knickerbocker culture, beginning in 1823, was the *New-York Mirror and Ladies' Literary Gazette*, edited by Samuel Woodworth and George Pope Morris. The *Mirror* balanced serious discussions of literature, art, drama, and music with fashion notes, toilet hints, and love stories. An editorial column commenting upon the contemporary Broadway scene gave the magazine a tone first sounded in *Salmagundi* and since echoed by most New York literary magazines down to today's *The New Yorker* with its "Talk of the Town." The *Mirror* survived and flourished as a light-hearted literary weekly that attracted literary contributions of a high level. Most distinguished of all were its art criticisms and its artistic, well-illustrated typography. It gained a nationwide readership and survived until 1857.

In 1833 Charles Fenno Hoffman started *Knickerbocker Magazine* as a light-hearted literary monthly, and a year later the foundering magazine was rescued by Lewis Gaylord Clark, a young man-about-town from upstate. Under Clark's editorship *Knickerbocker* thrived right along with the *Mirror* as a nationally recognized expression of New York urbanity, and Clark remained a commanding figure in Knickerbocker circles into the 1850s. Clark admired Washington Irving to the extent of paying him far more than the magazine could afford—two thousand dollars per year—to serve as contributing editor. Irving had put aside the whimsical humor of his early writings, but others continued in the tradition, including several of Irving's nephews. Among them John T. Irving Jr. achieved literary success with his "Quod Correspondence," which ran in *Knickerbocker* from

1841 to 1842, concerning one John Quod, "a tall elderly man, clad in a suit of rusty black," who was the spit and image of old Diedrich Knickerbocker, with "a slight stoop in his gait as if time were beginning to tell," and other whimsically depicted characteristics of the eccentric bachelor.[14]

As Knickerbocker writers aged they did their best to retain the skylarking youthfulness of their early style. Morris became editor of the *Mirror* at twenty-one, Clark took over the Knickerbocker at twenty-six, and other young men similarly took up editorial duties in their early twenties. Knickerbocker magazines featured "Joke Corners" and "Fun Jottings" and otherwise stressed humor. "The present age," Clark declared, "is emphatically the Age of Fun."[15] Clark himself was a past master at Knickerbocker humor, lightly addressed, "in good sooth" to the "gentle reader" from the "Editor's Table," regaling literate America with goings-on about Broadway.

Bachelors were almost as prevalent in Knickerbocker society as spinsters were in literary New England. Washington Irving remained a bachelor, although his bachelor retreat on the Hudson, Sunnyside, presently came to be filled up with adopted nieces. Other confirmed bachelors included Fitz-Greene Halleck, Lewis Gaylord Clark, Joseph Rodman Drake, Robert Charles Sands, and Charles Fenno Hoffman. Among them Halleck and Drake, "the Damon and Pythias of American poets," enjoyed exchanging extemporaneous verses with each other on a given subject. When these were published in the *New York Evening Post*, signed by "the Croakers," they created the same sort of literary stir that *Salmagundi* had inspired a generation before, becoming the talk of the town and inspiring hundreds to submit imitations to New York newspapers. Halleck later recalled this decade of the 1820s as "those happy days when we only lived to laugh."[16]

A characteristic literary man among the Knickerbocker set was the *single-song poet*, to use a Knickerbocker term, whose claim to immortality hung by the thread of a single lyric. Single-song poets included Samuel Woodworth ("The [Old Oaken] Bucket"), Clement C. Moore ("A Visit from St. Nicholas"), George Pope Morris ("Woodman, Spare That Tree!"), John Howard Payne ("Home, Sweet Home"), and Charles Fenno Hoffman, whose "Sparkling and Bright" was said to be "unsurpassed by any similar production in the language" but which appears not to have with-stood the test of time. The productive James Kirk Paulding remains per-haps best remembered for his "Peter Piper picked a peck of pickled pep-pers." The successful playwright Payne deserves to be remembered for more than "Home, Sweet Home," and the others all wrote more. Never-theless, in each case the single song served as the author's ticket to mem-bership in the literati.[17]

As editor of *Knickerbocker* Clark succeeded Joseph Dennie of *Port Folio* as the leading metropolitan literary bonhomme of the nation, gathering kindred literary spirits around him at his home, known as the Sanctum, and at various Broadway theaters, restaurants, and gathering places. A nasty opponent to those who crossed him or entered his cultural space without permission, Clark possessed the same sociability and talent for attracting friendships that had advanced Dennie's career before him. As with Dennie, his bright wit and genial manner cloaked a fierce loyalty to his magazine. Clark's political-social outlook was Dennie's as well; but where Dennie had commenced his career as an outspoken Tory, Clark avoided politics in print. In its literary opinions *Knickerbocker* was genteel and conservative, censuring all newfangledness in letters and ridiculing the Transcendentalists in particular. Despite Clark's strong Whig bias and particular admiration for Daniel Webster, the editor was obliged to ac-commodate a literary community in which the Democratic Party tended to prevail—from Bryant, Cooper, and Irving on down.[18]

Clark could not hope to dominate literary New York as Dennie had dominated literary Philadelphia. He could not even gain membership in the Sketch Club, though he attended from time to time as an invited guest and did become a charter member of its successor, the Century Club, in 1847. Nonetheless, in his column, "The Editor's Table," Clark successfully assumed the mantel of spokesman for New York culture, sharing his so-phisticated life with readers. "The Editor's Table" remained the most popu-lar feature of *Knickerbocker* and gave out-of-towners their main ideas about Broadway life. Over the years the spritely mix of book notes, gossip, and other comment grew to comprise a substantial part of the magazine.

The literary quality most prized by Knickerbocker literati was *Rabe-laisian*. As the Knickerbocker writers and critics understood the word, which remained a key term in their critical lexicon, no bawdy connotations were intended where literature was concerned—although conversational give and take among men of letters in the Sanctum was another matter. Washington Irving wrote that Rabelais was "an old French writer of admirable wit and humor, though too gross and obscene for female perusal."[19] Since a man's published writings inevitably came under female perusal, a genteel form of the Rabelaisian style was required in print, demanding extraordinary literary control to be properly brought off. Clark defined this conception of Rabelaisianism in praising the style of Charles Godfrey Leland:

> There is the same extraordinary display of universal learning, the same minute exactness of quotation, the same extravagant spirit of fun, the same capricious and provoking love of digression, the same upsetting of admitted ideas, by which trifles are seriously descanted upon, and bolstered up with endless authorities, until they expand into gigantic proportions, while time-honored truths are shuffled by with the most whimsical contempt.[20]

The Rabelaisian style was, in other words, very near to the intellectual style that Dennie and his circle in Philadelphia and the Anthologists in Boston had cultivated at their literary dinners, except that Irving had created a native tradition for it which gave the Knickerbocker literati their own special sense of place. Clark united the Rabelaisian ideal, by implication at least, with anti-Jacksonian social and political elitism. But Democratic Rabelaisians inhabited New York as well. Evart Augustus Duyckinck, a leading rival of Clark's in literary journalism, identified the virtues of the Rabelaisian style with the best elements of American democracy. Rabelaisian standards were suited not only to favorable comparisons with Boston prudery but also to favorable comparisons with effete aristocracy in England. Clark was decidedly Anglophile in his tastes; so was the Dutch-American Duyckinck. Duyckinck espoused a warm literary patriotism, Clark at least posed as a patron of American letters. Neither editor expected culture to emerge from the American backwoods, but the Rabelaisian style seemed to offer the proper synthesis of cosmopolitan civilization and American circumstances for the nation as well as for the metropolis.

⊰ III ⊱

NEW YORK'S LITERARY REPUTATION in the 1820s rested upon the three major writers associated with the city: Irving, who remained in Europe throughout the decade; Fenimore Cooper, who sailed for Europe in 1826 and remained abroad until 1833; and William Cullen Bryant of Great Barrington, Massachusetts, the only one of the three to demonstrate enduring loyalty either to New York City or to the cause of American literary nationalism. Bryant got along well enough with the other two, and Irving always made it a point to speak well of Cooper in public. But Cooper grew to detest Irving, the Anglophile, and there was continuing resentment, shared to some extent by all three, at being permanently grouped together in the public mind.

Like Irving, Cooper made his most influential contributions to the New York literary community during his salad days as a new and astonishingly successful novelist. Raised on his father's wilderness estate in upstate New York, Cooper attended Yale College for three years, joined the Navy and became a lieutenant, then resigned his commission in 1811 and settled with his bride in Westchester County. Ten years later, following publication of his highly successful *The Spy*, Cooper moved to New York City and immediately became the leading figure in the literary community. Several years after his arrival, Cooper started an informal club in a back room of his publisher's bookstore. This expanded into the Bread and Cheese Club—also referred to as the Lunch Club and the Cooper Club—which met regularly for hotel dinners. Never very formally organized, its amorphous membership included doctors, lawyers, merchants, scientists, and army and navy men, but writers and artists predominated. It revolved around its founder, who may have been the closest approximation to Samuel Johnson that America had produced. William Cullen Bryant, who was new in New York at the time of the Bread and Cheese Club, later recalled the "inexhaustible vivacity of his conversation, the minuteness of his knowledge, in everything which depended upon acuteness of observation and exactness of recollection."[21] When Cooper left for Europe in 1826, the club disintegrated after a year or so but was later followed by the Sketch Club. Thomas Cole and Bryant, who appear to have initiated the Sketch Club, originally met at the Bread and Cheese

Club dinners, and most of the writers and artists who joined the Sketch Club had earlier participated in Cooper's club.

Cooper could certainly not be charged with having "kissed a Monarch's —— hand," as Freneau wrote of Irving, and he drew no such criticism from literary nationalists while he was abroad. Indeed, while abroad, Cooper carried on the battle against the defamers of America in his *Notions of the Americans*. But he was dismayed by the American society he rediscovered upon returning to the United States in 1833, and he criticized it in novels and essays. Cooper's *A Letter to His Countrymen* (1834), *The Monikins* (1835), and *The American Democrat* (1838) expressed the creed of a gentleman who remained spiritually very much the lord of the manor at Cooperstown. Fenimore Cooper's rejection of his father's Federalism was based more upon his agrarian distrust of monocracy than on an egalitarian opposition to the now-vanishing Republic of Virtue and Talents. Cooper was repelled by this new America, where pseudo-democrats debased society with their leveling influences and insistence upon mass conformity. In *The American Democrat*, Cooper wrote:

> Some men fancy that a democrat can only be one who seeks the level, social, mental, and moral, of the majority, a rule that would exclude all men of refinement, education, and taste from the class. These persons are enemies of democracy, as they at once render it impracticable. . . . All that democracy means, is as equal a participation in rights as is practicable; and to pretend that social equality is a condition of popular institutions, is to assume that the latter are destructive of civilization

Cooper reasoned that popular institutions undermine civilization since, he believed, equality can be obtained only by reducing the entire community to the lowest standard of taste and refinement. In the four volumes of *Gleanings in Europe* (1837–38), Cooper compared English and American society and concluded that "a national character somewhere between the two, would be preferable to either."[22]

America's preeminent man of letters succeeded in arousing a storm of popular hostility in his homeland, accompanied by virulent abuse from the Whig press, to which Cooper responded with a series of libel suits, all of which he won. At the conclusion of his successful litigations, the avowed, if unrepresentative, democrat, Cooper, received a jubilant letter from his friend, the avowed monarchist, Fitz-Greene Halleck, congratulating him on his victories against the evils of the free press, evils which Halleck traced to John Milton, who had fostered slander with his defense of the liberty of unlicensed printing.[23]

⊷ IV ⊶

ON CHRISTMAS EVE IN 1824 William Cullen Bryant, then thirty, wrote his New York friend Charles Sedgwick from Great Barrington, Massachusetts, that he was determined to leave the law—"this beggarly profession," as he called it. For half of his short life, Bryant had mixed letters with law and in 1821 had seen the publication of his first volume of verse, which included "Thanatopsis." His effusions had won the warm encouragement of Boston's literati, especially Richard Henry Dana, an editor of the *North American Review*, which started to publish Bryant. More recently Bryant had contributed to the *United States Literary Gazette* a review-essay praising Cooper's romantic evocation of the nation's recent past but urging instead a national literature based on the "rich and varied" experience of the present age. Bryant had heeded his own call with a farce, *The Heroes*, that lampooned the antebellum chivalric code and its propensity for duels. Now the poet sought a reliable outlet for his prose in an arena big enough for his convictions.

Sedgwick recommended New York and suggested that Bryant contact the Athenaeum, a popular library and reading club that was thinking of sponsoring a journal. After several exploratory trips to the city, Bryant was engaged in 1825 as editor of a new monthly, the *New-York Review and Athenaeum Magazine*, at a commanding salary of one thousand dollars per year, twice his earnings from law.[24] Several months later he joined the staff of the *New York Evening Post*, rose to editor several years later, and continued his influential and profitable connection with that newspaper until his death in 1878.

Throughout his long career Bryant successfully pursued three separate and apparently ill-assorted vocations. First, he continued to write poetry, and while his verse remained slight in quantity and lacking in any perceptible development from his earliest attempts, it continued to be appreciated by readers and to be highly rated by critics. Second, as a crusading newspaper editor, Bryant engaged in endless local, state, and national contests as a Loco-Foco Jacksonian Democrat who later went Republican in the slavery issue. As editor of the *Evening Post*, he gathered about him a like-minded staff of Democratic intellectuals including William Leggett, Park Godwin, and members of the Sedgwick family. And third, despite the antagonisms engendered by his editorial activities, Bryant acted as a moderating and organizing influence within the literary-artistic community in particular and the civic community in general.

A striking characteristic of the creative community of New York City that Bryant joined in 1825 was the cordial relationship that existed among artists and writers, the relationship that Asher Durand famously evoked in his painting "Kindred Spirits," of his friends Thomas Cole, the painter, and William Cullen Bryant, the poet, communing together in a sylvan setting. William Dunlap—painter, playwright, stage manager, art historian, and organizer of kindred creative spirits from the days of the Friendly Club—was an early worker for closer relationships between artists and writers, but even without such furtherance the relationship seemed natural in New York City, where the two groups were joined by common enterprises in journalism and publishing and by a shared interest in achieving a profitable, professional, and gentlemanly social status. New York's three literary lions each shared close relationships with artists. Cooper enjoyed a hearty fellowship with Samuel F. B. Morse as well as with numbers of other painters who attended his Bread and Cheese Club meetings. Irving, who had taken up drawing at one point and considered becoming a painter, struck up friendships with Washington Allston, Charles R. Leslie, and American painters based in Europe. Bryant was on close terms with painters at home and abroad, beginning with Cole and Durand and including Dunlap, Morse, and Allston.[25]

Despite their similar professional goals, artists and writers faced different problems. For many writers, the composition of belles lettres was unquestionably a gentlemanly pursuit, a congenial avocation for the college educated. For others, writing was seen as a vocation that warranted professional status. Nathaniel Hawthorne, beginning his literary career in 1825, put it succinctly:

> I don't want to be a doctor, and live by men's diseases; nor a minister to live by their sins; nor a lawyer to live by their quarrels. So I don't see there's anything left for me but to be an author.

In this contest Noah Webster remained the inadequately appreciated pioneer, having almost single-handedly initiated copyright legislation in the individual states and in the federal Congress to secure for himself and other writers a legal right to the profits of their labors. Enforcement of these copyright laws was, of course, another matter, but Webster won lawsuits as well. However, the efforts to obtain an international copyright law in Jacksonian America found writers themselves divided on the issue, just as they were divided on the issue of professionalism in the business of literature.

Some who advocated an international copyright law called for a permanent writers' league to monitor it. But parochialism and backbiting mitigated against such an association. Similarly fraticidal tendencies had not prevented physicians or lawyers from forming medical and legal associations, at least locally, but these had been established to maintain professional standards. Writers, too, were concerned about standards, or the lack thereof, manifest in the shoddy novels and magazine stories, which continued to outsell serious literature. But consensus on the nature of literary trash proved more elusive than agreement on quackery, and few writers supported an association that would dictate standards of aesthetics or craft.[26]

Artists who sought to be seen as gentlemanly professionals faced quite different problems. Unlike writers, the artists' professional—or at least occupational—status was not questioned, but their gentlemanly status was. Historically, the painting of likenesses—*limning*—and the carving of figureheads for ships had provided livelihoods for craftsmen in the employ of gentlemen. While painters, together with other artisans, enjoyed a more substantial and negotiable market for their product than writers did, they lacked the social prestige that adhered to literary pursuits. They had customarily been viewed as common people, unless they had happened additionally to enjoy the advantages of social position and of either the college education or the European training that elevated them from artisans to the rank of gentlemen artists.

As portrait painting offered the surest source of income, artists were in the invidious position of being obliged to please wealthy patrons, who not only paid them for services rendered but also served as trustees of the municipal art institutions that sought to regulate their activities. Circumstance thus fostered a fraternity among New York's artists that had no parallel among the city's writers.

Young artists opposed to the patrician American Academy of the Fine Arts organized their own National Academy of Design in 1826. The American Academy, founded in 1802 as the Society of Fine Arts, had been the first such municipal academy established in the United States, though individuals—notably Charles Willson Peale in Philadelphia—had organized similar institutions privately. Chancellor Robert R. Livingston invigorated the society on returning to New York from France with "rare and beautiful objects." At a time when Americans had little or no opportunity to see either European works of art or reproductions of them, Livingston sponsored the acquisition of plaster casts of classical statues in the Louvre. Accordingly, the painter John Vanderlyn was sent to Paris to supervise the making of the casts and to copy or purchase copies of great paintings.[27]

The academy received support and guidance from leading men of the city: the Livingstons, Mayor DeWitt Clinton, and merchants and professional men who served as its directors. It failed to win strong public support, however, because it held itself aloof from the city's professional artists. Founded "as a place of rational amusement to our citizens and strangers, and a delightful study to the Amateur," the American Academy resisted appeals of professional artists to use its facilities until 1817, when it grudgingly opened its rooms to them from six to eight in the morning.[28] Young artists, who resented being treated like beggars, organized the National Academy of Design in 1826. Their academy combined aspects of a craft guild, a professional association, a producers' cooperative, an art school, and a public gallery, and it thrived from the first on public support. So enthusiastic was the response to its annual spring exhibition that the costs of the school and its exhibitions were paid for out of public admissions fees. As the patrician American Academy languished and died, the artisan National Academy prospered, and its leading artists rose to affluence and gentlemanly station in the community.

Even in the first decades of the century, when amateur gentlemen of the American Academy appeared to command the New York art world, Manhattan was establishing a national reputation as the working artists' capital. As the century wore on, the contrast between New York's enterprising creative community and the smaller communities of Boston and Philadelphia became more pronounced—particularly as Boston's Athenaeum and Philadelphia's Pennsylvania Academy of Fine Arts continued to cater to patrician patrons rather than professionals. "The artists of New York happily rid themselves from this thralldom of insolent corporate patronage more than twenty years ago," *Sartain's Union Magazine* declared in 1850, "and now occupy an enviable and commanding position," founded upon the only real art academy "in the western hemisphere."[29]

Although the National Academy continued to be operated by professional painters, architects, sculptors, and engravers, honorary memberships were extended to some writers, and two writers, Bryant and Verplanck, held appointments on the art school faculty.[30] A new occasion for professional relationships between writers and artists arose with the introduction of the literary annual to America by the Philadelphia firm of Carey and Lea. Initiated in 1825, *The Atlantic Souvenir: A Christmas and New Years' Offering* embraced contributions by artists and writers jointly. By 1829 at least seventeen literary annuals were being published, while magazines, led by the *Mirror*, became more and more extensively illustrated.[31]

The two communities commingled in recreation as well as creation, nowhere more famously than in Gotham's Sketch Club. In his "Prehistoric Notes of the Century Club," John Durand, artist and son of Asher Durand, traced the origins of the Sketch Club to an 1828 Christmas annual, *The Talisman*, edited by Robert Sands, Verplanck, and Bryant, who enlisted Morse, Cole, Durand, and other artists as illustrators. The association assumed a more permanent form when the group became the founding members of the Sketch Club, in 1829. Immediately famous, this select and cheerful confraternity of writers and artists devoted itself to extemporaneous composition of verse and prose and to sketching, skits, and merry high jinks, aiming always to keep itself simple as well as light-hearted. Formal dinners were interdicted, and suppers were to "consist of sandwiches, coffee and wine, or such 'dietics' as the caterer may deem necessary."[32] Durand told how a wealthy member violated this rule in 1829 by serving a formal supper during a meeting at his home, whereupon the club disbanded and reorganized itself without the rich man and with more detailed regulations.

As restraints on ostentation and suspicion of the rich relaxed over the years, opinion increasingly favored the acquisition of permanent quarters. Eventually, this led to the incorporation of the Century Club in 1847. Among its original forty-two members, ten were merchants, ten were artists, seven were gentlemen of the learned professions or of leisure, and four were professional writers. The Century Club expanded in size and prestige thereafter, enrolling actors and musicians as well as artists and literary men, until at the turn of the twentieth century, the National Academy of Arts and Letters could be selected principally from its extensive and distinguished membership. By then the literary men who had founded the Saturday Club of Boston had died, and they had been supplanted mainly by gentlemen from the business community whose most tangible literary credentials consisted of membership on the Harvard Board of Overseers.[33]

❧ V ☙

NEW YORK OFFERED ITS LITERATI sociability in variety and abundance. Salons, soirées, receptions, parties, and banquets were held in hotel clubs, in clubs that met in private homes, and increasingly in clubs that flew their flags above imposing private quarters. But sidewalks, restaurants, and taverns equally provided occasion for informal meetings. The publishing and theater district occupied a famous stretch of Broadway, sharing the street with eateries, saloons, commercial houses, art galleries, and private residences, all offering places for literary society to gather and gab. Among public houses, the old Shakespeare Tavern was favored by DeWitt Clinton, Robert Charles Sands, James Kirke Paulding, James Gates Percival, and Fitz-Greene Halleck.[34] Bohemians who favored Pfaff's Tavern, beginning in the mid-fifties, carried this practice to an extreme, gathering nightly. Not so the gentlemen of Knickerbocker circles, where steady barroom lounging was not countenanced. Before the Civil War flag-flying private social clubs were mainly harbingers of New York's future—the first founded was the Union Club, in 1836. As elsewhere, literary sociability was fostered chiefly in the parlors and dining rooms of private households.

On the conservative margin of New York's literary society, judges and lawyers of the Kent Club dined at members' houses on Saturday evenings. According to Philip Hone, their time was spent equally on wisdom and joviality, the division occurring at 10 P.M., after which "They seemed to condemn all law but that of passing the bottle."[35] Hone attended a half dozen such clubs that made more or less pretense at literary cultivation, including a bookless Library Club and ultimately a Hone Club. The Hone Club dined together on alternate Mondays and discussed American history and society from a Whig point of view, continuing to meet regularly until Hone's death.

Physicians remained active, as ever, in literary circles. While venerable Samuel Latham Mitchill continued to make the rounds of literary parties in the 1820s, young Dr. James De Kay engaged in Knickerbocker fun with some of the younger poets including Joseph Rodman Drake and Fitz-Greene Halleck, he and Halleck joining the Ugly Club, which vowed "to advocate ugliness in all its hideous forms."[36] Dr. John Wakefield Francis, who became the dominant figure in New York medical circles, managed to remain at the same time a peripatetic member of Knickerbocker literary society who kept on good terms with the sometimes bitterly contending factions within that society. Meanwhile his mentor and partner until 1820, Dr. David Hosack, presided over what was reputed to be the most lavish literary evening in town following his marriage to a wealthy widow in 1825.

Guests were invited to Hosack's parties by the evening or by the season. Thomas Cole received a printed invitation in November 1826 declaring that "Dr. Hosack requests the favour of Mr. Cole's company on Saturday evenings, during the winter." Other such seasonal guests included John Trumbull, William Dunlap, and John Henry Hobart, bishop of New York's Episcopal diocese. Jared Sparks, then editor of the Boston-based *North American Review*, noted in his diary in 1826 visiting "at Dr. Hosack's with a large company of literary gentlemen and others, Chancellor Kent, Dr. Mitchill, Halleck the poet, men of bar and clergy."[37] A year later Nathaniel Parker Willis, a senior at Yale with a published book of verse to his credit, gained entry to a Hosack evening.

On Saturday evening [Willis wrote] I went to a genuine *soirée* at the great Dr. Hosack's. This man is the most luxurious liver in the city, and his house is a perfect palace. You could not lay your hand on the wall for the costly paintings, and the furniture exceeds everything I have seen. I met all the literary characters of the day there, and Halleck, the poet, among them.[38]

Mistress of somewhat comparable ostentation was Mrs. Emma C. Embury, poet and scholar of wealth and station, who maintained a similarly elegant salon.[39]

For single women as well as for single men and married couples, New York offered numerous and varied occasions for mixed intellectual company conducted within the domestic sphere. Whether they were called *soirées, parties, salons, conversations, evenings,* or *receptions,* they were regularly scheduled occasions where hosts and hostesses were "at home" to a circle of acquaintances and their friends. Even single women might enjoy success as hostesses if they radiated sociability while remaining immaculately above reproach. Anna C. Lynch of Waverley Place, author of "Bones in the Desert" and other poems, was accounted the most successful of literary hostesses, both as a single woman and later as Mrs. Botta. "To be invited to the reception of Miss Lynch," wrote Elizabeth Oakes Smith, "was an evidence of distinction, and one in itself, for she was strict in drawing the moral as well as the intellectual line."[40]

Smith was herself at home to literary society every other Sunday evening, together with her husband, Seba Smith, author of the pseudonymous Jack Downing letters. The Smiths, from Portland, Maine, were among several New Englanders whose guests tended to be drawn from New York's sizable Yankee community. Yankees were also to be seen at the receptions of the Unitarian minister Orville Dewey and most notably at the town houses of Henry and Robert Sedgwick, who were visited for several months each winter by their novelist sister, Catharine Sedgwick, from her home in the Berkshires. It was the Sedgwicks who had invited William Cullen Bryant to New York, and it was at their houses that Bryant and the Connecticut Yankee Fitz-Greene Halleck became acquainted. Native New Yorkers frequently found visiting the Sedgwicks' included Gulian Verplanck, Robert Sands, Thomas Cole, and Fenimore Cooper.[41]

Drawing the moral line was always a problem, especially where un-married women were concerned. On the one hand, society demanded that a woman's reputation be absolutely spotless; on the other hand, most women of letters wrote poetry, the sphere and spur of passion in a romantic era. Brazen flirtation was bad form, but tender infatuation was not, so long as it was pure. Among ladies' men, masters of this etiquette generally popular among women, Nathaniel Parker Willis and Edgar Allan Poe were notable. Unfortunately for Poe, loves and jealousies he aroused in the hearts of admirers were beyond his control and contrib-uted to his downfall.

Also contributing to Poe's downfall was his series of articles on "The Literati of New York," for *Godey's Ladies' Book* in 1846. Among the thirty-eight brief biographical sketchs, twelve were of women.[42] The descrip-tions were not by any means reliable since Poe was settling old scores in some and mending fences in others. Nevertheless, the characterizations indicate the conventions by which literary women were appraised in mid-nineteenth-century America. Thus Caroline M. Kirkland was favor-ably presented as "frank, cordial, yet sufficiently dignified—even bold, yet especially ladylike; converses with remarkable accuracy as well as fluency; is brilliantly witty, and now and then not a little sarcastic, but a general amiability prevails." The poet Frances S. Osgood was "ardent, sensitive, impulsive," as befitted a lady poet, but also "the very soul of truth and honor"—she and Poe had been accused by a jealous poetess, Elizabeth Ellet, of having an affair—"a worshipper of the beautiful, with a heart so radically artless as to seem abundant in art—universally re-spected, admired and beloved."

By contrast a New England bluestocking reformer such as Lydia Maria Child did not appeal to Poe: "She is of that order of beings who are themselves only on 'great occasions.'" Of Catharine Sedgwick he de-clared similarly: "Her manners are those of a high-bred woman, but her ordinary *manner* vacillates in a singular way, between cordiality and a re-serve amounting to *hauteur*." But with Margaret Fuller, Poe seemed to be of two minds: She was

> looking at you at one moment earnestly in the face, at the next seem-ing to look only within her own spirit or at the wall; moving nervously

every now and then in her chair; speaking in a high key, but musically, deliberately (not hurriedly or loudly), with a delicious distinctness of enunciation.

In addition to private and semiprivate literary gatherings, the civic testimonial dinner afforded men of affairs in New York an opportunity to develop republican clubability on a grand scale. An obvious occasion for such a dinner—and the one that historically initiated the custom—was Irving's return from Europe in 1832, when the private dinner at Philip Hone's house was followed by the public dinner at the City Hall, attended by three hundred guests for six hours of food and oratory. A year after Irving returned, Cooper arrived and was met by a deputation of old Bread and Cheese Clubbers, including Bryant and Dr. Francis, who were

> desirous of testifying to you the continuance of their friendship, of the respect in which they hold your talents, and of their approbation of your manly defence, while abroad, of the institutions of our country [at] a dinner at such time as shall be agreeable to you.[43]

Cooper left town without waiting for such a dinner, but occasions arose for other dinners, and the biggest of them all in Boston as well as New York was honoring the arrival of Charles Dickens in America in 1842.

No dinner, not even Thackeray's rousing welcome a decade later, approached the scale of the Dickens dinners. Dickens enjoyed a popularity in America greater than any writer except Sir Walter Scott, and no English literary figure of Dickens' caliber had visited America before. Dickens evidently came—though he did not say so—because he had invested heavily in a bogus Cairo City and Canal Company that Darius B. Holbrook of Boston had advertised widely in Europe, and Dickens was furiously determined to go to Illinois to appraise the situation. On the way he passed through Boston and New York, where leading citizens planned testimonial dinners for him, and Philadelphia, where leading citizens declined to do so.[44]

In Boston the dinner for the thirty-year-old author was planned by a committee of "The Young Men of Boston," headed by Josiah Quincy Jr. and including James Russell Lowell, Oliver Wendell Holmes, and William Wetmore Story, then in their twenties or early thirties. The numerous testimonial addresses that followed the many courses praised Harvard and

Boston as well as Dickens and literature. Edward G. Loring told Dickens of the founding of Harvard College, which "made it its great duty to guard the purity of our English speech. Sir, if we have not profited in that respect by her teachings, it is our own fault." James T. Fields later remembered that

> We younger members of the dinner party sat in the seventh heaven of happiness and were translated to other spheres. . . . [F]requent messages came down to us from the "Chair" begging that we hold up a little and moderate if possible the rapture of our applause.[45]

In New York a public ball was held in Dickens' honor the evening after he and his wife arrived, followed by a testimonial dinner four days later. The ball, decorated with scenes and characters from *Pickwick Papers*, was organized by a "mixed committee, official, fashionable and literary, and some who aspired to all these distinctions," according to Dr. T. L. Nichols, an observer, and attracted an "immense crowd of the 'beauty and fashion' of New York." Twenty-five hundred tickets were taken at the door. The subsequent dinner was sponsored by forty-two leading literary and civic gentlemen, including Hone, Bryant, Irving, and the aged James Kent, former chancellor of the New York Court of Chancery. Two hundred thirty men sat down to it; at the same time a dozen wives and daughters, segregated with Mrs. Dickens in a room at the upper part of the hall, slipped out and regrouped behind the banquet president's chair "to the discomfiture of certain old bachelors and ungallant dignitaries," according to Hone.[46] "Boz" attended several smaller dinners, including one hosted by Lewis Gaylord Clark that Dickens later wrote was "the pleasantest dinner I enjoyed in America." In addition, Irving, Bryant, and Fitz-Greene Halleck breakfasted with Dickens. And then, off to Illinois and that mythical canal on the Mississippi. Meanwhile, Dickens had not pleased everybody. Irving was disgusted by his vulgarity at breakfast and always afterward held this against him. Others remained uncritically admiring until the next year, when *Martin Chuzzlewit* appeared with its unflattering account of New York and America. Hone found it difficult to believe that "such unmitigated trash should have flown from the same pen that drew the portrait of the immortal 'Pickwick.'" Cooper, who had viewed the Dickens welcome with contempt, wrote Rufus Griswold that Dickens was

> doing precisely what I looked for, from him. This country must out-grow its adulation of foreigners, Englishmen in particular, as children outgrow the rickets. It will not happen in your day,—much less mine.[47]

❦ VI ❧

AMONG THE STAUNCHEST BOOSTERS in the New York literary community were expatriate New Englanders like Bryant and Halleck, for whom Manhattan had proved a generous open city of opportunity. Writing in his weekly, *The New-Yorker*, in 1839, New Hampshire-born Horace Greeley asserted that

> New York has become the metropolis in our country, not only of commerce, but of literature and the arts . . . No man well acquainted with the history of Literature and Art in our country during the last ten years, can refuse to acknowledge that New York has towered above her sister cities.[48]

Such claims would have been construed as boorish boasts in Philadelphia or Boston, where the genteel code of the patrician classes set cultural standards.

But gracious silence in the realm of literary journalism by no means implied a faltering of civic pride. The young Knickerbocker writer J. T. Irving Jr., visiting Salem in 1832, was asked at dinner whether he preferred New York or Boston.

> I of course said N.Y. But I had no sooner said it than I had about a dozen up the table all singing out that N.Y. would bear no comparison with Boston. . . . A little red faced man opposite me was very indignant. . . . He said New York would never flourish whilst it had Boston on one side and Philadelphia on the other. . . . [H]e bellowed out his anger so loud as to draw the attention of too many so shut up.[49]

A dinner party of Philadelphians in 1832 would probably not have argued the cultural superiority of their city primarily on belletristic grounds.

The arenas of intellectualism that might more readily have come to mind would have been the Franklin Institute, the Philadelphia Medical Society, and the Law Association, where presentations and debates attracted city-wide attention. Nevertheless, there remained a case to be made for Philadelphian belles lettres, based upon the city's continued primacy in the field of literary publishing, its leadership in the publication of women's magazines that contained impressive literary content, and the signal contributions that Philadelphians made to the literature of the American theater, from Robert Montgomery Bird to George Boker.

Philadelphia continued to lead the nation in literary publishing through the enterprise of Carey & Lea, which wrote Fenimore Cooper in 1826 that Philadelphia did everything better in literary affairs than New York except produce novelists.[50] Already publishing Irving's books, Carey & Lea acquired Cooper and other writers impressed by the firm's unrivaled marketing operation. The annual gift book, *Atlantic Souvenir*, started in 1825, was an effective means of attracting such New York literati as Paulding, Bryant, Halleck, and Irving. Another lure was the *American Quarterly Review*, edited by Robert Walsh and published by Carey & Lea from 1827 to 1833.[51] The only American publisher of the eighteenth century to survive well into the nineteenth, Matthew Carey retired in 1822, leaving the firm in the hands of his son the economist Henry C. Carey, and his son-in-law Isaac Lea. In 1838 that partnership dissolved, and Philadelphia ceased to compete seriously with New York in literary publishing. The Harper brothers James and John founded their business in 1817 and by midcentury remained the oldest firm in the nation.[52] Together with Joseph and Fletcher, who entered the firm in the 1820s, the Harper brothers were hard-headed Methodist businessmen whose ventures into the literary field were supported by a steady trade in religious works. In the mid-1830s, as Carey & Lea declined, the Harper brothers signed contracts with Bryant, Poe, and Longfellow, as well as William Dunlap, James Kirke Paulding, Catharine Sedgwick, William Gilmore Simms, and others.[53]

Daniel Appleton entered New York publishing in 1838, followed by John Wiley, who later joined with George Palmer Putnam. Moses S. Dodd entered the trade in 1839. Boston, meanwhile, afforded its authors no publishing service that included marketing books outside of New England until James T. Fields developed the trade as a partner in Ticknor & Fields in the 1840s. How the New York publishers may have rated with the literary community before then may be indicated by the way Richard Henry Dana Jr.'s *Two Years before the Mast* was placed with a publisher in 1839. Working through their long-time New York friend William Cullen Bryant, the Dana family first approached the Harper brothers, then Appleton, then Coleman, and finally Wiley & Putnam. When all four publishers rejected the manuscript on terms that would have returned the author substantial royalties, it was sold outright to the Harpers, who made a handsome income from a book that sold briskly from the day of publication.[54] Among these publishers, Wiley and Putnam were distinguished by their appreciation of literature for its own sake and for the pleasure they took in literary fellowship. It was at Wiley's that Richard Henry Dana Sr. met Cooper and the poets James Gates Percival and Fitz-Greene Halleck in the 1820s, and it was there that Cooper started up his Bread and Cheese Club.[55]

Philadelphia publishers continued to excel up to the Civil War in the area of women's magazines that maintained a literary tone of sorts. The most successful of these—indeed, much the most successful magazine of the age—was *Godey's Lady's Book*, published monthly and edited by Louis Antoine Godey from 1830 and then edited by Sarah Josepha Hale from 1837 until 1877. A number of magazines were modeled on *Godey's*; of these *Peterson's Ladies' National Magazine*, founded in Philadelphia in 1842, was the most successful. Meanwhile, *The Casket: Flowers of Literature, Wit and Sentiment* ran on a monthly basis from 1826 to 1831 in Philadelphia and later achieved its greatest success as *Graham's Magazine* under George Rex Graham from 1838 to 1858, working with a series of distinguished coeditors, including Edgar Allen Poe, Ann S. Stevens, Rufus Wilmot Griswold, (James) Bayard Taylor, and Charles Godfrey Leland. No magazines emerged in New York to rival these, which were able to pay the best rates available to authors; although *Knickerbocker Magazine* maintained its ladies' departments, and the *Mirror* continued to dominate the field among the weeklies.[56]

Outside the area of ladies' magazines, New York dominated the field of literary weeklies and monthlies, the weekly *Mirror* being joined in 1848 by Evart Augustus Duyckinck's higher-brow weekly, *Literary World*. Literature and politics mingled in the *Democratic Review,* begun in 1837 and successful enough to draw opposition from the *Whig Review,* begun in 1845. Finally, in the 1850s the crowning achievement of American literary journalism, *Putnam's Monthly Magazine,* brilliantly illuminated the American literary renaissance of that decade. In Boston, meanwhile, the only literary periodical of quality to last more than a year throughout this period, other than the quarterly *North American Review,* was Joseph T. Buckingham's monthly *New-England Magazine,* published from 1831 to 1835, followed twenty-two years later by *Atlantic Monthly.*

In Philadelphia, a tradition of support for the theater had flourished since the pre-Revolutionary days of the Anglican proprietor John Penn and the Anglican proctor of the College of Philadelphia Reverend William Smith. By the late 1820s three theaters prospered in the city. On their stages were performed verse dramas written by members of the Philadelphia gentry, the most serious and talented of whom was Robert Montgomery Bird. Born in New Castle, Delaware, Bird had become a proper Philadelphian by the time he graduated from the University of Pennsylvania medical school in 1824. After school Bird put his medical career aside to write plays for the Philadelphia stage. His dramas proved financially as well as critically successful—the distinguished actor Edwin Forrest continued to perform Bird's *The Gladiator* and other Bird plays throughout his career—but the theater system did not permit Bird to earn an adequate income.[57] After four years of critical success and financial failure, Bird turned to writing novels, of which the best was *Nick of the Woods* (1837). But there proved to be little profit in fiction either—and even less honor, so far as Philadelphia was concerned. Novels continued to be frowned on by Robert Walsh and the Philadelphia society he represented; while, according to the historian of American drama, Montrose J. Moses, dramatic art was viewed in Philadelphia as "a grace rather than an earnest accomplishment."[58]

Until the late 1820s, the Philadelphia stage, dominated by the excellent Chestnut Street Theater—affectionately referred to as Old Drury—retained first place in the nation. But interference and internal dissension led to the bankruptcy of Old Drury in 1828. Four of the city's other acting companies failed during the following year, and in 1830 New York had

taken the lead in the American theater which it never relinquished thereafter. Fundamental to New York's ascendency in the theatrical, as in the
publishing and the art worlds was its emergence as the unrivaled commercial metropolis of the nation. Following completion of the Erie Canal
in the 1820s, the city established an unrivaled position as the national
entrepot for cultural as well as commercial products of Europe. Beginning in the 1820s great British actors and actresses played the American
stage, among them Edmund and Charles King, Junius Brutus Booth, and
Charles and Fanny Kemble, together with singers and actors from the
Continent, and these performers mainly played the New York stage.[59]
Their performances of British and European drama and opera contributed little to an indigenous American theater, but the number of original
American plays produced on the New York stage increased impressively
as well. According to A. H. Quinn's list, American plays premiering in
New York increased from thirty-three in the eighteenth century to sixty-
five in the 1830s. By comparison, original American productions in Philadelphia increased from sixteen in the eighteenth century to forty-nine in
the 1830s. Boston, which saw eleven productions of original American
plays in the eighteenth century, produced only eleven more in the 1830s.

≼ VII ≽

IN 1858 HENRY CLAPP OF Nantucket arrived in New York from the Left
Bank in Paris to start up a lively literary weekly, *Saturday Press*, and introduce *bohemianism* to America. Balzac in his 1840 "Prince of Bohemia" had
coined the term *Bohemians* to describe the liberated and impoverished artists and writers of Paris, and in 1848 Henri Murger's *Scènes de la vie de bohème*
presented a romantic study of these young Parisian intellectuals, who pursued art for art's sake and flaunted bourgeois morality. Murger asserted
that bohemianism could exist nowhere but in Paris; nevertheless, his book
inspired young artists and writers in other cities to create Bohemias of their
own. In New York bohemianism was fostered by the Panic of 1857, which
brought students and writers into the cheap boardinghouses in the Greenwich Village area and put some writers out of jobs, freeing them to adopt
the nonconformist attitudes of the Bohemians.[60]

New York Bohemians inherited the Knickerbockers' contempt for dour Puritanism and their robustly irreverent attitude toward conventional wisdom. By the 1850s the Knickerbockers themselves had matured into more sober Victorians, along with the English-speaking world generally. Yet even in their light-hearted youth, the Knickerbocker literati had been proper gentlemen where persons of the opposite sex were concerned, confining Rabelaisian ribaldry to gatherings of men only. Women of questionable virtue played active roles in Murger's Parisian Bohemia, and they came to play active roles in Clapp's New York Bohemia as well. According to the drama critic William Winter,

> Clapp was an original character. We called him "The Oldest Man." His age was unknown to us. He seemed to be very old, but, as afterward I ascertained, he was then only forty-six. In appearance he was somewhat suggestive of the portrait of Voltaire. He was a man of slight, seemingly fragile but really wiry figure; bearded; gray; with keen, light blue eyes, a haggard visage, a vivacious manner, and a thin, incisive voice. He spoke the French language with extraordinary fluency, and natives of France acknowledged that he spoke it with a perfect accent. He had long resided in Paris, and, indeed, in his temperament, his mental constitution, and in his conduct of life, he was more a Frenchman than an American. . . . Such as he was,—withered, bitter, grotesque, seemingly ancient, a good fighter, a kind heart,—he was the Prince of our Bohemian circle.[61]

Clapp's circle met nightly in Pfaff's beer cellar, under the sidewalk of Broadway near Bleeker Street. The circle's martyr was Edgar Allan Poe, who had died in 1849, and its genius was Walt Whitman, who was on hand almost nightly when he was in town and whose poetry appeared in Clapp's *Saturday Press*. Other poets who were regulars at Pfaff's were Fitz-James O'Brien, Bayard Taylor, Edmund Clarence Stedman, and Thomas Bailey Aldrich, who served as assistant editor on *Saturday Press* before finding more respectable employment as assistant editor, then editor of *Atlantic Monthly* in Boston. William Dean Howells had published verse in both *Saturday Press* and the *Atlantic Monthly* when he went east in 1860. He paid a call on Clapp's circle and went away disillusioned with American bohemianism, shocked by their behavior and by the hatred they vented against Boston. He later wrote,

> I had found their bitterness against Boston as great as the bitterness
> against respectability, and as Boston was then rapidly becoming my
> second country, I could not join in the scorn thought of her and said of
> her by the Bohemians.

He nevertheless retained some respect for the quality of *Saturday Press*,
which "attacked all literary shams but its own . . . and made itself feared
and felt."[62]

The most startling aspect of Clapp's Bohemian circle was its women,
led by the journalist-poet and would-be actress Ada Clare. There was nothing new about a group of literary men meeting in a New York saloon, but
there *was* something new about Ada Clare making herself welcome in
Pfaff's as a fellow Bohemian who viewed Knickerbocker—not to mention
Victorian—propriety with an easy insouciance. Born Jane McElhenny,
Clare was, like Poe, an orphaned but gently reared Southerner. In Charleston her cousin Paul Hamilton Hayne, the poet, had influenced her in her
own desire to write verse. Clare also entertained ambition to become an
actress. Supported by an independent income, she launched herself on
both careers in New York, with little success in either.

Clare was successful, however, in achieving notoriety through a love
affair with the concert pianist Louis Moreau Gottschalk, which she herself publicized, and through her role as queen of the American Bohemians. In both roles her beauty worked to her advantage. "She is," wrote
John Burroughs, "really beautiful, not a characterless beauty, but a singular, unique beauty." Clare went to Paris in 1857 and wrote articles for New
York newspapers about the impressions of a young woman traveling
abroad by herself. When she returned to New York, Clapp's circle welcomed her to its company. She involved herself publicly in new love
affairs, while continuing her grand passion for Gottschalk, by whom she
had a child. For this she was scolded in the respectable press. But national
notoriety did not discourage her Bohemian friends, who remained supportive. Clare was described as quiet in dress and dignified in manner, except that she chain-smoked cigarettes, drank large quantities of beer, and
indulged in off-color remarks. E. C. Stedman, in common with other men,
admired her appearance, and he was particularly taken by her delicate,
"tip-tilted nose," which to his mind was just "the right nose for a trim

little person with a past." Walt Whitman later concluded that she had been the New Woman, arrived early.[63]

Like Clapp, Clare could claim firsthand authority on the subject of bohemianism, based upon her Paris observations. To be a Bohemian, she explained, one needed an affinity for the arts and a cosmopolitan attitude unhampered by customary rules. It was not necessary, as "worldlings" supposed, that the Bohemian "must be poor, that he must take pleasure in keeping his boots and his cheese in the same drawer," or that he must drink to drunkenness or live in a garret. He or she was the sort who was naturally at ease in the world, living as he or she pleased, guided "by the principles of good taste and feeling," in a spirit of "easy, graceful, joyous unconsciousness." Other women joined Clare in Pfaff's, including Adah Menken, world famous as "the Naked Lady" for her American and European performances of the male role of Mazeppa in flesh-colored tights.[64]

Saturday Press folded for lack of funds in December 1860. But by then the Pfaff Bohemians had helped found a new weekly, *Vanity Fair*, working a lighter vein than *Saturday Press* and benefiting from more substantial financial backing than Clapp could command. Edited successively by Pfaffians Frank Wood, Charles Godfrey Leland, and Charles Farrar "Artemus Ward" Browne, *Vanity Fair* achieved distinction as the best humor magazine to appear in America to that time. The Civil War was not an auspicious time for humor magazines, however. *Vanity Fair* failed to gain circulation sufficient to support it, and its satirical commentary on the wartime scene attracted "bushels of anonymous letters, expressing the most exaggerated hatred, intensified abhorrence, and inmitigated malevolence towards us," as the editor wrote in the summer of 1862. The magazine went out of business a year later.[65]

After *Vanity Fair* ceased publication, a number of Pfaff Bohemians sought to escape the war by going west. In 1864 Ada Clare moved to San Francisco, followed by Gottschalk. So did other Pfaffians, including Adah Menken, Charles Farrar Browne, and Fitz Hugh Ludlow, author of *The Hasheesh Eater*. San Francisco was gaining a literary celebrity of its own, supporting the *Golden Era* and numbers of other literary magazines. Its wartime literary community included Mark Twain, Bret Harte, Ina Coobrith, Charles Warren Stoddard, and Joaquin Miller. However, when

Browne, as Artemus Ward, gave his first San Francisco lecture, some newspaper reviews were concerned that his humorous remarks had served no
moral purpose. The Pfaffians were out of place in the west, and the majority of them returned home, followed by the most successful of the
western writers.[66]

When the war was over, Clapp started *Saturday Press* up again, introducing eastern readers to Mark Twain with the publication of Twain's
"Jim Smiley and His Jumping Frog" in 1865 before the *Press* ran out of
funds and stopped for good. Once this scandalous magazine ceased publication, Victorian America positively expunged it from the literary record.
It was not merely that Henry Clapp, this cynical though kindly, drunken
though brilliant, American Voltaire soon became lost in the literary
shuffle of the Gilded Age. Beyond that, the very back issues of *Saturday
Press* itself were everywhere disposed of, despite their exceptional literary
content. Libraries retained their early files of *Atlantic Monthly*, which had
begun a year earlier than *Saturday Press*, but today not one single complete series of *Saturday Press* is known to exist anywhere. Whatever might
be said in his favor, Clapp was no moralist and no gentleman by American
standards. Having failed to meet the moral standards set by the nation's
literary classes, he apparently forfeited his place in the Republic of Letters
of Victorian America.

In 1845 another literary New Yorker from Nantucket Island, Charles F.
Briggs, had brought out *Broadway Journal*, so named, he had explained,
because

> Broadway is confessedly the finest street in the first city of the new
> World. All the dealers in intellectual works are here centered; every ex-
> hibition of art is found here. . . . New York is fast becoming, if she be
> not already, America, in spite of South Carolina and Boston.[67]

Against such New Yorkish boastfulness on the part of an ex-New Englander, Emerson may be considered to have made a Boston Brahmin's
reply in his essay, "Civilization." For Emerson the "true test of civilization
is, not the census, nor the size of cities . . . but the kind of man the country turns out." It was

> not New York streets, built by the confluence of workmen and wealth
> of all nations, though stretching outwards towards Philadelphia until

they touch it, and northward until they touch New Haven, Hartford, Springfield, Worcester and Boston,—not these that make the real estimation.

In seeking a "certificate of civilization," Emerson and his fellow Brahmins were inclined to look elsewhere than in the "great cities or enormous wealth" that New York had come to epitomize.[68]

❧ 5 ❧

BRAHMIN
BOSTON

There is . . . in New England, an aristocracy, if you choose to call it
so. . . . It has grown to be a *caste*,—not in any odious sense,—but by the
repetition of the same influences, generation after generation. . . . If
you will look carefully at any class of students in one of our colleges,
you will have no difficulty in selecting specimens of two different aspects of youthful manhood. . . . The first youth is the common country-
boy. . . . You must not expect too much of any such. Many of them
have force of will and character and become distinguished in practical
life; but very few of them ever become great scholars. A scholar is, in a
large proportion of cases, the son of scholars or scholarly persons.
    That is exactly what the other young man is. He comes of the
Brahmin caste of New England. . . . There are races of scholars among us,
in which aptitude for learning, and all these marks of it I have spoken
of, are congenital and hereditary. . . . [O]ur scholars come chiefly from
a privileged order, just as our best fruits come from well-known grafts.
                              — Oliver Wendell Holmes, *Elsie Venner* (1861)

DAZZLED BY MANHATTAN'S "opulence and splendor," Philadelphia's "trade
wealth and regularity," and the "exterior and superficial accomplishment
of gentlemen" from colonies to the south that he encountered at the
Continental Congress, John Adams, writing home to Abigail Adams, expressed painful awareness of the comparative backwardness of his beloved Boston and the comparative lack of polish among New Englanders,
owing "to the little intercourse we have with strangers, and to our inexpe-
rience in the world."[1] Boston had failed to keep up with cities to the south
in several respects. The Boston of Adams's youth had been the most
populous city as well as the foremost trading center of British America,
but it had been overtaken by Philadelphia in both respects since then and

by New York City as well. While Philadelphia had tripled in size from about thirteen thousand in 1743 to forty thousand in 1775, Boston's population had remained around sixteen thousand throughout the period.[2]

At the time of the Revolution, Boston remained somewhat isolated and out of touch with modern currents of thought by comparison to the region for which Philadelphia served as the metropolitan center, despite Boston's commercial dominance in the coastwise and West Indian trade. To the south, post roads and stagecoach lines connected the region from New Haven to the Chesapeake. By the eve of the Revolution, the most current learning in this middle region of the colonies was the Scottish, having entered America by way of the Virginia tobacco trade with Glasgow and the Scottish immigration to Philadelphia and surrounding areas. Scottish immigrants included those university-trained scholars who played so influential a part in the development of higher education and intellectual life generally. Scots were not welcome in Boston, however, and the Scotch-Irish who settled there were mainly segregated in ghettos.

Boston, with its learned clergy, its comprehensive system of education, and its well established and supported college, enjoyed a self-sufficiency in learning that remained rooted in its seventeenth-century origins and resistant to change. Josiah Quincy, president of Harvard from 1829 to 1845, wrote of that institution's condition a century earlier that

> The impulse given to science and literature in England, during the reign of Queen Anne, gradually extended to Massachusetts. . . . [B]ut the customs and rules of the College tardily yielded to the influences of the period; and it was not until after the middle of the eighteenth century, that effectual improvements were introduced.[3]

These improvements included the introduction of a course in England rhetoric and belles lettres in 1767, which may have reflected Scottish academic influence. But the significant introduction of Scottish scholarship to the Harvard curriculum appears to have been first initiated by the Reverend David Tappan, following his appointment as Hollis Professor of Divinity in 1792. It was Tappan who introduced the student William Ellery Channing to the three books that shaped Channing's thinking in college: Adam Ferguson's *History of Civil Society*, Francis Hutcheson's *System of Moral Philosophy*, and writings of the Welshman Richard Price.[4]

When John Adams arrived in Philadelphia, meanwhile, and met members of the American Philosophical Society, he entered a modern intellectual world that must have been something of a revelation to him, though he does not say so directly in his diary or his letters home. And at the age of forty, he apparently set about to educate himself in the Scottish Enlightenment, mastering the works of Adam Smith, Thomas Reid, Dugald Stewart, and others in the years to come.

Boston's growth was limited by its geography. The populations of surrounding suburban towns, including Cambridge, continued to grow, as did towns that shared Massachusetts Bay, including Salem and Marblehead. Boston differed in being situated on a peninsula that lacked both land for growth and the rich and developing hinterlands of Philadelphia and Manhattan. Under the circumstances metropolitan Boston could not hope to rival Philadelphia and New York in size. It might claim qualitative superiority—it remained the best-run municipality in English America—but during Adams's lifetime the city suffered more than its share of troubles. The depressions, battle casualties, and disasters suffered in Boston were worse than those in cities to the south. Boston had been ravaged by wars and epidemics, by hurricanes and fires as though it had been singled out by providence for especially rigorous testing.

Yet quantitative comparisons of the three largest American cities failed to do justice to Boston, because Boston differed in kind from the other two. Philadelphia—despite its origins as a Holy Experiment—and New York were essentially urban centers that had grown in response to favorable economic circumstances. Boston, by contrast, was an imperial city-state, one that had energetically settled Connecticut, Rhode Island, and upper New England. Beyond that, Boston had colonized the northeast with literate communities, from Long Island and Staten Island to Nova Scotia. Boston continued to exercise its intellectual hegemony in the Republic as New Englanders formed enclaves of Unitarian-Congregational-Presbyterian literacy in Cincinnati, Savannah, San Francisco, and Portland, Oregon, sending out schoolmasters, schoolmistresses, scholars, and college presidents across the continent. Comparatively few New Englanders settled in Philadelphia; yet the two Bostonians who did so most prominently—Benjamin Franklin and Joseph Dennie—formatively influenced the Philadelphia Enlightenment and the literary counterrevolution that followed it.

New York City attracted literati from throughout the nation, but New Englanders predominated among those who migrated there, and with the coming of the Civil War literary New York became a thoroughly Yankee Unionist society, however non-Yankee and divided on the war issue New Yorkers at large may have been.

Conceding to Abigail in 1776 that "My countrymen want art and address . . . knowledge of the world . . . the exterior and superficial accomplishment of gentlemen, upon which the world has set so high a value," John Adams insisted that New Englanders nevertheless excelled gentlemen to the south in "solid abilities and real virtues" and that, such being the case, his countrymen were duty-bound to remedy their more superficial imperfections. For "New England must produce the heroes, the statesmen, the philosophers, or America will make no great figure for some time." New England was equipped to fulfill this mission, he wrote Abigail, because of advantages it enjoyed over "every other colony in America and, indeed, of every other part of the world that I know anything of." These advantages were

1. "The people are purer English blood; less mixed with Scotch, Irish, Dutch, French, Danish, Swedish, etc., than any other."
2. "The institutions in New England for the support of religious morals and decency exceed any other; obliging each parish to have a minister, and every person to go to meeting, etc."
3. "The public institutions in New England for the education of youth, supporting colleges at public expense, and obliging towns to maintain grammar schools, are not equalled, and never were, in any part of the world."
4. The township system of government, which "gives every man an opportunity of showing and improving that education which he received at college or at school."
5. The law distributing intestate estates and preventing monopolies of land.[5]

New England comprised the most homogeneous and culturally distinctive region of Revolutionary America. The Yankee had already emerged in colonial times as a widely recognized, well-defined regional type, the like of which no other region had produced. When Hugh Henry Brackenridge, writing in Pennsylvania at the outset of the national period, required a comic type for *Modern Chivalry* to represent the American common man, he summoned up a stereotypical Irishman, Teague O'Regan, to serve the purpose, for the lack of a comparable American national type. However when the Bostonian Royall Tyler, writing in the same period, needed a comic type to represent the common man in his play *The Contrast*, he created the servant Jessamy, who evidently was as recognizably Yankee to the audience as O'Regan was recognizably Irish to readers of *Modern Chivalry*. Indeed, the Yankee remained the most recognizably American type, comic or otherwise, in 1846, when James Russell Lowell recreated him as Hosea Biglow to offer a down-to-earth Yankee argument against the Mexican War. Had a southern writer wished to respond to Lowell's attack on the same literary level, no similarly distinctive Southern regional type would have been available to him through which to present his rebuttal.

The Yankee may have remained the most clearly recognizable type in America, but that did not necessarily entitle him to represent America as a whole. A contrary line of argument was advanced by a contemporary of Adams, the French-American New Yorker, Michele de Crèvecoeur. Writing as J. Hector St. John in his essay "What Is an American?" Crèvecoeur considered New Englanders to be the least authentic Americans because they were the most English. Characteristic Americans, according to Crèvecoeur, were "a mixture of English, Scotch, Irish, French, Dutch, Germans, and Swedes. From this promiscuous breed, that race now called Americans had arisen," except in the region of New England, which remained populated by "the unmixed descendants of Englishmen."[6]

Crèvecoeur's new man, the ethnically mixed American, was a romantic and thoroughly admirable character—cosmopolitan, tolerant, provident, self-reliant, individualistic—and the ethnically mixed society Crèvecoeur described was idyllic. Yet Crèvecoeur's thesis does not appear to have won favor with literate Americans in the society it flattered so extravagantly, judging by the muted American reception of *Letters from an American Farmer*, in which the essay "What Is an American?" appeared. After going through several printings in London, the first American edition of *Letters* came out in 1793, and it was not followed by a second printing until 1904.[7] By that time Crèvecoeur's melting pot interpretation had been reconstituted by Frederick Jackson Turner, who made it an aspect of his frontier thesis, and by immigrant writers like Mary Antin. In this twentieth-century context, Crèvecoeur's essay came into its own as a classic interpretation of the American character.

However ethnically mixed American society south of New England may have been, English remained America's language, and England itself the fount of American civilization. A German-speaking culture might take root in western Pennsylvania and southward along the frontier, but its influence upon the dominant Anglo-American seaboard culture was at best indirect. Literate society in this seaboard region was predominantly English in its ethnic origins and thoroughly English in its cultural orientation. And with political independence from England, Anglo-Saxon race consciousness within this society increased rather than diminished. Nineteenth-century American school children were taught, in textbooks written largely by Yankees, that a well-defined racial hierarchy, together with its national subdivisions, existed in the world and that the Anglo-Saxon race, along with its American subdivision, led all the rest.[8] By this standard New England enjoyed a racial advantage over the rest of the nation, however open to criticism Yankees might be on other grounds. And to the extent that it remained culturally more English than other regions, New England earned the admiration, however reluctant, of Anglophile Americans elsewhere in the nation—which was most educated Americans, including Verplancks and Duyckincks in New York and Grimkés and Legarés in Charleston.

The Anglo-American homogeneity of New England and its superior literacy enabled the region to establish itself as the one most clearly representative of the national experience. When the new country's history came to be written after the Revolution, New England resistance to English tyranny, from Plymouth Rock to Bunker Hill, was depicted as the core and essence of the American struggle. This historical bias toward New England reflected the region's richer storehouse of preserved artifacts and scholars to interpret them—both owing to the virtues listed by Adams. What resulted from this regional scholarship was, however, more than a merely provincial interpretation of the nation's history. Following the Revolution historians in New York, Pennsylvania, Virginia, and South Carolina tended to accommodate themselves to the New England version as well. No other region offered as clear-cut and well-documented a narrative of the struggle for English liberties that culminated in the Revolution.[9]

The reputation of the Yankee outside New England—shrewd and rapacious in business, pious and no doubt hypocritical in morals—was not exemplary. Yet the Yankee did possess qualities that were widely admired, and they were those very qualities that John Adams had listed in his letter to Abigail. Jefferson admired the orderliness of New England's township system, and he was instrumental in extending the township system to the Northwest Territory. Yankees typically possessed more book learning than other Americans, and education commanded respect throughout America, however anti-intellectual American society might be in practice.

The system of public education that the Massachusetts General Court instituted early on and that Connecticut adopted as well provided for grammar schools maintained at the local level but kept up to provincial standards by inspectors. The system included Latin grammar schools beyond the regular grammar schools, preparing scholars for the publicly supported colleges Harvard and Yale. Boston Latin School, founded in 1635, served for over three centuries as the major preparatory school for Harvard, with more graduates matriculating in Cambridge down to the mid–twentieth century than any other private preparatory school.[10] Harvard remained the crowning intellectual establishment within the Commonwealth of Massachusetts, training the leadership of the Commonwealth in the areas of politics, religion, and literature. As John Adams summed it up for Abigail, there was "no one thing in which we excel" the provinces south of New England "more than in our University, our scholars and preachers."[11]

New England owed its educational system to institutions established "for the support of religion, morals and decency" that Adams mentioned, including the Congregational Church, maintained in every parish and strongly supported at the grassroots level. Early efforts to found public schools in New York and Pennsylvania, by contrast, had given way to the proliferation of sectarian schools. While these impressively reflected the intellectual vitality of sectarian religion, notably in eighteenth-century Philadelphia, they led to no coherent educational system. In the southern colonies, where the Anglican Church was established, the church assumed some responsibility for public education, but it lacked the grassroots support that the Congregational Church enjoyed in New England, and again no coherent system resulted. In New England itself during the early national period, the system of public education declined as children of the merchant gentry came increasingly to be educated in private institutions. But a revitalization of the common school occurred in the 1830s and 1840s under the leadership of Horace Mann and others, and the New England common school system became a model for the nation.

Although Yankee historians placed their region at the center of the national experience, New Englanders continued to be imbued with a provincial outlook that reflected the region's peripheral location at the northeast corner of the nation. Boston Brahmins came to accept a civilizing mission of national proportions in the age of Emerson, but they remained Bostonians first and foremost. As to New England's relationship to the nation as a whole, Margaret Fuller spoke the mind of the Boston Brahmins when she wrote in 1844 that New England should be viewed, not as a section of the nation but as "a chief mental focus," serving as the brain of the body politic, while other parts of the nation performed the functions of the lungs, heart, and other equally vital but less sensitive organs.[12]

❧ II ☙

HARVARD HAD BEEN FOUNDED IN 1636, in the famous words of the promotional pamphlet, *New England's First Fruits* (1643), "to advance *Learning* and perpetuate it to Posterity; dreading to leave an illiterate Ministry to the Churches, when our present Ministers shall lie in the Dust." This concern to maintain a learned ministry in the wilderness may well have been uppermost in the minds of the founders, but what they set out to establish was a liberal arts college to serve the requirements of the community as a whole rather than a theological seminary. Harvard was modeled upon Emmanuel College, Cambridge, which magistrates as well as ministers of the Massachusetts Bay Colony had themselves attended. The purpose of the college was officially described in 1650 as "The advancement of all good literature, artes and sciences," no mention being made of the ministerial training. Thus from the outset Harvard set itself the broad task of educating young men to become the ruling class of the province. Those who were to become ministers would study theology under a minister upon graduation; they would be offered no special courses as undergraduates that were not a part of the general curriculum. All students would together pursue a program of studies comparable to those offered by the liberal arts colleges of Cambridge University in England.[13]

From the outset of the Puritan experiment in Massachusetts, civil authorities had asserted their dominance over the clergy in worldly and even religious matters, as was demonstrated in the banishment imposed by John Winthrop and the magistrates upon the Reverend Roger Williams and upon the Reverend John Cotton's parishioner Anne Hutchinson. This exercise of civil power had carried with it the implication that, however profoundly learned the clergy might be, their intellectual domain was limited to spiritual matters, and even in that sphere their authority was open to question. This distinction between secular and religious authority had not initially seemed critical, as right-minded Puritans were expected to be of essentially one mind in matters of church and state. But as times changed and New England expanded and prospered, worldly affairs took increasing precedence over the spiritual. Ministers responded defensively, organizing ministerial associations from which laymen were excluded, emphasizing the importance of their calling and the status attached to it, and in other ways consciously professionalizing themselves.

In New England as elsewhere, the Great Awakening of the mid–eighteenth century revived religious feelings while at the same time it challenged the authority of pastors over their congregations. The emotionalism and disorderliness of revivalism offended the merchant gentry of eastern Massachusetts especially, and it was resisted by their churches, including the First Church of Boston, whose pastor, Charles Chauncy, attacked the Whitefield revival movement in what remained a classic statement of Massachusetts religious liberalism, *Seasonable Thoughts on the State of Religion in New England* (1743). Sermons should be well-styled lectures, serving to edify the congregation, Chauncy argued. They should eschew both emotional exhortations and doctrinal argumentation. Good conduct should be the test of conversion. Chauncy's pamphlet was directed against the writings of Jonathan Edwards, who defended revivalism and influenced a rising generation of "New Divinity" clergymen. In

Congregational churches where New Divinity ministers were installed, the naves resounded with homiletics reasserting the centrality of sin and redemption. This Calvinist style of religion alienated many church members, and a good many of the more affluent pewholders consequently left the Congregational church to buy pews in Anglican churches, where their virtue would not be questioned on Calvinist grounds. Others asserted control over their churches, notably in Boston, where congregations took care to select their own kind of enlightened pastors.[14]

Bright young men who might earlier have chosen ministerial careers, were meanwhile turning in increasing numbers to the newly developing legal profession. John Adams was one of those who entered college in the 1750s with an idea of training for the ministry and then discarded it for the law. Adams remained thereafter a faithful churchgoer, but to his mind the law had taken precedence over divinity both as a branch of learning and as an office of social responsibility. Adams ranked the ministers he heard mainly by the style of their sermons, as though they were specialists in rhetoric. He believed they ought, however, to know their place in society and confine themselves to it. Adams was emphatic on this point in expressing his disapproval of the one minister, John J. Zubly of Georgia, who shared membership with him in the First Continental Congress. Granting that Zubly was "a man of learning and ingenuity," Adams observed that

> as he is the first gentleman of the cloth who has appeared in Congress, I cannot but wish he may be the last. Mixing the sacred character with that of the statesman, as it is quite unnecessary at this time of day, in these colonies, is not attended with any good effects. The clergy are universally too little acquainted with the world and the modes of business to engage in civil affairs with any advantage.

Where they were learned, their very scholarship militated against them as men of affairs; for "those of them who are really men of learning, have conversed with books so much more than most men as to be too much loaded with vanity to be good politicians."[15]

The legal profession fattened on material progress in eighteenth-century Massachusetts more evidently than the ministry did. Affluence tended to undermine Calvinism, and while the gentry of Massachusetts Bay had not been strangers to luxury in the late colonial period, it was conspicuously in the Federalist era that Boston acquired the opulence John Adams had observed in New York and Philadelphia at the outset of the Revolution. The Revolution itself made fortunes possible for some like George Cabot who turned to privateering. The codfish industry languished together with the West India trade after independence, but new markets opened up, of which the most dramatic was the China trade beginning in 1784, while George Cabot was initiating trade with St. Petersburg. The men of Massachusetts Bay were meeting strangers around the globe and accumulating fortunes to spend on more gracious living than had been widely supportable in colonial times. Many of these fortunes were in the hands of new men—Cabots, Higginsons, Perkinses, Jacksons, Lees—sharing possession of the Commonwealth with members of the older merchant gentry who had survived dangerous times. More than any other state, Massachusetts had undergone a change in the ruling order during the Revolution, the list of Massachusetts loyalists having read, as Moses Coit Tyler wrote, "almost like a beadroll of the oldest and noblest families concerning the founding and upbuilding of New England civilization."[16]

The new men assiduously perpetuated the old ways, most noticeably in matters of dress, affecting cocked hats, scarlet cloaks, beaver gloves, and six-foot Surinam walking canes. The accoutrements surprised and amused visitors from New York and Philadelphia, where fewer accessories were required to make the man. For Boston's merchants, being seen in full regalia both affirmed one's consequence and expressed one's contempt for the modern, revolutionary French style in dress.[17] Among the pre-Revolutionary Massachusetts gentry, Puritan plainness had not been in vogue, nor had blue law decorum. Dr. Alexander Hamilton of Maryland, traveling through the Northern colonies in the mid–eighteenth century, found

> more hospitality and frankness shown here to strangers than either at [New] York or at Philadelphia. And in the place there is abundance of men of learning and parts; so that one is at no loss for agreeable conversation. . . . Assemblys of the gayer sort are frequent here; the gentlemen and ladies meeting almost every week at concerts of music and balls. . . . I saw not one prude while I was here.[18]

Following the Revolution, Boston's young matrons added the "Tea Assembly" to their round of regular dancing assemblies. Mixing card playing and wine drinking with dancing, tea assemblies aroused such old patriots as Sam Adams and John Hancock to call for their suppression.[19]

The Tea Assembly was enjoyed by one of the major figures of this era, the architect Charles Bulfinch. Bulfinch, Harvard 1781, traveled and studied in Europe for several years and then settled in Boston, where he designed the homes of the affluent, provided new street lighting and drainage systems, and introduced gracious urban appearances such as had appealed to John Adams on first seeing New York and Philadelphia. Bulfinch belonged to the fashionable younger generation that included Harrison Gray Otis and Robert Treat Paine Jr., who scandalized Boston with the Tea Assembly and plunged the city into the even more divisive theater issue. Following the repeal of an antitheater law in Philadelphia in 1789, the campaign for a Boston theater began, a writer in the Massachusetts *Centinel* arguing that "there is no town in America so large as this, that has so few public amusements." Following a violent controversy, the Federal Street Theater, designed by Bulfinch, opened in 1794. Gutted by fire four years later, it was immediately rebuilt, marking the triumph of the worldly order in Boston society.[20]

Other more respectable institutions made their appearances in post-Revolutionary Boston, including the Massachusetts General Hospital, the Boston Society of Natural History, the Massachusetts Historical Society, and the American Academy of Arts and Sciences. Then in 1807 the Boston Athenaeum was founded; a project of the Anthology Society, it grew to become the library, art museum, and leading cultural institution of Boston's gentry. In short, Bostonians acquired for themselves in the early national period cultural-philanthropic institutions such as the Philadelphia gentry had inherited from colonial times, and civic rivalry with Philadelphia was certainly a motivating force in the early stages. However, Boston did possess one cultural institution that far outshone anything Philadelphia possessed of a like nature.

Harvard College remained the oldest and most firmly established institution of higher learning in America, and in the nineteenth century it became the favorite object of benefaction for Boston's gentry. Down through the eighteenth century, however, the financing of Harvard had not been considered the personal responsibility of its alumni. The college had found other means to get by, including student fees, provincial funding, and lotteries. Such substantial endowments as had been made to it in the eighteenth century were contributions from non-Harvard men, notably members of the Hollis family in England.

Up through the Federal period, the teaching staff remained small and mainly undistinguished. At the time John Adams attended Harvard in the 1750s, each incoming class was assigned a tutor who instructed that class throughout the entire four-year curriculum. Beginning in 1767 instruction was assigned by subject matter: one tutor teaching Greek, one Latin, another logic, metaphysics, and ethics, a fourth natural philosophy and mathematics, and a fifth elocution, English rhetoric, and other parts of belles lettres.[21] By 1790 the staff had been expanded to include three professors in addition to the tutors. However, not until John Thornton Kirkland became president of Harvard in 1810 were contributions solicited from alumni and substantial gifts from men of wealth, enabling the school to attract a faculty worthy of what was becoming the nation's most richly endowed university.

Massachusetts gentlemen of the Revolutionary era were inclined to view their obligations as members of the established Congregational church rather casually. Regular church attendance on Sundays, once virtually compulsory, was no longer the rule for many. The large, loud voice of Jonathan Edwards' and George Whitefield's Great Awakening, with its emphasis on original sin and the terrors of eternal damnation, had swept through New England in the early 1740s, producing thousands of converts. The hysteria and convulsions so frequent in these mass conversions could not be sustained indefinitely, however, and by the 1780s many Bostonians were maintaining an attitude of indifference to, if not actual disrespect for, organized religion. Meanwhile, the excesses of the Great Awakening had provoked an opposite religious impetus, early expressed in the writings and sermons of Boston minister Charles Chauncy. Chauncy's *Seasonable Thoughts on the State of Religion in New England* (1743) opposed rhetorical eloquence in sermons as a pernicious appeal to emotions rather than to good sense. Rejecting the revivalists' dogmatic determinism, Chauncy substituted an incipient Unitarianism, emphasizing reason, tolerance, and the possibility of universal salvation.

While Congregational churches in Massachusetts edged closer to Unitarianism, the gentry started returning to the fold, partly in response to the French revolution. A half century after the Great Awakening and Chauncy's seasonable thought upon it, Robespierre assumed command of the second Committee of Public Safety, and through it revolutionary France, amid a Reign of Terror that demanded official worship of the goddess of Reason. These developments shocked New England Federalists, who began taking a second look at organized religion as a bulwark against French anarchy and atheism and the social and political demoralization associated with them. Timothy Dwight, Yale president and grandson of Jonathan Edwards, seized the moment to lead a "Second Great Awakening," rallying the forces of religion in support of Federalist and traditional Congregational principles. In Massachusetts, however, political conservatism and religious liberalism by this time went hand in hand; in Boston especially, Chauncy's influence remained in the ascendant. King's chapel in Boston broke with the Episcopal Church in 1796 and officially adopted Unitarianism. Within a generation, over two hundred Congregational churches in New England would follow suit. Influencing this shift were two of Harvard's brightest undergraduates, William Ellery Channing and Joseph Stevens Buckminster.

As presented by Channing and Buckminster, Unitarianism became preeminently a literary religion, avoiding doctrinal arguments where possible and emphasizing the oneness of aesthetic and moral truth and the spiritual authority of great literature as their repository. Buckminster's Harvard Phi Beta Kappa address of 1809 on "The Dangers and Duties of Men of Letters" called for a literary elite guided by high moral and scholarly ideals, able to withstand pressures for quick and popular success. Less elitist than Buckminster in emphasis, Channing stressed the universal receptivity of mankind to elevated sentiments and committed himself increasingly to humanitarian reform, especially to the cause of abolishing slavery, while devoutly pursuing parallel careers as literary critic and theologian. His brother, Edward Tyrell Channing, meanwhile taught literary method at Harvard to two generations of Unitarian and Transcendentalist men of letters.[22]

In the Unitarian era ministerial training led to politics as well as to literature. Edward Everett, whom Buckminster had disuaded from studying law, began his career at nineteen as minister of the Brattle Street Church. Following five years of study in Europe, he assumed the first professorship of Greek literature at Harvard. Unhappy with teaching, Everett entered politics at age thirty to become congressman, governor, ambassador to Great Britain, secretary of state, and senator from Massachusetts, distinguishing himself in all of his vocations as one of the most admired orators of the age. John Gorham Palfrey, the historian, similarly moved from the Unitarian ministry to a Harvard professorship to politics.

Harvard had meanwhile resisted a countermovement of Calvinists to control it, appointing an avowed Unitarian as Hollis Professor of Divinity in 1805. Conservatives led by Jedidiah Morse responded to this defeat by founding Andover Theological Seminary as the "West Point of Orthodoxy," amid the ongoing conflict between Calvinism and Unitarianism that disrupted church congregations in the commonwealth until the outbreak of the Civil War. Unitarianism remained secure with such affluent congregations as those of the Brattle Street and Federal Street Churches, but even in the university town of Cambridge, the moderately conservative pastor Abiel Holmes, father of Oliver Wendell Holmes, was removed by more conservative parishioners who objected to Holmes's way of sharing his pulpit with guest preachers who frequently were more liberal than he.[23]

Harvard Unitarianism might have been liberal, but it was not notably literary outside the rhetoric classes of Edward Tyrell Channing. Among Harvard's moral philosophers, Andrews Norton achieved particular eminence as pedagogical spokesman for an aging generation, against which a rising younger generation of ministers, instructed and inspired by the Channing brothers, staged their Transcendental rebellion. Emersonian Transcendentalism completed the transition from clergy to clerisy that Buckminster had espoused in "The Dangers and Duties of Men of Letters." Membership in this new intelligentsia all but required a Harvard education but not additional training at the Harvard Divinity School. Thus, in 1837 Emerson was joined by four other young Unitarian ministers and two laymen in forming the Symposium, or Transcendental Club; but in 1856 he stood alone as the only product of the ministry among the founders of the august Saturday Club, most of whom initially studied to be lawyers. Among Emerson's Concord circle only Emerson himself enjoyed unquestioned standing in Boston's Brahmin circles, nor were practicing ministers accorded the same prestige enjoyed by such ex-ministers as Edward Everett, John Gorham Palfrey, and John Sullivan Dwight.

A churchly quality nevertheless inhered in Boston's literary society, as it inhered in Bostonian culture as a whole. Henry Adams wrote of New England in 1850 that "Lawyers, physicians, professors, merchants were classes, and acted not as individuals, but as though they were clergymen and each profession was a church."[24] In this sense the profession of literature comprised a New England church, of which the Saturday Club came conspicuously to be the leading congregation.

III

HARVARD ENTERED UPON an unparalleled era of growth with the installation of John Thornton Kirkland as president in 1810. Appointed minister of the New South Church of Boston in 1793 at the age of twenty-three, Kirkland had gained a reputation as a scourge of French infidelity and was known as an ardent Federalist, so that Massachusetts Calvinists were slow to recognize the pronounced liberalism of his religious views. A prominent and popular member of the Anthology Society, Kirkland was chosen as its president the year he became president of Harvard, and as president of Harvard he drew upon his friendships in the business community for munificent endowments. Harvard's cause was also furthered when the friendly, Federalist state legislature in 1814 passed "An Act for the encouragement of literature, piety, morality and the useful arts and sciences" authorizing a substantial special funding of Harvard for a ten-year period. These munificent sources of income financed a large building program, including Divinity Hall and the Medical College in Boston, as well as an increase in professorships from ten to twenty-five. Kirkland changed Harvard from a provincial college to a national one with a growing enrollment of out-of-state students, especially from the south. Kirkland's vision was "a university upon the extended plan," which, beyond preparing young men for the professions, would achieve the "formation of the national character, and the elevation of the national spirit" and "the creating of the literary profession among us."[25]

The banner year for the expansion of the faculty at Harvard was 1815, when four additional chairs were endowed. Samuel Eliot, the self-made president of the Massachusetts Bank, anonymously endowed a chair in Greek language and literature, which was initially filled by Edward Everett. That same year, Isaac Royall endowed the Royall Professorship of Law; Benjamin Thompson, Count Rumford of Bavaria, who originally hailed from Woburn, Massachusetts, bequeathed the Rumford Professorship in Science; and Abiel Smith endowed a professorship in the French and Spanish languages, which was initially filled by George Ticknor.[26] Beyond endowing the Greek professorship, Samuel Eliot bestowed his daughters, Anna and Catherine, upon two prominent Harvard professors, George Ticknor and Andrews Norton, together with the wealth that permitted Ticknor and Norton to live lives of gracious splendor far beyond their own slender means. Other scholars of modest means who similarly wived wealthily were Edward Everett, George Bancroft, and Henry Wadsworth Longfellow.[27] This marriage of wealth and learning was emblematic of Boston-Cambridge relations. College dons and the merchant gentry of State Street were united in matters of religion and politics and in their common admiration for the gentleman's classical education. They shared an ideology that combined business-minded conservativism in politics—Federalist, Whig, Republican—with Unitarianism or liberal Congregationalism in religion.

Early in the Kirkland era, great expectations for the literary enrichment of the college rested upon four scholars—Edward Everett, George Ticknor, George Bancroft, and Joseph Cogswell. In the heady era following the War of 1812, Harvard sent the four to pursue studies at Göttingen that they might bring German humanism and university methods back to Cambridge. Little had been known of German literature and scholarship in America before the appearance of an American edition of Madame de Staël's *Germany* in 1815. Benjamin Franklin, who had published books for the Pennsylvania Germans, visited Göttingen in 1766 and later was instrumental in founding a German Institute at the College of Philadelphia (disbanded after the establishment of Franklin College in 1787).[28] In New England, John Quincy Adams retained an interest in German literature that he had acquired while serving as American minister to Prussia. But most of Adams's fellow Brahmins thought poorly of German culture, associating it with the Hessian soldiers of the Revolutionary War. It was Madame de Staël's work that chiefly changed their minds. Although *Germany* was not actually reliable reportage, it was enthusiastic, and the author's reputation among young American readers invested her account with considerable authority. The book inaugurated an era of American admiration for things German that lasted for one century to the year.

In preparation for his European education, George Ticknor visited American notables with European connections, including John Adams, Benjamin Silliman at Yale, William B. Astor in New York, and Thomas Jefferson at Monticello. Armed with letters of introduction in Europe, he visited Wordsworth, Scott, Robert Southey, Madame de Staël, Chateaubriand, Alexander von Humboldt, Friedrich and August von Schlegel, Byron, Goethe, and many more. With less preparation but hardly less successfully, Everett, Bancroft, and Cogswell joined this intellectual celebrity hunt and found a ready welcome from Europeans who were curious to know what American scholars might be like.[29] The American impressions of coarse and materialistic yet scholarly and academically stimulating Göttingen were mixed, but they returned to Cambridge with enlarged views of higher education that Harvard was far from ready to accept.

The travelers returned to a college where rote instruction remained the rule, and attempts to introduce the lecture system aroused opposition from faculty and students alike. All but Ticknor were required to live in Cambridge, where they were subject day and night to student bullyragging. Bancroft left after one year of classroom disruptions and nighttime window-smashings. Cogswell left after two years of duties that "might as well be performed by any shop boy," eventually to fulfill his scholarly purpose as the creator of the New York Public Library. Everett remained for five years, during which he persistently sought an exemption from the faculty residence requirement and tried to find other work that would be "respectable."[30] Of the four, Ticknor alone was exempted from the residence requirement, thanks to the terms of the Smith Professorship he held, which also freed him from much routine classroom instruction. Made wealthy by his advantageous marriage, he took up elegant residence at Nine Park Street in Boston and put in the necessary minimum appearances at Cambridge to deliver formal lectures and supervise the instruction of modern languages. From that favorable vantage point, Ticknor retained his connection with Harvard for seventeen years, attempting from the outset to achieve sweeping reforms in curriculum and in discipline—the first necessary stage, to his mind, being conversion of the existing institution "into a thorough and well-disciplined high school."[31] In these reform efforts Ticknor won little sympathy or support from other faculty members, who were burdened with onerous chores and circumstances from which he was exempted.

Nor did German learning fare very well at Harvard, even though the university remained more committed to teaching German than any other American university. Although Ticknor chose to study in Germany, he later selected Spanish as the language of his major research, as did the historians William Hickling Prescott and John Lothrop Motley (like Washington Irving earlier). Francis Parkman chose French; while George Bancroft, an enthusiastic student of German culture and author of the brief but scholarly *Studies of German Literature*, ultimately settled upon the English-language subject of American history. Except for Longfellow, who became a serious German scholar, Harvard men tended to avoid that language in favor of the Latin tongues for which their classical training had better prepared them. Among the Transcendentalists, the American intellectuals most committed to German philosophy and literature, Margaret Fuller mastered the language, while Frederick Hedge possessed the most scholarly knowledge of the field, having been sent to Germany in the care of Bancroft at the age of thirteen. Emerson conceded that he ought to be knowledgeable in the language of transcendental philosophy, but he never became fluent in it.[32]

Conditions at Harvard were at their most promising during the years when the four scholars returned from Europe, but the intellectual climate deteriorated thereafter. Kirkland became well known for his lax permissiveness toward students and their dissipations and rebellions, and his reputation was reflected in declining enrollments. Matters came to a head with the Great Rebellion of the class of 1823, which resulted in the dismissal of thirty-six seniors and the public questioning of Kirkland's abilities. Kirkland's Federalist Party had meanwhile lost control of the state legislature, and when the special funding of Harvard came up for reconsideration, the bill was defeated, confronting Kirkland with a financial crisis and a hostile Harvard Corporation. Leading the opposition to Kirkland in the corporation was Nathaniel Bowditch, the brilliant, self-taught astronomer, mathematician, and hard-headed businessman from Salem, whose interference was resented then and later by alumni such as Emerson on grounds that Bowditch was not himself a Harvard graduate and ought not to have been granted authority over it. Bowditch nevertheless forced Kirkland's resignation in 1828 and was instrumental in arranging the appointment of Boston mayor Josiah Quincy in his place.[33]

Quincy assumed responsibility for an institution in the throes of crises, facing the possibility of bankruptcy amid declining enrollment; students who were out of control; a restive, discontented faculty; a hostile state legislature; and alumni that were sharply divided over who should be president and what course he should pursue. Except that he was a layman assuming a position traditionally reserved for ministers, Quincy possessed impressive qualifications for the position. A member of one of the oldest and most esteemed Massachusetts families, he was, according to John Adams, "a rare instance of hereditary eloquence and ingenuity in the fourth generation . . . with every advantage of family, fortune and education."[34] Quincy had set out to become a politician of national stature, but as a congressman before the War of 1812, his impolitic, outspoken Boston prejudices had isolated him even from other representatives of New England. It was as mayor of Boston in the 1820s that he had conspicuously demonstrated the administrative abilities that impressed members of the Harvard Corporation.

Draconian reforms soon restored Harvard to solvency under Quincy. But crises continued in his dealings with students and faculty at a time when surprisingly close relations were developing between these groups. Among the faculty, opposition to Quincy was led by Karl Follen, a former member of the radical student movement in Germany who had emigrated to Boston, become an instructor at Harvard, married a Cabot, and advanced to a temporary professorship in German literature that his father-in-law endowed. Amid social feuds between Cabot and Quincy women in Cambridge, the Follen's home became a meeting place for students, opening Follen to the charge of fomenting the student rebellion that erupted in 1834.

Whatever its cause, that rebellion gave faculty opponents of the autocratic president, led by Edward Everett, occasion to oust Quincy from office and replace him with someone more amenable to their opinion—someone such as Everett himself. Quincy was rescued from expulsion by the vigorous support of John Quincy Adams. If Quincy's vindication was won by a slender margin of power, it nonetheless affirmed the fact that control over the university rested with the president and the Boston businessmen who served on the corporation of Harvard, not with the faculty and students. His position solidified by this victory, Quincy went on to side with faculty members who had been advocating curricular reforms away from the traditional required classical curriculum. During the next decade virtually all courses above the freshman level were made part of a system of electives. Quincy's successors Edward Everett and Jared Sparks abolished the sophomore and junior options, and a return to a three-year elective system awaited the post–Civil War presidency of Charles William Eliot.[35]

Meanwhile the town of Cambridge during the administrations of Kirkland and Quincy had grown to become an extended learned community unmatched elsewhere in the nation. Faculty members may have lost the fight to control the college, but in other respects they advanced considerably after the eighteenth century, rising to positions of high standing in the Commonwealth. Harvard instructors in 1800 had been described as "little better than Monks," full of "enmity and suspicion," to be compared with "the crew of a Privateer."[36] Thirty years later professors, instructors, and tutors had grown in number to about thirty, and they had grown in affluence and cultivation as well.[37] European visitors found them a "brilliant and fascinating society" and Cambridge a "fashionable oasis." A British journalist who had known a good number of "academical dignitaries," wrote that among them "the Professors of Harvard College were, as a body, the pleasantest. They are all men of scholarly education, some of them of European repute, and yet they are also men of the world."[38] They lived graciously on substantial Cambridge estates, assisted in a good many cases by the propensity of "our rich girls to buy themselves a professor." As a European visitor remarked, unlike most American businessmen, Boston "bankers and money kings pride themselves in being connected, by family-ties, with the aristocracy of intellect."[39] Cambridge provided an intellectual hothouse for children raised in its society, notably

Oliver Wendell Holmes, James Russell Lowell, Margaret Fuller, Thomas Wentworth Higginson, Charles Eliot Norton, and Charles Pierce. All were the children of scholars or scholarly persons, whom Holmes no doubt had particularly in mind when he coined the phrase "Brahmin caste of New England."

During the Kirkland era and afterward, Samuel Eliot's sons-in-law Andrews Norton, in Cambridge, and George Ticknor, in Boston, presided over their respective realms, setting the proper social tone. When George Bancroft paid Norton a call after returning from Europe, he offended his former teacher by the familiarity of his manner and the impropriety of his dress, and Norton severed social relations with him forthwith.[40] Ticknor assumed the more ambitious responsibility of serving as arbiter of Brahmin society in Boston, together with his wife, Anna Eliot Ticknor, who commanded the bearing that befit the first matron of Boston.

The Ticknors presided nightly at Nine Park Street over a stream of visitors from abroad, mixing with a select list of socially acceptable Boston Brahmins. On the basis of his years in Europe, Ticknor remained the American with the most distinguished list of European worthies, and Europeans of literary consequence were directed to his address, where highest standards of gracious opulence were maintained. The daughter of the Ticknor's pastor wrote of Anna Ticknor that

> from the beginning of her married life, until her death she was queen. There was only one Mrs. Ticknor, by implication, and greatly honored were those who had access to her home,—to the parlor and the library upstairs, the throne room as it were. There she and Mr. Ticknor received nightly. . . . The nobility and the scholars of Europe met there as nowhere else. . . . I have never seen any society equal to what was there, great cordiality shading off into degrees of high-bred courtesy in discussion and courtly grace of movement.[41]

There was no place in Ticknor's Boston for the informal intellectual conviviality that had attracted the Maryland physician Alexander Hamilton when he visited Boston in the eighteenth century. Edward L. Pierce wrote of nineteenth-century Boston that

> There was but one society at that period to which admission was sought, and everyone in it knew everyone else who was in it. It was

close and hard, with a uniform stamp on all, and opinion running in grooves.[42]

Ticknor presided with diminishing authority over this society for a half century, systematically ostracizing offenders of propriety. When George Bancroft became a partisan Democrat, Ticknor excluded him, as he did Charles Sumner and an increasing number of others. George Hilliard, a friend of both Ticknor and Sumner, protested Ticknor's banishment of Sumner from his circle. But Ticknor was unmoved, replying that the principles of Boston society

> are right, and its severity towards disorganizers and social democracy in all its forms, is just and wise . . . and is the circumstance which distinguishes us favorably from New York and the other large cities of the Union, where demagogues are permitted to rule, by the weak tolerance of men who know better, and are stronger than they are.[43]

As the slavery issue came to divide opinion in Boston, Ticknor drew the line against the reformers generally. He warned the young Harvard instructor Nathaniel Shaler that admittance to the Ticknor household carried "certain disabilities." He explained to Shaler that he

> should find my way to the houses of the Lawrences, to those of Mr. George Hilliard and Judge Parker and Professor Parsons of Cambridge, but that I should not enter those of the Lowells or the Quincys or that of Mr. Longfellow.[44]

That Shaler should avoid the company of Emerson's circle in Concord hardly required mentioning. The rise of this younger generation in the 1830s disturbed Ticknor and Norton exceedingly. After tea at the Nortons with the Ticknors in 1838, Longfellow noted in his journal that they "all hold in great contempt apparently, all peepings and movings of the wing among the young and sometimes extravagant young writers of the day."[45] By the eve of the Civil War, the Ticknors had isolated themselves from Boston's most distinguished literary elite, who were ensconced together, unthreatened by Nine Park Street, in the nation's most exclusive and rarified literary association, the Saturday Club of Boston.

↝ IV ↜

FORMIDABLE AS THE TICKNOR evenings were, they remained for many years the most consistently authoritative expression of literary sociability in town. Although educated Bostonians knew each other, as Henry Adams said, "to the last nervous center," they did not necessarily fraternize. As an English visitor noted, Boston society was fragmented into family sets or clans, each of which established its own standards, unlike the London sets who aped the higher aristocracy. "Grandchildren," Samuel Eliot Morison wrote, "mixing constantly with cousins in family parties and outings were apt to marry within the clan despite meeting other young ladies and gentlemen at dance assemblies, Harvard commencements and private balls."[46] There were the Essex County set, the Adams-Brooks-Quincy-Cranch set, the Forbes-Perkins set, and the Lawrence-Peabody-Loring set. These clan relationships extended the woman's sphere of activity and enlarged women's social authority. "The Jacksons came up from Newburyport to Boston, social and kindly people, inclined to make acquaintances and mingle with the world pleasantly," Colonel Henry Lee wrote. *"But they got some Cabot wives, who shut them up."*[47]

While men held intellectual sway over women, women enjoyed social authority over men, arranging their "circle of friends," as these social sets were called. Thus intellectual compatibility was apt not to be an important criterion for marriage. Late in life Oliver Wendell Holmes remarked that although his relations with Lowell had always been pleasant, they had "never sat long alone" nor walked a mile in company because they "did not live within easy reach" of each other. Fanny Longfellow regretted the infrequency of "regular, nourishing" contacts between her husband and other literary people, Longfellow "being especially social by nature." It seemed strange to her that with "so many men of high culture" about, one could not enjoy their company because they were "too busy, or too domestic," so that hardly anyone but the Swiss scholar Louis Agassiz was "to be relied on for any social purposes." Lowell complained that Bostonians seemed to have only two notions of hospitality, "a dinner with people you never saw before nor ever wish to see again, and a drive in Mount Auburn cemetery."[48] Edward Everett wrote that in Boston "it is scarcely possible to say anything which will not bring you into personal collison with your acquaintances." Even among friends, Catharine Sedgwick wrote, Bostonians "were afraid to speak lest they commit themselves for life"; while Longfellow declared that Boston was a "great village. The tyranny of public opinion there surpasses all belief."[49]

Nor did the academic setting of Cambridge prove conducive to social intercourse. Of Harvard in the 1870s, Henry Adams wrote

> Several score of the best-educated, most agreeable, and personally the most sociable people in America united in Cambridge to make a social desert that would have starved a polar bear. The liveliest and most agreeable of men—James Russell Lowell, Francis J. Child, Louis Agassiz, his son Alexander, Gurney, John Fiske, William James and a dozen others . . . While all these brilliant men were greedy for companionship, all were famished for the want of it. Society was a faculty-meeting without business.[50]

In the late 1830s two Harvard-trained lawyers, Charles Sumner and George Hilliard, and three faculty members, Longfellow, Cornelius Conway Felton, and Henry Cleveland, organized themselves into The Five of Clubs at a time when all but Hilliard were unmarried. The Saturday dinner meetings where they discussed each others' writings came to be referred to in newspapers as "The Mutual Admiration Society." However, Cambridge society remained mainly the society of family groups, as in Boston, and in the 1830s it was dominated by competition between the Josiah Quincys with their four unmarried daughters and professor Karl Follen's wife, the former Eliza Lee Cabot, with her two unmarried sisters-in-law, all "given to hospitality."[51]

The historian William Hickling Prescott was, like Longfellow, gregarious by nature and took part in all social events that Brahmin Boston afforded. The Prescotts themselves gave elegant dinners on Sunday evenings at 55 Beacon Street.[52] Prescott, whose great reputation in English literary circles as a scholar and a gentleman greatly impressed and pleased George Ticknor, was the exceptional Brahmin who attended Ticknor's functions while remaining on friendly terms with partisan Democrats like George Bancroft and Nathaniel Hawthorne. Nineteenth-century Bostonians appear to have traveled more extensively in Europe than did other educated Americans, in part to escape what Julia Ward Howe referred to as "the frozen ocean of Boston life." Once abroad they sought out other Bostonians, who flocked happily together in London, Paris, Rome, and Florence, free of the immediate restraints of Boston's civilized order.

Genial Oliver Wendell Holmes became the famous toastmaster to those he named the Brahmins. And even more effective master of the social art, responsible for a substantial measure of the sociability in Holmes's community, was James T. Fields, a self-made outsider from Portsmouth, New Hampshire. Fields arrived in Boston in 1831 with a common school education and an ambition to rise in Brahmin society. Finding employment in the staid book firm of Ticknor and Company, he joined the Boston Mercantile Library Association, went to lectures at the Lyceum, and attended William Ellery Channing's Federal Street Church on Sundays. Fields accumulated a fine personal library and a wide circle of friends, and as he advanced himself in the firm, he worked to attract local authors away from their New York and Philadelphia publishers by addressing himself to the marketing of books outside Boston as other Boston publishers did not bother to do. In time the firm became Ticknor & Fields. Fields became the trusted friend of Boston writers and also the genial proprietor of the Old Corner Book Store, where literary men might drop by to chat with one another or with literary visitors from out of town. Longfellow was among the most regular and appreciative frequenters of the Old Corner, while the less sociable Hawthorne valued Fields as a worldly guide so far as the practical side of authorship was concerned. It was at the Old Corner that Emerson and one or two other men began to organize the Saturday Club.[53]

On business in England, Fields broadened his circle of literary acquaintances, and it was he who persuaded William Makepeace Thackeray to undertake a lecture tour in America. When Thackeray arrived in Boston, Fields saw to it that he was introduced to everybody and widely entertained in small groups rather than at the more customary formal banquet. For instance, Lowell arranged with Fields to invite a half dozen of his friends, including Longfellow, to his house to meet Thackeray. Fields arrived with Thackeray two hours late, and as the wine flowed freely, an evening of hilarity followed featuring the endless punning then prevalent at gatherings of literary wits. "Will you take some port?" Lowell asked Thackeray. "I dare drink anything that becomes a man," Thackeray replied. "It will be a long time before that becomes a man," another quipped. To which Professor Cornelius Felton retorted, "Oh no; for it is fast turning into one." According to Longfellow, who recorded these good-natured ripostes, this tempo was kept up until one in the morning.[54]

Atlantic Monthly founder Nathaniel Parker Willis, who loathed Boston society, wrote warmly of

> the classic locality happily termed "Parnassas Corner," the bookstore of Messrs. Ticknor & Fields. . . . Here congregates . . . a score of authors worth peeping at. . . . FIELDS, the publisher, [is] the hub in which every spoke of the radiating wheel of Boston intellect has a socket— the central newsgiver, listener, sympathizer, gossip and advisor—his little desk behind the green curtain . . . and the half circle of two or three seats around it the snug retreat for many a confidential interview, many a stirring chat by bright spirits over the leading topics of the day, many an introduction of chance strangers to intellectual celebrities.

At the urging of Longfellow and the Reverend George Ellis of the Harvard Divinity School, Harvard awarded Fields an honorary Master of Arts, which Fields sent to his high school to hang on its walls as "an example of what any other hard-working honest Portsmouth boy might achieve."[55]

Boston's literati occasionally went in for civic celebrations. One such was the welcome in 1842 of Charles Dickens by Fields and his young friends. When a new public water system was completed five years later, ceremonies were presided over by Mayor Quincy, Daniel Webster, Nathaniel Hawthorne, and Ralph Waldo Emerson, seated upon a platform that had been raised over Frog Pond. After a parade of townspeople, a jet of water was released, and a school chorus sang an ode Lowell had written for the occasion, "My Name Is Water."[56] The annual civic celebration that traditionally involved the whole community was the Harvard commencement festival. At one time riotous, the festival lost its carnival atmosphere after the Kirkland era.[57]

On visiting Boston in 1831, Alexis de Tocqueville was surprised to discover that, while "the prejudice against people who do nothing is strong," there nevertheless were "a certain number of people who, having nothing to do, seek out the pleasures of the mind."[58] The Calvinist concept of calling had not died out in Boston, but well-cultivated idleness was itself a recognized calling in Brahmin circles. Richard Henry Dana Sr., who briefly edited *The Idle Man* in New York, was one such gentleman, who trained himself in the law and devoted himself to literature, for a time as coeditor of *North American Review*. Another man of leisure was Francis Calley Gray, who "never tired of repeating that intellectual and moral culture was the object worthiest of highest ambition."[59]

Longfellow's brother-in-law, Thomas Gold Appleton, a founding member of the Saturday Club, devoted his life to literature, conversation, and travel. To his father's invitation to enter the family business, Appleton replied, "No, thank you! Arts and letters are what I care for. I will not waste my life." Dabbling in the arts led Appleton in time to the conclusion that "I have the temperament of genius without the genius." But that did not deter him from continuing in his chosen course. As he wrote his father

> I cannot see that a man improving his character and mind, living modestly on a moderate income is wholly despicable. If he tried to do good, and to find the truth and speak it, I cannot see that he is inferior to a man who only toils, nobly, to be sure, but still without leaving himself time for much of these.[60]

Most Harvard-educated Bostonians were not Brahmins, as Holmes defined the term, and a quality of Boston Brahminism that remained alien to the Harvard-educated merchant gentry was the pious conviction that the cultivation of one's own sensibilities might constitute in itself a laudable vocation for a gentleman. Not all Boston intellectuals shared this view, for that matter. Although Josiah Quincy pursued literary and scientific interests throughout his life, his intellectual pursuits remained subordinate to his public duties, and it was his public career that justified his existence. Such was not the case with Quincy's son, Edmund, however, nor with his sons-in-law, the Reverend Robert Cassie and Dr. Benjamin Greene. Cassie remained a minister without a parish and Greene a physician without a practice; Edmund Quincy remained an idle man who dabbled in literature and donated his services to the abolitionist movement. He wrote an English friend in 1846 that "There is nothing in this country except anti-slavery that is worth a gentleman's notice. Our politics are a kennel in which the dirtiest dog that rolls in it gets the most bones."[61]

⊸ V ⊱

WHILE OLIVER WENDELL HOLMES conspicuously served as master of ceremonies in festivities involving Boston Brahmins, it was Holmes's friend Ralph Waldo Emerson who unobtrusively but most effectively applied himself to the task of organizing literary society and fostering sociability among its members, not only in Concord but in Boston as well. Emerson's gently reserved temperament together with his unsociable philosophical themes of individualism and solitude have disguised his gregarious nature and the extraordinary social talents he so effectively employed. Social talent seems to have run in the Emerson family; Emerson's father was secretary of the Anthology Society, and his brother William, living in a Concord-like setting on Staten Island, was a founder and secretary of the Sketch Club in New York. Emerson himself was the instrumental founder of the Saturday Club in 1856, the first such association of Boston literary men to emerge since the disintegration of his father's society forty years earlier.

Enjoying close relations with his three brothers, all of whom became lawyers, Emerson grew up with familial assumptions that remained more fundamental to his conduct of life than the expression of the Self he consciously cultivated. Emerson was by habit a community man as well as a family man. Upon settling in Concord he assumed more than his share of civic duties. Beginning as hog reeve, he was next elected to the school committee, where he served as both chairman and secretary. He joined the library social committee and later served as its president. He preached occasionally in the local church and lectured for the local lyceum. Full recognition of his acceptance in the community came, five years after his move to Concord, when he was elected to the town's Social Circle, a group of about twenty of the better sort of villagers and farmers. Years later, in discussing the meeting time of what became the Saturday Club, Emerson ruled out Tuesday evenings since that was the evening the Social Circle met in Concord. While avoiding involvement in the rough-and-tumble of the town meeting, Emerson became an active member of Concord's cultural elite at the same time he was judiciously assembling his own transcendentalist coterie.[62]

The Concord immortalized in the writings of Emerson and his

protégé Thoreau was a rural village, close to nature. For Emerson's own purposes Concord was something else as well: a comfortable suburb of Boston. Unlike most of his literary village associates, Emerson was emerging in the 1840s as a leading Brahmin. A Bostonian by birth, upbringing, and conviction, he had evidently chosen to live in the village of Concord because its peripheral proximity to the city—a two- or three-hour ride by stage—allowed Emerson to remain a Bostonian while gaining a personal freedom such as Boston's townspeople did not enjoy. No one was better acquainted with Boston's social conformity than Emerson. At the same time nobody valued Boston culture more highly than he. By locating himself in Concord, Emerson gained a freedom of action within Boston society that was denied his Brahmin friends from Boston and Cambridge.

In Concord, Lydia and Waldo Emerson presided over a gracious household that functioned as the unobtrusive center of Emerson's carefully and patiently cultivated Concord literary circle. The Emersons' domestic ambience encouraged men and women as egocentric and contentious as Margaret Fuller and Henry David Thoreau to lend their support to the harmony of the whole. The popular author and antislavery feminist Elizabeth Oakes Smith spent several weeks in the Emerson household while on a speaking tour. Transplanted New Yorker and expatriated New Englander, Smith was no follower of Emerson's, yet she found herself very much at home there. "It was, indeed, a model household," she wrote, "everything fresh as a rose . . . the wholesome and tempting breakfast, and the long talks over the coffee, Mr. Emerson so quietly breathing out his precious aphorisms." Smith believed one ought to be able to make a fair estimate "of the quality of the man, by the quality of the household; and here Mr. Emerson may be fairly regarded as a model man, a sort of family Socrates without a Xantippe."[63] Such three-week visits by persons with whom the Emersons were but distantly acquainted provided Emerson with the pleasant means of enlarging his familial circle.

Women were more prevalent and enjoyed greater intellectual liberty among the transcendentalists than among other intellectual circles in America, excepting those expressly dedicated to the humanitarian causes considered appropriate for women to pursue. This is not to say that

Emerson considered intellectual women the social equals of intellectual men. Lydia Maria Child, who admired Emerson, recognized that his gentle and tolerant high-mindedness cloaked an inflexible double standard where women were concerned. Child wrote of Emerson's lecture "Being rather than Seeming" that the sentiments expressed were beautiful but that the motives behind them were pernicious as applied to women.

> *Men* were exhorted to *be*, rather than to *seem*, that they might fulfill the sacred mission for which their souls were embodied . . . but *women* were urged to simplicity and truthfulness, that they might become more *pleasing*.[64]

Emerson was able to come to terms with feminists as he was able to come to terms with a wide variety of New England eccentrics by treating "the men and women of one idea, the Abolitionist, the Phrenologist, the Swedenborgian, as insane persons with a continual tenderness and special reference in every remark and action to their known state."[65] His admiration for Fuller and sympathy for her aspirations led him to accept her not on her own terms but as he sympathetically reconstrued them.

It was not originally intended that the women of Emerson's circle would be included in the Symposium or Transcendental Club, which Emerson together with George Ripley and three other ministers, Orestes Brownson, and Bronson Alcott organized in 1837. However, when fourteen male members of the informally organized club were invited to the Emerson home that year, following his delivery at Harvard of his Phi Beta Kappa "American Scholar" address, they found Margaret Fuller and Elizabeth Hoar together with Lydia Emerson and Sarah Ripley included for the occasion, which consisted mainly of an elaborate dinner prepared by Lydia. Thereafter Fuller not only became a member of the club but was chosen to be editor of its proposed journal, *The Dial*, when Emerson declined to assume responsibility for editing it with Fuller as his assistant.

In due time Emerson applied his talent for cultural politics to Boston as well. The prominent Brahmins whom he had offended, especially by his Harvard Divinity School address in 1838, came from an older generation that was fading in influence. When old Andrews Norton denounced

Emerson and his address, the author was not disturbed but more concerned to remain on good terms with young Charles Eliot Norton. Emerson cultivated his own generation of Brahmins while keeping a watchful eye upon the young men annually graduating from Harvard.

As a Harvard undergraduate James Russell Lowell held the unworldly Emersonians in mild contempt. But when the university disciplined Lowell by rusticating him to Concord for a season, Emerson gently took him in hand. Lowell never accepted Fuller or Thoreau or William Henry Channing, but he remained an Emerson man from then on. Similarly, when Hawthorne moved to Concord, he entered Emerson's circle despite his hostility to the ideas of the transcendentalists. No individual Brahmin could presume to speak for the whole caste, but in the 1850s Emerson was probably on as good personal terms with elite Brahmins as any other of their number was.

Returning from London's literary social whirl in 1848, Emerson condescended to it publicly in the account he included in *English Traits*. At the same time he sought to recreate some semblance of its more positive aspects in Boston. His initial plan was to form a Town-and-Country Club on a broad basis. Although supported by Lowell and Longfellow, nothing came of his efforts until several years later, when a lawyer, Horatio Woodman, heard Emerson discuss his plan for such a club during one of Emerson's regular Saturday visits to Ticknor & Fields's Corner Book Store. Woodman himself was an outsider of no real standing in the Brahmin community, but he was tolerated as an adept "genius broker" among the Brahmins, and with Emerson's support he succeeded in making the necessary arrangements.[66]

In 1857 the club came into existence with eleven members: Emerson, Lowell, Richard Henry Dana, Julia Ward Howe's brother Sam Ward, Louis Agassiz, John Lothrop Motley, music critic John Sullivan Dwight, jurist Ebenezer Rockwood Hoar, literary critic Edwin Percy Whipple, and Woodman. To this group Holmes, Longfellow, and Professor Cornelius Felton of Harvard were shortly added. Six additional members were admitted between 1858 and 1860: William Hickling Prescott, John Greenleaf Whittier, Hawthorne, Thomas Gold Appleton, Charles Eliot Norton, and a merchant, John Murray Forbes. Meeting monthly for dinner at the Parker House on Saturday afternoons from three until about nine, together with selected guests, the Saturday Club, quietly and without drawing public attention to itself, became known and esteemed throughout cultivated American society.

Among the regular members the most ebullient conversationalists were reputed to be Agassiz, Holmes, and Tom Appleton, while Hawthorne appeared to be the most conspicuously ill at ease. Emerson remained in the background but regularly in attendance and always the model of gentlemanly sociability. "Emerson is an excellent dinnertable man," Dana wrote in his diary at the time the Saturday Club was being planned, "always a gentleman, never bores, or preaches, or dictates, but drops and takes up topics very agreeably, and has even skill and tact in managing his conversation." He added, "So, indeed, has Alcott; and it is quite surprising to see these transcendentalists appearing as men of the world."[67]

In the literal sense Emerson was actually less a man of the world than a man of Boston. Emerson believed that American civilization was rising indigenously as English civilization entered an inevitable period of decline. He believed, too, that within America civilization radiated out from Boston and not very far out, hardly existing beyond the Appalachians. Considering St. Louis during a lecture tour at midcentury, Emerson privately expressed doubt that a single reading man existed among its eighty thousand people.[68] East of the Appalachians, literary society was distributed throughout New England as nowhere else, but the proximity of New York had evidently proved fatal to literary culture in Connecticut; while New York, despite its recruitment of literary New Englanders, could not cultivate a literary community that would win Emerson's blessing.

Elizabeth Oakes Smith had moved with her literary husband, Seba Smith, from a small but lively literary community in Portland, Maine, to the large and lively literary world of New York, and she did not regret having passed Boston by. When Emerson asked her how she thought Boston society compared with New York's, she told him that it was very inferior since "society for general social purposes is almost lacking in Boston." To her mind,

> The women seem all propagandists, and the men leaders in something or other. They all seem to have a specialty and go out to promote it, [whereas New Yorkers] go into society to please and be pleased.

Emerson replied, "Perhaps for that reason society in New York is more shallow and the knowledge more superficial," but Smith did not think so. New Yorkers, she explained, "have not the intense admiration for each other that Bostonians have; they are not cliquish; they are not so pedantic."[69] Emerson did not agree, but to have pursued the disagreement further would have been contrary to his style of civilized discourse as well as his obligations as host.

◄ VI ►

LITERARY SPINSTERS WERE almost as common in Boston and New England as literary bachelors were in New York City. By the mid–nineteenth century, an increasing disproportion among the sexes in New England, and particularly a shortage of socially eligible gentlemen, offered justification for failure to meet women's traditional responsibility to marry and raise children. It became honorable, if unfortunate, for Brahmin women to remain single so long as profound disappointment in love was the spur that led them to devote themselves to letters or, better yet, humanitarian causes. Some independent-minded women took advantage of this loophole in the social contract, but they took care to do so under the aegis of family or of a respected father-figure in the community.

The revered and moderately feminist theologian of Boston Unitarianism, William Ellery Channing, served as patron to a number of ambitious women in the community, including the educator Elizabeth Palmer Peabody and the reformer Dorothea Lynde Dix. He employed each of them as secretarial assistant and Dix as governess of his children while supporting them in their efforts to invent vocations for themselves as single women. When at the age of thirty-six, Peabody conceived the plan of opening a book store in the front parlor of her family's home on West Street, she went to Channing to request his permission as well as his financial support to become a businesswoman. The venture, as she planned it, would retain a domestic character; the customers, including her many personal acquaintances, would be admitted to her private library, where books would happen to be for sale. Though Channing questioned the efficacy of the scheme, he provided the moral and monetary backing Peabody wanted, desiring "to see a variety of employments open to women" and seeing "nothing in the business inconsistent with your sex."[70]

Channing proved justified in his doubts of Peabody's business competence; the West Street Book Store was not profitable, and Peabody took in boarders—a time-honored domestic occupation for American women —to make ends meet. Meanwhile the store did serve as a literary social center where women were at home as they were not at home in James T. Fields's Old Corner Book Store. Peabody's bookstore provided the meeting place for the most famous and successful bluestocking sociability to surface in antebellum America, the "conversations" of Margaret Fuller.

At the age of twenty-nine, Fuller had firmly established her reputation in Boston as the bluestocking's bluestocking, and she was able to attract the most prominent literary women of the community, whom she charged the very substantial fee of twenty dollars for ten meetings. Fuller would designate the subjects under discussion and guide the "conversations," in which everyone was intended to participate. Twenty-five women enrolled in the first series in 1839. The meetings continued for four years, attracting forty women in all, including the Peabody sisters, Elizabeth Hoar, Lydia Maria Child, Sarah Ripley, the Mmes. George Bancroft, Theodore Parker, and Josiah Quincy, and Lowell's fiancée, Maria White.[71]

After more than a year of highly successful conversations on Saturday mornings at eleven, Fuller undertook to present a Monday evening series open to men as well as women and attended by Emerson, Bronson Alcott, George Ripley, and others of the transcendental circle. The experiment was a dispiriting and disagreeable failure. The women fell respectfully silent, except for Elizabeth Peabody and one or two others, and the men carried on the discussion among themselves, despite Fuller's persistent efforts to direct the flow of the conversation. Emerson issued arbitrary opinions with an uncharacteristic bruskness that did not admit of polite dissent; he later wrote Fuller a letter of apology. When Fuller resumed the conversations for women only, they immediately regained their original vitality and popularity.

Sarah Margaret Fuller was notorious during her lifetime—and she remains uniquely interesting—as the woman who exerted herself most radically to achieve equality with men in the American Republic of Letters. Trained from infancy by her widower father to become an intellectual giant, she grew up in the Cambridge area among the intensely motivated, precocious boys and girls of the nation's oldest, largest, and most prestigious academic community. Oliver Wendell Holmes and Richard Henry Dana Jr. were her classmates. William Henry Channing and James Freeman Clarke, members of the Harvard class of 1829 that Holmes celebrated in song and story, were early friends. Among her own sex, Fuller was mothered as a growing girl by concerned Cambridge faculty wives, and she tended thereafter to be attracted to somewhat older women, including the English writer Harriet Martineau and Elizabeth Peabody, through whom Fuller's initial visit with the Emersons was evidently arranged.

Maintaining a grueling schedule of studies in languages and literature, Fuller prepared herself single-mindedly for a career as an intellectual. Whatever extent her physical attractions to men—a much mooted subject—she early decided to be "bright and ugly" and live by her intellect. Uncertain of her writing ability, she gained confidence in her powers as a conversationalist, an estimate of herself shared by others. In the mid-1840s she became a successful editor, literary critic, and foreign correspondent for Horace Greeley's *New York Tribune*, pioneering as a woman in each of these fields. But Fuller exerted the greatest influence though her *Women in the Nineteenth Century* (1845), a feminist classic, and especially through the Boston "conversations" series that provided the material for that work. It was through the art of conversation that she made the deepest impression, favorable and otherwise, upon her generation.

A literary romantic and an emotional woman, Fuller was compelled by her chosen role to calculate her moves and pursue her social strategies in a manner inconsistent with her temperament. Marriage to another American intellectual would have entailed subordination to husband and family by law, custom, and community consensus. At the same time, in pursuing her egalitarian aims Fuller was necessarily dependent upon males as a lone female seeking a place among men of letters. Her progress in this society depended upon the good offices of men, including particularly her patron, Emerson, who effectively became her guardian in the intellectual community. Later Horace Greeley took her into his New York home and established her in the male profession of journalism. Finally her lover, the marquess Giovanni Angelo Ossoli, facilitated her assimilation into the Italian revolutionary movement, in Rome. With the marquess, Fuller became wife and mother, and she was returning to America in 1850 in this state of domesticity when she and her family drowned in a shipwreck off Fire Island on 19 July. In a stroke the nation lost a mind that like no other might have redefined horizons of the possible for evey bold and thoughtful wife and mother.

For Fuller the Emerson household in Concord had offered just the familial security a young woman needed while making a name for herself in the Republic of Letters. There she found the freedom and security shared by all members of the transcendentalist family so long as Emerson remained head of the household—including the freedom to behave waywardly when she was of a mind to. If she sought liberation from even these benign bonds of familial restraint, then in the opinion of Emerson and of civilized society generally, she sought in vain, denying the inescapable face of her womanhood.

Fuller's progress beyond Concord and Emerson began in 1843 with a wagon trip to Oregon in the company of her Cambridge friend James Freeman Clarke and his sister, Sarah. The travel book Fuller wrote after the trip, *Summer on the Lakes, in 1843*, attracted the interest of Horace Greeley, whose wife had attended Fuller's Boston conversations. When Greeley offered her a job on the *Tribune*, she accepted—to the dismay of her Brahmin friends. Emerson, in fact, made no attempt to disuade her, but he wrote Carlyle that "this employment is not satisfactory to me."[72] Initially uneasy about Fuller's presence in his house, which his wife had suggested, Greeley soon became her enthusiastic friend and admirer, introducing her to a career in New York that irretrievably broadened her horizons beyond the confines of Concord. Meanwhile, her critical reviews in the *Tribune* and her *Women in the Nineteenth Century* established her as a prominent member of the New York literati, presently with an apartment of her own and access to the leading salons and literary households of the city.

Invited to travel to Europe with a wealthy New York couple, Fuller took her savings, borrowed money from the artist-banker-lobbyist Sam Ward, whom she had known since his Harvard days, and with an assign ment as foreign correspondent from Greeley and a letter of introduction to Carlyle from Emerson, she sailed for England in the summer of 1846. It was while visiting the Carlyles in London that she met the Italian patriot Giuseppe Mazzini. There she became attracted to the cause of Italian independence, as might not have been the case, had she been introduced to the subject by the expatriate community of Bostonians and Englishmen in Florence and Rome.

In Rome she met Ossoli, an impecunious nobleman ten years her junior, and instilled in him the desire for Roman liberty that Mazzini had given her. They became lovers and patriots and parents, all of which came to be revealed to her old friends in Boston and Concord when the revolution failed and the Ossolis decided to sail to America. Their arrival was naturally awaited with embarrassment, anxiety, and foreboding by her friends. Under these circumstances, they wondered, how could she find a place for herself, not to speak of her consort and child, in respectable American society? Considering the problem she had created for herself, Emerson viewed her drowning at the age of forty as a timely and perhaps even welcome event. He wrote Carlyle that

> she died in a happy hour for herself. Her health was much exhausted. Her marriage would have taken her away from us all & there was a subsistence yet to be secured, & diminished power, & old age.[73]

Her death returned her to the guardianship of her Concord friends, who set about to prepare a memoir of her. "Without either beauty or genius," Emerson wrote Carlyle a year later, "she had a certain wealth & generosity of nature which have left a kind of claim on our consciences to build her a cairn."[74] Margaret Fuller Ossoli's literary remains were accordingly bowdlerized by her well-intentioned literary executors— Emerson, William Henry Channing, and James Freeman Clarke—to strip away their most pronounced assertions of her individuality. These protective gentlemen went through her papers with scissors and paste and india ink, expurgating passages in which her thought and character offended Victorian transcendental propriety. The resulting *Memoirs of Margaret Fuller Ossoli* conformed to the standards of womanhood that these gentlemen shared with educated Americans generally.

⊰ VII ⊱

WHEN THE PUBLICATION OF *Uncle Tom's Cabin* (1852) vaulted Harriet Beecher Stowe from the obscurity of domestic life to the highest reaches of world renown, her unique literary status confronted Brahmin Boston with a social problem for which there was no precedent. Within months of the publication of the novel, Stowe became the most acclaimed person of letters in America. In Europe her work was read even more widely than Cooper's Leatherstocking stories had been in the 1820s; virtually all educated people took up the novel. Had Stowe been a man, she would have been accorded her place at the head of the American literary community as a matter of course. But in the American literary community, the position of first among equals was not intended for a woman.

The literary world of England was something else again, however. Touring Great Britain in 1853, Stowe was lionized everywhere: by crowds in railroad stations, by dukes and earls on country estates, and at soirées, levees, breakfasts, luncheons, teas, and dinners. When she and her husband, the reverend Calvin Stowe, arrived in London, the lord mayor stole the march upon literary society with an impromptu dinner for which Dickens was hastily recruited. A plethora of dinings-out followed, interspersed with visits from persons of consequence, literary and otherwise.

The success of *Uncle Tom's Cabin* had been no less swift and overwhelming in America than in Europe, but Stowe's visits to New York and Boston following its publication had not occasioned the literary sociability that whirled about her in Glasgow, Edinburgh, London, and points between. Indeed, England acquainted her with forms of sociability she had not known about, such as the late morning "breakfast" given the Stowes by Sir Charles and Lady Trevelyn. Trevelyn's fellow historians Thomas Macaulay, Henry Milman, and Henry Hallam were there, as was a lady well acquainted with the novelist Charles Kingsley, whom Stowe much admired; a brilliant and animated, though venerable, erstwhile companion of the English abolitionists William Wilberforce and Thomas Clarkson; and various other ladies and gentlemen whom Stowe did not have the chance to meet or identify. "Looking around the table, and seeing how everybody seemed to be enjoying themselves," Stowe wrote, "I said to Macaulay, that these breakfast parties were a novelty to me; that we never had them in America, but that I thought them the most delightful form of social life." And so, off to lunch at Surrey parsonage.[75]

The Stowes' five whirlwind months touring Britain and the Continent were concluded with a final farewell breakfast given by the mayor of Liverpool. Returning to America they resumed their accustomed social round of church attendance and visits with family and friends. Following a second trip abroad to see to the English publication of the novel *Dred*, the Stowes planned yet a third voyage in 1859, and on this occasion literary Boston finally bestirred itself to honor the first lady of American letters with a dinner party.

Atlantic Monthly, which had made its appearance in 1857, owed its very existence to Stowe since it had been her promise to contribute to its pages that had secured the necessary backing from a publisher.[76] As was customary with some literary magazines, dinners were periodically held by *Atlantic*, where editors and contributors celebrated recent issues and planned future ones. Being a woman, Stowe had never been invited to an Atlantic Club dinner, just as she had never been invited to the Saturday Club, where a number of the same gentlemen regularly dined together. Although delighted at being the guest of honor at dinners in England, Stowe was not similarly happy about the idea of attending such a dinner in Boston, and she accepted only on condition that no wine be served. This was agreed to, and invitations were sent out to other women authors who had been published in *Atlantic*. None came except the young poet Harriet Prescott. She and the Stowes arrived on time, and after the reverend joined the men the two Harriets were left by themselves for three quarters of an hour while dinner was held up on the chance that other of the invited women would come. During that time, according to Prescott, the two waited in silence, broken only when Stowe "once asked me what o'clock it was, and I told her I didn't know."[77]

When it was decided to delay no longer, Oliver Wendell Holmes escorted Stowe to the table, while Thomas Wentworth Higginson escorted Prescott. Then, according to Higginson,

> The modest entertainment proceeded; conversation set in, but there was a visible awkwardness, partly from the presence of two ladies . . .

and moreover, the thawing influence of wine was wanting. . . . [V]ari-
ous little jokes began to circle *sotto voce* at the table.

Finally the aristocratic abolitionist Edmund Quincy called a waiter, who
took his water glass and returned it filled with a rosy liquid. Others followed suit, and the party warmed up. Holmes, sitting next to Dr. Stowe,
put forward the argument that profanity originated in the free use made
by the pulpit of sacred words and phrases. Lowell, within earshot of Harriet Stowe, argued that *Tom Jones*, with all its lusty sex, was the best novel
ever written. Afterward, Dr. and Mrs. Stowe confided to John Greenleaf
Whittier that while the company at the club was no doubt distinguished,
the conversation was not quite what they had been led to expect.

There were, to be sure, other women of letters in America who would
have relished the Atlantic Club dinner and improved it as Stowe did not.
Among the antislavery literati, Maria Chapman would have carried it off
with éclat and so would Julia Ward Howe, who was once accorded the ul-
timate accolade from the toastmaster of Boston himself, Oliver Wendell
Holmes, who told her, "Mrs. Howe, I consider you eminently *clubable*."[78]
Howe was, indeed, the consummate woman of letters. Accomplished in
art, music, languages, literature, and philosophy, she became active in
major reform movements of her time, especially abolition and woman's
rights. And she represented both the most culturally advantaged society
of her native New York City and the Brahmin society of Boston into
which she married. As the daughter of Samuel Ward, a wealthy and cultivated New York banker, and as the sister of Sam Ward, the internationally celebrated bon vivant and "king of the lobby" at Albany, Julia Ward
grew up to be "a frequenter of fashionable society, a musical amateur,
and a dilletante in literature," as well as a serious student of philosophy.[79]
Marriage to the Boston humanitarian and reformer Dr. Samuel Gridley
Howe introduced her into the literary and reform circles of Boston and
Concord, to which she contributed lectures and essays on German philosophy while publishing books of verse and travel sketches.

Although Julia Howe assisted her husband in editing the antislavery
paper *The Commonwealth* for several years, she did not become absorbed
in the work with the blind that chiefly absorbed his attention. Before the
Civil War slavery was the social issue that commanded her energies. Julia

Ward had brought to her marriage a New Yorkish prejudice against the Garrisonian abolitionists as being tiresome fanatics. But in Boston she found that they improved upon acquaintance, and she entered into their movement in the 1850s, a time when Harriet Beecher Stowe and other literary intellectuals became similarly committed. After the Civil War, Howe became increasingly identified with feminism, serving for several decades as president of the New England Woman Suffrage Association and of the New England Woman's Club, all the while writing and lecturing extensively on women's rights and other social issues and editing *Woman's Journal*.

Howe occupied a world in which the male and female spheres intersected more equitably than they did under most other literary women's heavens. An admiring gentlewoman of letters, Grace King of New Orleans, who observed Howe in an administrative capacity, thought Howe seemed "the embodiment of the Victorian idea of womanhood . . . with a poise of exquisite dignity"; she handled her assignment "with impeccable ease and polish of manners, and proceeded to organize it with what used to be called 'masculine competence.'"[80] When the American Academy of Arts and Letters was organized in 1908, it honored the old American rule against admitting women to the best literary company; but it made an exception for the lively eighty-nine-year-old author of "The Battle Hymn of the Republic," making her the lone woman to be elevated to that fifty-member assembly.

Julia Ward Howe's public accomplishments were achieved despite her physically and emotionally demanding domestic careers as wife and mother of six children. Dr. Howe, internationally famous as a humanitarian reformer when young Julia met him, held staunchly nonreformist views concerning the familial role of women. He settled his wealthy and sociable bride in a house in South Boston and left her there to cope with unfamiliar and increasingly arduous household chores while he devoted himself to his work with the blind and later the feebleminded as well. He resented her independent wealth and took steps to remove it from her control. The publication of her first book of verse, *Passion Flowers* (1854), upset him dreadfully, leading him repeatedly to broach the question of a separation agreement to terminate their marriage—a dire threat to Julia Ward, who believed that "Marriage, like death, is a debt we owe to nature."[81]

New public ventures by Julia Ward Howe were met with renewed objections to her unwifely behavior on the part of a husband who grew increasingly obstreperous with advancing age. Not surprisingly, Dr. Howe complained when his wife proceeded from abolitionism, which he himself championed, to woman suffrage. He did not deny that women ought to have the vote, but he wrote an old friend that

> zeal in pursuit of [suffrage] does not justify neglect of domestic relations and occupation; nor attempts to abolish those differences in our political and social sphere and duties, which spring out of differences in the very organization of the sexes.[82]

In the literary republic, as in the republic at large, nearly everyone in their various ways continued to maintain the distinction between a man's world on the one hand and a more circumscribed and duty-laden woman's sphere on the other.

LITERATI IN DEMOCRATIC-WHIG AMERICA

BOTH FEDERALISTS AND JEFFERSONIANS believed that a natural aristocracy of virtue and talent should rule the new Republic. But in 1828 the new Republic went its own way, rejecting John Quincy Adams for the autocratic populist Andrew Jackson. The organization of a Jacksonian Democratic Party, geared to secure the popular vote, provoked the opposing Whigs to develop these tactics further to secure the election of another war hero, William Henry Harrison, in 1840. Lacking a platform and any unifying issue besides opposition to the Democrats, the Whigs adopted the then-novel strategy of marketing their candidate with pins, placards, campaign hats, events, and entertainment, including a portable log cabin where men could find hard cider. Thus with the Whig victory in 1840, the model of the philosopher-president was replaced by the model of the party man and populist. The idea of government by a college-educated ruling class had already been rejected at the state level. White manhood or taxpayers' suffrage and direct election of public officials, including governors, became the rule in most new states admitted after the Constitution. By the eve of the War of 1812, this rule applied to most of the older states as well. Massachusetts, Virginia, and South Carolina continued to maintain an elite ruling class, but in this they went against the prevailing trend of popular rule secured by elections frequently held at state and local levels.

Up through the War of 1812, the notion persisted that the president, at least, should be a gentleman and perhaps a scholar, even if this was not required of congressmen. But even at the level of president it ceased to be a generally accepted criterion after the War of 1812. When Andrew Jackson emerged as a presidential candidate in 1824, opponents argued that he was unqualified for the position, possessing only a rudimentary frontier education and legal preparation and brought up in the western school of hard knocks, punctuated by duels and street brawls. Yet William H. Crawford, with a similarly rudimentary frontier education and a similar history of frontier brawling and dueling, had emerged as a serious contender for the presidency in 1816 and received the nomination of the congressional caucus, together with Jefferson's support, eight years later. Had Crawford not suffered a stroke during the campaign, he might well have won the presidency in 1824. As it turrned out, the presidency went to a man who had trained for the office from birth on the assumption that the office would seek the man of virtue and talents.

Following diplomatic assignments in Netherlands and Prussia, John Quincy Adams returned to America in 1801 to follow his defeated father to the presidency. He was quick to realize that the Federalist Party would serve him poorly beyond the political confines of Massachusetts, and as U.S. senator he pursued an independent course that alienated him from the ultra-Federalist senior senator of his state, Timothy Pickering. In 1803, when Pickering felt impelled by the Louisiana Purchase to consider the secession of New England from the union, Adams supported the purchase with some reservations. In 1807 Adams supported Jefferson's embargo bill and openly associated with the Republicans in Massachusetts, leading to his expulsion from the Federalist Party and his forced retirement from the Senate in 1808, before his term was up.

For a difficult year thereafter, Adams remained in political limbo, left to twist in the wind by the Jefferson administration he had supported. Then Jefferson retired to Monticello, and his successor, Madison, rewarded Adams with appointment as minister to Russia and later as a delegate to the peace negotiations in Ghent. In 1817 Monroe appointed Adams as his secretary of state, advancing Adams's claims to candidacy for the presidency in 1824. His rise in Jefferson's party did nothing to ameliorate John Quincy's personal bitterness toward the Sage of Monticello, however. Years later Adams reflected upon Jefferson's "craft and duplicity" and concluded that

> His success through a long life, and especially from his entrance upon the office of Secretary of State under Washington until he reached the presidential chair, seems, to my imperfect vision, a slur upon the moral government of the world.[1]

When Monroe received the nomination in 1816, John Adams complained that, although there was "not a more fit man in creation for the Presidency" than his own eldest son, it appeared that the candidacy of John Quincy Adams would be delayed "till all Virginians shall be extinct."[2] However, in 1825 the office finally sought Adams out, even though Jackson received more electoral votes. As provided for in the Constitution but never implemented before or since, the nominations of the three top candidates—Jackson, Adams, and Crawford—were submitted to the House of Representatives. Henry Clay, who had won thirty-seven electoral votes in the election as Kentucky's favorite son, supported Adams and ensured his election. Upon taking office, Adams appointed Clay secretary of state, and the campaign for the election of 1828 was launched at once amid charges of a "corrupt bargain" between a puritan and a swindler—"Blifil and Black George," as Virginia's John Randolph put it—to cheat Jackson out of the presidency.

From brilliant success in diplomacy, Adams advanced to inept failure in presidential politics. Ignoring the practical requirements of party politics, as he had in 1807, Adams acted upon the assumption that party loyalty, so important in times of conflict, should yield to constructive, rational discussion in business as usual. In his inaugural address, Adams asserted that "Ten years of peace, at home and abroad, have assuaged the animosities of political contentions and blended into harmony the most discordant elements of public opinion." He called upon those who still harbored the party spirit to discard "every remnant of rancor against each other" and yield "to talents and virtue alone that confidence which in time of contention for principle was bestowed only upon those who bore the badge of party communion."[3]

Adams thereupon outlined his radical program of expanded Federal involvement in the national life and entered upon a period of rancorous politics that persisted until he was voted out of office four years later. In addition to "laws promoting the improvement of agriculture, commerce, and manufactures," Adams recommended legislation promoting "the elegant arts, the advancement of literature, and the progress of the sciences, ornamental and profound." But it was the portion of his program affecting business that drew the main fire. By comparison his cultural programs seemed hardly worth worrying about, although his reference to projected federally funded observatories as "lighthouses in the sky" attracted derisive comment.

The national university that Adams proposed—as it had been proposed by every president before him—had no more chance in Congress than his more novel suggestions for federal patronage of learning. Benjamin Rush had been among the staunchest early supporters of such a university, and his son Richard Rush, serving as Adams's secretary of treasury, loyally supported the scheme in 1825, as he supported all of Adams's ambitious cultural and economic programs. With the rejection of these programs, the dream of the national university died, an outworn symbol of the lofty conception of a Republic of Virtue and Talents that had guided the framers of the Constitution and afterward the administrations of Washington, Adams, Jefferson, Madison, Monroe, and lastly John Quincy Adams.

During John Quincy Adams's vexed administration, Senator Martin Van Buren of New York had taken the lead in organizing a new political party geared to Jackson's great popularity, and in 1828, against an incumbent who refused to pursue party methods, Jackson won by a landslide. Naturally Adams men went out and Jackson men came in; this was to be expected, although it was furiously denounced. What shocked gentlemen more than the rotation in office itself was Jackson's defense of it as a matter of principle. Jackson explained in his first annual message to Congress that periodic changes in government personnel freed the nation of the evils of entrenched bureaucracy. To argue that public offices should remain in the hands of those trained by education and experience to perform them, Jackson continued, was to call into question the democratic nature of American political society. Nor did the conduct of government require the services of an educated elite. "The duties of all public offices are, or at least admit of being made, so plain and simple that men of intelligence may readily qualify themselves for their performance."[4] In practice Jackson refrained from authorizing sweeping changes in personnel for the purpose of rewarding friends and punishing enemies, but he defended the spoils system in principle against the traditional ideal of government by a virtuous and talented elite. His argument was taken by genteel opponents to mean that the age had passed when the patrician

Republic of Virtue and Talents was held as a high ideal and that the debased democratic age of the unlettered common man was at hand.

Jackson's administration got off to a memorable start with an inauguration celebration that was overwhelmed by thousands of uncouth, uninvited supporters who caused much property damage in the White House before the premises were cleared by opening the windows and laying out tubs of punch on the lawn. To hostile observers that vulgar episode fit all too well with the President's subsequent defense of the spoils system. Otherwise Jackson's conduct in office, although assertive, gave his opponents little cause for alarm until 1832, when he vetoed a bill to extend the charter of Nicholas Biddle's Bank of the United States. The bank bill veto bristled with ideology, attacking monopolists and other vested interests, including those of sinister foreign investors, who sought to bend the government to their selfish purposes. Against this money power Jackson presented himself as the representative and champion of the nation's humble working people. In the election of 1832, Henry Clay campaigned in support of the bank against Jackson and followed John Quincy Adams down to devastating defeat.

Following his second triumph at the polls, Jackson conducted a ceremonial tour of the nation, just as Washington and Monroe had done during their presidencies. Washington had made his tour early in his second administration, as Jackson did; Monroe had done so shortly after taking office in 1817, amid the lingering afterglow of the Battle of New Orleans and the Peace of Ghent. Monroe's warmly welcomed state visits to the populous northern regions of the Republic remained recent enough to offer a contrast to that of Jackson sixteen years later. Monroe's tour had been an unqualified triumph for himself personally and for the Republican system he presided over. Monroe was a courteous Virginia gentleman who, according to Abigail Adams, had captivated everyone by his "agreeable affability," his "unassuming manners," and "his polite attentions to all orders and ranks." His Northern tour attracted large and enthusiastic crowds at every stop, but the climax of adulation had come in Federalist Boston, where an estimated forty thousand had lined the streets to view his progress to Boston Common. On his last day of the week spent in Boston, Monroe visited the Boston Athenaeum and afterward drove to

Harvard, where he was awarded an honorary doctor of laws degree. That evening he dined at Braintree with former president John Adams, who had invited forty other guests. Altogether, it remained a notable event in the annals of Boston. A local newspaper improved on the occasion by coining a phrase, declaring that Monroe's visit signaled "an era of good feelings" in the republic.[5]

When Jackson paid his state visit to the northern cities in 1833, still larger crowds cheered him all along the way. In New York, according to Philip Hone,

> Broadway from the Battery to the Park formed a solid mass of men, women, and children, who greeted their favorite with cheers, shouts, and waving of handkerchiefs. . . . The President is the most popular man we have ever known. Washington was not so much so . . . he was superior to the homage of the populace, too dignified, too grave for their liking, and men could not approach him with familiarity. Here is a man who suits them exactly. He has a kind expression for each—the same for all, no doubt, but each thinks it intended for himself.

Hone recalled that President John Quincy Adams had occasionally visited New York, and although the newspapers announced his visits, "no huzzas rent the air when he made his appearance," though he was

> in all the qualifications which constitute his fittness to fill the office of a ruler of this great republic, twenty times superior to Jackson. . . . Adams is the wisest man, the best scholar, the most accomplished statesman; but Jackson has most tact. So huzza for Jackson![6]

In Boston, Jackson was as attractive to the populace as he was elsewhere. To the Whig political leadership, he was an embarrassment. He was anathema to the Boston merchant gentry following his veto of the bank bill, but he was also President of the United States and the one who recently had vindicated the union against South Carolina nullification. The memory of Monroe's visit was still green in Boston, and it had established precedents that would unavoidably apply to Jackson's visit. The Harvard Corporation met and concluded that since Monroe had been awarded an honorary degree under the same circumstances, it would be necessary to confer an identical degree upon President Jackson. President

Josiah Quincy of Harvard was an archconservative who continued to identify himself as "Federalist" in politics until his death in 1861, but he had trained himself to be a professional politician in a way that John Quincy Adams never wished to be, and he was capable of doing what had to be done in practical affairs. One thing Quincy had to do was to visit John Quincy Adams and prepare him for the fact that he would receive an invitation to attend the ceremonies. Adams informed Quincy that Jackson's ungentlemanly conduct toward him during and after the election of 1828 had been such as to prevent him from accepting the invitation. Adams informed Quincy, according to his diary account,

> Independent of that, as myself an affectionate child of our Alma Mater, I would not be present to witness her disgrace in conferring her highest literary honors upon a barbarian who could not write a sentence of grammar and hardly could spell his own name.

Quincy had admitted that Jackson was "utterly unworthy of literary honors" but said it had to be done and went ahead and did it, with the professional cooperation of his fellow Brahmin politicians Edward Everett and Daniel Webster.[7]

◈ II ◈

AFTER TWENTY-FOUR YEARS of one-party rule by the Virginia dynasty, which was returned to office quadrennially by nominations of the Republican congressional caucus, a second two-party system emerged, beginning with the free-for-all campaign of 1824 and culminating in the Log Cabin and Hard Cider campaign of 1840. In 1824 a great reservoir of votes existed in the states that had not found their voice in Monroe's uncontested election four years earlier, and the new two-party system began with the discovery of Andrew Jackson's drawing power in this potential electorate. Martin Van Buren and other professional politicians organized a new party in Congress and throughout the states, based upon Jackson's popularity, that swept John Quincy Adams from office in 1828 and overwhelmed Henry Clay in 1832. In the years of Jackson's second administration, those who had lost ground to his party organized an opposing Whig

Party. With no acceptable national candidate in 1836, the Whigs put forward favorite sons in the hope of depriving the Democratic candidate, Van Buren, of a majority in the electoral college. They failed in this, but the election revealed a popular old military hero among the Whigs—William Henry Harrison, who had successfully fought back a Shawnee attack at the Battle of Tippecanoe in 1811. Behind Harrison the Whig Party won in 1840, in the first campaign to draw substantially on the voting potential of the nation.

Politics had been a dirty business during the era of the Federalist-Republican two-party system, marked by exchanges of scurrilous slanders against candidates in rival newspapers and by skulduggery at the voting places. These unsavory practices had continued at the state and local levels throughout the so-called era of good feelings that Monroe presided over to 1825. With a return to the two-party system, presidential campaigns again became mud-slinging matches, none more so than the campaign of 1828, where the past sexual conduct of the candidates' wives was among the personal issues raised by both sides. Plainly, the two-party system did not provide a political mechanism suitable for promoting a Republic of Virtue and Talents. It was recognized that the overriding motive of both parties was the quest for office and the spoils of office. Few believed that the two-party system could fulfill or further America's constitutional blueprint in the years when the system was taking form.

Parties competed by pandering to masses of voters who, judging from electioneering methods, were assumed to be ignorant and gullible. It might be supposed that those repelled by these widespread practices might have been alienated from the republic that encouraged them. Not so at all. While politics remained a dirty business, political leaders like Webster, Clay, Calhoun, and Jackson remained heroes to their supporters. Nor did the squalor of politics bring into question the grandeur of the republic itself. James Russell Lowell advised Henry James in later years that James had erred in depicting a fictional American of the early republic as being embarrassed by his nationality while abroad in Europe.

> Americans of that generation [Lowell explained] hadn't that snobbish shamefacedness about their country—and especially if they were well-born as you represent W. to have been. It is a vice of the *nuova gente* altogether. The older men took their country as naturally as they did a

sunrise. There was no question . . . as to whether their country were the best in the world or no—they *knew* it was.

Speaking as a patriotic intellectual, however, Lowell found it "not real paradox to affirm that a man's love of his country may often be gauged by his disgust in it."[8]

Arthur M. Schlesinger Jr.'s *Age of Jackson* (1945) proposed that the second-party system opposed a Democratic Party of the people to a Whig Party of property. Subsequent studies substantially demolished this thesis by documenting varying economic-social alignments of the two parties from state to state and an overall pattern in both parties of political control in the hands of men of wealth. Nevertheless, the idea that the Jacksonians were more democratic than the Whigs was shared by supporters of both parties at the time and was expressed in the rhetoric of contemporary political campaigns.

Neither Democrat nor Whig adopted an ideology that overtly abandoned virtue and wisdom in favor of popularity. The Jacksonians in the midst of commercial and industrial change defended ancient republican virtues against the machinations of the "money power," which for them was incarnate in the Bank of the United States. Social philosophers of the democracy did, however, embody wisdom and virtue in the will of the people more positively and explicitly than appears in the writings of Jefferson. A romantically unequivocal statement of this ideology was voiced by George Bancroft at the outset of his dual career as historian and Democratic Party bureaucrat. In an address delivered at Williams College in 1835 titled "The Office of the People in Art, Government and Religion," Bancroft argued the transcendental superiority of the democratic mind over the mind of the educated elite.

> There is a *spirit in man*; not in the privileged few. . . . The spirit, which is the guide to truth, is the gracious gift to each member of the human family. . . . Beauty, like truth and justice, lives within us. . . . [W]ho are the best judges in matters of taste? Do you think the cultivated individual? Undoubtedly not; but the collective mind. . . . In like manner the best government rests on the people and not on the few. . . . It is when the multitude give counsel, that right purposes find safety; theirs is the fixedness that cannot be shaken; theirs is the understanding that exceeds wisdom.[9]

This romantic collective mind of the people provided the grand theme for Bancroft's history of American settlement and struggle for independence and nationhood, published in ten volumes over a forty-year period beginning in 1834. During that period, Bancroft served as collector of the Port of Boston under Van Buren, secretary of the navy and minister to England under Polk, and presidential advisor and minister to Germany under Andrew Johnson. "Office of the People" based its argument upon a transcendental conception of reason, absorbed by Bancroft at Göttingen, very like the one that Emerson arrived at through Carlyle and Coleridge, following his earlier study of Dugald Stewart.

Like the Democrats the Whigs appealed to ancient virtues as their guide to political conduct in a changing society. But where Democrats pursued egalitarian themes, Whig arguments tended to be traditionally elitist, continuing in the English country party tradition of civic humanism, as embodied in John Quincy Adams's Republic of Virtues and Talents and argued by Daniel Webster, William Henry Seward, and other Whigs directly out of classical texts from Harrington and Bolingbroke. The paternalism of eighteenth-century Whiggery echoed in the principles and practices of American Whigs from the 1830s until absorbed into the very different rhetoric of the fledgling Republican Party. Certainly, it was absent from the rhetoric of Abraham Lincoln. Both Democrats and Whigs laid claim to the principles of the Revolutionary Founders in coping with the problems and opportunities of an enterprising capitalist society.[10]

If, as Schlesinger argued, the nation's literary intellectuals rallied to the support of the Jacksonians, this was in part because Jacksonian populism made a stronger emotional appeal to literati than the Whig claim to represent the nation's cultural as well as economic elite. Even in Boston, where Daniel Webster commanded the party of the gentry, Jacksonians appealed to a distinguished minority of Brahmins—Bancroft, Nathaniel Hawthorne, and George Ripley among them—for whom the Democratic Party expressed America's democratic genius. Emerson was loath to accept Bancroft's interpretation of Jackson as a divine instrument of the collective mind. To Carlyle he wrote of Jackson that "a most unfit man in the presidency has been doing the worst things."[11] Yet Emerson, like other major writers, was ambitious to express the spirit of his age, which he knew to be democratic. Publicly he split the difference between the parties, asserting that "one has the best cause, and the other contains the best men." He accepted the superior egalitarianism of the Democratic Party, "facilitating in every manner the access of the young and the poor to sources of wealth and power." But Daniel Webster remained his political hero, until Webster delivered his traumatic "Seventh of March Speech," defending the fugitive slave bill in 1850.[12]

During Van Buren's administration, certain of Emerson's public statements encouraged Bancroft, Orestes Brownson, and other literary Jacksonians to suspect that the gentle philosopher of Concord was on the verge of committing himself to the party of the people. But Emerson was privately of a very different mind. Following the Log Cabin and Hard Cider Campaign of 1840, he wrote his brother William:

> I am but an indifferent Whig & do not care for Mr. Harrison, but since the election of J. Q. Adams I do not remember any national event that has given me so much content as this general uprising to unseat Mr. Van Buren and his government.

So much for the hopes of Bancroft and of literary New Yorkers as well that Emerson was entering their camp. Though he saw no good reason to take public issue with his Jacksonian friends, Emerson privately looked upon Jackson's party as a national disgrace. On the eve of the election of 1832 he confided to his journal: "Yet seemeth it to me that we shall all feel dirty if Jackson is reelected."[13]

<h2 style="text-align:center">∾ III ∾</h2>

UNTIL THE BANK BILL VETO upset their complacency, literary gentlemen in Philadelphia achieved a dignified and constructive modus vivendi with the increasingly democratic republic. Pennsylvania consistently cast its vote for the more democratic presidential candidate, producing no serious contender of its own until James Buchanan; Philadelphians were thus spared the welter of disturbing ambitions and machinations that surrounded favorite-son politics in Virginia, Massachusetts, New York, and elsewhere. The characteristically Pennsylvanian contribution to national statesmanship had been the financial role created by Robert Morris, Thomas Willing, and William Bingham during the Revolutionary era and adapted to Jeffersonian Republicanism by Albert Gallatin, Alexander James Dallas, and Richard Rush. In appointing Nicholas Biddle to the board of the second Bank of the United States, Monroe was following an already established tradition of reliance upon the services of politically liberal and financially respectable Pennsylvanians.

Under these circumstances the city's leading literary lawyer-businessmen enjoyed comfortable social relationships that were seldom disturbed by political differences. During the harmonious early decades of the nineteenth century, members of this gentry tended to move closer to one another in a residential area that straddled Chestnut Street. Old and recently arrived denizens of this neighborhood included Robert Vaux; John Vaughan, who hosted a regular literary soirée; Robert Waln, a Quaker merchant who became locally prominent in polite letters; Caspar Wistar of the Philosophical Society and the Wistar Parties, who moved to the area in 1814; the lawyer William Meredith, who had been Joseph Dennie's closest friend; Charles Jared Ingersoll; Horace Binney; Alexander James Dallas; and William Tilghman, the chief justice of the state supreme court.[14]

This era of brotherly love ended with Jackson's attack on the Bank of the United States and its parent bank in Philadelphia. Under pressure of the Bank War, Biddle, Horace Binney, and other supporters of the Bank of Philadelphia sought to destroy the standings of those longtime associates who now opposed them on this issue. Biddle and Robert Vaux were members of the older gentry who had cooperated cordially for a generation in a variety of civic philanthropic enterprises, but in 1834 Biddle's circle ejected Vaux from office in one community organization after another: the State Temperance Society, the Institution of the Blind, the Apprentices Library Company, and the Pennsylvania Hospital. "Now for the first time since this was a city," Vaux declared, "do we find intolerance brought into the affairs of scientific & charitable bodies."[15]

The Biddle circle ousted Richard Rush from the American Philosophical Society and blackballed a candidate whom Charles Jared Ingersoll put up for membership. Then, as Biddle's countermeasures against Jackson depressed Philadelphia's economy, leading supporters of Biddle turned on him, Binney now finding Biddle to have been "entirely deficient in details . . . destitude in capacity . . . a very vain man."[16] The Bank War disrupted Philadelphia's comfortably civilized community to its pre-Revolutionary roots. Later the controversy over slavery would open new wounds in the Quaker City, but not with the savagery of the Philadelphia Bank War.

Literary society appeared to survive by the law of inertia in the conservative Philadelphia circles associated with the Wistar Parties, the Walsh Soirees, and later the Carey Vespers, conducted by the publisher-economist Henry C. Carey. Initiated by Caspar Wistar, physician and president of the American Philosophical Society, the Wistar parties survived their founder's death under the aegis of the Wistar Association. As the Wistar parties survived Wistar, so did the Carey Vespers survive Carey. In addition, during Carey's lifetime a group of Philadelphia men met at his house every Sunday afternoon—until reduced in number to four members with a combined age of 351 years. Carey joined another group of twelve men for dinner once a year. Surviving the other eleven, Carey continued to hold the annual dinner alone until he himself died in 1879.[17]

In science Philadelphia remained at the forefront with the founding of the Academy of Natural Science in 1812 and the Franklin Institute in 1824. In literature it drifted to the rear, despite its continued leadership of the magazine and publishing businesses well into the nineteenth century. The literary-intellectual outlook of Philadelphia revealed itself pointedly in 1842 on the occasion of Charles Dickens' celebrated trip to America. While Boston and New York outdid themselves in welcoming this popular literary lion, literary Philadelphia, thoroughly Anglophile though it was, extended no civic invitation to him, and Dickens passed unheralded through the city on his way west.

In 1842 James Russell and Maria White Lowell honeymooned in Philadelphia, where Maria was acquainted with Quaker abolitionists from a previous visit. Lowell found Maria's friends pleasant and kind but "proportionately narrow compared with our New England breadth which God knows is narrow enough." Lowell required harsher words to describe the city's most venerable scientific circle, the Wistar Club. Invited to a club meeting by a distant relative, Lowell was "hideously struck by the want of intellect" among its members.[18] However, modern science was no more Lowell's forte than modern literature and criticism were the forte of the Wistar membership. In the years after the Lowells' honeymoon visit, Philadelphia's scientific intellectuals joined with like-minded intellectuals in the Middle Atlantic states to take on Massachusetts' literati in a contest over the proposed Smithsonian Institution. At stake was the very nature of the new national institution. Debate hinged on the meaning of *science*, a term whose connotations were becoming more focused during the early decades of the nineteenth century as modern paradigms of knowing and knowledge emerged. In 1826, when the English chemist James Smithson bequeathed a fortune to found an institution in Washington, D.C., "for the increase & diffusion of knowledge among men," *science* was still broadly construed to encompass many kinds of knowing, including those based in intuitive expression rather than experimental method. Empirical and inductive science had long been known as *natural* philosophy, to distinguish it from other, often more deductive ways of knowing, among them mathematical proofs and the pure reason of Kant's transcendental philosophy.

Once the least practical of the higher studies, by 1840, when the word *scientist* was coined in England, the branch of natural philosophy called physical science was already well known for the far-reaching utility of its results. But during the eighteenth century advances had also been seen in other areas of human inquiry, not least in the political sphere, where rhetoric, forensic science, and political science had given birth to forms of public discourse and legal mechanisms suitable for governing a democratic republic. It was thus with a sense of indignation rather than apology that congressional advocates for a Smithsonian Institution honored humanistic learning. Their leader in the Senate was the distinguished lawyer, colorful orator, and classical scholar Rufus Choate of Massachusetts. Choate objected to any definition of *knowledge* (the goal of science) that limited the term to the objects of natural philosophy. "This is knowledge, to be sure," Choate observed, "but it is not all knowledge, nor half of it, nor the best of it." Choate fought vainly to "vindicate art, taste, learning, genius, mind, history, ethnology, morals—against sociologists, chemists, & catchers of extinct skunks."[19]

Following his retirement from Congress in 1845, Choate urged Charles W. Upham, a Unitarian minister turned congressman from Massachusetts, to pursue the fight in the lower house. Upham chose to advance the literati's cause by playing the role of a strict constructionist. "The word *science*," Upham warned, "is getting to be quite generally used to denote what are called the physical sciences, excluding the political, moral, and intellectual science—excluding history, the arts and all general literature." When Smithson stipulated that his bequest be used to increase and diffuse "knowledge among men," Upham averred, he intended the broader construal of *knowledge* that was characteristic of his time. By extension, Smithson likewise would have expected science to comprise more than physical knowledge. Smithson therefore would have been surprised by the narrowing of meaning and astonished by the restrictions now being urged upon the disposition of his bequest.[20]

The law Congress enacted in 1846 was a compromise of sorts, but a rather poor one for Upham and the literati. Though their interests were not entirely ignored in the institution's mandate, they were addressed in the most general terms: the Smithsonian would include a "library composed of valuable works pertaining to all departments of human knowledge." As a sop, Choate was made trustee-at-large of the Smithsonian. In contrast, the act explicitly authorized the construction of a chemical laboratory, lecture rooms, a museum of "objects of art and of foreign and curious research." Most importantly, it vested the power to name the Smithsonian's head in Alexander Bache, a great-grandson of Benjamin Franklin and professor of physical science at the University of Pennsylvania. For administrator of the Smithsonian, Bache chose another physicist, the distinguished Joseph Henry of Princeton University. Henry's researches were fundamental to the development of the electromagnet and its practical applications (the basic unit of electrical inductance, the *henry*, takes his name), and he had no doubt that, so long as scientific research was freely shared, it would work far more effectively on mankind's behalf than any number of essays, novels, or epic poems. Accordingly, in his first report to the board of regents, Henry outlined a program for the Smithsonian that allocated all of the institution's operating budget for basic research and publication to make freely available the results of research.

The founding of the Smithsonian Institution in 1846 as a scientists' preserve demonstrated beyond the confines of the academy that the physical sciences had seceded from the Republic of Letters and that most literary men were willing to see them go. Interest in scientific subjects re mained keen among educated Americans, as was evidenced by the huge popularity of scientific lectures at the Lowell Institute in Boston and the Franklin Institute in Philadelphia. However, attendance at such lectures could only serve to impress upon the intelligent layman the increasing distance between the specialized world of the adepts, who consented to popularize their subjects for the many, and the broader world of those liberally educated men who had passed through a laboratory-free natural philosophy course to acquire a nodding acquaintance with the physical sciences on the way to their bachelor of arts degrees.

The literati might or might not keep abreast of major scientific developments and incorporate new findings into their own worldviews. Edgar Allen Poe was among those who attempted to do this by studying the writings of Newton, Laplace, Alexander von Humboldt, and others in a systematic effort to understand the universe. Yet Poe did not become a scientist, as Franklin, Jefferson, and other enlightened American men of letters had in the previous century. Nor was acquaintance with the works of leading scientists necessarily helpful to Poe's reputation as a literary intellectual. Senator Choate had spoken for a good many literary gentlemen when he asserted that science, narrowly defined, omitted the better part of knowledge. Literary intellectuals would continue to pursue the best of it, leaving the scientific intellectuals to their increasingly arcane researches.

⟣ IV ⟢

LITERARY MEN OF NEW YORK bruised themselves in the Bank War and in other political and literary encounters. It went with the territory. William Cullen Bryant was a poet, not a fighter. But when a rival editor slandered him, he was talked into defending his honor in the New York manner by confronting the villain and giving him a public thrashing. The villain, after sustaining several blows, took Bryant's whip away and left with it, while Mayor Philip Hone viewed the sidewalk scene from his front window with the contempt appropriate to an anti-Jackson gentleman. Several years later Bryant directed a campaign against the Bank of the United States in his *Evening Post* that was sufficiently offensive to cost him for a time his friendship with Gulian Verplanck. Bryant tired of the campaign after a year of it, and he turned the paper over to his more robustly belligerent assistant editor, William Leggett (who had talked him into the whipping encounter), and escaped to Europe for an extended visit.[21]

Bryant, Leggett, Theodore Sedgwick Jr., and other writers for the *Evening Post* played a major role in formulating Locofoco economic theory, the antibank, antimonopoly, antitariff doctrine that assumed the guise of Jacksonian radicalism and aroused emotional opposition from conservative quarters. The Locofocos advocated equality of economic opportunity against special privilege, pressing for passage of uniform incorporation laws in banking, for instance. Locofocos believed that any group of men who met certain uniform qualifications should be allowed to enter into banking wherever they chose to without being required to obtain a special charter from the legislature or to respect the special conditions that other banks had obtained in their charters. The Locofocos' ideas aroused passionate controversy during the long, hard depression of 1837, which consumed the entire administration of New York's first U.S. president, Martin Van Buren. Yet sociability was as characteristic of New York's literati as infighting and catcalling. Hone and Bryant remained on speaking terms and furthermore shared a sense of loyalty to their disorderly city that was also characteristic of the New York literati.[22]

The Whig Party discovered a worthy political-literary antagonist to Bryant and his *Evening Post* in Horace Greeley of the weekly *New-Yorker*, later of the daily and weekly editions of the *Tribune*. Arriving in New York City from upper New England with some newspaper experience, twenty-three-year-old Greeley started the *New-Yorker* in 1834 as "A weekly Journal of Literature, Politics, Statistics and General Intelligence," assisted by three other newcomers to the city: Park Benjamin from Massachusetts, who went on to a varied editorial career; Rufus W. Griswold from Philadelphia, who became an editor, anthologist, and arbiter of American verse; and Henry J. Raymond from western New York, who founded the *New York Times* in 1851. Greeley's staunch and pungently expressed Whig views on tariffs, banks, internal improvements, and other issues impressed Thurlow Weed, William Seward, and other New York Whigs, who arranged for Greeley to edit a campaign paper in the election year 1840. A year later Greeley merged that paper with the *New-Yorker* and another weekly into the *Weekly Tribune*, which from the outset enjoyed a large circulation, making Greeley perhaps the best known and most popular writer of the day throughout rural America. At the same time, Greeley started the daily *Tribune*, which argued Whig issues and advocated a wide range of humanitarian reforms and utopian projects, running a daily column by the Fourierist utopian Albert Brisbane, hiring transcendentalists Margaret Fuller and George Ripley as reporters, and taking Karl Marx on as a columnist. The literary-political contests of the *Post* and the *Tribune* remained a continuing New York attraction, even after both papers ended up together in the 1850s on the side of antislavery and the Republican Party.[23]

In 1837 a New York literary lawyer, John L. O'Sullivan, joined with his brother-in-law Samuel D. Langtree to begin the *United States Monthly and Democratic Review*. The monthly periodical was founded to advance the cause of democratic letters, much as Joseph Dennie had years earlier established a viable literary magazine, the *Port Folio*, by advancing the cause of *anti* democratic letters. For decades the *Port Folio* had enjoyed the distinction of being the only literary journal in America to survive financially without relying upon love stories to attract female readers in the manner of *Knickerbocker*, which Langtree had briefly edited. The *Democratic Review* countered such sentimentality with content that promoted red-blooded male loyalty to America's destiny, to American literature, to democratic principles, and to the Democratic Party. Its informing purpose would, according to the editors, give a "vast circulation" to a journal containing "nothing but matter of distinguished excellence."[24]

O'Sullivan was an ardent admirer of Nathaniel Hawthorne, whose first collection of stories, *Twice-Told Tales*, appeared in 1837, and he wanted the *Democratic Review* to "afford Mr. Hawthorne what he has not had before, a field for the exercise of his pen, and the acquisition of distinction worthy of the high prominence" of his writings. In line with its democratic theme, the magazine was initially published in Washington, D.C., during the Van Buren administration. Following Van Buren's defeat in 1840, it suspended publication for six months while O'Sullivan relocated to New York; there the review continued publication until the eve of the Civil War. The years of its major literary influence were those under O'Sullivan's editorship, which continued until 1846.

A spread-eagled nationalist who coined the phrase *manifest destiny*, O'Sullivan sought submissions from all who reflected credit upon American literature and were not overtly opposed to democracy. His natural alliance in New York was with Evert Duyckinck's Young American circle of patriotic Democrats; and Duyckinck and William A. Jones remained the leading contributors to the columns of literary criticism in the *Democratic Review* until 1848, when they acquired a more genteel, less contentious vehicle of their own in *Literary World*. Bryant contributed also, as did his associates on the *Evening Post* William Leggett and Parke Godwin. Another newspaperman, Walter Whitman, contributed eight stories that emulated Hawthorne's manner while expressing convictions very like those of the young America circle.

O'Sullivan was also attracting contributions from New England writers, beginning with Hawthorne and George Bancroft and in time including Whittier, Emerson, and Thoreau. This penetration of the Brahmin community created bitter feelings in Boston. John Quincy Adams, who had helped launch Dennie's *Port Folio* in 1801 with his account of travels in Silesia, turned down O'Sullivan's invitation to contribute to the new *Democratic Review* by brusquely paraphrasing his father: "literature . . . must always be aristocratic; the democracy of numbers and literature [are] self-contradictory." Longfellow, who preferred not to mix politics with poetry, wrote a friend in 1839 of the *Democratic Review* that the "*Loco-focos* are organizing a new politico-literary system," which praises Locofoco authors but speaks "coolly of, if they do not abuse, every other. They puff *Bryant* loud and long; likewise my good friend Hawthorne." When Brahmin George Sumner published an article on Greece in O'Sullivan's magazine, he found that "because that article appeared in the *Democratic Review* it is trodden under foot, and I am denounced as 'an Administration man.'" George Ticknor told Sumner he "was sorry to see it in such company"; Joseph Story was "troubled"; Sumner's brother Charles regretted George's connection with such a "leaky craft"; and Nathan Hale refused to reprint the article in his Boston *Daily Advertiser*. "God *damn* them all!!!" wrote George Sumner, "and yet I cannot but laugh, roars of horrid laughter, on thinking of all these things."[25]

Orestes Brownson joined his *Boston Quarterly Review* with the *Democratic* in 1842 but separated the next year over disagreements on political policy. In general, the mixing of politics and literature became increasingly difficult with the approach of the Mexican War. In 1846 O'Sullivan was forced to sell out, and with his departure went most of the contributors who had given the magazine its literary distinction. Its success had by then brought a rival into the field, the *American Review: A Whig Journal of Politics, Literature, Art and Science*, which continued from 1845 to the Whig debacle of 1856. Edited by a Yale graduate, George H. Colton, the *Whig Review*, as it was called, included fiction and verse by leading writers, including Poe and Lowell, Whig-oriented literary and art criticism by Henry T. Tuckerman and others, and political essays by Daniel Webster, Edward Everett, John C. Calhoun, Horace Greeley, and Henry Raymond. Old John Quincy Adams, whose sympathy for the Whigs overcame any reservations, was contributing to the *Whig Review* just before his death in 1848.

Lewis Gaylord Clark's monthly *Knickerbocker* magazine remained apolitical in content but implicitly Whiggish in its editorial tone. The enemies Clark made tended to be in the camp of the Democratic Party, especially including the "Young America" expansionists and literary nationalists. Chief among his enemies was the New York literary critic and editor Evert Augustus Duyckinck. The well-to-do son of a leading New York bookseller, Duyckinck had attended Columbia and taken the grand tour before settling down to the life of a literary gentleman in New York. The nucleus of his circle was a small group of Columbia men who formed themselves into the Tetractys Club, including William A. Jones, a leading literary critic, and Cornelius Mathews, a widely ridiculed playwrite, novelist, and critic whom Duyckinck doggedly defended for years. Together these three men edited *Arcturus: A Journal of Books and Opinion*, which sustained a brilliant but brief career in 1840–42. In 1847 Duyckinck returned with a weekly, *Literary World*, that ended in 1853 as a semiannual publication. Duyckinck edited other periodicals briefly and later exerted influence over literature as a literary critic and as an editor for the publishing houses G. P. Putnam & Son and John Wiley.[26]

It was by his reputation as New York's leading gentleman of letters among the magazinists that the honorable and friendly Duyckinck distinguished himself. Lowell wrote of him in *A Fable for Critics*:

I'm happy to meet
With a scholar so ripe, and a critic so neat,
Who through Grub Street the soul of a gentleman carries.

Mathews, on the other hand, Lowell depicted as "a small man in glasses" who followed a few steps behind, "dodging about, muttering, 'Murderers! asses!'" The southern novelist and poet William Gilmore Simms later consoled Duyckinck for the failure of *Literary World*, arguing that it had been too gentlemanly for New York. "For tastes, such as yours & the tone & temper of such a work you required a *select* circle; and the proportion of refined in New York to the bulk of the population was too small to give you such a circle."[27] The avuncular Duyckinck became the presiding figure in a widening circle of Lewis Gaylord Clark's literary enemies. Besides Jones and Mathews this circle included Poe as well as Simms, who traveled to New York from Charleston almost annually to oversee the publication of his numerous literary works and to escape the South Carolina summers. As editor of the *Southern Literary Messenger*, Poe had dealt savagely with a novel by Simms; Simms had done much the same to Mathews. Yet against the clever, pretentious, vindictive, conniving, aggrandizing Clark, the truculent trio made common cause.

The columns of the *Democratic Review, Arcturus, Literary World*, and some other New York periodicals were home to the Young America school of criticism, united by its central theme of the democratic spirit in literature. William A. Jones was perhaps the most prolific and representative member of this school, which included Duyckinck, O'Sullivan, William Leggett, and Park Godwin. The periodicals that ran these reviews tended to share a New Yorkish animus against straitlaced Boston; yet the literary credo they espoused elevated Boston's poets to the pinnacle of critical estimation of literature. Poetry for the Young America school represented both the highest and the most typical and democratic form of literature. A critic for the *Democratic Review*—probably Leggett—asserted that

All poetry, indeed, is essentially democratic. . . . Poetry can never be made the instrument of oppression, and the poetry of England, in particular, has gloriously contributed to swell the mighty current of democratic feeling which is now spreading over the world.

Most leading American poets were New Englanders, and their writings displayed the New Englander's love of ideas, "the predominance of intellect." Among this group, according to an 1847 *Democratic Review* essay, "First, by right undeniable, we have placed the name of RALPH WALDO EMERSON, whom there is little risk in pronouncing the most original, not only of American poets, but of living writers."[28]

Glorious as was Emerson in their view, Young America critics were on the lookout for a "great Poet of the People," a "world-renowned bard," a "Homer of the mass." One candidate that appeared to be a possibility to Jones was John Greenleaf Whittier, chiefly based upon Whittier's 1850 collection *Songs of Labor.*[29] An occasional contributor of fiction to *Democratic Review* and peripheral member of the Young America circle, the young printer-editor Walter Whitman must surely have been influenced by this company to envision himself as the coming Homer of the mass. But when *Leaves of Grass* appeared in 1855, it was ignored or condemned by these same Young America critics while being discovered and praised by Emerson and Charles Eliot Norton of Boston.

V

YOUNG AMERICA WAS NOT altogether misled in heralding Emerson as a poet of the democratic spirit, even though Emerson, the birthright Federalist-Whig-Republican, concealed from them his antipathy to Jackson, and Van Buren, and the Democratic Party. To the extent that Emerson articulated a political theory, his views were closer Jefferson's than to those of any Federalist or Whig Party spokesman. He believed that the best government was the one that governed least, that the best society was the one closest to the soil.

> Where the statesman plows
> Furrow for the wheat,—
> When the Church is social worth,
> When the state-house is the hearth,
> Then the perfect State is come,
> The Republican at home.[30]

To the extent that Emerson held an economic theory, he believed that "Gold and Iron are good / To buy iron and gold" and good for no more than that; a coercive institution like the Bank of the United States, in Emerson's view, imposed unworthy restraints upon individual liberty.

Brahmin Boston as a whole was politically Whig as a matter of course. One was not expected to be politically active on behalf of the Whig Party, but to take up cudgels for the Democrats as Bancroft and Hawthorne did, was considered an offense to civilized values, and Bancroft particularly faced ostracism as a consequence. Hawthorne was less affected by his political deviance, having lived only briefly in Boston while serving as a weigher in the customhouse during Van Buren's administration. Besides this, Hawthorne was not very sociable by nature, and his rising literary reputation abroad won him respect among Brahmins. When the Saturday Club formed, Hawthorne was its lone Democrat.

The generation of Boston Brahmins that included George Ticknor, Josiah Quincy, and Andrews Norton responded to Jacksonian Democracy by maintaining their standards—literary, political, and social—against all democrats and reformers through the power of ostracism, such as it was. That their effort might be a losing one certainly occurred to them as they observed changes in the nation's political discourse and the emergence of a subversive younger generation at Harvard. Ticknor remembered all his life the sense of "evil foreboding" that the mathematician and astronomer Nathaniel Bowditch conveyed to him one day in the early 1830s when Bowditch observed

> in a manner so impressive that I remember the spot where I stood, and rarely pass it without recalling the circumstances, "We are living in the best days of the republic."[31]

The rising younger generation of Brahmins was not generally disposed to contest the Whig Party, but its members did tend to respond to the reforming spirit of the age, unlike the old guard. This responsiveness took a largely literary form in the case of Emerson; among his friends it manifested itself in two movements, one for utopian communitarianism and one for humanitarian reform. Both utopianism and humanitarianism were associated with the Whig Party nationally as well as in Massachusetts, and both were implicitly critical of Jacksonian democracy. The Jacksonians typically stood for free enterprise and a society in which the rise of the common man would not be impeded by forces of monopoly and special privilege. Utopian communitarians argued, to the contrary, that better forms of society might be achieved through cooperation rather than competition. Criticism of Jacksonian democracy was even more pronounced among humanitarian reformers. The objects of their solicitude were defenseless members of society, over whom the indiscrimate egalitarianism of the Jacksonians tended to run roughshod: the lame, the blind, the insane, the uneducated, and increasingly the enslaved, whose masters held the upper hand in the Democratic Party.

During the Revolutionary era, humanitarian reform had drawn its inspiration from the ethical rights idealism embodied in the Declaration of Independence. The main center for these reform movements had been Philadelphia, where they were enlightened by the Quaker spirit of brotherly love. During the democratic era that emerged a half a century after the Revolution, Quakers remained prominent in humanitarian reform, along with natural rights idealists, but the newest inspiration to improve the condition of mankind was the spirit of perfectionism that swept through both the evangelical and liberal churches alike, professing faith in the perfectability of the individual and the perfectability of society as well. An emergent center for this second great wave of humanitarian reform was Boston, where the Unitarian Church offered a philosophy of reform and provided leadership in the fields of education, women's rights, treatment of the insane and of the blind, as well as leadership in the two predominant movements of temperance and abolition.[32]

The romantic spirit of immediatist, millennialist perfectionism revived reform movements that had originated during the Revolutionary era and transformed the evangelical societies that had organized since the War of 1812 to restore clerical authority over the threatened moral order. The Bible Society, the Tract Society, the Sunday School Union, the Temperance Union, and the Home Missionary Society were among those benevolent societies that had been organized, as the editor of the Boston *Congregationalist*, Edward Beecher, explained in 1835, "To abolish all corruptions in religion, and all abuses in the social system, and, so far as it has been erected on false principles, to take it down and erect it anew."[33]

So revolutionary an undertaking as this could not, as it turned out, be kept securely in the control of the clergy. What emerged was a *religious party*, as Emerson termed it, that imbued the individual with decisive moral authority and brought all social institutions, including the newly created benevolent societies, under the scrutiny of perfectionists, for whom no human institutions were sacred.

In his 1844 lecture "New England Reformers," Emerson drew the attention of his listeners to

> the signs that the Church, or religious party, is falling from the Church nominal, and is appearing in temperance and non-resistance societies; in movements of abolitionists and of socialists; and in very significant assemblies called Sabbath and Bible Conventions; composed of ultraists, of seekers, of all the soul of the soldiery of dissent, and meeting to call in question the authority of the Sabbath, of the priesthood, and of the Church.

In the course of "this din of opinion and debate there was a keener scrutiny of institutions and domestic life than any we had known," and amid "plentiful vaporing, and cases of backsliding," there emerged "the adoption of simpler methods, and an assertion of the sufficiency of the private man."[34] As to the political sufficiency of the private man, Thoreau wrote that "any man more right than his neighbors, constitutes a majority of one already" and need not wait for an actual majority of one to support him and those who support him "before they suffer the right to prevail through them."[35]

Belief in the perfectability of societies led to a wide variety of communitarian experiments during the democratic era. "We are all a little wild here with numberless projects of social reform," Emerson wrote Carlyle in 1840. "Not a reading man but has a draft of a new Community in his waistcoat pocket."[36] Dozens of such communities were operating or in the planning stage at that time. The best known, founded by and for literary intellectuals was Brook Farm, conveniently situated near the western edge of Boston in West Roxbury, Massachusetts. In 1840 its organizer, George Ripley, was attempting to persuade Emerson to cofound the community, as he had joined Riply to cofound the Transcendental Club several years earlier. Emerson valued his privacy too much to exchange it for residence at Brook Farm, but he became a regular visitor from the time it opened in 1841, along with Margaret Fuller, Theodore Parker, Bronson Alcott, Orestes Brownson, and other more conservative Brahmins, a number of whom sent their children to be educated there. Among the most distinguished regular members of Brook Farm were George and Sofia Ripley, Elizabeth Peabody, Nathaniel Hawthorne, and John Sullivan Dwight; younger members who later distinguished themselves in the Republic of Letters included the literary journalists George William Curtis and Parke Godwin, the future editor of the New York *Sun* Charles A. Dana, and the later convert to Catholicism and cofounder of the Paulist Fathers Isaac Thomas Hecker.[37]

Ripley drew upon a variety of contemporary examples in creating "The Brook Farm Institute of Agriculture and Education" as a cooperative society engaged in teaching, farming, and manufacturing. In consultation with Albert Brisbane and Horace Greeley, Ripley converted Brook Farm into a Fourierist phalanx in 1844. In so doing he parted company philosophically with Emerson, who had advised Fourierists and other utopians that

> a grand phalanx of the best of the human race, banded for some catholic object [is] excellent; but remember that no society can ever be so large as one man.[38]

The utopian socialist François-Marie-Charles Fourier had argued that humans have no integral soul but only a partial one and therefore individuals can achieve personal integrity only when banded together with others. Accordingly, at the restructured Brook Farm greater emphasis was placed on the collectivist experience as an end in itself. There was also a sense of being part of a larger movement, functioning internationally according to Fourier's principles. Some members left when this conversion occurred, but most remained until a disastrous fire in 1846 led to the disbanding of the association a year later. By then the vogue for utopian experiments had largely passed for New England intellectuals, who were becoming increasingly drawn to national political issues by the Mexican War, the subsequent cession of western lands, and the question of slavery and its threatened expansion into the newly acquired territories.

New England's fame as a center of mid-nineteenth-century utopianism

rests chiefly upon Brook Farm, despite the fact that Brook Farm was neither a pioneer effort among such communities nor an outstandingly successful example of them. It remains famous because it attracted the New
England literati, who afterward incorporated it into American literature.
Somewhat similarly, the reputation of mid-nineteenth-century New England as a center for humanitarian reform owed much to the association
of the reformers with the literati. Emerson refused to involve himself actively in humanitarian reforms, but his essays on the subject immortalized the New England reformer, three of whom achieved signal prominence and came to personify the movement in standard historical accounts:
Samuel Gridley Howe, Horace Mann, and Dorothea Lynde Dix. Howe
entered upon his career as a reformer when he returned to Boston in 1831,
after serving for six years as a soldier and surgeon in the Greek revolution,
to engage in his life work of educating the blind. Mann abandoned a law
practice and promising political career in 1837 to become secretary of the
newly created Massachusetts Board of Education. In this role he devoted
himself to developing common schools that would adequately educate a
democratic society. Dix entered upon her career to improve treatment of
the insane in 1841, following an initial career as a schoolmistress. Each of
these three reformers became an illustrious example of Thoreau's "majority of one," pursuing reform as a matter of individual commitment.

❦ VI ❦

BOSTON GAVE LITTLE SIGN that it was about to become a center for moral
and antislavery reform at the time William Lloyd Garrison launched his
abolitionist *Liberator* on 1 January 1831. Nor, for that matter, was there
much indication at the time that an emerging literary generation in Boston was about to upset the status quo, contributing to a coming American
renaissance of letters and enabling Boston to rival and then surpass New
York City as a center of this renaissance. On the face of it, Boston in 1831,
together with Josiah Quincy's Harvard, appeared to be, in Emerson's
terms, all "establishment" and no "movement." In literature Boston was
represented by its lone literary periodical, the staid *North American Review*.
In the area of humanitarian reform, Boston, in common with other Ameri-

can cities, supported a number of benevolent societies for widows, paupers, and other distressed members of society, and charitable associations continued to be organized as new social problems arose in the community. However, in 1831 Boston could not rival Quaker Philadelphia as an urban center for humanitarian reform.

The potential of Boston's Unitarian Church for social reform remained as yet largely unrealized. Its foremost minister, William Ellery Channing, internationally distinguished in the fields of theology and literature, had not spoken out on public issues generally or on the antislavery issue particularly. Calvinists then took the lead in social reform efforts. In 1826 the Congregationalist minister Lyman Beecher took a church in Boston to lead the evangelists against the array of Unitarian liberalism. Beecher proceeded to initiate the temperance movement that during the next decade became a seedbed for a wide range of humanitarian reforms, including antislavery reform. It was the evangelical but unclerical—indeed often belligerently anticlerical—Garrison, however, who effectively initiated an era of moral reform in Boston that continued from the 1830s to the Civil War.[39]

Born in Massachusetts, Garrison first came to general notice at age twenty-five when he joined the Quaker Benjamin Lundy in editing an antislavery paper in the slave state Maryland. Imprisoned for libel, Garrison was released through the efforts of a New York merchant and abolitionist sympathizer, Arthur Tappan. Back in Boston, Garrison became a charismatic leader who attracted and retained the personal loyalty of his New England following against antiabolitionists in New England and anti-Garrison abolitionists elsewhere. His movement differed significantly from abolitionist groups emerging in New York, Pennsylvania, Ohio, and other states. The most distinctive tenet of the Garrisonians was *immediatism*, which called for the immediate and unconditional end to slavery in America and attacked abolitionists who wished to work against slavery within the American political system. While the Garrisonians offered no practical means of ending slavery, their incendiary writings and orations won them national attention, especially in the South. Garrisonians dismayed abolitionists elsewhere by integrating their movement racially. Where abolitionist societies outside New England tended to be strictly segregated, Garrison invited blacks into his organization from the outset;

indeed, it was black support that early on provided Garrison his main financial assistance.[40]

Garrison's conception of oppression was broad, his sympathies catholic. In the *Liberator*, he simultaneously pursued temperance reform, women's rights, and the peace movement along with abolition. The columns of the *Liberator* were open to other reforms as well; those who assisted Garrison in getting out the *Liberator* were free to write much as they pleased and to advance causes of personal concern to them. Abolitionists outside New England criticized Garrison for uniting other social causes with antislavery reform rather than concentrating on the single issue of abolition. However, these auxiliary causes, particularly women's rights, positively influenced the development of the Garrisonian movement by attracting the active support of energetic, well-educated, articulate, and socially respectable women in Salem, Boston, and elsewhere. They in turn were apt to be effectively positioned to exert influence upon men of their own class. Wendell Phillips and James Russell Lowell were among the converts to abolitionism who had been encouraged to commit themselves by militantly abolitionist wives or sweethearts.

As the association of abolitionism with women's rights and other causes broadened the basis of support for Garrison among New Englanders, some came to see in Garrison an image of inclusive social idealism. On this basis Garrison was able to appeal more to literary intellectuals than he might have managed to do as a one-issue reformer. At the same time, the ideologically uncompromising if perhaps impractical advocacy of immediate abolition appealed to idealistic intellectuals in New England—increasingly so following the annexation of Texas, the Mexican War, the Mexican cession, and most of all the Compromise of 1850 with its Fugitive Slave Act, committing New Englanders personally to the enforcement of slave society in America.

To be sure, intellectuals outside New England were also attracted to the abolitionist movement and the Garrisonian movement. Surveys of the abolitionist leadership nationally indicated that one-half to two-thirds were college men, with Harvard, Yale, and Oberlin degrees predominating. The typical abolitionist leader was a Protestant from the Northeast, especially New England, who was associated with "one of the professions concerned with the communication of ideas or information." Broadly speaking, this placed the typical abolitionist leader in the class of the nation's intellectuals; yet he might still not be a "reading man" as Emerson used the term to include scholars of widely ranging intellectual interests such as Unitarianism fostered in Boston. The Garrisonian movement notably distinguished itself by the increasing influence it exerted over such literary men and women in New England.[41]

Garrison entered the abolitionist movement at the bidding of the Quaker reformer Benjamin Lundy, and Lundy remained a formative influence upon the Garrisonian movement thereafter. The first American antislavery society had been founded in 1775, and antislavery societies had proliferated in New England, as elsewhere in the nation. Slavery itself was abolished in Massachusetts in 1780. All of that was buried nearly a half century in the past, however, when Benjamin Lundy traveled to Boston in 1828 to give witness against slavery, winning from among his generally hostile listeners one major convert in William Lloyd Garrison. Active antislavery reform had been everywhere a thing of the past in 1815, when Lundy started out alone in St. Clairsville, Ohio, upon an extraordinarily influential career as an itinerant antislavery evangelist-printer-editor-lobbiest. Lundy became, after years of struggle, the catalyst who converted the old and defunct antislavery movement into the new and revolutionary abolitionist movement of the 1830s. In 1828 Lundy converted the evangelical reformers Arthur and Lewis Tappan to the abolitionist cause, and they went on to lead in the founding of the New York movement. Following Garrison's conversion in the same year, the young temperance reform editor followed Lundy to Baltimore to serve as associate editor on Lundy's *Genius of Universal Reform*. When Garrison returned to Boston in 1830, he was militantly committed to Lundy's Quaker objectives of abolition, feminism, and peace, to be pursued with a Quakerish adherence to the principle of nonresistance, but with a most un-Quakerish pugnacity. When Lundy died in 1839, Garrison acknowledged the debt he owed his mentor: "I feel that I owe everything, instrumentally and under God, to Benjamin Lundy."[42]

As a Quaker, Lundy represented a continuing libertarian tradition that spanned the enlightened eighteenth century and the romantic nineteenth. William Ellery Channing's antislavery efforts, initiated in the 1830s, similarly represented a persistence of enlightened thought in romantic America, as did John Quincy Adams's parallel fight for the right of antislavery petitioners to be heard in Congress, and both Channing and Adams were indebted to Lundy for guidance in that new evangelical era of reform. Channing based his influential public letter to Henry Clay opposing annexation of Texas in 1837 upon Lundy's *Origin and True Causes of the Texas Revolution* (1836), the pamphlet that also aroused Adams to oppose annexation. Thereafter Lundy kept Adams supplied with material for Adams's campaign on the floor of the House of Representatives. As Samuel Flagg Bemis wrote, "Single-handedly Adams manned an anti-Texas battery in Congress, and Lundy passed the ammunition."[43]

Lundy's libertarian and humanitarian pursuit of emancipation through constitutional means accorded more closely with John Quincy Adams's approach to the problem than it did with the immediatist approach of Garrison, an approach inspired by British rather than American sources. Lundy's influence upon Garrison in other respects had been facilitated by Lundy's tolerance for Garrison's militant advocacy of immediate and unconditional emancipation while Garrison had worked with him on the *Genius of Universal Reform*. "Thee may put thy initials to thy articles," Lundy had informed Garrison, "and I will put my initials to mine, and each will bear his own burden."[44]

In his appeals to women for support against slavery, Garrison followed the example of Lundy but moved aggressively beyond Lundy's modest appeals. Lundy had recruited a Philadelphia Quaker, Elizabeth Chandler, to edit a Ladies' Department in the *Genius of Universal Emancipation*, and Garrison created a similar department for *Liberator*, reprinting much of Chandler's material from the *Genius*. Then in 1832, after a year of publication, the *Liberator* appealed to women to organize on their own in the abolitionist cause.

Women in Salem responded immediately with a Female Antislavery Society. Later that year, following the organization of the New England Antislavery Society, twelve women organized a Boston Female Anti-Slavery Society that, under the leadership of Maria Weston Chapman, was soon exerting an independent and very disturbing impact upon Boston society as a whole. Women of the Boston Female Anti-Slavery Society, including Chapman and her sisters, Anne and Caroline Weston, belonged to Boston's respectable families. Chapman herself was a wealthy, beautiful, and aristocratically bred young woman who had spent much of her early life in London in the family of an uncle who was a partner in Baring Brothers, the foremost banking firm in the British Empire. Over the objections of their pastor, William Ellery Channing, Maria Chapman and her husband, Henry, entered the Garrisonian camp. Joining them were a scattering of prominent lawyers, merchants, and ministers and many of the Boston blacks who had provided Garrison's *Liberator* with its earliest and most needed support. Garrison's most notable early recruit was Lydia Maria Child, nationally known writer of children's stories, who shocked her admirers and lost her privileges in the Boston Athenaeum by writing *An Appeal in Favor of That Class of Americans Called Africans* (1833).

When abolitionists from New England joined those of Pennsylvania and New York in forming the American Anti-Slavery Society in December 1833, the Tappans's New York group asserted its dominance and its disapproval of Garrison's abrasive, self-serving tactics. The divisions were already evident that would split abolitionists into two rival national organizations in 1840. In Quaker Philadelphia a large Female Anti-Slavery Society was organized in 1833, out of which Lucretia Mott emerged as the nation's leading figure in the womens' antislavery movement. At the same time Garrison and Boston women were gaining their own celebrity in the fight to permit Prudence Crandall to conduct a school for black children in Connecticut and in the dramatic episode of 1835, when a mob suppressed a meeting of the Boston Female Anti-Slavery Society and roughed up Garrison, leaving him to spend the night in jail, where the mayor of Boston lodged him for his own safety. Wendell Phillips, the son of the previous mayor, had read Child's *Appeal* and happened to witness the humiliation of Garrison by the mob. Two years later Phillips committed himself to the Garrisonian movement at a meeting held in Fanieul Hall to protest the murder of the abolitionist editor Elijah Lovejoy by a mob in Alton, Illinois.

The mobs that manhandled Garrison in Boston, murdered Lovejoy in Alton, and terrorized and suppressed abolitionist meetings in New York City and elsewhere in the north were organized and manned by gentlemen of standing in the community who believed themselves to be entirely justified in taking extraordinary measures to suppress activities that threatened to sever society from its moorings. It was his outrage at these purportedly respectable mobs that occasioned the commitment of Phillips, together with his fellow Boston aristocrat Edmund Quincy, to the abolitionist cause at the Lovejoy protest meeting in 1837. Two years earlier it had been the violence of an antiabolitionist mob in Utica, New York, that had determined the cultivated, aristocratic, and wealthy Gerrit Smith to dedicate his life and fortune to the cause of abolition and related reforms. In Utica as in Boston, the mob had been made up of the supposedly respectable class rather than the "rough-scuff." But by the elevated social standards of Gerrit Smith, Wendell Phillips, or Edmund Quincy, these mobs had hardly comprised gentlemen of the first rank.[45]

Phillips was a brilliant orator who frequently engaged in daring and dextrous jousting with hostile audiences on behalf of victims of social injustice. Like other patrician humanitarians of the age, Phillips was less a democrat responding to his times than an aristocrat asserting noblesse oblige: the responsibility of the socially privileged to protect the least fortunate members of society against the ruthless egalitarianism and majoritarianism of the common man, whose sovereignty had lately been proclaimed. The underclasses would always need guidance and protection, for as the young Samuel Gridley Howe wrote,

> Knowledge, alone, can free men from error, and it is impossible that the diffusion of this should ever become so general, as to produce the effect; for the lower classes always have, and always must, continue in ignorance and be the dupes of others.[46]

In the process of devoting themselves to the underclasses, these elitist humanitarian reformers liberated themselves from confinement in that "frozen ocean" of respectable Boston society that Julia Ward Howe and many others complained so bitterly of. Reform ostracized them from stuffy evenings at the Ticknors and gave them access to the exotic world of the "dangerous" classes, while the righteousness of their motives protected their reputations in society, even where their activities were censured. Garrisonian abolitionists were dedicated but not necessarily dour. Phillips and Quincy in particular were gay blades, frequently brimming with wit and good humor. Nor was abolitionism as dangerous an adventure in Boston as Garrisonians liked to pretend. Nobody was injured by the famous Boston mob of "gentlemen of standing" that shut down

Maria Chapman's meeting of the Boston Female Anti-Slavery Society and paraded Garrison through the streets in 1835. Furthermore, no such mob was ever again organized against the abolitionists in Boston, once Maria Chapman put that one tartly to shame. The social respectability of many Garrisonians secured the safety of the movement, no matter how outrageous it might continue to appear to conservative Bostonians.

Within the Garrisonian camp Phillips, Quincy, Maria Chapman and her sisters, and various others from time to time referred to themselves as the Boston Clique remaining a breed apart from most of their coworkers —although charismatic Garrison always remained the acknowledged leader to whom they tendered their unwavering loyalty. As for the rest, some were socially and intellectually their peers, while the others were a mixed bag. Discrimination on racial grounds was naturally to be avoided, but the movement attracted odd sorts from whatever race. Maria Chapman observed that "The good Lord uses instruments for his purpose I would not touch with a fifty-foot pole."[47] Edmund Quincy, another member of the clique, belonged to the class of Boston gentlemen who cultivated a refined idleness as an honorable calling in itself, studying, traveling, developing taste in the arts, in polite letters and conversation, and in food and wine. As a gentleman of leisure, Quincy could donate much time and energy to the abolitionist cause, writing and editing the *National Antislavery Standard* in New York and assuming responsibility with Phillips and others for publication of the *Liberator* when Garrison was absent from Boston.

Members of the clique, who were in their late twenties when they committed themselves to the cause, took to rebellion joyfully. Phillips told his fellow reformers that "if we never free a single slave, we have at least freed ourselves." Nor did they pay a high price in social ostracism. As for the "*cold shoulders*," Edmund Quincy wrote, "there was not much of it that was forced on my notice." Lydia Maria Child calculated that she was "a gainer decidedly" in exchanging the society of the "respectables" for the firm friendship of their moral and intellectual betters. Nor could she see that the sales of her books had suffered noticeably from the bad reputation of their author.[48] Meanwhile, antislavery opinion continued to gain ground in Brahmin Boston as the British emancipated their West Indian slaves in 1844 while the United States annexed Texas as a slave state, fought a war with Mexico, and most dangerously acquired new territory west to the Pacific, thus reopening the question of slavery in the territories that the Compromise of 1820 had effectively settled for a generation.

⊰ VII ⊱

IN SIGNING THE Declaration of Independence, learned patriots had believed they were contributing to Western civilization, not writing themselves out of it. Jefferson followed Franklin as president of the American Philosophical Society and also as the foremost American *philosophe* in the international community of letters. But as the colonies broke with England politically, so did America separate from Europe culturally, over time, despite the best intentions of its philosophical founders. Educated Americans growing up after 1800 could not ignore the gulf dividing the age of Metternich and the age of Jackson, no matter how hopeful some might have been that America's libertarian example would exert a liberalizing influence upon monarchical Europe.

Americans became a race apart. As a young Bostonian armed with letters of introduction from Jefferson, and from John and John Quincy Adams, and from other traveled Americans, George Ticknor gained swift access to most of Europe's leading literary men and women—the more easily for his being an exotic figure in 1815, a representative of the new and still little known American republic. Yet Ticknor did not become a cosmopolitan man as a consequence; he returned to Boston and for several decades remained at home to distinguished European visitors. Among leading American literati of Ticknor's generation, Washington Irving was perhaps the last—indeed, the last before the Civil War—to play the part of a citizen of two worlds. And the Anglophile Irving, reviled as well as honored for his cosmopolitan sensibilities, withdrew in time to the respectably provincial life of an American gentleman at Sunnyside on the Hudson.

Writers of the American republic faced the task of improvising a literature that would be authentically American while still rooted in the Old World past. The literary civilization of the Continent posed no problems for American writers. The classical texts of Greece and Rome remained the common heritage, and recent European literature had imperceptible influence in American literary culture, even if works by certain Continental writers were read widely. The living English-language heritage of Milton and Shakespeare was another matter. The Anglo-American literary community was bound to England by a common historical past, common social, political, and legal institutions, and above all a common canon of literature. Literary culture in America was grounded in Milton and Shakespeare, Addison and Dryden, Pope and Johnson, and beyond that—political independence notwithstanding—it was a response to Wordsworth, Coleridge, Dickens, and Thackeray.

British critics in the nineteenth century continued to treat American literature as a colonial branch of English literature. Under these circumstances, Americans were hard put to establish their independent existence as a Republic of Letters. The call to create an American literature went forth with the Revolution and remained a crying issue down to the Civil War, punctuated by unnumbered literary declarations of independence. But declarations could not resolve the problem. The literary community was inescapably situated at the fork of its own, peculiarly American dilemma: its native tendency pointed in the direction of the antiliterary Republic of the Common Man, and its civilized tendency pointed in the direction of imperial London. For literary Americans, London represented both their cultural heritage and their continuing colonial status as writers.

The best approach to this dilemma—there was no solution to it—was to affirm Anglo-American literary culture as an American birthright, discover native themes in American nature and society, and avoid entangling alliances with the English literary establishment so far as that might be possible. One could not ignore the judgments of the British literary magazines since they remained as authoritative with the American reading public as with the British themselves. The best that American writers could do was to keep their distance from London's literary society, and this they did. Except for those serving in diplomatic posts, leading literary men after Washington Irving approached London's richly laden literary banquet warily and supped with a long spoon. Meanwhile, the rising American cultural nationalism of the 1820s was sufficient to deter subsequent American literary aspirants from following Irving's example and seeking their literary fortunes in London.

When James Fenimore Cooper arrived in London in 1826, his literary

reputation was already internationally established, his hostility to aristocratic and decadent English culture confirmed, and he visited London for
business reasons only. Initially Cooper remained only long enough to sign
up with a reliable publisher before departing for France. When he returned two years later, it was to arrange for publication of his *Notions of
the Americans*, an argument written in reply to scurrilous English travel
accounts of America. Upon seeing *Notions* through the press three months
later, he was off to the Continent again.

Although dozens of letters of introduction had been pressed upon
Cooper when he went to Europe, he never used any of them, either on the
Continent or in London. Nevertheless, callers appeared as soon as he had
established a London residence for his brief stay in 1828, and he was drawn
into London's literary social swirl in spite of himself. He even came to enjoy himself at Holland House, where women praised his books and men
listened to his political opinions. He did not give in altogether, however.
The racy conversation of Lady Holland and other aristocratic women
offended him, and he remained on his guard against veiled condescension
from everybody. One gentleman advised another to call Cooper out as soon
as he was introduced, because it would come to that before long anyway.[49]

George Bancroft was similarly imbued with patriotic Jacksonian animus toward aristocratic England when President Polk appointed him
minister to the Court of St. James in 1846. Bancroft was not the doughty
combatant that Cooper was, however, and he yielded to the hospitality of
Lord and Lady Palmerston and to the flattering and glittering receptions
at Holland House and elsewhere. He joined Macaulay, Henry Milman,
Henry Hallam, and other fellow giants of his profession at weekly "historical breakfasts" and savored the elegant life, which had appealed to
him from his student days in Germany, however incongruously it may
have sorted with his democratic persuasion. Then he returned to America
in 1849 and withdrew from public life to get on with his history of the
Revolution, where American equality and brotherhood again triumphed
over English aristocracy and tyranny.[50]

A year later Bancroft's fellow historian William Hickling Prescott arrived in London. A moderate Whig, Prescott was predisposed in favor of
his English hosts rather than against them. At the time his *History of the
Conquest of Mexico* had appeared, in 1843, many British investors had re-

cently been hurt in the American Panic of 1837, when Pennsylvania and other states repudiated state bonds. Awaiting British reviews amid British outrage against America, Prescott wrote a friend in England to ask whether he thought that "the English Aristarch will visit the sins of repudiation on a Yankee author." He worried unnecessarily. The major British reviews could not have praised *Conquest of Mexico* more highly, the *Edinburgh Review* comparing it favorably with Scott and Thucydides in describing its style and use of incident.[51]

When he visited London in 1850, Prescott consequently experienced "the most brilliant visit ever made to England by an American citizen not clothed with the *prestige* of official station," according to George Ticknor. Macaulay found it incredible that Prescott could turn his back on London society after six weeks of such social success and return to his provincial community across the Atlantic. But Prescott, who had thoroughly enjoyed his London visit, was more than content to return home. He wrote that England was the most truly civilized place on earth but that Englishmen were nevertheless irredeemable "islanders, cut off from the great world," including his own American world. They all traveled, "yet how little sympathy they show for other people or institutions, and how slight is the interest they take in them."[52] The home-grown parochialism of Boston suited him better than the metropolitan parochialism of the British islanders.

Nathaniel Hawthorne, after writing a campaign biography of Franklin Pierce (1850), was rewarded with the office of U.S. consul in Liverpool from 1853 to 1857. He accepted the post because he needed the money, not because he expected to benefit from the English experience. Like Cooper and Bancroft he opposed the British system on ideological grounds. But Hawthorne was less politically oriented than they and far more ambivalent in his attitudes toward the country he called "our old home." Hawthorne's reactions to his situation reflect the ambivalence of literary America as a whole to its English heritage. Hawthorne, who detested his office work and disliked Liverpool, toured the English countryside extensively and appreciatively, with "a singular sense of having been here before." In *Our Old Home* he described feeling

> like the stalwart progenitor, a person returning to the hereditary haunts after more than two hundred years, and finding the church, the hall, the farmhouse, the cottage, hardly changed during his long absence.

Yet England remained a foreign country. Sitting in his English house not long after arriving in Liverpool, "with the chill, rainy English twilight brooding over the lawn," the realization came to him that he would "never be quite at home here."[53] Hawthorne remained critical of English society and institutions and patriotic toward an America he regarded with mixed emotions.

> After all the slanders against Americans [he wrote from England] there is no people worthy even to take the second place behind us, for liberality of idea and practice. The more I see of the rest of the world, the better I think of my own country (not that I like it very enthusiastically either).

It was when his wife was away on an extended visit toward the end of his stay in England that the full "bitterness of exile" came over him. "I am like an uprooted plant," he wrote, "wilted and drooping."[54]

A trip to France cheered him up after his four-year stint in England was over. There he learned that "London is not to be mentioned, nor compared even, with Paris." He did not take a liking to the French people he saw. "But they do grand and beautiful things in the architectural way; and I am grateful for it." He enjoyed Florence and appreciated Rome when he was in the mood to, and he remained for a year in Italy, followed by another year in England, while seeing *The Marble Faun* through the press and making arrangements that would return him royalties from England. In 1860 he returned with utmost eagerness to New England and upon arriving sank immediately into a black depression.

In his gentler way, Ralph Waldo Emerson viewed England as antagonistically as Cooper did. Emerson paid his first visit to Europe in 1832 after he had resigned his pastorate, giving "health" as the reason for the trip.[55] Emerson required an excuse more than most, because he scoffed at the idea that travel was broadening. Those who thought to acquire experience through travel were only carrying "ruins to ruins" in his opinion. However, he had been

> much indebted to the men of Edinburgh and of the *Edinburgh Review*—to Jeffrey, Mackintosh, Hallam, and to Scott, Playfair, and De Quincey; and my narrow and desultory reading had inspired the wish to see the faces of three or four writers—Coleridge, Wordsworth, Landor, De Quincey, and the latest and strongest contributor to the critical journals, Carlyle.

Among them, he later concluded that only Carlyle had been worth visiting.[56]

On the basis of that visit and a subsequent one during the winter of 1847, when he was invited to address some English Mechanics' Institutes, Emerson wrote *English Traits* (1856), the only integrated book-length study he ever composed. In contrast to Hawthorne's *Our Old Home* (which would appear in 1863), Emerson's *English Traits* kept its subject at arm's length, even while recounting anecdotes from his visits. Emerson boned up sufficiently in reference works to present his account in the form of a natural and civil history of English civilization at the time when "British power has culminated, is in solstice, or already declining." In Emerson's account English civilization, including English literature, is discussed as though it were something altogether foreign to Americans.

Emerson's description of Stonehenge, which he visited with Carlyle, brings him to Carlyle's complaint that Americans in England

> dislike the coldness and exclusiveness of the English, and run away to France and go with their countrymen and are amused, instead of manfully staying in London, and confronting Englishmen and acquiring their culture, who really have much to teach them.

Emerson replied that he was easily dazzled by Englishmen but that when he returned to Massachusetts he would

> lapse at once into the feeling, which the geography of America inevitably inspires, that we play the game with immense advantage . . . and that England, an old and exhausted island, must one day be contented, like other parents, to be strong only in her children.[57]

Emerson's second visit falling "in the fortunate days when Mr. Bancroft was the American Minister in London," he had easy access through Bancroft and Carlyle

> to excellent persons and to privileged places. . . . I saw Rogers, Hallam, Macaulay, Milnes, Milman, Barry Cornwall, Dickens, Thackeray, Tennyson, Leigh Hunt, D'Israeli, Helps, Wilkinson, Bailey, Kenyon and Forster; the younger poets, Clough, Arnold and Patmore; and among the men of science, Robert Brown, Owen, Sedgwick, Faraday, Buckland, Lyell, De la Beche, Hooker, Carpenter, Babbage and Edward Forbes. It

was my privilege also to converse with Miss Bailie, with Lady Morgan, with Mrs. Jameson, and Mrs. Somerville.

The company was to Emerson overwhelming rather than uplifting. He concluded

> It is not in distinguished circles that wisdom and elevated characters are usually found, or, if found, they are not confined thereto; and my recollections of the best hours go back to private conversations in different parts of the kingdom with persons little known."[58]

So much for Society, which London boasted and Boston lacked. It was not London that attracted Bostonians or other literary Americans when they flocked to Europe. When James Russell and Maria Lowell decided in 1850 that they could finance a trip to Europe by selling some of Maria's property, they set out for Italy, where many of their friends were living. In fact, fourteen Lowells were in Rome at the time, permitting Lowell to explain as he left Boston that he was going abroad to become acquainted with his family.[59] Paris lacked profundity by comparison to Rome, but it did not lack Bostonians. James T. Fields wrote home that "It is almost like returning to Boston to come to Paris. At any time and on every stair we meet Boston friends." Emerson had planned to brush up his French while in Paris, but he met Oliver Wendell Holmes there and others from Boston and found little opportunity to use the native language.[60]

A brilliant literary society remained ready at any time in London to welcome Lowell and other American literary lights to the Athenaeum, to the Reform Club, to Holland House, and to other circles, societies, homes, castles, and country seats. Longfellow, Holmes, and others knew they were welcome, but like Emerson these American cousins took a chary view of English cultural hospitality and little or no advantage of it.

✥ VIII ✥

MOST OF THE CONTINENT was unknown country to educated Americans at the time of the Revolution. Business had brought merchants and planters to the Low Countries, and the sons of wealthy Maryland planters were educated there and in Portugal. Paris was known by reputation, but hardly any Americans had seen it for themselves. From an American standpoint, Franklin was exploring darkest Europe when he visited Heidelberg. Benjamin West, the Pennsylvania Quaker, was as much a novelty to the Romans who greeted him as Red Jacket, the Seneca chief, would have been. The Revolution sent a few Americans to Paris and drew many Frenchmen to America. It also created a scattering of diplomatic posts for literary men, from St. Petersburg to the Barbary Coast. The renegade Connecticut Wit and poet-entrepreneur Joel Barlow settled in Paris and was joined after the turn of the century by the painter-entrepreneur Robert Fulton. Others visited Paris to study its art collections, and medical students had studied there as well as in other Continental universities. Nevertheless, it was only in London that an American intellectual community may be said to have maintained itself abroad in the early years of the Republic.

London did not decisively cease to be the home metropolis for American artists and writers abroad until the second war for independence, waged from 1812 to 1814, settled America's separate nationality beyond question. Irving sought literary success in England in 1815—and achieved it after five unhappy years as an unnoticed outsider. When Irving sought to sustain the success of *Sketch Book* with the yet more Anglicized *Bracebridge Hall*, he was met with harsh criticisms in the British reviews that sent him packing to the Continent and to new successes as a historian and observer of Spanish civilization. Meanwhile in 1815 international recognition had come to Harvard graduates George Ticknor, Edward Everett, and Joseph Green Cogswell not for literary achievement but simply for their pioneering efforts as American graduate students at Göttingen. There, as representatives of the distant and novel American republic, they achieved an instant celebrity such as Irving could not achieve in England with *Salmagundi* and *Knickerbocker History* already to his credit.

Carrying letters of introduction from Göttingen professors, Everett and Ticknor visited Goethe and lesser German luminaries in Weimar. Then it was on to Paris for Ticknor. Armed with letters from Jefferson, John Adams, and other older travelers, he met August Wilhelm von Schlegel, Alexander von Humboldt, Robert Southy, and many more illuminati. Then to Spain and Italy with more letters to meet more luminaries, including Byron near Venice. It was only after this conquest of the Continent that Ticknor advanced upon Great Britain with his letters of introduction to visit Wordsworth near Grasmere, and Scott in Abbotsford, and the host of titled and literary men and women in London. Everett followed much the same course, journeying from Goethe and other Germans to Byron in Italy, to Paris, London, Edinburgh, and thence Abbotsford. Cogswell's itinerary similarly included Weimar, Paris, and Abbotsford. George Bancroft arrived at Göttingen in 1818, then roamed on to Weimar and Paris. These heady years of American literary lion hunters in Europe soon passed, but they inaugurated an enduring era in which peregrinating American students and tourists were commonplace on the Continent.[61]

The age of the Grand Tourist was beginning as well; though the volume of both travelers and students remained small by comparison to the later volume of overseas travel in the steamship era. Upon the conclusion of the Napoleonic wars, scheduled packet ships had entered the business of providing direct and reliable transatlantic passenger service, opening Europe for the first time to an affluent tourist trade. In 1828 Philip Hone noted in his diary that every member of a recent New York dinner had been to Europe. In former times, Hone observed, the few who had made the trip had been accorded the respect due "learned pundits." But times had changed:

> Now the streams of accumulated knowledge may be obtained at innumerable fountains: the Abraham Schermerhorns, the James J. Jones, the Gibbses, the Primes do pour forth streams of intellectuality.[62]

The higher priority of Paris, Rome, Venice, and Florence over London and Edinburgh on the Grand Tour implied no superior regard for the French or Italian peoples. The tour ostensibly concerned itself with the glories and grandeurs of the past more than with the attractions of the present. Parisian culture was Gallic, which is to say charming and often brilliant but not altogether substantial nor altogether moral. Paris was nevertheless a "must" for its museums, beginning with the Louvre and the Luxembourg, as well as for its boulevards and gardens and the nearby Palace of Versailles. There was obviously more to Paris than the cultivated past, however, and few would practice self-denial to the point of resisting the pleasures of its theaters and restaurants. Among Boston Brahmins, Holmes was a somewhat singular case, having lived in Paris as a medical student and having openly relished it, even in letters to his conservative father, the Reverend Abiel Holmes, in Cambridge. Holmes afterward became noted in Boston for his characteristic gaiety, which served him as Boston's leading toastmaster. The more customary view of Paris from Boston was that, while delightful to visit, it was corrupt and ought to be taken seriously only for its artifacts. Nevertheless Longfellow's brother-in-law Thomas Gold Appleton, a cultivated man of leisure who knew both Paris and Bostonians in Paris, observed that "All good Bostonians expected when they died to go to Paris."[63]

London and Rome, like Paris, offered tourists the requisite lessons in civilization through museums and art galleries, historic streets, gardens, public buildings, cathedrals, and ruins. London taught Americans their English heritage. Rome taught them their classical as well as their Christian heritage. In Rome, colorful festivals, religious processions, and music provided splendid spectacles for sightseers; but Protestant Americans naturally associated this with papist superstition. American tourists valued the Eternal City primarily for the grandeur of its ancient remains, which returned a civilized person to her Greco-Roman and Christian roots.

The American colonies in Florence and Rome were Bostonian colonies for the most part, and the original settler was the Boston-bred sculptor Horatio Greenough, a protégé of the painter Washington Allston. Greenough sailed for Rome in 1825 during his senior year at Harvard. After an interval back in Boston, Greenough returned to Italy, eventually settling in Florence in 1833, where he remained until shortly before his death in 1851. He was joined in 1837 by Hiram Powers of Vermont and recently Cincinnati, who had completed commissions to model the heads of Webster, Jackson, Calhoun, and others and had journeyed to Florence to finish them in marble. An eminently sociable man, Powers became the leader of the Florence community. The sculptors were joined by American artists, attracted by the Tuscan countryside, which was reputed to be more beautiful than any to be found in America, or, in any event, more appropriate for the painter's art.

Meanwhile, Rome enticed its share of gifted Americans. The young New York sculptor Thomas Crawford, brother-in-law of Julia Ward Howe, settled in Rome in 1835 and was presently joined by other sculptors, including Harriet Goodhue Hosmer, the bohemian daughter of a Watertown, Massachusetts, physician. William Wetmore Story, son of the Harvard Law School professor and Supreme Court justice Joseph Story, first went to Florence, but in 1856 Story moved to Rome, where he remained the center of American social life until nearly the end of the century. Story had practiced law for a decade in Boston and had produced two major legal treatises before quitting the profession after his father's death to devote himself to poetry and sculpture.[64]

In both Rome and Florence, most foreign residents were English, and most English residents embarrassed their American cousins. Whereas the Americans typically wished to be accepted by the Italians without rancor and in some cases entered Italian social and political life, the English characteristically treated Italians as inferiors. Whichever attitude one took toward the Italian people, the Italians acquiesced to the presence of the foreign element in their society, retaining a familial privacy yet permitting the free development of alien communities that relished the ambience of Italian wine and song. This colorful setting was one in which Boston Brahminism could readily transplant itself.

Mid-nineteenth-century Americans in Italy viewed Italian Catholicism with gradations of antipathy ranging from condescension to hatred, and they almost universally considered the ubiquitous monks to be degraded to the point of bestiality. On the other hand there was admiration and sympathy for the Italian patriots Giuseppe Garibaldi and Giuseppe Mazzini and for the risorgimento. Active involvement in the movement for Italian nationalism by Americans was led by women—not only Margaret Fuller but also Catharine Sedgwick and Julia Ward Howe. Just as Fuller had met Mazzini in London, so Sedgwick's and Howe's involvement began in their meetings with political exiles in New York, where they first became acquainted with Italian nationalists, before sailing for Italy.

Although Americans preferred not to be mistaken for the often haughty and seemingly eccentric English, a union developed among English-speaking artists and writers, centering especially around Robert and Elizabeth Barrett Browning, who wintered in Florence from 1847 to 1861. The Brownings became the Storys' closest friends in Italy. And as it was customary for all Brahmins to visit the Storys when in Europe, so did it become customary for New England Brahmins to visit the Brownings at their homes in both Italy and England. The Lowells, Longfellows, Holmeses,

Nortons, Adamses, Hawthornes, Bancrofts, Beechers, and Jameses all came. Under John Ruskin's influence, Charles Eliot Norton led fellow Brahmins back beyond that "period of pure immorality, the Renaissance," to Giotto, Fra Angelico, and the high medieval world of Dante. In 1861 Norton formed the Dante Club with Lowell and Longfellow. In 1874 the chair of the history of art was created for Norton at Harvard, and there, together with Lowell and Longfellow and a few others, he took refuge against Gilded Age materialism in a circle devoted to translating and appreciating Dante.[65]

Athens did not offer travelers and expatriates the amenities of Paris or Rome, and conditions remained unsettled in Greece even after its liberation from the Ottoman Turks at the close of the 1820s. Greece accordingly remained off the main routes traveled by American tourists. But the Greek revolution fired American imaginations and inspired the Greek revival that furnished Jacksonian America with its most characteristic architectural style. Most educated and traveled Americans of the 1830s, 1840s, and 1850s evidently were satisfied to read about Greece in the travel accounts of Nathaniel Parker Willis and Bayard Taylor. For the more dedicated literary men, the pilgrimage to Hellas became almost de rigueur. "Anybody who comes to Europe and not to Greece," the clergyman Phillips Brooks wrote home to Boston in 1866, "is very much a donkey."[66]

Even before the Greek revolution of the 1820s, a very few ardent Hellenists penetrated the forbidden country. Among the few who did, Nicholas Biddle was the first to leave a record. Having graduated from Princeton at fifteen and studied law, the twenty-year-old Biddle was serving as secretary to the American minister in France and traveling in Italy in 1806 when the possibility of finding passage on a ship to Greece occurred to him. Acting on the thought, he "touched the holy soil of Greece" in May and proceeded upon a two-month tour of Corinth, Delphi, Thermopylae, Thebes, Aegina, Salamis, Marathon, Athens, and other storied places, returning to France by way of Trieste.

More than a decade followed before another literary American, Edward Everett, repeated the trip. Together with George Ticknor, Everett had conceived the idea while visiting Byron in Italy. But Ticknor's father had written his son that Athens was "not worth exposing your life, nor the money you must spend to see it," to which George had replied, "I willingly give up Greece."[67] Supplied with letters of introduction from Byron and accompanied by Theodore Lyman Jr., a fellow Bostonian at Göttingen, Everett set forth in 1819 on what proved to be an agreeable tour of the ancient country. The two men enjoyed the hospitality of hosts and the tolerance of Turkish officials, for whom they were as much objects of curiosity as Benjamin West had been to the Romans six decades earlier.

In 1821 the Greek revolution broke out, attracting the services of American philhellenes such as the young Harvard Medical School graduate Samuel Gridley Howe. Hellenists were followed by relief workers, then by missionaries when the revolution came to its squalid end with a mutually distrustful British-French-Russian protectorate inhibiting further fighting among factions. To literary America the most notable active participant in the revolution had been Lord Byron, who died in Greece at age thirty-six. The most notable imaginative participant turned out to have been Edgar Allan Poe, whose "To Helen" compellingly evoked the post-neoclassical emotional appeal of Hellenism to romantic America.

Beyond Greece the Ottoman Turks ruled the Mediterranean fringe of the classical and the biblical world, and Constantinople (today's Istanbul) remained the eastern terminus of civilization as Americans understood the word. Beyond Constantinople lay the Orient, a mysterious region that most well-educated Americans gave little thought. The old China trade had brought New England in direct contact with Cantonese civilization from the early years of the Republic, and Herman Melville was among the sailors who entered the South Seas aboard New England whalers. Missionaries followed merchants and fishermen to China, Korea, South Sea islands, India, and finally Japan, creating an American market for Asian curios but not a corresponding scholarly American interest in Asian culture.

The most celebrated American scholar with a penchant for Oriental literature, Ralph Waldo Emerson, had come to the subject through his study of classical Greek philosophy rather than from his contact with Boston's China trade, though that may have influenced his thinking as well. Neoplatonism led Emerson from Athens to Alexandria and thence eastward to the literatures of Arabia, Persia, India, and China. Among these, Emerson found Chinese Confucianism the least rewarding, seeing the eponymous founder as a "middleman" for a materialistic and rigidly formal society. It was the mysticism of India and of Hindu literature that most enriched his own poetically Unitarian conception of an unqualified and immutable oversoul. As with Emerson's eclectic reading generally, however, his gleanings from Oriental literature served illustrative purposes without altering his philosophy in substantive ways.

Emerson devoted his life to becoming someone other than the "improvised European" of Henry Adams's epithet. Having "listened too long to the courtly muses of Europe," he sought to draw upon "the breadth and luxuriance of Eastern imagery and modes of thinking . . . to unbind and animate the torpid intellect," extending its range beyond the bounds of classical Christian civilization while rooting it firmly in native American soil.[68] Emerson did not count himself among the "Authors we have, in numbers, who have written out their vein, and who, moved by a commendable prudence, sail for Greece or Palestine, follow the trapper into the prairie, or ramble around Algiers, to replenish their merchantable stock." Rather he would "plant himself indomitably on his instincts, and there abide," as the American scholar in Concord and Boston, sitting "at the feet of the familiar . . . The meal in the firkin; the milk in the pan; the ballad in the street; the news of the boat;" wise in the knowledge, drawn from books as well as nature, that "the near explains the far."[69]

Even so, Emerson's efforts to become something other than an improvised European were hardly likely to be better realized than Henry Adams's more arduous efforts to become something in the world other than a Bostonian. In his journals Emerson quoted a contemporary German newspaper:

> In the American backwoods there is nothing of those social and artistic enjoyments which ennoble man, whilst they dissatisfy him. What man would live without the poesy of sounds, colors, and rhymes! Unhappy people that is condemned to this privation!

Boston Brahmins had been brought up to be improvised Europeans, and so had all college-educated Americans as well as all self-educated Americans who entered the American Republic of English letters.

❧ 7 ❧

THE SOUTH IN THE
LITERARY REPUBLIC

EDUCATED SOUTHERNERS WERE FAR better acquainted with the North than
New Englanders were with the South. Yankees probably traveled as widely
as Southerners, but they did not travel much in the South. Among those
who did, there were the ubiquitous peddlers who did much to earn New
England its bad name nationally; Bronson Alcott, for one, peddled alma-
nacs for a time in Virginia and the Carolinas. There were also those Yankee slave traders and overseers who operated in the South in fact as well as
in the fiction of *Uncle Tom's Cabin*, and there were Yankee teachers. William Ellery Channing served as tutor in a Virginia household in 1798, before settling permanently in Boston. There were visits by New Englanders
for nonbusiness reasons as well. Emerson once spent a winter in Charleston
and St. Augustine for his health, and Lowell once visited a college classmate in Charleston. In neither case did the firsthand acquaintance appear to
influence the visitor's later perception of the South, however. The New
York Yankee Frederick Law Olmsted was unique among Northern writers in dealing with the antebellum South as a subject for serious systematic firsthand study.[1]

Like it or not, literate Southerners belonged to Northern culture as
literate Northerners did not belong to the culture of the slave states. Throughout the period from the Revolution to the Civil War, many young gentlemen of the South went north to college rather than to Great Britain, as
had been customary in colonial times. In the course of that period, an
increasing number of Southerners attended the proliferating colleges and
universities of their own region. But even in Southern colleges they were
apt to take instruction from Northerners. Beyond that, the Southern reading public remained altogether dependent upon the North for its reading

matter. It imported its books from New York, Philadelphia, and Boston as well as from London, and it imported its newspapers and magazines from the North along with the books.

Southern literary gentlemen were capable of introducing quarterlies such as the *Southern Review* that compared favorably with the *North American Review* in quality if not longevity, while the monthly *Southern Literary Messenger* managed to survive for thirty years, from 1834 to 1864. What the South could not successfully turn out were general magazines and women's magazines such as *Graham's* and *Knickerbocker* and *Godey's* and *Harper's*, all of which sold well in the South along with the leading New York newspapers. As editor of the *Messenger* in 1861, Dr. George W. Bagby complained that "Southern patriotism never was proof against Northern newspapers and picture magazines." Bagby could conceive of nothing that would have

> hindered the hottest secessionist from buying the *New York Herald* and subscribing for *Harper's Magazine.* Southern patriotism is, and has always been a funny thing—indeed the funniest of things. It enables a man to abuse the Yankees, to curse the Yankees, to fight the Yankees, to do everything except quit taking the Yankees papers.[2]

The South lacked metropolitan centers sufficiently large and literate to support its own publishers of books and periodicals in competition with the North. Urbanization altered the South only on its periphery, in New Orleans, St. Louis, Cincinnati, Baltimore, Charleston, and Savannah. Five Southern states in 1860 did not have a single town with a population of ten thousand. Richmond, which served as the metropolitan center of Virginia, to the extent that there was one, numbered 5,730 in 1800 and grew gradually to 27,550 fifty years later. As the literary center of the Old Dominion, Richmond, despite its small population, attracted notable literary lions, including Dickens and Thackeray, and it was in Richmond that Thomas W. White, a local printer, founded the *Southern Literary Messenger* and published it for ten years, after which a series of other Richmond printers assumed responsibility for it. It was not the planters of Virginia who supported literary culture in the state capital and were on hand to greet distinguished visitors, however. Richmond culture was the concern of the business and professional men of the community.[3] The cultural life of the planters remained on the plantations, and it remained a private matter of the individual planter for the most part.

Virginia had traditionally been noted for its learned men and also for its sociability, but not for its combining of these qualities into scholarly sociability. Gentlemen displayed their learning in politics, notably in political oratory; otherwise there was little provision made for intellectual intercourse. The gaiety of dances, balls, and barbecues and the masculinity of gambling, drinking, hunting, and horse racing were not conducive to intellectuality. The Southern gentleman tended to pursue his scholarly interests in private, if he pursued them at all upon completion of his formal education. The model mid-eighteenth-century Virginia gentleman-intellectual, William Byrd II of Westover, rose early each morning to read his lines of Hebrew, Greek, and Latin before entering the world around him. Thereafter he gave himself over to business followed by social life, in a round of activities that were divorced from his daily solitary periods of study. Several generations later, the widower Jefferson created a world for himself in Monticello that combined business, sociability, and learning in a life that was uniquely Jeffersonian—a *tour de force* rather than a representative example of southern planter culture.

Joseph Le Conte, a Harvard-educated Georgian, taught geology at the University of South Carolina and fought in the Confederate army before going on to a distinguished career at the University of California, where he remains memorialized in Le Conte Hall. In his *Autobiography*, Le Conte recalled a "hot and heavy" discussion with the South Carolina planter Langdon Cheves in 1858 that illustrated the privacy of the intellectual lives of Southern aristocrats. As a student of Louis Agassiz, Le Conte supported the theory of creation by design that Darwin's *Origin of Species* would refute a year hence. Cheves, on the contrary, advanced the theory of the development of new species by transmutation. When Le Conte raised

> the apparently unanswerable objection drawn from the geographical distribution of species and the manner in which contiguous fauna pass into one another, i.e., by substitution instead of transmutation, his answer was exactly what an evolutionist would give to-day—viz., that intermediate links would be killed off in the struggle for life as less suited to the environment; in other words that only the fittest would survive.

As to why Cheves had not published his idea, Le Conte wrote:

> No one well acquainted with the Southern people, and especially with
> the Southern planters, would ask such a question. Nothing could be
> more remarkable than the wide reading, the deep reflection, the refined
> culture, and the originality of thought and observation characteristic
> of them; and yet the idea of publication never even entered their minds.
> What right had any one to publish unless it was something of the great-
> est importance, something that would revolutionize thought?[4]

Southern gentlemen who did venture into print did so in the uneasy knowledge that, in the opinion of other Southern gentlemen, they were violat-
ing the proprieties by displaying their ideas and literary talents in public.

Organized religion—chiefly Anglican and Presbyterian—provided the
main basis for organized intellectual endeavor in Virginia, but it failed to
win the cordial support of the planter class in general, and it suffered se-
verely from Jefferson's anticlerical animosities in particular. In the Southern colonies, Anglican pastors had served virtually as employees of the
planters, who had administered the local parishes and hired and fired ministers through the office of vestryman. Southern planters might be devout
Christians in private or they might not, but few were devoted churchmen.
For gentlemen of the planter class, religion was typically seen to be a private matter that was not amenable to institutional regulation. During the
Revolution, Jefferson drew up an Ordinance of Religious Freedom that
was the basis for disestablishing the Anglican Church in Virginia, an achievement which Jefferson ranked with the Declaration of Independence and
the founding of the University of Virginia as one of the three deeds for
which he most wished to be remembered.

Disestablishment of the Anglican Church forced its successor, the Episcopal Church, to compete for membership with sects that had developed
without state assistance. The new church retained the nominal membership of the planter class as a whole, but whether it would manage to survive in the South on this basis remained in doubt for more than a generation. The evangelical churches meanwhile flourished throughout the South,
and among them the Presbyterian Church energetically supplanted the
Anglican-Episcopalian as the leading religious agency in the field of higher
education, organizing Washington College and Hampden-Sydney in Vir-

ginia and strongly supporting the campaign that led to the founding of the University of Virginia.

Surveying the evangelical clergy of Virginia in 1817, the Presbyterian minister John Holt Rice estimated that there were only ten or twelve "men of some literary attainments" among four or five hundred Baptist preachers and that Methodists were "about equal in point of learning"; whereas among the Presbyterians, forty or fifty ministers were "furnished with the best education that the literary institutions of the state will afford, and anxious to diffuse religious knowledge."[5] Among these, Rice himself was preeminent. The son of an impecunious Virginia lawyer, he had acquired sufficient learning to be appointed professor of theology at Hampden-Sydney College and to be offered the presidency of the College of New Jersey at Princeton, which he declined. In addition to teaching, preaching, and planting, Rice busied himself as a publisher who nearly bankrupted himself with a luxurious edition of John Smith's *True Travels* and *Generall Historie*, and as an editor of the *Virginia Literary and Evangelical Magazine* from 1818 to 1828. Consciously modeled on "the best" Scottish literary journals, Rice's magazine was the only such review to appear in Virginia until the *Southern Literary Messenger* started up in the 1830s.[6]

Jefferson had benefited from the staunch support of Presbyterian clergymen in his campaign to disestablish the Anglican Church. Furthermore, as the devoted student of "Dr. William Small of Scotland" at William and Mary, Jefferson had been taught the same Scottish-oriented "system of things" that students studied at Hampden-Sydney and Princeton. On these grounds, Jefferson might have made common cause with Rice where intellectual matters were concerned. Jefferson did not limit his anticlerical views to established churches, however, and he was especially suspicious of the pretentions of the Presbyterians in the field of education and learning, partly because these pretentions paralleled—or rivaled—his own.

Although Jefferson had found himself allied with Presbyterians in the attack on the Anglican establishment, he had never trusted these allies. Publicly he acknowledged their services to religious liberty; privately he noted his opinion that "Presbyterian wd. open just wide enough for hims." He conceded that the Presbyterians had "a little more monkish learning than the clergy of other sects," but in his view that made them all the more dangerous to the Republic of Letters since it encouraged them to interfere in the world of learning. In education as in other matters, Jefferson believed that the Presbyterians wanted "nothing but license from the laws to kindle again the fires of their leader John Knox, and give us a 2nd blast from his trumpet."[7] Whatever might be suspected of Methodists and Baptists in this regard, they devoted themselves to saving souls in society at large and did not interfere extensively in literary matters as Presbyterians did.

Presbyterians supported the plan to create a state university and did not oppose the appointment of Jefferson as "rector," with wide authority to shape the institution. But they were bound to differ with the aged deist of Monticello over matters of importance. Rice broadly indicated the nature of these differences in his comparison of "the Rational religionists and the Evangelical preachers." The rational religionists, he wrote,

> generally affect superior learning, and refinement, and taste: they dwell much on the small moralities of this world; they speculate in a very cool, philosophical manner on virtue, and the fitness of things, and the inconvenience of vice &c. &c.

The evangelical preachers, by contrast, were the sounder intellectuals for being "no enemies to true learning, to sound criticism, to refinement in taste, and to all the graces of literature," without forgetting that all is "but loss in comparison with the excellency of the knowledge of Christ Jesus."[8]

It was Rice who drew Jefferson's fiercest attacks upon the Presbyterians by leading the opposition to Jefferson's appointment of the English Unitarian minister Thomas Cooper to the University of Virginia faculty on grounds, Rice wrote, that Cooper's "prejudices appear to us violent; and all his liberality is reserved for his own party." The same might have been written of Jefferson or of many other learned Southern gentlemen who nourished the same unreconstructed anticlericalism that Jefferson did. Rice was successful in heading off Cooper, who then accepted the post of president of South Carolina College, which he retained from 1820 to 1833, until Presbyterians and others finally managed to force his resignation on religious grounds.

By the mid–nineteenth century, Presbyterians controlled a fourth of all institutions of higher learning in the nation, while numbers of other colleges and universities were administered by presidents who had trained in Presbyterian institutions, and all public institutions of learning were subjected to the kind of Presbyterian pressure that followed Cooper from Univeristy of Virginia to South Carolina College. Despite this unparalleled influence upon higher education, however, the Presbyterian Church did not exert an influence upon literary society in the South or elsewhere comparable to the influence of the smaller Congregational Church or of the very small Unitarian denomination in New England. Insufficiently evangelical to compete on equal terms with Methodists and Baptists in society at large, the Presbyterians were evidently too evangelical for the taste of the religious liberals, who tended to predominate in literary circles in the South and elsewhere.

⊰ II ⊱

THE DECENTRALIZED CHARACTER of planter society in Virginia may have served to inhibit intellectual society, but Charleston, South Carolina, offered the paradox of an anti intellectual society of ostentatiously learned plant ers and merchants. Of 114 American students who attended the Inns of Court in London during the colonial period, forty-six were from South Carolina. In particular, Charleston produced some peerless classical scholars in the process, from Thomas and Charles C. Pinckney in the Revolutionary era to Hugh Swinton Legaré in the Jacksonian era to Basil Gildersleeve in the Gilded Age. Yet Legaré warned an American student at Heidelberg not to overdo his foreign studies. He himself, Legaré wrote the student, had "found my *studies in Europe* impede me at every step of my progress." It had turned out that "Nothing is more *perilous* in America, than to be too long *learning*, and to get the name of bookish."[9]

With the wealthiest gentry on the colonial American mainland, Charleston on the eve of the Revolution supported the most urbanely cultivated activity of any colonial city, with its theater, concert hall, bookstores, and libraries, its dancing assemblies, race meets, taverns, and clubs. The Charleston Library Society, founded in 1748, acquired the "large collection of very valuable books, prints, globes, &c." that much impressed Josiah Quincy of Boston when he was shown around the library of Charles C. Pinckney, "a man of brilliant natural powers, and improved by a British education at the Temple." The oldest musical institution in Anglo-America, the

St. Cecilia Society, was founded in Charleston in 1762, supporting an orchestra that presented concerts every two weeks during the winter and spring seasons for society members.[10]

The Charleston gentry patronized the arts and letters, but the practice of them was customarily left to their social inferiors, from the hired musicians of the St. Cecilia orchestra to the small circle of Scottish physicians—attracted to the area by a wealthy clientele in a debilitating climate—whose botanical studies lent international distinction to Charleston in the natural sciences. Dr. Alexander Garden was a leading figure in this circle, and Garden for his part looked contemptuously upon "the gentlemen planters, who are absolutely above every occupation but eating, drinking, lolling, smoking, and sleeping, which five modes constitute the essence of their life and existence."[11] The planters themselves considered politics as well as planting to be occupations suited to their station, and they favored the public exercise of intellectuality among themselves chiefly in the exercise of forensic powers.

Nevertheless, the high value placed by the gentry upon expensive classical educations and upon London fashions, including fashions in the arts, fostered an intellectual tradition that in turn nourished a small, beleaguered literary society in Charleston from the late colonial period to the Civil War. In Revolutionary times Christopher Gadsden resigned from the Charleston Library Society because the librarian had stopped buying classical works, for the reason that nobody was reading the ones on the shelves.[12] In the national period South Carolina produced a peculiar breed of fiercely loyal yet fiercely alienated Charleston intellectuals, from Legaré and James Lewis Petigru in the nullification era to William Gilmore Simms followed by Paul Hamilton Hayne in the times of secession, Civil War, and Reconstruction.

Legaré was the leading classicist of Charleston at the time he served simultaneously, in 1830–32, as attorney-general of the state and editor of the *Southern Review*. Educated at Edinburgh and on the Continent following graduation from South Carolina College, Legaré returned to enter politics and pursue a highly successful law practice. He declared that Charleston's society was culturally superior to Boston's, and he wrote George Frederick Holmes in 1833, "I ask of heaven only that the little circle I am intimate with in Charleston should be kept together while I live"—adding, however, "We are (I am quite sure) the *last* of the *race* of South Carolina. I see nothing before us but decay and downfall."[13]

William Gilmore Simms entered Charleston's cultural and political life as a poet and Unionist editor at the time the nullification crisis was taking shape in the late 1820s and learned that "in our city, a man betraying the most remote penchant for poetry, is regarded as little less than a nuisance." Class distinctions, meanwhile, barred him from membership in Legaré's circle. Legaré praised some of Simms's verse, but he did not publish it in the *Southern Review*. Nor could he think of Simms as in any way his equal. Although Simms eventually married into the planter class, he was an outsider by birth and lacking in the classical education that was the substance of intellectual life for Legaré. The circle that Legaré cherished "were mostly men of mature age, elegant, refined, aristocratic . . . who looked upon literature as the choice creation of gentlemen," as Paul Hamilton Hayne wrote; so when Simms broke in upon them with his verse, they "treated the maiden effusions of our author with good-natured contempt."[14] Simms outlasted them, however, to form a circle of his own in Charleston, and in the meantime he retained his friendships in New York and came to know leading literary intellectuals of Virginia. Nationally, as well as among certain Charlestonians, he gained recognition as the unrivaled man of letters of the deep South.

By the eve of the Civil War, Simms had gathered around him a small literary group that met at his house and at John Russell's bookstore. The circle included several literary lawyers, including the young Göttingen graduate Basil L. Gildersleeve, who would become a Johns Hopkins professor and the nation's most respected classicist; a newspaper editor; several professors; and two "literary bohemians," the poets Henry Timrod and Paul Hamilton Hayne. At suppers at Simms's home, the Wigwam, members of this group planned *Russell's Magazine*, which ran monthly under the editorship of Hayne with the backing of "Lord John" Russell. Concerning itself with local as well as national and universal cultural matters, *Russell's Magazine* lasted from 1857 to March 1860, when, as Hayne later wrote, "our small and audacious craft . . . struck upon breakers and sank, like a shot, to Davy Jones' locker."[15]

Earlier in the 1850s Hayne had visited Boston while arranging for publication of his poetry and had enjoyed the company of leading men of letters there. In 1860, following the collapse of *Russell's Magazine*, Hayne wrote Horatio Woodman of the Boston Saturday Club, declaring,

> I love Boston. . . . As for Charleston, & So. Carolina generally . . . The people are intensely provincial, narrow-minded, and I must add—igno-rant. Literature they despise. . . . If the opportunity ever presented it-self, I shall take a final farewell of the South, and "pitch my tent" not far from "Bunker Hill."[16]

Then the war came, and Hayne took up the lost cause and consigned himself to literary exile.

In the upper South literary society showed signs of life in the booming city of Baltimore during the early national period. In 1816 the Delphian Club was founded by a small group of lawyers, physicians, and professors, including Tobias Watkins, physician and editor of the *Federalist Gazette*, who undertook to edit a literary magazine, the *Portico*, to which Delphians contributed. Among the original members was John Pierpont, merchant-poet who soon left for Boston to become a Unitarian minister, and his associate John Neal, the self-educated literary man from Maine who would soon achieve notoriety as a brilliant though erratic critic and novelist.

Neal contributed extensively to the *Portico* during the two years it lasted, and the *Portico* and the Delphian Club served him as his institution of higher education. In his novel *Randolph* Neal wrote,

> You have heard of the Delphian Club. I was there last night and never was it my misfortune to see such a heap of intellectual rubbish and glitter in all my life. . . . [T]he chief entertainment of the society ap-peared to consist in calling each other by hard names. . . . The members read essays, chase puns, wrangle vehemently and noisily about noth-ing, talk all together.

In his autobiography, Neal wrote that it had been

> to them, and to that association, that I am indebted for the best part of my doings, and a larger portion of happiness that I enjoyed in the South. High-minded, generous, unselfish men, they were both intellectual and com-panionable, indulgent, and with all their whims and freaks, congenial.[17]

The Delphian Club disbanded in 1826, and from then until the Civil War, the responsibility for intellectual sociability in Baltimore and Chesapeake society generally was assumed by the novelist-biographer-politician John Pendleton Kennedy. With the appearance of *Swallow Barn* in 1832, Kennedy, a prominent Baltimore lawyer, won recognition as the most graceful stylist among Southern writers and the leading man of letters in Chesapeake society. Nor was this distinction purchased at the cost of arduous literary labors and bitterly frustrated ambitions, as with Simms in South Carolina. Kennedy was gifted with the literary and social talents required of a polished man of letters and with the disposition to appreciate the role in life that his talents had earned him. James Russell Lowell wrote of Kennedy, "He was in the highest sense a genial man. He had a singular gift for companionship, for being something better than his books, and his finer qualities were lured out by the sympathy of the fireside."[18] Praising Kennedy for being "something better than his books" may have been Lowell's way of condescending to the gentleman from Maryland, but it described an ideal that Southern men of letters held up to themselves.

Kennedy grew up in the city and summered in Virginia on the Pendleton plantation of his mother's family. Following study at Baltimore College and service in the War of 1812, he had entered law practice and politics, while inditing light essays for the *Portico*. He became a protégé of two giants of the American bar, William Wirt and William Pinckney, and his affairs prospered from the outset, Wirt, the biographer of Patrick Henry, remaining his model of the literary gentleman. Kennedy later married the daughter of a wealthy Baltimore textile manufacturer, and his economic ties remained those of the business community, which no more appreciated his literary talents than Charleston appreciated those of Simms—for as Kennedy explained, "fine writing falls on the business world like water on a duck's back."[19]

In addition to his early literary associations with members of the Delphian Club, Kennedy had organized his own club of younger lawyer friends, while he remained close to his cousins in Virginia, Philip Pendleton Cooke and John Esten Cooke, who shared his interest in writing. He entered politics as soon as he entered law and widened his circle of literary friends at Annapolis and Washington, D.C. He met Irving, whose *Bracebridge Hall* had been a model for *Swallow Barn*, the year the book was published, and he met Simms in 1840. During a tour of New England in the 1840s, he came to know Longfellow, Prescott, and other of the Brahmins, while he made friends with John Quincy Adams and Daniel Webster in Washington. An early Jacksonian turned Whig in 1833, Kennedy was obliged for family reasons to decline the diplomatic posts abroad that were offered him, though he served as secretary of the Navy under Fillmore. In 1863 he was awarded a doctor of laws degree by Harvard College as the most distinguished southern author on the Union side.

Although the Chesapeake literary society over which Kennedy presided did not seem sufficiently substantial to support a major literary magazine of its own, Thomas W. White started the *Southern Literary Messenger* in 1834 against the advice of friends and kept it going. Its early issues were honored by contributions from Beverley Tucker of William and Mary and his colleague Thomas R. Dew, but they included little to attract the educated general reader. Kennedy was among those from whom White hoped to receive contributions, but Kennedy refused his solicitations, as he did those of Simms in Charleston, not wishing to involve himself in what may have seemed to him the rather nasty work of literary reviewing. What Kennedy did contribute to White was the services of his young protégé Edgar Allan Poe.

During the year and several months that Poe edited the *Messenger*, it was distinguished by his own contributions of reviews, short stories, and verse, while otherwise retaining its pedestrian character. One reason Poe and the magazine parted company was that White's conception differed from Poe's execution. White was not ambitious, as Poe was, to rival the British reviews and monthlies and enter Northern literary quarrels. The magazine that White had in mind was to be primarily regional in outlook, a vehicle that the Chesapeake gentry would support and contribute to and be proud of, and in this he succeeded sufficiently to keep his magazine alive. While Northern writers, including Longfellow, Elizabeth Oakes Smith, and the ubiquitous Mrs. Signourey began to appear in its columns, the quality of regional contributions improved, with increasing help from the oceanographer Matthew Maury and from the Cooke brothers.[20]

ᴈ⩥ III ⩤ᴈ

SOUTHERN LITERARY GENTLEMEN, some of whom considered it presumptuous to speak of American literature at all, hardly expected to create a literature of their own apart from the rest of the nation. Nor did their literary magazines seek to foster literary disunion. John R. Thompson, who edited the *Messenger* from 1847 to 1860, observed, as he was taking his leave of the magazine, that

> We have endeavored to cultivate kindly feelings between the two divisions of the country, believing that in the Republic of Letters at least there should be no strifes and bickerings. . . . The magazine has been prompt to recognize the highest merit alike in all quarters of the land, and the sins of Bryant, the editor, have not deadened us to the beauties of Bryant, the poet.[21]

Even *Russell's Magazine*, launched in the year of Bleeding Kansas and the Dred Scot decision, studiously attempted to avoid anti-Yankee bias in literary reviews.

There remained the institution of slavery that was peculiar to the Southern states, however, and that required Southerners to remain ever vigilant in the face of an expanding free-state population to the north and west. In 1787 southern members of the Constitutional Convention had expected the population of the slave states to increase more rapidly than that of the free states as time went on, but such had proved not to be the case. By the time of the Missouri Compromise debates three decades later, the South had lost its position of parity in the House of Representatives and was fighting desperately to retain it in the Senate. Whether slavery was to be considered a necessary evil or a positive good, it remained the legal right and shaped the society of a conscious minority within a predominantly free nation. In 1828 John C. Calhoun's *South Carolina Exposition* and *Protest* signified the readiness of members of Charleston's gentry to secede from the Union to defend its vital interests.

In January 1831 Garrison issued the first number of the *Liberator*, which immediately became notorious in the South, where its abusive attacks were widely reprinted in local newspapers. Later in 1831 Nat Turner organized a rebellion in Southampton County, Virginia, killing 57 whites, mainly women and children. Representatives of western counties, where few farmers owned slaves, responded to the rebellion by introducing a resolution in the state legislature calling for the abolition of slavery. Following a full debate, eastern planters overwhelmingly defeated the resolution, and Professor Thomas R. Dew of the College of William and Mary improved upon the occasion by writing a *Review of the Debate*, which comprised an extended scholarly defense of the institution of slavery on biblical, anthropological, sociological, and historical grounds. Emancipation ceased to be open to public discussion after the Virginia debate, and the learned vindication of slavery established itself as the most broadly rewarding field of scholarship open to southern intellectuals.

What appeared to be an aggressive slavocracy to Northern abolitionists seemed divided, defensive, and vulnerable to those Southerners who necessarily identified their culture with the peculiar institution and who now came under open attack from Northern abolitionists. In reaction to the abolitionists, the South imposed censorship upon itself with the aid of President Jackson and the federal post office to keep subversive literature out of the hands of Southern blacks, while stricter legal codes circumscribed the activities of free negroes and of slaves. James DeBow, as editor of *DeBow's Review*, meanwhile attempted with little success to do something about the economically fragmented character of the slave states and their abject economic dependence upon the North.

There were "fire eaters" in the South such as Robert Barnwell Rhett of South Carolina and Edmund Ruffin of Virginia, who were as unrestrained in their fulminations as were Wendell Phillips in Boston and Gerrit Smith in Utica, New York, whom they resembled in elitist temperament as well as reckless ideological commitment. They were condemned by moderates in the South, however, just as Phillips and Smith were condemned by moderates in the North, and so long as there appeared to be hope for a Union that would remain viably half slave and half free, literary men in the South tended to keep their distance from the fire eaters, even when engaged in defending slavery against the attacks of abolitionist critics. Hugh Swinton Legaré and his associate on the *Southern Review*, James Lewis Petigru, remained strong Unionists during the South Carolina nullification crisis and afterward. William Gilmore Simms, who assumed a leading role in Charleston's subsequent literary periodicals, remained Unionist until 1856, when he collided with hostile audiences on a northern lecture tour and returned in fury to cast his lot with the secessionists.

In addition to producing numerous volumes of historical novels and verse and literary essays, Simms contributed writings in defense of slavery to the body of proslavery literature that remains the primary product of

Southern antebellum literary nationalism. To Northern antislavery men, this growing literature was abominable evidence of the overweaning aggressiveness of the slavocracy. To the more literary of the Southern men who contributed to this argument, such writing tended to be viewed as an unfortunately necessary defense against the irresponsible slanders of the abolitionists.

The Southern intellectuals who essayed a defense of American slave society formed a closely interlinked group that included Simms, William Harper, James Henry Hammond, and William Grayson of South Carolina and Thomas R. Dew, Nathaniel Beverley Tucker, George Frederick Holmes, and George Fitzhugh of Virginia. Simms and Holmes in particular made it their responsibility to keep in touch with others of the group and with each other. All were planters, as befitted Southern gentlemen of letters. Dew, Tucker, and Holmes were also college professors, and Harper and Hammond were in politics, Hammond as governor of and senator from South Carolina. Simms was the only professional literary man among them, but then except for a few magazine editors, Simms could be considered the only professional man of letters in the whole intellectual community of the South.[22]

Responsibility for the defense of slavery by no means rested with these intellectuals alone. Ministers formulated elaborate religious justifications. Physicians, led by Dr. Josiah Nott of Alabama, argued the separate creation of the races, and anyone else who had an idea on the subject and could write it down was welcome to do so. However, there was particular pressure upon recognized Southern intellectuals to contribute their learning to the cause. The German-American scholar Francis Lieber, who taught at South Carolina College until the eve of the Civil War, was sure that his failure to contribute to this literature put the presidency of the college out of his reach. "Nothing," he explained, "would give me greater renown than a pamphlet written for the South especially in favor of slavery."[23] President Thomas Cooper of the College of South Carolina, the English Unitarian minister whom Jefferson considered the most learned man in America, became a learned expounder of the virtue as well as the necessity of slavery.

Cooper appears to have relished the popularity his advocacy brought him in his adopted state, but he was no Southern gentleman. Those Southern gentlemen who responded to this demand upon their talents placed themselves in the awkward position of seeming to be catering to popularity, and the resulting popularity embarrassed and in some cases irritated them. For the prolific Simms in particular, the admiring attention paid to his proslavery writings presented a bitter contrast to the comparative disinterest on the part of the Southern reading public in his literary productions. Nor were these men always able to approach the subject as honestly as they might have wished to. The one proslavery argument that all agreed upon was the unacceptability for them of emancipation. Hammond wrote Simms of slavery:

> As to the thing *per se*, I do not love it. I believe it a political and social blessing, taking government and society at large. As an individual, I would far prefer tenants to slaves. But that system is wholly impracticable now and abolition would be simply to *ruin* all things.[24]

Jefferson remained an awkward problem for proslavery advocates, who did not wish to repudiate the honored philosopher of the agrarian South but who could not accept the open-ended egalitarianism of the Declaration of Independence or the antislavery bias of *Notes on Virginia*. William Smith of South Carolina explained away the argument for emancipation in Jefferson's *Notes* as "the effusions of the speculative philosophy of his young and ardent mind" and argued that it was "impossible when his mind became enlarged by reflection and informed by observation, that he could entertain such sentiments, and hold slaves at the same time."[25] Jefferson's natural rights theory and his criticisms of slavery came to be dismissed as the passing influence of French philosophy upon him, which he later outgrew as the despotic consequences of that philosophy in France revealed themselves. After Jefferson's death, Southern writers demolished the argument of the Declaration line by line, as Joseph Dennie and other northern arch-Federalists had earlier done.

Emancipation was unthinkable, so proslavery writers put the best possible face on slave society, ignoring its gross evils, which were obvious even to them. Beyond the basic fact of involuntary servitude, the most painfully evident of these evils were the cruelties practiced by some masters, the licentiousness that betrayed itself in a large and growing mulatto population, and the sundering of slave families to satisfy the supply and demand of the slave trade. To deny or to minimize these evils, as all pro-slavery writers resolutely did, hardly served as a positive defense of the peculiar institution, however. To assert that blacks were naturally and happily suited to slavery or that the institution served to civilize and Christianize barbaric peoples was to defend the institution more positively so far as the slaves themselves were concerned. Yet this, too, did not answer the charge that slavery demoralized and retarded Southern society as a whole. Inevitably the defense of slavery required that comparisons be made with nonslave societies, to demonstrate that the former was as good as or superior to the latter.

Proslavery writers were thus compelled for comparative purposes to examine and analyze free society in a systematic way that reformers in free society did not themselves feel called upon to do. Sociology as a scholarly concept in America originated in the course of the proslavery argument. The first two American books to contain the term in their titles were both proslavery works published in 1854: the Mississippian Henry Hughes's *A Treatise on Sociology* and the Virginian George Fitzhugh's *Sociology for the South.* George Frederick Holmes, who corresponded with Fitzhugh, also corresponded with Auguste Comte and was probably the most scholarly follower of Comte in antebellum America. In later years, when slavery no longer remained to be defended, Holmes published a more sophisticated sociology text of his own, *The Science of Society*, which appeared in 1883, the year that Lester F. Ward's *Dynamic Sociology* was published.

Although Fitzhugh achieved widest recognition as a proslavery social philosopher, he was not honored accordingly by his fellow advocates. Among the leading Southern intellectuals, Holmes was closest to Fitzhugh, and even Holmes became disaffected toward him, concluding that Fitzhugh was chiefly a "great egoist." Unlike Holmes and others of his circle, Fitzhugh made little pretense to being a scholar. In *Cannibals All! or, Slaves without Masters* (1857), he dismissed philosophy as a waste of time, and he admitted to Holmes that he had never read Aristotle; though he later did and was pleased to find Aristotle in agreement with him.[26]

Those whom Holmes associated with as equals included Beverley Tucker, Edmund Ruffin, James Hammond, and William Simms. These five men made up "the Sacred Circle," as Simms called them, of Southern intellectuals, who thought of themselves as sharing a vocation more elevated than that of apologists for the institution, however necessary that role might be. In their own minds these five men constituted the intellectual elite of the South, and as such they shared the duty to guide and shape Southern civilization. "Duty," Tucker declared, required the intellectual to be a "safe guide to blind but honest ignorance," while Simms explained that "Superior endowments were specially conferred by Providence" upon him and his circle for the "tuition and patriarchal guardianship" of humanity, and "The true business of genius is to lift and guide a race."[27] Their grandiose aspirations proved impossible to realize, but more modest aims would perhaps have proved equally unattainable. The sacred circle was united by a common sense of alienation from their own society.

Some of these men were early and ardent secessionists, as with Beverley Tucker and Edmund Ruffin, but others were not. Senator Hammond wrote Simms from Washington, D.C., in 1860 that he avoided the North-South issue, because anything he might add to the discussion would be "rather more against the South than the North." The secessionists, in his opinion, expressed "the insanity of one-idea *Enthusiasts*, the weak folly of besotted *Ignorance*." By the time South Carolina pulled out of the Union, however, Hammond was acknowledging "all honor & glory to that wide & noble Convention."[28] When war came, Hammond as well as the erstwhile nationalist Simms entered enthusiastically into the creation of a Confederacy where their intellectual stewardship might prove more influential than had been the case in the southern section of the federal Republic.

John C. Calhoun, who dominated South Carolina politics and who constructed a political science for the South, was not a member of the sacred circle or of any intellectual coterie. He lacked the necessary quality of sociability, and he displayed little interest in pursuing learning for its own sake. He devoted his mind to statecraft, or perhaps simply to politics. That he possessed a brilliant mind and a masterful command of it southern intellectuals conceded; yet they were made restive by his iron authority and his abrupt changes in political direction. The extended essays that capped Calhoun's reputation as a political thinker were not published until his death. Calhoun died during the debates over the Compromise of 1850, where, unlike Webster, he defended the integrity of the section he represented rather than that of the nation.

ᚱ IV ᚲ

HAVING IMPRESSIVELY DEFENDED American slavery in his *Review of the Debates in the Virginia Legislature* (1832), Thomas R. Dew of the College of William and Mary turned his attention to womanhood. In a series of three articles contributed to the first volume of the *Southern Literary Messenger* (1835), Dew presented "Dissertation on the Characteristic Differences between the Sexes, and on the Position and Influence of Women in Society."[29] In his defense of black slavery, Dew had refrained from presenting arguments based upon supposed racial differences between blacks and whites, and in considering the role of women in society, he explicitly rejected the argument that females were inherently different from males either mentally or emotionally. He observed that so-called masculine traits of character were in many individual cases more perfectly developed in women than in men, and taking the female sex as a whole, he declined to speculate on "whether their moral and intellectual differences are wholly due to education or partly to nature."[30]

Having disavowed arguments based upon supposed psychological and mental differences between the sexes, Dew presented an argument for male supremacy based upon the indisputable physical differences of women and men—most decisively, the relative lack of bodily strength that placed women in the position of physical subordination to men. The evident physical differences of the sexes were sufficient to account for the natural subordination of women to men that was everywhere observable. Consequently,

> Women are precisely what men make them, all over the world. . . . The greater physical strength of man, enables him to occupy the foreground in the picture. . . . Her inferior strength and sedentary habits confine her within the domestic circle. . . . She must rely upon the strength of others . . . by the exhibition of those qualities which delight and fascinate. . . . Grace, modesty and loveliness are the charms which constitute her power.[31]

In short, the ideal of Southern womanhood simply represented the natural subordination of women to men arising from the physical differences of the sexes.

Dew went on to argue that the intellect of women benefited in important ways from their domestic situation, by comparison to men, whose

> intellectual characters are, to a very great degree, modelled by their employments. . . . Woman is in general, except so far as affected by her husband, free from this influence, which is so unfavorable to that varied and brilliant conversation suited to promiscuous society.

Such being the case, Dew regretted "the practice prevalent among the married and elderly gentlemen of separating themselves from the rest of the company at dinner parties and evening gatherings to talk among themselves" on the comparatively narrow topics of particular concern to them. Meanwhile, "For the same reason that woman surpasses man in conversation, she is superior to him in epistolary comment," her letters generally being more varied and interesting than those of men.[32] It would appear to follow from this that women were naturally superior to men in belles lettres generally, but Dew limits his consideration to the literary skills of women in private correspondence.

Dew quoted Joseph Addison as suggesting

> that had women determined their own point of honor, it is probably that wit or good nature would have carried it against chastity, but our sex have preferred the latter, and women have conformed to the decision.

Chastity was the point of honor, rather than wit and good nature, respecting women in the North as well as in the South. But in the South black slavery added dramatic emphasis to this point of honor. Wilbur J. Cash wrote that the brute fact of widely prevalent miscegenation in Southern society inspired obsessive Southern defensiveness:

> On the one hand, the convention must be set up that the thing simply did not exist, and enforced under penalty of being shot; and on the other, the woman must be compensated, the revolting suspicion in the male that he might be slipping into bestiality got rid of, by glorifying her; the Yankee must be answered by proclaiming from the housetops that Southern Virtue, so far from being inferior, was superior, not alone to the North's but to any on earth, and adducing Southern Womanhood in proof.[33]

Miscegenation aside, it remained true, as a Southern gentleman explained, that "The Slave Institution of the South increases the tendency to dignify the family. Each planter is in fact a Patriarch—his position compels him to be a ruler in his household." And throughout this slave society, "Domestic relations become those which are most prized." Within this system, qualities of feminine dependence were rated highly by men. In Fitzhugh's words:

> As long as she is nervous, fickle, capricious, delicate, diffident and dependent, man will worship and adore her. Her weakness is her strength, and her true art is to cultivate and improve that weakness.[34]

Fitzhugh warned that changes in either the dependent role of woman or the slave status of the black would disrupt the family and destroy society.

Paradoxically, this ideal Southern woman was as practical and masterful as she was capricious and delicate. As the Virginian John Esten Cooke described a fictional heroine,

> She was, indeed, all woman in her organization—both timid and firm, both pliable and unbending. Under the shy manner you could see this force of character, and felt that if the moment came this girl would be capable of opposing her will with unfaltering nerve to any obstacle in her path.[35]

The mistress of a large plantation and mother of many children required such will and stamina to perform her manifold plantation-keeping duties while comporting herself graciously as the lady of the manor.

This all-capable mistress of the plantation appears throughout the fictional accounts of the old South, whether written by Northerners or Southerners. "If we are to believe the novelists," William R. Taylor wrote, "the plantation house was populated by generous hearted but improvident or indolent men and single-minded and domineering women and their incipiently Amazonish daughters."[36] Indeed, the circumstances that confronted the bride of a Southern planter virtually required her to establish practical authority over a domain that might in many cases be more meaningfully compared with a European duchy than with upper-class Northern households such as those the Cabot women dominated in Boston.

Beyond this domestic domain, Southern gentlewomen circulated in "the *fashionable* world," together with marriageable maidens who, according to the South Carolina reformer Sarah Moore Grimké, had been taught that

> to attract the notice and win the attentions of men, by their external charms, is the chief business of fashionable girls. They seldom think that men will be allured by intellectual acquirements, because they find, that where any mental superiority exists, a woman is generally shunned and regarded as stepping out of her "appropriate sphere."[37]

Women in these circumstances could not expect to be taken seriously. The Scottish traveler Mrs. Basil Hall observed of Southern society that "Women are just looked upon as house-keepers in this country" and that "there appears to be no sympathy between the sexes. They have no subjects of conversation in common." Once married, they had little reason to converse with each other; hence the vile custom at social gatherings Mrs. Hall attended in the South of women herding together and men segregating themselves.[38] Outside the fashionable world, according to Grimké, Southern girls were brought up to consider marriage as "a kind of preferment" and to look upon housekeeping for a husband as "the end of her being." To this end, Southern girls were trained "to regard themselves as a kind of machinery . . . of little value as the *intelligent* companions of men."

For literary diversion, Grimké added, women were stultified by "the novels which inundate the press, and which do more to destroy her character as a rational creature, than anything else."[39] Southern women wrote as well as read the women's books that inundated the press. Among the most successful writers of bestsellers in America, E.D.E.N. Southworth, August Jane Evans, Eliza Ann Dupuy, and Mary Jane McIntosh were all native Southerners, while Caroline Gilman and Caroline Lee Hentz were transplanted New Englanders who began their writing careers after marrying into Southern society. Women poets meanwhile appeared abundantly in the South as elsewhere in the nation, Mary Elizabeth Lee of Charleston being the most successful among them in placing her verse in magazines and gift books.

This literary activity went against paternalistic Southern disapproval of female authorship. Professor Dew's colleague at the College of William and Mary, Beverley Tucker, wrote that "The feeling which disposes woman to see her name in print is hardly less meritricious than that which makes her show her ankles." Rather than showing off creatively, woman should, averred Tucker, bask in the creative influence of her husband. As a gentleman in Tucker's novel, *George Balcome,* explained, "Even should her faculties be superior to his, he cannot raise her so high but that she will still feel herself a creature of his hands."[40] In deference to Southern moral values, many women did submit their literary offerings modestly under pseudonyms, but many more were disposed to see their names in print (and perhaps to show their ankles as well) against the disapproval expressed by Tucker.

These successful Southern authoresses mainly entered the field in the 1850s, following the appearance of Harriet Beecher Stowe's extraordinarily successful *Uncle Tom's Cabin,* and their writings were more remarkable for popularity than for literary quality. None of these women earned a literary reputation comparable to Stowe's. The Southern women of the era whose literary reputations stand highest today are Sarah Moore and Angelina Emily Grimké, who went north before writing their essays on abolition and women's rights in the 1830s, and Mary Chesnut, who aspired to be a novelist but ultimately achieved literary distinction with her carefully revised Civil War diary, posthumously published in 1905.

The writings and activities of Chesnut and the Grimké sisters demonstrate the independence of mind that might be achieved by privileged Southern women raised in families where the head of the household allowed daughters to be educated beyond the requirements of domesticity. Chesnut's *diary* records friendships or acquaintances with the leading men of letters of South Carolina: William Gilmore Simms, who supported her husband politically; members of Simms's circle, including Henry Timrod and Paul Hamilton Hayne; the LeConte brothers and other scholars of the College of South Carolina; and such cultivated political men as Langdon Cheves Jr. and Robert M. T. Hunter. Serious discourse with these gentlemen was quite in order on a one-to-one basis but was otherwise banned from mixed company.

Thus with Chesnut, while visiting Charleston in 1861:

I dined tête-a-tête with Langdon Cheves. So quiet. So intelligent. So very sensible withal. There never was a pleasanter person or a better man than he. While we were at table Judge Whitner, Tom Frost, and Isaac Hayne came. They broke up our deeply interesting conversation—for I was hearing what an honest and a brave man feared for his country. And then the Rutledges dislodged the newcomers and bore me off to drive on the Battery. On the staircase met Mrs. Izard, who came for the same purpose. On the Battery, Governor Adams stopped us. He had heard of my saying he looked like Marshal Pelessier—and he came to say at least I had made a personal remark which pleased him, &c&c, for once in my life.

Later Chesnut "received orders that I was not to walk any more with men on the Battery. Is not all this too ridiculous at my time of life?"[41] Intellectually sober discussion did not suit the style of Southern sociability in general, and in particular it was not permitted to intrude itself upon the ladies.

Chesnut felt free to speak her own mind about issues as well as personalities, apparently all the freer for the fact that as a woman she did not count politically. She seems never to have been constrained to conceal her hostility toward slavery or toward the oppression of women that she associated with it. An overseer on the Chesnut plantation, who accepted her assertion that most Southern white women were "abolitionists in their hearts, and hot ones too," added, "Mrs. Chesnut is the worst. They have known that here on her for years."[42] Chesnut's aristocratic status evidently entitled her to outspoken opinions that would not have been permitted in lower-class women, and her impressions of the extent of abolitionist opinion among Southern women may have unduly reflected the views of women of her own class, whose husbands had such ready access to their slave quarters.

Chesnut's criticisms of slavery necessarily took the form of private opinions rather than public pronouncements. When Angelina Grimké published her abolitionist *Appeal to the Christian Women of the Southern States* in 1836, it was publicly burned by the Charleston postmaster, while the Charleston police warned Angelina's mother that they had orders to arrest and deport Angelina should she come home for a visit, as she had been planning to do. The police also warned that Angelina might be the victim of mob violence before they could take her into custody. This may have been a scare tactic. Chesnut, who was entering her teens at the time, appears never to have become aware of the pamphlets of the Grimké sisters nor of public outrage against them. Nevertheless, the views of these Charleston gentlewomen on slavery and on the condition of women closely resembled the private views Chesnut came to record in her journal a generation later.

Like Chesnut, the Grimkés grew up in an aristocratic South Carolina family where serious attention was paid to the educations of daughters— up to a point. Sarah's father, the prominent planter-politician Judge John Faucheraud Grimké, did not accede to her request that she be allowed to study with her brother while he prepared to meet the classical college entrance requirements (as Judith Sargent had done with her brother in Gloucester, Massachusetts). Sarah nevertheless acquired a sound education and later assisted in the education of her younger sister, Angelina.

The radicalization of Sarah chiefly began at the age of twenty-seven, when she accompanied her father to Philadelphia and became attracted to the doctrines of Quakerism, in particular to its "witness" against slavery and the oppression of women. Sarah converted Angelina to the Society of Friends, whereupon the more activist Angelina led Sarah into the Garrisonian abolitionist movement over the protest of more conservative Quaker friends. Finally, most scandalously of all, the abolitionist movement led the Grimké sisters to the rostrum, where they shattered universally accepted standards of decency by entering the arena of public life as contestants in the manly art of oratory.

The one well-remembered American precedent for so blatant a breech of propriety had been a lecture tour undertaken by a Scottish-born woman, Frances "Fanny" Wright, in 1828 in a number of American cities. Wright was a freethinker who had founded a community for free blacks in Tennessee and who in her lectures mixed attacks on conventional views of religion, marriage, and family with calls for the emancipation of slaves. With Robert Dale Owen, she published the *New Harmony Gazette* at an Indiana utopian community, later moving the paper to New York City and renaming it the *Free Enquirer*. Wright's varied and remarkable pursuits brought her name before a growing public. But it was her physical presence at the rostrum that earned her national notoriety. The unprecedented brazenness of these performances attracted rude audiences of curiosity seekers and extensive coverage in the national press. Wright's defiance of convention won her few public expressions of support, and afterward it seemed inconceivable that respectable American women might follow the example of this Scottish Jezebel who defied Saint Paul's explicit injunction to women against public speaking.

In contrast to Frances Wright, the Grimké sisters advanced meekly to the public platform at the urging of others. While visiting New York City, they had responded to invitations to address small parlor gatherings of women on slavery as they had known it, against the advice of Philadelphia Quakers, with whom they were beginning to part ways. The parlor gatherings attracted larger audiences of mixed company, and as word spread of the sisters' eloquence as well as firsthand knowledge, antislavery societies in New England requested the sisters to speak to their groups as well. In New England the sisters advanced with great trepidation from parlor performances to public meetings, and there they encountered furious opposition from the Council of Congregational Ministers of Massachusetts. The council issued a public pastoral letter concerning the Grimkés' activities, explaining that "The power of woman is her dependence, flowing from the consciousness of the weakness which God had given her for her protection" and warning that

> If the vine, whose strength and beauty is to lean on the trellis-work, and half conceal its cluster, thinks to assume the independence and the overshadowing nature of the elm, it will not only cease to bear fruit, but fall in shame and dishonor into the dust.[43]

Armed in righteous causes and by aristocratic upbringings, the Grimké sisters responded in kind, Angelina expressing herself through the columns of Garrison's *Liberator* and a further *Appeal to the Women of the Nominally Free States* (1837), Sarah through magazine articles published as *Letters on the Condition of Women and the Equality of the Sexes* (1838). Until confronted with the issue of free speech for women, Sarah and Angelina had drawn upon standard antislavery arguments, supported by their own personal knowledge of slave society. With their responses to attacks upon them as female public speakers, they found themselves in an uncharted area of controversy giving rise to the original lines of argument by which they formulated a distinctively American ideology of equal rights, that *"whatsoever it is morally right for a man to do, it is morally right for a woman to do."*[44]

The Grimké sisters had "leaped from 'their spheres,'" as the Boston abolitionist Maria Weston Chapman wrote, leading the way for growing numbers of women who were presently lecturing to mixed audiences on any subject of public interest, right along with the men.[45] In 1848 at Seneca Falls, New York, the more radical among them joined Elizabeth Cady

Stanton in advocating woman suffrage. But such demand for admission to the ballot box posed no threat to the existing manly order in the foreseeable future. More immediately challenging were the women who were actually ascending to the speakers' platforms of lecture halls and churches to participate in that most masculine, noble, intellectual, elevated, and eloquent branch of the civilized arts, the statesman's art of public speaking.

Meanwhile down in the plantation South, Mary Boykin Chesnut wrote in her diary that she had "Tried to read Margaret Fuller Ossoli, but could not."[46] Chesnut shared areas of intellectual interest with Ossoli, being a voracious reader of serious literature and holding zealously feminist opinions in the privacy of her journals, but the assertive Yankee bluestocking must have seemed an impertinent if not alien figure to the South Carolina planter's lady. Chesnut belonged to the sorority of Southern womanhood, and she remained inextricably bound by its code of behavior, regardless of her wealth and high station. In an overwhelmingly agrarian economy that depended upon a black slave labor system, white women of whatever conditions were hardly in a better position to contest the domestic institutions of the region than were the slaves beneath them. They accommodated themselves as a matter of course to the patriarchal social order that prevailed throughout the slave states.

ఇ V ఈ

CHARLESTON EMERGED IN 1828 as the center for secessionist sentiment in the South with Calhoun's anonymous *South Carolina Exposition*, attacking the "tariff of abominations" and arguing the sovereign right of an individual state to nullify such federal enactments. Although the immediate issue was tariff legislation, the underlying issue was slavery. While the upland cotton country of South Carolina had entered upon an economic decline, the lowland planters continued to thrive on the culture of rice and sea island cotton. Aristocratic willfulness in Charleston was fostered by continued prosperity rather than threatened poverty. This prosperity depended upon a labor force of black slaves that greatly outnumbered the white population, however, and in 1822 the Charleston gentry had been traumatized by the discovery of Denmark Vesey's well-organized, widely ramified conspiracy of slaves and free blacks to overthrow their masters. Vesey had read antislavery speeches made in Congress by Northern politicians during the Missouri Compromise debates—the same politicians who were now plundering the agrarian South through protective tariffs.

Members of the tightly knit Charleston gentry came to see themselves as the elite guardians of Southern institutions against Northern manufacturers, democrats, and abolitionists. In 1832, led by Calhoun, they elected a legislature that called a state convention to declare the tariff of 1832 null and void within the state. President Jackson responded with a Force Act, authorizing use of federal troops against the offending state, together with a somewhat face-saving compromise tariff. The nullifiers had expected other Southern states to follow their lead. None did, and opposition within South Carolina itself threatened to develop into armed rebellion. Isolated and beleaguered, the Carolinians withdrew their ordinance against the tariff, while vaingloriously passing another one against the Force Act. Victory was claimed by all sides, but the Charleston fire-eaters had suffered a humiliating defeat from which some of them did not recover. From that time forward a group of men among the Charleston gentry remained, in the phrase of the Charleston classicist Basil Gildersleeve, like a fetus in a bottle, unchanged by passing events, waiting obsessively for the opportunity that finally came following Lincoln's election in 1860 to lead the South out of the Union.[47]

Meanwhile, during the Mexican War, Congressman David Wilmot of Pennsylvania provided Southern fire-eaters with an issue calculated to unite the South against the North when he introduced the Wilmot Proviso to Congress, proposing to prohibit slavery in all territory to be acquired from Mexico. The proviso passed the House, where the free states enjoyed a substantial majority, but it was blocked in the Senate, where equality of representation had been maintained between free and slave states. The proviso remained a hot emotional issue on both sides, as the Mexican Cession of 1848 extended the western boundaries of the nation from the Rocky Mountains to the Pacific and as the free-slave parity in the Senate became threatened by the impending admission of California as a free state. Under these circumstances, Calhoun sought to create a united Southern front at a Southern convention called in Nashville in 1850.

There still were prominent South Carolinians who remained Union-

ist in sentiment, but they had lost political power in the state to the secessionists. The issue that effectively divided South Carolina's political leadership by 1850 was whether to secede under any circumstances, as Robert
Barnwell Rhett urged, or wait for secessionist support to mature in other
Southern states, as Langdon Cheves wished to do. As it turned out, the
Charleston secessionists failed to control the Nashville convention, which
awkwardly straddled the issue. Furthermore, the convention was itself
overshadowed by the debate over the Compromise of 1850 as it made its
way through Congress, highlighted by Senate speeches of Webster, Calhoun, Clay, Douglas, and others. The omnibus of unrelated measures that
made up the Compromise of 1850 appeared for several years thereafter
successfully to have weathered the crisis. It failed to appease secessionists
in the south, however, and it included a new fugitive slave law that further
enflamed antislavery sentiment in the north.

James D. B. De Bow was a Southern nationalist from Charleston whose
major concern was the Southern economy and its dependence upon Northern business enterprise. De Bow moved to New Orleans and in 1846 founded
the *Commercial Review of the South and Southwest,* which became known as
De Bow's Review. In it he encouraged Southern manufactures, development
of Southern trade with Europe, and the organization of Southern commercial conventions. A Southern cultural nationalist as well, he supported
Southern colleges and Southern publishers seeking to lessen the intellectual dependence of the South upon the North. Encouraged by De Bow,
the Southern Commercial Convention at Memphis in 1853 passed a resolution recommending to Southerners

> the education of their youth at home as far as practicable; the employ-
> ment of native teachers in their schools and colleges; the encouragement
> of a home press; the publication of books adapted to the educational wants
> and social conditions of these States, and the encouragement and support
> of inventions and discoveries in the arts and sciences, by their citizens.[48]

In 1856 the Southern Commercial Convention meeting in Savannah
returned to the cause of encouraging native cultural institutions, appointing a committee to prepare a "series of books in every department of
study, from the earliest primer to the highest grade of literature and science." The erstwhile Brook Farm resident and belle lettrist George Will-

iam Curtis, writing in *Putnam's Magazine*, ridiculed the idea of a slave society fostering its own literature and cited William J. Grayson's *The Hireling and the Slave* as an unhappy example of such a literature. Noting the absence of William Gilmore Simms from the textbook committee, Curtis invented a resolution of his own for the convention: "*Resolved*, That there be a Southern literature. *Resolved*, That William Gilmore Simms, LL.D. be requested to write this literature."[49]

Simms had ventured north in 1856 on what proved to be an ill-timed lecture tour. Several months earlier Senator Charles Sumner of Massachusetts had insulted Senator Andrew Butler of South Carolina. Butler's relative Congressman Preston Brooks of South Carolina had responded by caning Senator Sumner into insensibility, and the temperature of the sectional controversy had risen on both sides of the Mason-Dixon Line. Simms meanwhile set forth on a series of speaking engagements that had been planned with the idea of renewing old acquaintances in the North as well as earning needed money. He had enjoyed success lecturing throughout the South on literary topics such as "The Moral Character of Hamlet" and on historical subjects such as "South Carolina and the Revolution," and it was hoped that Northerners would enjoy them as well.

Welcomed north by Evart Duyckinck and other of his New York literary friends, Simms began his schedule in Buffalo before an initially friendly audience of twelve hundred. He later wrote his friend Senator James Hammond of South Carolina that there had been nothing in his lecture on South Carolina in the Revolution

> which should have given offense. . . . I made no allusion to Brooks, directly or indirectly. I did to Sumner, as the wanton assailant of S.C. . . . I had to do this, in order to show why & on what points, I had undertaken to correct the vulgar mistakes or misrepresentations of her history.[50]

Simms evidently remained unaware of how bellicose he actually became in the course of his lecture. Weathering the storm of outrage that followed, Simms repeated the talk in Rochester and New York City, then canceled the rest of his tour when his lecture committee informed him "that they could not only sell no tickets, but could not succeed in *giving* them away." Returning hurt and uncomprehending to his plantation, this erstwhile literary nationalist now counseled "constant recognition & assertion of a *Southern Nationality*.[51]

Southern men of letters tended to be reluctant rebels at best, even in the secessionist hotbed of Charleston. During the nullification crisis, the aristocratic gentlemen associated with the *Southern Review*, including the "Union Man of South Carolina," James L. Petigru, had led the opposition to nullification, Hugh Swinton Legaré writing from Europe that "If the Union should go to pieces, it will be one hideous wreck—of which, excepting New-England, no two parts will hold together."[52] Simms's Sacred Circle of self-appointed spokesmen for slave society and the South included such Virginia fire-eaters as Beverley Tucker, who lamented the failure of the Old Dominion to support nullification, and Edmund Ruffin, the agricultural scientist and long-time secessionist, who committed suicide when the Confederacy went down to defeat in 1865. For Simms himself secession was a sad business, separating him from his literary friends in the North and from the region where his books had been published and sold and far more widely read than in his native South.

A considerably more reluctant secessionist than Simms was his literary associate Paul Hamilton Hayne, poet and editor of *Russell's Magazine* during its valiant four-year effort to foster literature in Charleston in the late 1850s. Hayne's uncle, Robert Young Hayne, brought the family name its most enduring national recognition through his U.S. Senate debate with Daniel Webster in 1830, upholding the state's rights interpretation of the nature of the Union. Paul Hamilton Hayne, on the other hand, succumbed to the charms of Brahmin culture during two visits to Boston in the mid-1850s, while arranging with Ticknor and Fields for publication of three volumes of his poetry. Depressed by the dearth of literary companionship in Charleston, Hayne was writing Northern friends complaining of his sense of isolation and expressing his desire to move to Boston as late as the summer of 1860, four months before South Carolina seceded from the Union.[53]

Neither were the leading literati of the Chesapeake region distinguished by secessionist zeal. John R. Thompson, the Richmond lawyer-poet who edited the *Southern Literary Messenger* for thirteen years to 1860, pursued an editorial policy of sympathy for Southern literary nationalism together with a defense of Southern slave society that became increasingly aggressive over the years. Like Haynes, however, Thompson valued a growing friendship with Northern writers, especially New Yorkers, including Richard Henry Stoddard, Rufus Griswold, and Frank R. Stockton, who contributed to the *Messenger*. He left Richmond for Baltimore in 1860 but returned when war broke out, writing that "every consideration of filial and patriotic duty would oblige me to remain and share in the fate of my native Virginia, apart from any convictions I might entertain of the original folly of secession."[54]

Thompson's successor as editor of the *Messenger*, the physician and dialect humorist George William Bagby, showed greater enthusiasm for the war at first, joining the army and fighting at Bull Run despite severe physical disabilities, which resulted in his discharge in 1861. He soon lost confidence in Jefferson Davis and the prospects for the Confederacy, however, and at the conclusion of the war attempted to relocate in New York, only to be forced back to Richmond by bad health. John Esten Cooke of Richmond, among the most prolific contributors of prose and poetry to the *Messenger* as well as to Northern periodicals, was neither proslavery nor anti-Yankee in sentiment. He nevertheless decided for secession following Lincoln's election and fought from Bull Run to Appomattox, chiefly as a cavalry officer. However, "My first thought on the surrender," he wrote, was to "get my two horses fat on grass—sell them—then to N.Y.—write, and look Paris-ward."[55]

Cooke's cousin John Pendleton Kennedy had rendered an appealingly sentimental version of the slave plantation in *Swallow Barn*, but Kennedy was a Baltimore businessman and Whig politician who viewed slavery as a reactionary institution that was inhibiting material progress in the South. In 1860 Kennedy sided unquestioningly with the Unionists, denouncing secession in South Carolina as "a great act of supreme folly and injustice . . . which history will record as the most foolish of blunders as well as the most wicked of crimes."[56]

North-South literary friendships survived the war, and at war's end Bryant, Duyckinck, and other literary men of New York stood ready to resume old ties and to assist old friends in reestablishing themselves. The surviving Southern literati of the antebellum years had in most cases been ravaged by war, however, and they were now seeking to survive in a Reconstruction atmosphere of hostility or indifference on the part of the Northern reading public and Northern publishers. Cooke, who survived four years of combat without a wound, proved to be one of the luckier ones, securing writing assignments with the *New York World* and resuming a profitable relationship with Appletons. Simms also resumed publication of books and articles in New York, but he was poorly paid for what became hackwork for second-rate periodicals. During the war his house and plantation had been destroyed and rebuilt and destroyed again, together with a library of more than ten thousand volumes. He wrote Hayne in 1869, the year before he died, "I do not now write for fame or notoriety or the love of it, but simply to procure the wherewithal of life for my children" at the cost of "a continued strain upon the brain" that was doing injury to his health.[57]

Hayne's house and library had also been destroyed during the war and the large fortune he had inherited had been invested in Confederate enterprises and currency, which defeat rendered worthless. Ill and nearly penniless at war's end, he resettled with his family on a few acres of land in the Georgia pine barrens near Augusta, and lived there for twenty years until his death in 1886. He remained productive as a poet and as a correspondent with literary friends in New York, Boston, and the South. He continued, as before, to be read more widely in the North than in the South, but in the North he failed to experience the popularity and critical acclaim that came to be accorded to a younger generation of Southern writers of the New South, led by Joel Chandler Harris, Thomas Nelson Page, and George Washington Cable, authors of sentimentalized versions of the Old South that appealed especially to Northern readers.

≈§ 8 Ȝ

BOSTONIZATION OF THE
LITERARY REPUBLIC

ANTISLAVERY SENTIMENT HAD BEEN on the rise in Boston's literary community during the 1840s, stimulated in 1844 by the emancipation of slaves
in the British West Indies at the very time the U.S. government was preparing to admit the slave state of Texas to the Union. Literary men in Boston were predominantly opposed to the Mexican War, which provided
Thoreau with the occasion for his night in jail for refusing to pay taxes to
the state as a protest against its involvement in the war and for his subsequent essay on "Civil Disobedience." Lowell, who had entered the antislavery movement during his courtship of the abolitionist Maria White,
wrote for the *Pennsylvania Freeman* and the *National Anti-Slavery Standard*
and contributed his popular *Bigelow Papers* to the antiwar effort. It was the
Fugitive Slave Act of 1850 and Senator Daniel Webster's defense of it that
rallied literary Boston against the slave power.

Perhaps paradoxically, it was in defense of their provincial rights as
Yankee members of the Commonwealth of Massachusetts that the New
England literati extended their moral authority over the national Union
as a whole. The Garrisonian vindication of the rights of freeborn Yankees
against the encroachments of the slave power, which Wendell Phillips
had so effectively articulated, had been simultaneously and separately
pursued by Congressman John Quincy Adams. In contesting Southern
objections to his reading of antislavery petitions addressed to him by his
Massachusetts constituents, Adams broadened the antislavery issue to include the principle of free speech and the rights of all persons, including
nonvoting women, to petition governments concerning their grievances.
Single-handedly in session after session of the House of Representatives,
Adams attacked the "gag resolution" against antislavery petitions, which

Southerners had passed in Congress in 1836. Northern opinion gradually rallied to Adams's support, forcing the repeal of the gag rule in 1844. As a matter of personal conviction, Adams was an antislavery man, but as the representative of Quincy, Massachusetts, in Congress, Adams rallied Northern sentiment not against slavery itself but against surrendering native liberties to the slave power.

The Fugitive Slave Act of 1850 required Northerners to assist in the apprehension of runaways. This legal provision for the submission of Northern freemen to the authority of Southern slaveholders was enacted into law by a Southern-dominated Congress with the eloquent support of the supposed paladin of New England's liberties, Senator Daniel Webster. For a generation Webster had been the pride of Massachusetts, its peerless orator and foremost national statesman. Now in what was remembered as his Seventh of March Speech, Webster spoke for the preservation of the Union and for the fugitive slave bill as a necessary price of union. Webster was widely praised for his speech at the time, in Massachusetts and throughout the nation, but the adverse reaction of New England's literati was galvanic. Emerson wrote of the Seventh of March Speech that "There never was an event half so painful occurred in Boston."[1]

It was Whittier, the Quaker poet and dedicated abolitionist of long standing, who immortalized Webster's apostasy for this literati in his most powerful poem to date, "Ichabod." But much else was written on the subject, publicly and in private. Bostonians were reminded that Webster was an outsider whom the commonwealth had adopted and honored with high office, having been born and raised in New Hampshire and educated at Dartmouth. Following Webster's speech the normally even-tempered young Whig Charles Francis Adams wrote in his diary:

> It is a deep and damning spot on the good name of Massachusetts that a profligate adventurer from another state shall be able to come into this and beslave so many honest citizens with his bitter poison. For thirty years he has done much to corrupt the hearts of the young and the minds of the older community.[2]

Emerson was among those who had preferred not to be involved in the slavery question. Under pressure from friends and admirers, however, he made a pronouncement on the subject in 1844, avoiding the disturbing

Texas question and choosing as his text the emancipation of British West Indian slaves, which, he affirmed, gave rise to "the proud discovery that the black race can contend with the white." Then in 1851, when the Fugitive Slave Act effected the involvement of Massachusetts citizens in the enforcement of the slave system, Emerson gave notice that he would join those who refused to accept this dictate from slaveholders. Emerson delivered an attack on Webster and the Fugitive Slave Act in Concord in 1851 and again in New York City in 1854, arguing in both speeches in defense of Massachusetts rather than in opposition to slavery. Emerson told his New York audience that he "had never in my life up to this time suffered from the Slave Institution. Slavery in Virginia or Carolina was like Slavery in Africa or the Feejees, for me," until the new act "required me to hunt slaves," indicating moreover "that Slavery was no longer mendicant, but was become aggressive and dangerous." It proved to Emerson that the Garrisonians had been right all along, "the Cassandra that has foretold all that has befallen, fact for fact."[3]

Emerson's commitment to antislavery in 1850 was hardly calculated to influence popular sentiment on the subject in the nation at large, however it may have stirred up discussion within Brahmin Boston. By contrast, Harriet Beecher Stowe's similar response to the Fugitive Slave Act in 1850 resulted in an upheaval of national and international sentiment inspired by her extraordinarily popular and influential *Uncle Tom's Cabin*. Like Emerson, Stowe had never previously found reason to oppose slavery publicly, although she had lived close to slave society for eighteen years in the border city of Cincinnati, where she observed at first hand the system she depicted in her novel. In 1850 Stowe returned to New England when her husband accepted an appointment at Bowdoin College. It was in response to the urging of friends, following passage of the Fugitive Slave Act, that she agreed to write a few stories in opposition to slavery. Once started on them, she did not stop until *Uncle Tom's Cabin* was completed.

Uncle Tom's Cabin was difficult for Southern literary men to cope with effectively. First, it was cast in the accepted Southern literary form of a plantation novel, after the manner of John Pendleton Kennedy's *Swallow Barn* (1832); second, it attacked Northern as well as Southern involvement in slavery. Indeed, Stowe's leading villains, beginning with the Vermonter Simon Legree, were Northerners, while exploitative Yankee business was contrasted unfavorably with the paternalism of the Southern plantation. Stowe had intended, she later explained, to turn Southerners against slavery and not to turn North and South against each other. Stowe's revolutionary departure from previous literary models was in focusing her attention upon "life among the lowly," as the subtitle of the novel indicated. Where slaves had played supporting roles in previous plantation fiction, Stowe raised them to stations of equality as persons in her narrative without asserting any argument for racial equality against those racial assumptions about blacks that prevailed in the North as well as in the South.

Uncle Tom's Cabin was a novel about family life in a slave society where slaves were denied the right to those basic familial relationships out of which society is created and maintained. Stowe's narrative suggested further that the negation of the sanctity of family relations among blacks served to injure white family relationships as well. Seen from this point of view, slavery became a moral and social evil threatening the familial fabric of a nation that was already worried about the ability of the American family to survive in good moral health the changing circumstances of national life. The slaves as Stowe depicted them became the most dramatic human victims of that disintegration of family life which already preyed upon the minds of many Southern as well as Northern readers of novels. Uncle Tom's Cabin inspired a wave of Northern sentiment against slavery among many readers who had dismissed or condemned Garrisonians and other abolitionists as fanatical troublemakers.

The astonishing, earthshaking popularity of Stowe's novel persuaded a publisher to fund a new Bostonian literary magazine with an antislavery viewpoint, Atlantic Monthly, which Emerson, Longfellow, Lowell, Holmes, Motley, and several other Brahmins sought to found. They were able to do so in 1857 only after they had gained Stowe's commitment to contribute to the magazine.[4] By that time the literary gentlemen associated with the new enterprise were themselves at the forefront of the literary campaign against the extension of slavery, if not against the very existence of slavery anywhere in America. The Brahmin literati were driven to increasingly drastic commitments by the violent struggle over slavery in Kansas Territory and by the brutal caning of their friend, hero, and national spokesman Senator Charles Sumner at the hands of Congressman Preston Brooks of South Carolina.

In contrast with the immigrant from New Hampshire, Senator Daniel Webster—now denounced by antislavery Brahmins as a betrayer of their trust—Senator Charles Sumner, his successor, had belonged from Harvard days to the inner circle of Brahmin literary elite. A brilliant protégé of Joseph Story's at Harvard Law School, Sumner enhanced his reputation as a scholar and a gentleman during three years of subsequent study abroad. By his smashing acceptance in British society, Sumner won the admiration of George Ticknor's Boston upon his return. Together with his law partner, George Stillman Hillard, Sumner enjoyed membership in the Five of Clubs, or Mutual Admiration Society, together with Dr. Samuel Gridley Howe and Professors Longfellow and Cornelius Felton of Harvard. As the slavery issue increasingly divided Boston, however, all members of the Five of Clubs found the going difficult in Ticknor's Boston. Sumner's respectability meanwhile suffered from his failure to marry or to do well at the law professionally. He seemed to be making little of his life.[5]

Then in an 1845 Fourth of July oration, "The True Grandeur of Nations," Sumner surprised and egregiously offended leading Boston Whigs with a pacifist attack on all wars, an attack that seemed on that patriotic occasion to reflect upon the American nation's own Revolutionary heroes themselves. The speech won Sumner a following among pacifist and antislavery reformers, however, and thereafter he increasingly allied himself with the Conscience Whigs against the mercantile Cotton Whigs. And having discovered himself as an orator, Sumner entered politics, winning Daniel Webster's Senate seat on a Free Soil-Democratic ticket in 1851, when Webster vacated his seat to enter Fillmore's cabinet as secretary of state. Ostracized by leaders of the merchant gentry, Sumner won support from fellow literary intellectuals, who had been shocked by the Fugitive Slave Act and Webster's support of it.

Inexperienced in politics and unskilled in debate, Sumner depended for his effect as a senator upon carefully prepared orations, rich in indignation and classical references. Such an oration was his laboriously prepared "The Crime Against Kansas," which ran 112 pages in the printed version and was delivered on two successive days in May 1856. In the speech Sumner directly attacked several senators, including Andrew Butler of South Carolina. He denounced Butler as a Don Quixote whose mistress was the harlot slavery and who "touches nothing which he does not disfigure—with error, sometimes of principle, sometimes of fact," as "with incoherent phrases" he "discharged the loose expectoration of his speech." As for South Carolina, its whole history evinced less merit than was contained in the brief history of free Kansas in its struggle against oppression.[6]

This was poetic license exercised by a man of romantic letters, as was Emerson's subsequent assertion that the entire population of South Carolina was as nothing compared with the solitary man that one member of that population had struck down. It was also thoroughly and meanly slanderous to Butler, and to Congressman Preston Brooks's equally romantic way of thinking, honor required that Sumner's insult to his kinsman Butler be suitably avenged. A duel was out of the question since Sumner would reject it, and Brooks was no match physically for the six-foot-four senator from Massachusetts, so a frontal assault would not do, either. Brooks therefore chose to come up behind the seated Sumner and administer a sound thrashing. As it happened, Brooks lost control of himself and beat Sumner senseless, leaving him with injuries that required three years to heal.

News of the caning electrified and polarized the nation. Brooks won rousing support in the South. In Charleston he was almost universally celebrated as the very pink of Southern chivalry. In the North he was denounced as a craven coward and homicidal slavocratic rake. Throughout the North indignant citizens held protest rallies. In Massachusetts, according to Edward Everett, news of the caning

> produced an excitement in the public mind deeper and more dangerous than I have ever witnessed. . . . If a leader daring and reckless enough had presented himself, he might have raised any number of men to march on Washington.[7]

News of the caning reached Kansas on the day that John Brown was planning a "radical retaliatory measure" against proslavery men on Pottawatomie Creek that would involve "some killing." Brown and his brothers "went crazy—*crazy*" at the news of the caning, according to Brown's son Salmon. "It seemed to be the finishing touch."[8] There followed the cold-blooded midnight murders of five proslavery men that came to be known as the Pottawatomie Massacre.

The Garrisonians still preached nonresistance, but other Boston abolitionists had been aroused by news of the war in Kansas to finance and supply free Kansas fighters, especially their hero, John Brown. Brown went east to Boston on a fund-raising tour in January 1857. There he met and vastly impressed the antislavery literati, including Emerson and Thoreau, and a group of antislavery intellectuals were inspired by Brown to organize themselves into the Secret Committee of Six in support of his activities. The New England Emigrant Aid Society was already financing and arming Kansas settlers openly, but in addition the Secret Six supplied Brown with funds to assist him in Kansas and later at Harpers Ferry. The Secret Six were Samuel Gridley Howe, Thomas Wentworth Higginson, George Luther Stearns, Franklin Benjamin Sanborn, Theodore Parker, and Gerrit Smith. All but the New Yorker, Smith, were from Boston. Parker and Higginson were Unitarian ministers, Stearns was a businessman, Howe a physician, and Sanborn a recent Harvard graduate who as a reporter in Kansas helped to build Brown's reputation.[9]

Although Brown was a secretive and dissembling man, the Secret Six evidently knew pretty well what he had been up to, including the terrorist murders at Pottawatomie, Kansas, and they more or less knew what he planned to do next. Following Brown's capture at Harpers Ferry, the discovery of papers in his possession implicating his backers spread panic among them. Meanwhile, Emerson and Thoreau, who were not implicated in Harpers Ferry and not accurately informed about Pottawatomie, came forth immediately to glorify Brown as a transcendental saint.

There was a world of difference between the vivid metaphors of Emerson and Thoreau and the bloody deeds of the literal-minded Brown, and it was to be the poetic rather than the literal Brown who survived in the transcendental legend. Still, the transcendental image of Brown that emerged from their eulogies was not entirely a figment of their imaginations. Brown seems to have reeducated himself in the meaning of his fight against slaveholders as he read accounts of his exploits in Republican newspapers and as he realized the remarkable impression he was making on eastern intellectuals. Brown effectively presented himself as a hero to men whom he knew to share a different frame of mind from his own. In the process he evidently became in his own mind ultimately like the hero that his intellectual supporters took him to be. While awaiting trial

Brown had the opportunity to read what was said of him by his transcendental sympathizers and to gain a new understanding of himself and his mission. In his famous last speech to the court that convicted him, he fabricated an account of himself that bore little relation to his earlier motives and conduct but instead offered an image of him that accorded sympathetically with the consensus of the antislavery literati.[10]

The speeches of Emerson and Thoreau embarrassed Wendell Phillips and other Garrisonians whose doctrine of nonresistance had restrained them from supporting Brown. They now brushed aside such reservations and joined in the eulogy of the martyred hero. The defense of Brown let them discharge what they felt to be their moral obligation as intellectuals to represent the national conscience—much as Émile Zola and European intellectuals would later do in the Dreyfus case or Felix Frankfurter and American intellectuals would do still later in the Sacco-Vanzetti case. Wendell Phillips declared the chief merit of Emerson's life to have been the fact that, having talked about heroism all his life, he recognized the hero when John Brown appeared and rose to the occasion. Emerson would probably not have agreed, but in the history of the American intellectual community, his defense of Brown remained an act of signal importance, indelibly validating the priestly authority of the intellectual as moral guardian in America's democratic society.

❧ II ❧

THE NEW YORK CITY THAT William Gilmore Simms had known from frequent business trips and had come to bank upon before his ill-fated speaking tour in 1856 was the business-minded metropolis and publishing center of the nation. New Yorkers tolerated social and political diversity as a fact of metropolitan life. As a commercial center for the Southern cotton trade, New York had developed social as well as commercial ties that had been strengthened among the merchant gentry by intermarriages. Abolitionist agitation struck directly at this commercial nexus, and the earliest abolitionist meetings in New York City, as elsewhere in the state, faced mob opposition. Thereafter the abolitionists went on about their activities without much interference, adding to the often rancorous diversity of New York City life.

New York appears to have led the nation in recruitment of abolitionists. Nearly half of the delegates to the American Anti-Slavery Society in 1835 were from New York. The Liberty Party was born there in 1839, and in 1844 New Yorkers cast more than 15,800 of the 62,300 votes for the Liberty Party candidate, James Gillespie Birney. The strength of the movement was in upstate New York rather than the city, however, and its membership was substantially recruited from New England immigrants and their children. Two-thirds of the abolitionist leaders of the state were Yankees; nearly half of them had been born in New England.[11] The seventeenth state, Ohio, became a major staging ground for the evangelical leadership of the abolitionist movement through the leadership of men like Charles G. Finney and Theodore Dwight Weld, who married Angelina Grimké. But Ohio was a world apart from Manhattan. In New York City, Arthur and Lewis Tappan, founders of the statewide abolitionist organization, were immigrants from Massachusetts who had made their fortunes as merchants in New York.

Between Simms and the evangelical Tappan brothers, any meeting of the minds might be unthinkable. But the more politic antislavery stance of another Yankee New Yorker, the *New York Evening Post* editor, William Cullen Bryant, was no bar to Simms's friendship. The two literary men remained friends at the time of Simms's disastrous New York speaking tour in 1856, and Bryant made a point of renewing their friendship in 1868. Bryant's views on the politics and morality of slavery were at least approximately shared by his associates on the *Evening Post*, John Bigelow, Parke Godwin, and Theodore Sedgwick Jr. Similar convictions were held by the liberal faction of the Democratic Party in New York, known as the Barnburners in opposition to the conservative and proslavery Hunkers.[12]

Bryant viewed the slavery issue primarily as a political issue and only secondarily as a moral issue. No matter how reprehensible this system of human subjugation might be, Bryant disapproved of abolitionist agitation that threatened to disrupt the whole national democratic society. On the other hand, he opposed himself equally to aggressive designs on the part of slaveholders to extend slavery and to dominate national politics in the interests of the slaveholder. As a Democrat, Bryant viewed the issue as a party matter, the Democratic Party normally being the majority party and at the same time the party that was always subject to Southern domination. Bryant supported John Quincy Adams's attack upon the gag resolution that Southern congressmen had imposed against the reading of antislavery petitions in the House of Representatives.

Bryant opposed the abolitionist Liberal Party in 1840 and again in 1844, arguing the necessity of working within major parties to bring about reform. However, the aggressions of the Polk administration temporarily changed Bryant's mind about the futility of third parties. Bryant and a substantial number of the Barnburners had opposed annexation of Texas, opposed war with Mexico, and opposed the extension of slavery into the newly acquired territories. The Barnburners meanwhile remained without influence in these matters, having been shunted aside by the Polk administration in favor of William Learned Marcy and the Hunkers. In 1848 the Barnburners bolted the Democratic Party in New York, while the Conscience Whigs in Massachusetts broke with the Cotton Whigs and joined the Free Soil Party, nominating Van Buren as its presidential candidate and young Charles Francis Adams as his running mate.

Campaigning on the slogan "Free Soil, Free Speech, Free Labor, and Free Men," the party launched the political campaign against the extension of slavery and the pretentions of the slave power, a party line that the Republicans would adopt six years later. In 1852 Bryant and the *Evening Post* half-heartedly returned to the Democratic Party to support Franklin Pierce. Nathaniel Hawthorne, who had attended Bowdoin College with Pierce, believed Pierce would be a great president and wrote a campaign biography to argue the case for him. Bryant only hoped that Pierce would be better than Polk on the slavery question. Bryant abandoned this hope in 1855 and brought the *Evening Post* to the side of the recently organized Republican Party.

In aligning himself with the Republican Party, Bryant joined political forces with his editorial rival, Horace Greeley of the *New York Tribune*. Greeley had opposed slavery more vigorously than Bryant had; he had vigorously supported a wide range of humanitarian reforms and utopian schemes, and he had identified these issues with the Whig Party, for which he had been a stalwart champion against the damnable Democratic Party of Bryant and the slaveholders. As Bryant himself turned against the Democratic Party and the slaveholders during the Polk administration, he continued to oppose Greeley and the *Tribune* editorially, falsely charging Greeley with willingness to permit slaveholders a share of the Mexican Cession. Greeley responded with understandable heat, declaring, "You lie, villain! Wilfully, wickedly, basely lie!" Years later Bryant refused to exchange greetings with his abusive rival when they met at a breakfast, as a consequence of this particular exchange.[13]

In New York City as elsewhere, the issue regarding slavery in the new territories generally and in Kansas especially remained heated; New York, like Boston, was disturbed by a series of incidents after 1850 involving alleged runaway slaves. However, in New York there was much else going on to distract attention from the slave issue. Business was booming in 1850, and the city was expanding to incredible proportions, its population grown to more than half a million at mid-century, not counting Brooklyn and other extensions of the burgeoning metropolis. Broadway was flourishing in the era of Edwin Forrest, Edwin Booth, and P. T. Barnum, the last of whom operated his museum in New York and brought Jenny Lind from Sweden in 1850 for a concert tour. *Uncle Tom's Cabin* was playing to full houses on Broadway soon after the book was published. America's first World's Fair was hosted by New York in the summer of 1853, it's centerpiece the futuristic Crystal Palace, made of glass and iron. Construction of Central Park began in 1853, and Castle Garden was established to accommodate the swelling horde of immigrants two years later. In the year of the clipper ships and California gold, the chances were slim that the Compromise of 1850 could absorb the attention of any but a few New Yorkers for long.

The *New York Times* started up in 1851 to compete with Greeley's *Tribune* and James Gordon Bennett's *Herald*, the leading morning papers. Manhattan had advanced beyond Philadelphia in publishing except in the field of ladies magazines, where Philadelphia remained dominant. The house of Harper brought out *Harper's Monthly Magazine* in 1850. It enjoyed immediate success, based mainly upon the literary offerings that it was able to pirate from British publications in the absence of an international copyright law. As a literary monthly the only competition it faced was Lewis Gaylord Clark's sadly deteriorated *Knickerbocker Magazine*. The opportunity was there for a new magazine that would embody New York's variety, vitality, and sophistication, as *Knickerbocker* had once done with some success, a new magazine that would buy the best American literature of the day rather than pirating the best that British writers had to offer.

American literary nationalism triumphed amid sectional discord. The climax of national literary creativity occurred between the stopgap Compromise of 1850 and the national collision over Kansas midway through the decade. Poe died just before the decade began, at the age of forty. But between 1850 and 1855 there appeared Emerson's *Representative Men* (1850), Hawthorne's *The Scarlet Letter* (1850) and *The House of the Seven Gables* (1851), Parkman's first volume of history, *History of the Conspiracy of Pontiac* (1851), Melville's *Moby Dick* (1851) and *Pierre* (1852), Stowe's *Uncle Tom's Cabin* (1852), Thoreau's *Walden* (1854), Fitzhugh's *Sociology for the South* (1854), Simms's *Southward Ho* (1854) and *The Forayers* (1855), Whitman's *Leaves of Grass* (1855), Longfellow's *The Song of Hiawatha* (1855), Timothy Shay Arthur's *Ten Nights in a Barroom and What I Saw There* (1854), George Boker's poetic drama *Francesca da Rimini* (1855), and the first volume of Irving's *Life of George Washington* (1855).[14] Of the three authors upon whom the literary republic had earlier depended for its reputation, Cooper died at the beginning of the decade and Irving at the end, while Bryant continued to write verse, edit the *Evening Post*, and preside over literary occasions until his death in 1878. The arrival of America as a literary nation together with the arrival of New York as a national metropolis suggested to some the possibility of publishing an unprecedented metropolitan and national literary magazine.

In 1845 Charles F. Briggs, a Nantucket sailor and author of the popular sea tale *The Adventures of Harry Franco* (1839), started up the *Broadway Journal* as a literary weekly that would capture the spirit of Broadway, on the confident assumption that New York City had itself become a subject of national interest.[15] Investing his earnings from *Harry Franco* and other writings in the project, Briggs hired Poe as assistant editor. What followed remains unclear except that five months later Briggs found himself ejected from the magazine, and Poe was in charge. Two months after that, *Broadway Journal* ceased publication, leaving Poe with personal debts to Horace Greeley and others that he never repaid.

It was Poe's last chance to be his own magazine editor before he died in 1849, but Briggs moved into other editorial jobs after *Broadway Journal*, including management of a magazine that failed, where *Harper's Monthly* succeeded, in pirating English fiction. The Harper brothers had built up one of the world's largest publishing businesses by reprinting English literature without compensation to the authors, and they extended this practice with *Harper's Monthly*. The magazine came at once under criticism in the name of the uncompensated British authors and also in the name of unpublished American authors, whose writings were not published in *Harper's Monthly* because they could not be pirated. In 1852 Briggs approached the Harper brothers' leading rival, George Palmer Putnam, with the proposal for a monthly that would cater to America's best writers and would provide a recognized national medium for America's ascendant literary culture.

Whereas the Harper brothers were hardheaded merchants who prided themselves on their Methodist probity and enterprise, Putnam was a Harvard-educated man of letters for whom literary publishing was a way of life as well as a livelihood. He took up the project with enthusiasm and in 1853 launched *Putnam's Monthly Magazine*, edited by Briggs with the assistance of George William Curtis and Parke Godwin. Business reverses forced Putnam to sell the magazine after three years, and it was merged out of existence in 1857. But for the five years that Briggs edited it, *Putnam's Monthly* became the focal point of literary America, a unique achievement up to that time and one which in some ways has hardly been equaled by any American literary magazine since.[16]

Southern writers looked askance at this Whig-oriented venture, and Simms, who was editing the *Southern Quarterly Review* at the time and contributing to the *Southern Literary Messenger*, attacked *Putnam's Monthly*. So did editorials in *De Bow's Review* and *Russell's Magazine*. Under these circumstances the editors of *Putnam's Monthly* did the best they could, soliciting from Southern Whigs, including John Pendleton Kennedy and William Swinton, who agreed to write for them, and making a point of including at least one Southern author in each issue. In New England Hawthorne agreed to consider sending something but never did, very likely because of the magazine's anti-Democrat bias and its attacks on Hawthorne's Bowdoin classmate President Franklin Pierce. Whitman's

Leaves of Grass received a cautious rave (as a remarkably successful amalgamation of "Yankee transcendentalism and New York rowdyism" that no woman should see), but Whitman was keeping a studied distance from the literary world and did not contribute. Otherwise, virtually every writer in the nation whose reputation survives contributed to *Putnam's Monthly*. Among these, the most extensive early contributors were Longfellow, Lowell, Thoreau, and Melville. Thoreau's "Excursion to Canada" and "Cape Cod" were serialized, as was Melville's *Israel Potter*. Other authors were Bryant, the travel writer Bayard Taylor, the poet Richard Henry Stoddard, the essayists Charles Eliot Norton and Charles Dudley Warner, the Swedenborgian philosopher Henry James Sr., the political scientist Francis Lieber, and Fenimore Cooper, one of whose naval histories was published posthumously. Briggs infused the magazine with a New York-ish quality by drawing extensively upon the services of leading newspapermen of the city, including Horace Greeley, Charles A. Dana, George Ripley, and Clarence Cook.

Putnam's Monthly paid all contributors well by current standards and, as Frank Luther Mott wrote, the magazine was "edited with a certain degree of freedom from the inhibitory fears of the time, with a cultivation and intelligence that would have given it standing in any period of our history."[17] Following the scandal caused by the incestuous plot of *Pierre*, Melville's prospects were poor for marketing his stories, but Briggs published numbers of his short stories in addition to *Israel Potter*, while gently returning "The Two Temples" with the explanation that "My editorial experience compels me to be very cautious in offending the religious sensibilities of the public, and the moral of the Two Temples would array against us the whole power of the pulpit."[18]

Editorially antislavery and hostile to the Democratic Pierce administration from the outset, *Putnam's Monthly* answered the charge of being a Republican Party organ, without remaining consistent to this purpose, with an article by Parke Godwin on "American Despotisms."[19] The most oppressive of despotisms was slavery, but there were others, Godwin wrote, including the tyranny of political parties, of "our ecclesiastical organizations," and of general public opinion. He argued that public opinion did not assert itself with overt majoritarian force, as Tocqueville supposed, but rather through a general uneasiness that affected the reading public when it was exposed to widely ranging free expression of ideas. Criticisms of the monthly's eclectic character were a case in point, Godwin argued: readers were expressing concern over the mixing of discussions of politics, science, and religion with less sober matter. Against this genteel tyranny Godwin issued a declaration of intellectual freedom. It had never been the intention of the editors of *Putnam's Monthly* to offer a magazine for milliners, he explained. "No! we had other conceptions of the variety, the importance, the dignity, and the destiny of literature." Writers and artists constituted a priesthood, and "a free scope must be given to the action of their genius; and such as we trust they will ever find in the pages of this Monthly."

Political conditions were bad for such a free-spirited enterprise in the year of the Kansas-Nebraska Act, however. Economic conditions worsened with the Panic of 1857, and in that year *Putnam's Monthly* was forced to merge with a much less distinguished rival. A month after *Putnam's* merged into oblivion, the *Atlantic Monthly* breathed the first breath of what proved to be enduring life in Boston. It was almost as if the spirit of the national literary culture had transmigrated from New York to Boston. In fact, the demise of *Putnam's Monthly* represented the failure of New York's literary culture to speak for the nation; the stable growth of the *Atlantic Monthly*, on the other hand, evinced the success with which Boston's regional literature, amid Civil War and Reconstruction, was expanding to become the accepted voice of Victorian civilization in Gilded Age America.

⊰ III ⊱

THE DURABILITY OF THE *Atlantic Monthly* could not have been anticipated given the history of literary journalism in Boston. Except for quarterlies, led by *North American Review*, no literary magazine had survived for much more than a year in Boston since Park Benjamin had moved the five-year-old *New-England Magazine* to New York in 1835. James Russell Lowell, the founding editor of the *Atlantic Monthly*, had previously edited *The Pioneer*, which had begun brilliantly and ended disastrously in 1843 after three issues, leaving Lowell with crippling financial obligations. Oliver Wendell

Holmes had been studying law at Harvard in 1830, the first year of *New-England Magazine*, and he had written a column in it under the heading of "The Autocrat of the Breakfast Table." Twenty-six years later Holmes resumed the Autocrat column in the *Atlantic Monthly* with the opening line: "As I was just going to say when I was interrupted—."[20]

The *Atlantic Monthly* owed its inception to an outsider in Boston's literary community, Francis Henry Underwood, the son of a farmer in Enfield, Massachusetts. After a year at Amherst, Underwood taught school in Kentucky and returned to Massachusetts in 1850, fired with antislavery sentiments and literary aspirations. Cultivating the acquaintance of Lowell and other Brahmins, Underwood collected promises of contributions from leading writers and received the backing of the Boston publisher of *Uncle Tom's Cabin* to start a literary and antislavery magazine in 1853, but the publishing house went out of business before the first issue could appear. In 1856 Underwood took his proposed magazine, as well as his services as literary editor, to Phillips, Sampson, and Co., the publishers of Harriet Beecher Stowe's latest work, *Dred*. With Stowe's support and her promise to contribute, Underwood persuaded the firm to undertake the risk.

At a Parker House dinner given by the publisher Moses D. Phillips in 1857, he and Underwood were joined by the leading authors whom Underwood had interested in the venture—except, of course, Stowe. They were Emerson, Longfellow, Lowell, Holmes, Motley, and James Elliot Cabot. Seated at the far end of the table, Underwood watched his magazine take shape during the dinner and pass out of his possession. Lowell was urged to accept the editorship, which he agreed to do, providing that Holmes would promise to contribute regularly. Holmes promised he would do so and suggested the name *Atlantic Monthly*, which the others accepted. Underwood had no hope whatever of Phillips's support for his claim to the editorship. Phillips, who referred to Underwood condescendingly as "our literary man," sat in awe of the distinguished Brahmins at the table, "leaving himself and his 'literary man' out of the group," as he later modestly wrote.[21]

The name *Atlantic Monthly* particularly suited the magazine as Lowell and presumably others at the table conceived of it. Another national literary magazine such as *Putnam's Monthly* was not what he had in mind. Rather the *Atlantic Monthly* would unite the transatlantic cultures of New

England and Old England. Underwood was appointed as Lowell's assistant and sent to England to collect submissions and promises from English writers. Charles Eliot Norton, who was in England at the time, was instructed to collect what he could and bring it home with him. Norton returned with a trunkful of manuscripts by admittedly undistinguished English writers, but he unaccountably lost the trunk between the New York dock and his hotel, thereby sparing the editor, as Norton later wrote, the trouble of rejecting the unworthy lot of them.[22]

Other English writers whom Underwood approached took offense at Lowell's assertion of his right to reject their submissions, the novelist Charles Reade informing Lowell that "The stories you do publish in the *Monthly* could never have been selected by any judge competent to sit in judgment on mine. We had better wait a little."[23] After waiting a little Lowell abandoned the transatlantic idea, and the *Atlantic Monthly* became essentially a Bostonian magazine. During the first fifteen years of the *Atlantic*, two-thirds of the contributors were from New England—most living within commuting distance of Boston—and together they wrote much more than two-thirds of the material.

The only member of the defunct *Putnam's Monthly* to write extensively for the *Atlantic* was Parke Godwin, who agreed to do a series of political articles until Lowell offended him by drastically editing a piece on "Mr. Buchanan's Administration" and then added six pages of his own to express more forcibly the "contempt" and "humiliation" that Buchanan aroused in right-minded people. Godwin wrote Underwood that he did not think much of Lowell as a political commentator and "would prefer to put my writings before the public without his 'improvements.'"[24] Another author who came under Lowell's editorial knife was Thoreau, whose first and only submission had been blue-penciled to delete a sentence about a pine tree: "It is as immortal as I am and perchance will go to as high a heaven, there to tower above me still." Lowell had feared that the sentence might give offense on religious grounds. Thoreau considered Lowell's censorship "very mean and cowardly," but Lowell, who disliked Thoreau and disputed his literary pretentions, was happy to be rid of an author whom he could not arbitrarily exclude without offending Emerson.[25] Lowell did not consider that he was editing a monthly for milliners either, but neither did he intend to allow authors a free scope for their genius as

Putnam's Monthly had attempted to do. Lowell established the *Atlantic* as a genteel periodical, and James T. Fields continued this tradition when he assumed the editorship in 1861.

Underwood went on managing the office and corresponding with authors for the absent-minded Lowell. When Fields took control as editor and publisher, he fired Underwood. Thereafter Underwood remained in Boston as a writer of short stories, novels, and biographies of Lowell, Longfellow, and Whittier, and he remained active as a founder and president of the Papyrus Club, a kind of lesser Saturday Club. In 1886, during the Cleveland administration, Underwood succeeded Bret Harte as American consul in Glasgow and thereafter lived out his days in Scotland. In 1875 Francis Parkman had written Underwood a letter of apology for the treatment he received from Parkman's fellow Brahmins. Parkman wished

> that your connection with the *Atlantic* could have been continued long enough to give your literary powers and accomplishments a fair chance of just recognition. It is for the interest of us all that men like you should be rated for what they are worth. Harvard and its social allies answer a very good purpose in defending us—to some extent—against the literary clap-trap and charlatanry which prosper so well throughout the country, [but it works injustice upon others who are] neither Harvard men nor humbugs.[26]

In 1860 young William Dean Howells traveled from Ohio to visit New York, where the *Saturday Press* had published his verse, and Boston, where the *Atlantic* had done likewise. His campaign biography of Lincoln was just out, assuring him a friendly reception in Boston as well as securing him a position in the new government as consul in Venice. In Boston, the city of his dreams, Howells met Lowell, Holmes, Hawthorne, Thoreau, Emerson, and Fields, to whom he offered his services as assistant editor of the *Atlantic*. At war's end Fields sent for Howells, who rose to the editorship of the *Atlantic* and to lofty distinction as author, critic, and literary statesman, remaining the generally acknowledged dean of American letters to his death in 1920.[27]

Reviewing the American literary scene of 1860 long afterward in *Literary Friends and Acquaintance* (1900), Howells recalled that "Philadelphia had long counted for nothing in the literary field," while "In the South there was nothing but a mistaken social ideal, with the moral principles all standing on their heads in defense of slavery." In the East many periodicals

> had lately adventured in the fine air of high literature [and] gasped and died. . . . The best of these, hitherto, and better even than the *Atlantic* for some reasons, the lamented *Putnam's Magazine*, had perished of inanition at New York, and the claim of the commercial capital to the literary primacy had passed with that brilliant venture.

Boston chiefly, if not Boston alone, remained the center of a vigorous intellectual life among the nation's leading authors (in which group, to be sure, Howells did not include Melville or Whitman, to name two unorthodox non-Bostonians).[28]

Educated opinion in Boston was far more unified in support of war in 1861 than was the case with the literary classes of New York or Philadelphia or of Baltimore, Richmond, or Charleston. There were a few dissenters in Boston, to be sure. The most eloquent of these was Nathaniel Hawthorne, who warned his countrymen in 1862 that "For ourselves, the balance of advantages between defeat and triumph may admit of question," and that "No human effort, on a grand scale has ever yet resulted according to the purposes of its projectors," the advantages being always incidental. "Man's accidents are God's purposes. We miss the good we sought and do the good we little cared for."[29] The *Atlantic Monthly* refused to publish a second such article by Hawthorne, who died before the war was over. Meanwhile, a representative of the Boston literati more typical than the dour Democrat Hawthorne was Emerson, who crammed his journal with thoughts on war, heroism, morality, and freedom. "If the abundance of heaven only sends us a fair share of light and conscience," he wrote a friend, "we shall redeem America for all its sinful years since the century began."[30]

The war tested a generation of privileged young men who had enjoyed the comforts and luxuries of a kind of affluence unknown in America before the factory and the railroad. Older Americans raised in harder, simpler times had been concerned about the softening influences of this life upon the moral fiber of youth. In this respect the Civil War was welcomed as a test of the new generation, and the noble response of Brahmin heroes vindicated the opinion of Boston Brahmins in their continued legitimacy as a ruling class. Robert Gould Shaw, a Yankee Brahmin from Staten Island, became the most heralded of Brahmin heroes in July 1863 when he went to his death leading the nation's first regiment of black troops against Fort Wagner. Great care had been taken in selecting the appointment for this unique post, with "reference not only to military capacity, but to personal character and social position," according to a Boston merchant who had sponsored this regiment. The honor had gone to Shaw, a "youthful looking, fair-haired commander—the very type and flower of the Anglo-Saxon race"—and Shaw had responded in such a manner as to inspire two of Emerson's most memorable lines of verse: "When Duty whispers low, *Thou must*, / The youth replies, *I can*." And so it was with Charles Francis Adams Jr., Charles Lowell, thrice-wounded Oliver Wendell Holmes Jr., Thomas Wentworth Higginson, who also commanded black troops, and others.[31]

When Lincoln signed the Emancipation Proclamation of January 1, 1863, the war to preserve the Union became explicitly a war to abolish slavery. No slaves were freed by the proclamation since it applied only to areas currently in enemy hands. However, in the subsequent history of Reconstruction, there would never again be so clear-cut and unsullied a victory for the antislavery cause as this. Accordingly, on the occasion of the signing, Boston's literary community held a meeting in Music Hall to celebrate this triumph for liberty and also for Boston. Emerson read his "Boston Hymn," and a chorus rendered Holmes's "Army Hymn." When word arrived that the President had signed the proclamation, the audience gave three cheers for Lincoln followed by three cheers for William Lloyd Garrison, who was present at the celebration.[32]

⇥ IV ⇤

UNLIKE BOSTON, NEW YORK CITY had never corporately presented itself as a moral city, and the posture it maintained during the Civil War, as the metropolis of the Union, left much to be desired. Its public officials remained openly disloyal to the Lincoln administration as well as flagrantly corrupt. Leading merchants remained dogmatic Southern apologists until secession and war cut them off from the cotton kingdom and invalidated Southern business debts to them. Manhattan's populace responded to conscription in 1863 with four days of draft riots that left hundreds dead in their wake. The municipal government responded to the riots by voting three hundred dollars from the city treasury for every drafted resident who could not afford to buy his own way out of the Army.[33]

Aside from treasonable conduct high and low, the national metropolis lacked a history and civic character that fitted it to embody the idealistic purposes of the war to preserve the republic and cleanse it of slavery. New York remained first and foremost what it had always been: a commercial center with an interest in national union that was most evidently a business interest. So far as Manhattan had succeeded in evolving a distinctive civic ideology beyond its proverbially unrestrained business ethic, it had been the Knickerbocker tradition, fondly and whimsically nurtured by leading literary gentlemen during the half century since Washington Irving invented it. Even the young antebellum New York Bohemians, who scoffed at their Knickerbocker elders, were themselves committed to a flippant view of life that owed a good deal to the established Knickerbocker mode of Rabelaisian wit.[34]

Nathaniel P. Willis, whose "Pencillings" and "Dashes of Life with a Free Pencil" had earlier been models of New Yorkish élan, was now a penciller of unacceptably frivolous chitchat. Willis had long since outlived his formerly brilliant reputation when he died in 1867 at the age of sixty-one. Likewise, Lewis Gaylord Clark's sophisticated literary gossip was no longer wanted and he was dropped from *Knickerbocker* by the backers of the magazine in 1861. Clark was briefly rehired two years later and then permanently let go. During his last years Clark earned his living working in the New York Customs House, where Herman Melville survived the Gilded Age in even greater obscurity. The literary backbiting that had characterized the world of Lewis Gaylord Clark did painful injury to him and others in the long run. The extreme of this vindictiveness had been represented by the Vermonter Rufus Griswold, who had used his position as Poe's literary executor to slander the poet's reputation and if possible enhance his own. Griswold had made his living compiling literary anthologies, chiefly of living poets, whose personal loyalties he sought to secure against competing anthologists or editors. He seems to have borne Poe no particular animosity personally, but he became obsessively jealous of Poe's literary acclaim.

Poe's suffering in Griswold's hands was at least posthumous. Griswold's most distinguished and devastated living victim was his old rival Evart Duyckinck. In 1855 Duyckinck, together with his brother George, produced a monumental two-volume *Cyclopaedia of American Literature*, which was praised by reviewers as a definitive work that served its subject well by doing it full scholarly justice. Griswold responded with an exhaustive *New York Herald* review, later published in book form, itemizing innumerable errors of fact as well as syntax and substantially destroying the high reputation for erudition and exactitude that Duyckinck had carried into this magisterial enterprise. His friend William Gilmore Simms urged Duyckinck to put Griswold's review to good use in preparing a revised and corrected edition, but Duyckinck had no stomach for such a project anymore. His Young America literary circle had already disintegrated under excruciatingly bitter personal circumstances, and the sectional struggle was cutting him off from Southern friends and disrupting polite literary society in the city. Pursuing a series of undemanding editorial projects, Duyckinck survived Griswold, who died a lonely, lingering death in 1859. Duyckinck ended his days comfortably as a literary columnist for the *New York Times*. He was coediting an edition of Shakespeare with William Cullen Bryant when the two men died in 1878.[35]

New Englanders and native New York Yankees from Staten Island, Long Island, and upstate had filled the ranks of New York's literary community since the early years of the Republic. With the coming of the war, these Yankees advanced to assume command of Manhattan's cultural affairs. Henry W. Bellows of Boston, the leading Unitarian minister in New York City, emerged at the outset of the war as the de facto leader of the Unitarian Church nationally. Spokesman for the conservative wing of Unitarianism, Bellows delivered the Harvard Divinity School Address in 1859, attacking the regrettable tendency in the church toward radical individualism, a tendency that had been carried to the extreme in "the Emersonian and transcendentalist school" and that was "Protestantism broken loose from general history, taken out of its place in the providential plan and made the whole instead of the part."[36] Contemptuous of the abolitionists and the other romantic humanitarians in his church, Bellows led in the organization in 1861 of the wartime Sanitary Commission to institutionalize voluntary benevolence, from the rolling of bandages to the sanitary inspection of camps and the building of hospitals, bringing a wide range of activities under the coordinated direction of a managerial elite. Serving Bellows as executive secretary of the commission was the Connecticut Yankee from Staten Island, Frederick Law Olmsted, an architect of Central Park, editorial manager of *Putnam's Monthly* after Briggs's departure, author of a classic series of journalistic accounts of antebellum Southern life, and a leading member of New York's cultivated society in the Gilded Age.

Other cultivated New York Yankees who dedicated themselves to the work of the Sanitary Commission were the chemist Wolcott Gibbs of the New York College of Physicians and Surgeons and the Lawrence Scientific School at Harvard and the lawyer George Templeton Strong. Both the Gibbs and the Strong families had arrived in New York from Massachusetts in the colonial era by way of Long Island. Strong was one of eight founders of the New York Union League Club in 1863. As treasurer of the Sanitary Commission, Strong labored unremittingly and effectively to apply New York business methods to nonprofit patriotic benevolence.

The literary community of New York was not as readily rallied to the war effort as the business community, and some literary men did not survive the grim age as writers at all. The best place for a literary man to be during the war was with one of the leading daily newspapers: James Gordon Bennett's *Herald*, Greeley's *Tribune*, Henry J. Raymond's *Times*, or Bryant's *Evening Post*. By the time he retired and passed his paper on to his son-in-law, Parke Godwin, Bryant had edged his way into the millionaire's circle. Profits were made on publishers' row as well, but in the field of literary journalism, they were made only by the house of Harper with its monthly magazine, which had by then taken to paying British contributors and accepting American writings, and *Harper's Weekly: A Journal of Civilization*, started in 1857.

Fletcher Harper managed both of Harper's magazines for a generation. He faced the problem of reconciling the Democratic Party loyalty of the Harper brothers with political circumstances of the war. In the case of *Harper's Monthly*, it remained possible and profitable to pursue a nonpolitical course. The weekly was by its nature more involved in current events, however, and in 1862 Fletcher Harper committed the weekly to a staunchly Unionist and Republican position with the appointment of Thomas Nast as illustrator and George William Curtis as editor.

Curtis, a Rhode Islander, had preferred a year at Brook Farm to college. He followed it with four years in Europe, then settled in New York in 1850 to begin a career in journalism on the *Tribune*. Modeling his early writing upon the hugely popular travel accounts of Nathaniel Willis, Curtis enjoyed immediate success as author of a travel book, *Nile Notes of a Howadji* (1851), and a satire on New York society, *Potiphar Papers* (1853). Having established himself as a leading literary man-about-town, Curtis married into the Brahmin Shaw family of Staten Island and put aside shallow sophistication for serious literary journalism. While editing and writing for *Putnam's Monthly*, Curtis managed to coauthor the Editor's Easy Chair feature in the rival *Harper's Monthly*. When *Putnam's* went under, Curtis took entire possession of the Editor's Easy Chair and for forty years maintained it as the most popular literary department in American journalism. He is remembered today chiefly as the genteel liberal Republican who served as chairman of a reformist civil service commission during the Grant administration.[37]

In 1864 Yankee Brahmins crowned their wartime occupation of literary New York by ousting Gulian C. Verplanck as president of the Century Club and installing George Bancroft of Boston in his place. Member of a Dutch-English merchant family of long standing in the city, Verplanck had grown up in Manhattan and combined literary and scholarly activities with a political career, serving for four terms in the House of Representatives. A genial, generous, and optimistic personification of Knickerbocker culture, Verplanck had been the cofounder with his friend Bryant of the Century Club in 1847, and he remained the heart, soul, and president of the club until Civil War issues led to his ouster. A Democrat who grew increasingly active in opposition to the war and in support of the peace movement, Verplanck aroused the bitter hostility of younger members of the club, who led an attack against him that even old friends felt impelled to support for patriotic reasons. George Templeton Strong complained of "How unpleasant it is to vote for a snob like Bancroft against my old friend Verplanck. But Verplanck's Copperhead talk is intolerable."[38]

At war's end efforts to revive several old literary magazines ended in failure. Henry Clapp's attempt to reestablish his Bohemian *Saturday Press* in the Reconstruction era did not last long. But while it did last, it served to introduce Mark Twain to an eastern audience for the first time. The efforts of Charles Briggs to resurrect *Putnam's Monthly* seemed more promising but failed anyway after two years, despite the abilities of three successive editors, Briggs, E. C. Stedman, and Parke Godwin. In 1870 the magazine was absorbed by *Scribner's Monthly*, which came to dominate literary journalism in Gilded Age America.

Meanwhile, Frederick Law Olmsted had made up his mind during the Civil War that New York should have a more rigorously intellectual journal of opinion than Curtis's popular *Harper's Weekly*, and he drew up plans for such a magazine. Called away to California to manage some mining properties, Olmsted left the project in the hands of his friend the Anglo-Irish immigrant Edwin Lawrence Godkin. Olmsted provided Godkin with a letter introducing him to Charles Eliot Norton, whom Olmstead wished to bring into the enterprise. By the close of the war these men had joined their project with one being advanced by abolitionists in Boston and Philadelphia, the launch of a magazine called the *Nation* serving the interests of the freed slaves. The two groups formed the Nation Association, raising half of the necessary capital in Boston and the rest in New York and Philadelphia. The *Nation* began publication in 1865 under the editorship of Godkin, after Curtis and *Tribune* editor Whitelaw Reid had both declined the position.[39]

An American correspondent for the *London Daily News*, Godkin owed his appointment as editor to his friend Olmsted, who gained Norton's support over the objections of the abolitionist backers from Boston and Philadelphia. As it happened, the abolitionists' misgivings turned out to be entirely justified. As editor of the *Nation*, Godkin made it an organ of his own personal opinion, which was straight Manchester liberalism with a chaser of Anglophile disdain for American democratic and materialistic culture. As a liberal, Godkin had opposed slavery without qualification, but he retained little interest in the welfare of the freedmen once the institution of slavery had been abolished. When George L. Stearns of Boston, a militant abolitionist from the days of John Brown, led a fight against Godkin among the stockholders in the magazine, Godkin, with the support of Olmstead and Norton, withdrew from the Nation Association and formed E. L. Godkin and Company to publish the *Nation*. Freed from the abolitionists he set forth on his remarkable career as the self-appointed but widely accepted authority within the national intellectual community on all matters affecting American civilization.

Rivaling Godkin in influence as a political and cultural mentor to the liberal Republican literary class was the German immigrant Carl Schurz. Upon emigrating to America from Germany following the suppression of the Revolution of 1848, Schurz gained influence as a representative of German-American opinion in the Republican Party. He served as a field general in the Civil War, and he increased his influence as U.S. senator from Missouri and outspoken conscience of the Republican Party thereafter. Schurz served as the *Nation's* anonymous Washington correspondent while in the Senate, and several years after the death of William Cullen Bryant, in 1878, he joined with Godkin to take over the *Evening Post*. The collaboration proved damaging to the reputation of both men. Godkin presently ejected Schurz from the paper under circumstances that reflected against Godkin's business honesty on the one hand and against Schurz's reputation for journalistic competence on the other. Schurz went on to be a leader of the Mugwumps, who supported Cleveland against Blaine in 1884, and in 1892 he succeeded George William Curtis as president of the National Civil Service Reform League and also as editorial writer for *Harper's Weekly*.[40]

Immigrant intellectuals in antebellum America, including the chemist and free thinker Thomas Cooper, the political scientist Francis Lieber, and the naturalist Louis Agassiz, had achieved positions of prestige and influence among the American literary classes, but none had enjoyed such commanding influence as Godkin and Schurz attained among the educated elite of the nation during the post–Civil War decades. The readiness of American intellectuals to defer to these two pundits from abroad appears to have been symptomatic of a wavering confidence in themselves and their nation. These, "the best men" in society, saw themselves as the lineal descendants of the aristocracy of virtue and talents that had existed in the golden age of the early Republic and as the defenders of civilization during the Civil War. In the dynamic new zeitgeist that followed the war's end, these intellectuals discovered themselves to be strangers in their own land amid the corrupt, industrialized, urbanized, immigrant-operated society of the Gilded Age.

While literati of antebellum New York met unhappy and untimely ends or lingered on in mean obscurity, the Boston Brahmins remained enveloped in national veneration to their deaths: Emerson and Longfellow in 1882, Lowell in 1891, Whittier in 1892, and Holmes in 1894. Longfellow, Lowell, and Whittier remained productive in their later years, and Lowell reached the widest audience of any of his generation of Brahmins with *Among My Books* and even other postwar volumes of essays. He himself viewed these later writings as inferior efforts, but amid the ungenteel commotion of the Gilded Age, a wider and more appreciative public existed for them than ever had before. Emerson, whose memory began to fail him during the Civil War years, lived on in the bosom of his family and friends, serenely accepting adoration and international honors to the end of his days.

No younger generation of Brahmins emerged in Boston to replace these literary gentlemen when they died. Indeed, among those elected to succeed these elder Brahmins in Boston's Saturday Club, only a few achieved literary distinction, the most notable being two successive editors of the *Atlantic Monthly*, William Dean Howells and Thomas Bailey Aldrich. Reviewing the literary situation of New England and the nation in 1900, Howells observed that New England was no longer producing a national literature, and he supposed that it would "probably be centuries yet before the life of the whole country, the American life as distinguished from the New England life, shall have anything so like a national literature." That being the case, Howells believed it would "be long before our larger life interprets itself in such imagination as Hawthorne's, such wisdom as Emerson's, such wit and grace as Holmes's, such humor and humanity as Lowell's."[41] For Howells, these Boston Brahmins had been without equals in the Literary Republic, and as acknowledged dean of national letters, he approvingly certified the literary Bostonization of an otherwise woefully unrefined Gilded Age America.

⊰ EPILOGUE ⊱

THE ACADEMY OF ARTS
AND LETTERS, 1904–1909

WHEN THE U.S. SENATE FAILED to support the bill presented by Charles Sumner of Massachusetts in 1864 to incorporate a National Academy of Literature and Art, plans for any such association were postponed indefinitely. Sumner's suggested list of members to the academy appears to have been based substantially on Boston's Saturday Club membership. Had the bill received serious consideration, senators from New York, Pennsylvania, and elsewhere would no doubt have questioned its Bostonian orientation, betraying the provincialism that historically had characterized the nation's literary society. As it was, not even those who would have been honored by membership showed much interest in the plan. In response to an appeal from Senator Sumner, Ralph Waldo Emerson attempted to arrange a meeting with Longfellow, Lowell, Holmes, Richard Henry Dana, and George William Curtis to discuss the project, but only Lowell and Holmes found the time to make themselves available.[1]

The National Academy of Moral and Political Sciences, which Sumner's bill would also have incorporated, similarly failed to win Senate support. However, the idea of it was kept alive by Boston literati. While the climate of the Civil War had not proved amenable to the advancement of literature and art, it had proved powerfully favorable to the promotion of plans to reconstruct society along lines suggested by the newly evolving intellectual discipline of social science. Accordingly, socially conscious Boston literati went ahead on their own to found the American Social Science Association in Boston in 1865.

The stress upon moral individualism associated with the old Transcendental Club was dated by then. Most of the original participants in the Symposium of the 1830s had turned from contemplation of self to social reform. Among them, the clergyman Theodore Parker became a militant abolitionist as well as a champion of the working classes. He was joined by others who took antislavery positions also. At the same time a greater commitment tended to be made to supporting workingmen's rights by George Ripley, James Freeman Clarke, and Orestes Brownson. During the Civil War, the United States Sanitary Commission, by efficiently organizing hospitals and medical care for the military, demonstrated to educated humanitarians the efficacy of bureaucratic social reform over individual dedication. That something should be done for the urban and industrial masses and that intellectuals should face the problems of industrial society became the point of view of the informally constituted Radical Club of Boston after the Civil War. Included among its regular members were Emerson, Wendell Phillips, Thomas Wentworth Higginson, Whittier, Julia Ward Howe, and Samuel Gridley Howe together with younger members such as the teleologist John Fiske and most influentially the journalist Franklin B. Sanborn.

The youngest member of the Secret Committee of Six, which had helped finance John Brown's raid on Harper's Ferry, Sanborn had written a biography of Brown that did much to establish Brown's image as a transcendental saint. Later Sanborn wrote biographies of his literary friends as well: Emerson, Thoreau, and Hawthorne, and Samuel Gridley Howe. Beyond that, he became the guiding participant in the Radical Club and founder of the organization that provided a national forum for the concerns of Radical Club members, the American Social Science Association (ASSA).

As the association's name indicates, these Brahmin idealists were attracted to the notion, implicit in the new term *social science*, that mankind could be helped through new ways of gathering, generalizing, and applying knowledge of society. There was as yet no general agreement as to what this successor to moral philosophy comprised exactly. But the Civil War Sanitary Commission had demonstrated social science in practice, and the statistician Carroll Davidson Wright said that it warranted "the attention of men and women who were willing to aid in the cause of humanity for the sake of humanity." George William Curtis attributed "all advance from Barbarism" to "the development of social science." And Johns Hopkins president Daniel Coit Gilman observed that, if the ASSA accomplished its program, it would achieve "an earthly paradise, an enchanted ground."[2] One might acquire a faith in social science as the way to earthly salvation without necessarily comprehending what it was. Sanborn himself had "never seen or heard of a person who could concisely define" the concept "or state wherein it differs from other branches of human knowledge. It seems, indeed, to be neither a science or an art" but something more eclectic that shades off "easily and imperceptibly into metaphors on the one side, philanthropy on another, political economy on a third, and so round the whole circle of human inquiry."[3]

Literary intellectuals might be content with this general approach, but a professional class of academic social scientists presently emerged to assume authority over this area of knowledge and demarcate it. Geared to the university system and to the German mode of linking scholarship with public service, these professionals differed heatedly among themselves over questions of social theory but shared a professional outlook that shaped them into a breed apart from the literary-philanthropic gentlemen of the ASSA, just as the new social science disciplines of sociology, political science, and economics differed from the ministerial, parent discipline of moral philosophy, which had belonged to the traditional liberal arts college curriculum.

While the American Social Science Association was viewed with increasing condescension by the new academic professionals and scientific philanthropists, it was simultaneously losing relevance for the sort of literary-intellectual reformers who had originally founded it. In 1897 the visibly deteriorating ASSA came under the presidency of Simeon Baldwin, a Yale law professor, judge, and gentleman scholar of the old school. Under Baldwin's direction, the ASSA, with its own impending demise already in view, rather remarkably arranged to organize an entirely new society, one that would be not unlike the proposed National Academy of Literature and Art that Senator Charles Sumner had attempted to legislate into being during the Civil War.

The ASSA appointed an ad hoc committee to select 150 members who would form a National Institute of Arts and Letters. The new institute would thereafter proceed on its own, independent of the parent organization, and would represent national culture at its highest level. Accordingly, the ad hoc committee proceeded to select the nation's leading writers of fiction, poetry, drama, and history as well as its leading painters and sculptors, its leading composer of music, and its leading scholarly authorities on these subjects.[4]

In making its selections, the ASSA committee evidently compiled much of its list from the membership of the New York Century Club, supplemented with a few additions from the Boston Saturday Club. That must have seemed the best as well as the simplest and most obvious way to go about it. During the half century of its existence, the Century Club had pursued a policy of extending membership to the most prominent writers and artists in the nation, more and more of whom were coming to live in the general area of New York City. In 1897 the list was fairly definitive, by Century Club standards. The Saturday Club, on the other hand, had limited its membership from the outset to about twenty members. And while the Saturday Club membership had remained select, its initially brilliant quality declined as its original members died and were replaced by men of generally lesser note. Departing members were in some cases replaced by younger men of comparable literary distinction, including Francis Parkman, William Dean Howells, William James, Thomas Bailey Aldrich, and John Fiske. But selections increasingly tended to run to comparatively obscure Harvard professors and to members of the business community who were also honorable members of the Harvard Corporation.[5]

Brought into being with no clearly defined purpose in view, the Institute of Arts and Letters organized itself in New York and held occasional dinner discussions in addition to annual meetings. In its first six years, the institute expanded its membership from 150 to 250 to accommodate various worthies whom the ASSA ad hoc committee had left out. Then in 1904 the institute voted to advance in the direction of greater selectivity by creating a thirty-member Academy of Arts and Letters drawn from its membership. Seven members were to be initially elected by the institute as a whole; then those seven would select eight more, these fifteen would choose an additional five, and that total of twenty members would add the final ten. This procedure having been carried out, the thirty members decided to choose twenty more, bringing to fifty the membership of the completed academy that convened in Washington, D.C., for the first time, in 1909 under the presidency of William Dean Howells.

The event attracted little outside attention. Howells wrote his fellow Academician Henry James in England that the learned papers presented at the conclave "were really fine, but I think the public did not care in the least."[6] Nor did the public learn to care much about it thereafter. The academy achieved its widest recognition in 1930, when Sinclair Lewis attacked it in his Nobel laureate's speech as a stuffy little group that admitted nonentities and ignored certain of the nation's outstanding writers. Nevertheless, the initial creation of this academy in itself constituted a significant event in the social history of high culture in America. It came into being toward the close of the only era when one fifty-man academy could plausibly represent the nation's cultural elect to educated Americans. Such consensus has not occurred in the national community of letters before or since.

The forty-nine men and one woman—Julia Ward Howe—who made up the original academy presented a homogeneous portrait of high culture in America: the image of a well-educated, Protestant, Anglo-American gentleman of advanced age who lived in an urban area of northeastern United States. Geographically this charter membership of the Academy of Arts and Letters did not penetrate west of the original English settlements. Except for Joel Chandler Harris, author of the Uncle Remus stories, who lived in Atlanta, none of the members lived south or west of Washington, D.C. Three lived in London, two in Italy, and the rest were scattered from Washington to Maine; but twenty-four of the fifty lived in and around Manhattan. In addition to Harris the academy included four men born in the Confederate south: Mark Twain of Missouri, Thomas Nelson Page of Virginia, George Washington Cable of Louisiana, and Basil Gildersleeve of South Carolina. Except for Harris, however, all had left their native states by the time they won admittance to the academy: Gildersleeve was professor of Greek at Johns Hopkins University in Baltimore; Page was writing about old Virginia in nearby Washington, D.C.; Cable was memorializing Creole folk culture from Massachusetts; and Twain had long since moved to Elmira, New York; Hartford, Connecticut and Manhattan, becoming the most "desouthernized" Southerner that his friend William Dean Howells believed he had ever met.[7]

The academy was a gerontocracy. The median age as well as the average age of its members was sixty-five. Ages ranged from forty-five to ninety-one. Only two members were fifty years of age or under, and one of these youngsters had just completed his second term as President of the United States. The representatives of the fine arts tended to be somewhat younger than the men of letters: the average age for artists was sixty, while for literary gentlemen it was sixty-eight. The lone woman was eighty-nine. If the academy offered an accurate picture of the contemporary American Republic of Letters, then American high culture of the progressive era represented the fruition of the generation of writers, artists, and scholars that had come to manhood a half century earlier, in the golden age of America's literary renaissance. Scholastically it was the product of the old-time liberal arts college with its traditional classical curriculum, where the composite member of the academy had been enrolled on the eve of the Civil War.

⩓ II ⩔

FROM THE DEMOGRAPHICS of the academy's membership, one might suspect that writers and artists of established reputation were being excluded on grounds of femaleness, youth, and transappalachian location. In fact, such does not appear to have been egregiously the case, given the standards that prevailed in Victorian and Edwardian America. There were brilliant dissenters from this cultural consensus who were not elected to the academy, including artists Mary Cassatt, Thomas Eakins, and Albert P. Ryder and architects Louis Sullivan and Frank Lloyd Wright. Additionally the academy ignored a whole school of journalistic critics led by James Gibbons Huneker and including Ambrose Bierce, William Marion Reedy, and Percival Pollard. Admission was quite evidently limited to respectable worthies.

Had the Academy admitted members without distinction to sex, Sarah Orne Jewett might reasonably have been expected among the charter members, while in the years immediately ahead Edith Wharton and Ellen Glasgow would presumably have been elected rather than Booth Tarkington, Owen Wister, and James Whitcomb Riley. In any event, few if any literary women were notably eligible except Jewett at the time the selections were made. And granting that a case might be made for writers beyond the Alleghenies, western claims were not compelling either. Indiana offered General Lew Wallace in addition to Riley and Tarkington; Chicago boasted the novelists Henry Blake Fuller, Hamlin Garland, Mary Catherwood, Robert Welch Herrick, Will Payne and, with one novel to his credit, Theodore Dreiser, together with journalistic humorists, George Ade and Finley Peter Dunne. Ambrose Bierce and Jack London belonged to San Francisco's literary bohemia along with the humorist Gelett Burgess, the poet George Sterling, and the novelist-playwright George Cram Cook. None of these literary men suited the requirements of the academy. Membership for distinguished blacks like Charles Chesnutt and W. E. B. DuBois was, of course, out of the question.

A younger generation of writers had, indeed, appeared during the 1890s, but by the next decade its most brilliant figures were gone, including Harold Frederic, who died in 1898 at forty-two; Stephen Crane, who died in 1900 at twenty-nine; Richard Hovey, who died in 1900 at thirty-six; Frank Norris, who died in 1902 at thirty-two; and Paul Laurence Dunbar, who died in 1906 at thirty-four. These premature deaths cut short the end-of-the-century rebellion against the genteel tradition in American arts and letters, a rebellion that Howells had carefully fostered but whose partisans were otherwise beneath the notice of the academy.

In selecting its Southern men of letters, the academy naturally chose those whose writings appealed most to Northern readers, but that remained the only substantial readership available to Southern writers. Although literary magazines came and went frequently in the post–Civil War South, Southern readers remained as unsupportive of local talent as in antebellum days. The popularity and prestige of Joel Chandler Harris's Uncle Remus stories, George Washington Cable's accounts of old Creole days in New Orleans, and Thomas Nelson Page's descriptions of "ole Virginia" reflected much the same romantic appeal of the old South to Northern readers that had existed "befo' de war," as a book of dialect verse by Page put it, an appeal that revived in the North during the 1870s, following the end to Reconstruction.

Basil Gildersleeve had been a stalwart Confederate who managed to pursue a distinguished career in classical studies that outwardly appeared to be little affected by the war. Gildersleeve had been proud to say that he was "a Charlestonian first, a South Carolinian next, and after that a

Southerner."[8] In pursuing a well-established South Carolina tradition, he became the nation's foremost classicist. Following studies at Princeton, Berlin, and Bonn, he served as professor of Latin at the University of Virginia from 1856 to 1876, when he accepted an appointment as professor of Greek at the newly founded graduate university of Johns Hopkins in Baltimore. In 1908 Gildersleeve became the elected authority on classical civilization among the members of the Academy of Arts and Letters.

Antiquated as it was, this gerontocracy of arts and letters conveyed a substantial impression of legitimacy in 1909. These gentlemen continued to represent the accepted cultural establishment of the nation, and not even their critics could much doubt it. Ellen Glasgow visited New York as a young, little-known writer from Virginia at the time the academy was being assembled. She was taken to the Author's Club, where she

> met the various authors who would soon become, by self-election . . . [the] Immortals of the American Academy. . . . They were important, and they knew it but they were also as affable as royalty; and no one who valued manners could help liking them. . . . [They] had created both the literature of America and the literary renown that embalmed it. They constituted the only critical judgment, as well as the only material for criticism. . . . [The more I] saw of these agreeable authors, the more I liked them. The trouble was that I thought of them as old gentlemen, and they thought of themselves as old masters. . . . [They represented to me] a world that was dominated by immature age. Not by vigorous immaturity, but by immaturity that was old and tired and prudent, that loved ritual and rubric and was utterly wanting in curiosity about the new and the strange.[9]

❧ III ❧

THE INSTITUTE OF ARTS AND LETTERS had limited its role in creating the academy to the selection of the initial seven members, and these were intended to encompass the full range of cultivated pursuits that the institute itself encompassed. Robert Underwood Johnson, *Century Magazine* editor and secretary of the institute, reported in 1904 that in selecting these seven members, we have done what we could to honor literature and the arts by choosing as the fathers of the Academy our most distinguished and representative men, against whom, known as they are even beyond the limits of language and the arts, there can be no cavil.[10]

The select seven were composer Edward MacDowell, sculptor Augustus Saint-Gaudens, artist John La Farge, author and critic William Dean Howells, author and lecturer Mark Twain, poet and stockbroker Edmund Clarence Stedman, and author-statesman John Milton Hay.

MacDowell was a generation younger than his six fellows, and his inclusion among the select initial members of the academy may have seemed a slight to the older John Knowles Paine, then the dean of American composers. Paine had found a strong personal voice in his symphonies and oratorios, the first such American works to make a reputation in Europe, but from the institute's standpoint MacDowell had at least two advantages over Paine. First, by virtue of his long association with Harvard, Paine was seen as an academician; MacDowell, on the other hand, had made his reputation as a virtuoso and creative artist while in Germany, and a recent concert tour and scrape with the administration at Columbia had only confirmed his discomfort with the placid conformity of university art. Thus, at the time of his selection in 1904, he resembled the other initial members of the National Academy of Arts and Letters in not being an academic.

MacDowell's second advantage over Paine was the size and international scope of his audience. Paine had poured his best music into large works for large ensembles with the result that these works were seldom played. In music perhaps more than any other creative medium, American art was felt to be most characteristic when least ambitious: Americans made music for play, not contemplation, and the very notion of a great American symphony seemed an oxymoron to the nation's concert associations as the twentieth century began. MacDowell knew this, and after returning to the U.S. from Germany he ceased writing works for orchestra (with one exception). Instead, MacDowell put his best music into piano solos that he himself could play, publically and privately, as often as he liked. Thousands of Americans—and, more important, Europeans— bought and attempted MacDowell's character pieces and four sonatas on their parlor uprights. MacDowell's singular focus paid off. His piano works were written during a period when most composers of the German school reserved their best musical ideas for chamber ensembles, symphony orchestras, or opera stages and "wrote down" to parlor-bound soloists. MacDowell didn't and thereby gained an international reputation as well as admission to the academy.

MacDowell was born in New York City in 1860. He studied music there, as well as in Paris, Frankfurt am Main, and Darmstadt, where he began his teaching career. Returning to America in 1887, he settled in Boston, where Paine and his students Horatio Parker and Arthur Foote together with George Whitefield Chadwick and later Amy Beach formed the talented core of the German school's American outpost. MacDowell returned to his native New York in 1896 when President Seth Low offered him the first professorship of music at Columbia University. During his first years at Columbia, MacDowell made some small headway toward integrating musical studies into the general curriculum of the university, at that time a novel idea. During MacDowell's seventh, sabbatical year, a new university president reversed MacDowell's hard-fought changes while the composer was absent. An exchange of charges and counter-charges ensued in the New York press, followed by MacDowell's abrupt resignation. MacDowell subsequently fell into a profound midlife depression in 1904. His election to the National Academy might have presaged a welcome shift in fortunes, but shortly afterward the composer was struck by a cab and seriously injured while crossing a New York avenue. A subsequent period of physical and mental deterioration ended with death in 1908. Paine had meanwhile died in 1906. His old student Horatio Parker, then teaching at Yale, was called to replace MacDowell when the Academy convened in Washington in 1908.

The fine arts were integral to native high culture in America as music was not, and the two artists elected by the Institute were men of elevated reputations. The sculptor Saint-Gaudens and the painter, muralist, and worker in stained glass La Farge had been young rebels of the 1870s who had become the arbiters of American taste in the 1890s. When the Academy of Design rejected works submitted by European-trained La Farge and Saint-Gaudens, they had joined other young artists in founding the rival Society of American Artists, which held its first exhibition in 1878.

The new society was bound to prevail over the Academy of Design since it represented the dominant contemporary trends in European art. La Farge became president of the society and led it to ascendency in matters of national taste. The society's achievement was enshrined in the "White City" of the 1893 Columbian Exposition in Chicago. Saint-Gaudens, viewing the company of artists recruited for the fair, pronounced it "the greatest meeting of artists since the fifteenth century,"[11] and nothing that was to happen in American art during the next ten or fifteen years would challenge this assessment, so far as the cultivated men of the National Institute of Arts and Letters were aware.

Stedman earned admission to the Academy of Arts and Letters as its first poet by being generally ranked first nationally in a field of four poets that included Richard Henry Stoddard, Bayard Taylor, and Thomas Bailey Aldrich. As a poetry critic Stedman wrote the most influential appreciations of Poe and Whitman to appear in America in the nineteenth century together with criticism of other American and British poets. His criticism has remained more highly regarded than his verse. Late in his career he extended his friendship to a new generation of poets, including Edwin Arlington Robinson, Ridgely Torrence, and William Vaughn Moody, assisting them in their efforts to survive as poets in Gilded Age New York.

By the time Mark Twain was elected to the Academy of Arts and Letters, he had become the most celebrated American man of letters since Benjamin Franklin, while William Dean Howells was nationally the most widely respected literary statesman in the history of the Literary Republic. Furthermore, among critically acclaimed American literary men of the Gilded Age, Twain and Howells were the two leading moneymakers by a wide margin. Closely associated with one another in their personal as well as literary careers, they were together in the first choice of the institute to represent the art of fiction in the academy.

As a literary man Twain had earned his unique distinction by transforming the frontier humor of the old southwest into the literary art of *Huckleberry Finn* and then by recreating this art on the lecture platform. Twain relished this acclaim and played to it. Yet he did not believe in the judgment of the multitude, and he had doubts about his own literary legitimacy. Indeed, the more he was honored by mankind, the more pessimistic he became concerning the human race and its probable future.

While Twain despaired for the common world from which he came, he accepted the standards of mugwump gentility as being right and proper and beyond serious criticism.

An early supporter of Twain's claims to literary recognition, Howells continued in later years to exert himself on behalf of his friend's reputation—perhaps from force of habit—at a time when Twain was basking in an extent of national and international adulation, both critical and popular, greater than any other American writer has ever experienced. Wherever Twain traveled on his worldwide lecture tour, crowds recognized him as a familiar figure and as the undoubtedly representative American genius. Twain was at the pinnacle of his fabulous reputation in 1904 when members of the institute selected him to be a founder of the academy.

Twain's friend Howells stood first among equals in the academy, his election as its president being virtually a foregone conclusion. Indeed Howells's position of authority in the American Republic of Letters, from the 1880s to his death in 1920 has never been equaled by any other man of letters. American letters had been too provincial before the Civil War to sustain even a Franklin, a Jefferson, a Bryant, or a Lowell as the presiding spokesman for the entire national literary community. As for the era following World War I, Sinclair Lewis's complaints against the Academy of Arts and Letters in 1930 indicate the difficulties that any later pretender to Howells's position would have encountered. Howells was maintained in his unique office by that genteel consensus which assumed nationwide proportions during and after the Civil War.

Several years after Howells's death, H. L. Mencken wrote an essay, "Want Ad," discussing the nonexistence of any candidate suitable to succeed Howells as "dean of national letters," either among the list of "mystic nobles of the American Academy of Arts and Letters" or elsewhere. The joke of it was that Mencken himself came closer than anybody else to succeeding Howells as the most influential arbiter of national letters, and Mencken was a rowdy iconoclast who represented the aesthetic anarchy that had followed Howells's death. Gone was the "decorous and orderly era in American letters" that had persisted for almost half a century, from the Reconstruction era to the pre–World War I Greenwich Village revolt, without serious disturbance.[12]

This genteel half-century of Victorian American culture was encompassed by Howells's career, from the time the self-educated twenty-three-year-old printer, having placed his verse in *Saturday Press* and *Atlantic* and having published his campaign biography of Lincoln, set out from his home town in Ohio in 1860 for New York, Boston, and Venice. Returning from Italy in 1865, where his campaign biography of Lincoln had won him a consulship, Howells served as James T. Fields's assistant editor on *Atlantic* until 1872, then as editor-in-chief until 1881, fostering the careers of Mark Twain, Henry James, and many others in that period. Howells's literary activities drew him to New York in the 1880s, and his departure from Boston marked the decline of that city as a literary center in relation to New York. In New York he became an editor for *Harper's Magazine*, contributing its column "The Editor's Study" while contracting to write one novel and one farce per year for Harper's publishing firm.

Following a series of successful novels of manners, often featuring young Americans abroad, Howells discovered Tolstoy and Turgenev. Thereafter, he became a militant champion for realism, writing and promoting fictions in which protagonists' fortunes were not superposed upon nor separable from the precisely rendered textures of their worlds. Like other American writers of his generation, Howells shied away from frank treatment of sex found in writings of the French naturalists, but he was the first to praise similar treatments in novels by younger Americans, as in Crane's *Maggie* or Norris's *McTeague*, and in his final novel, *The Leatherwood God*, Howells himself tried to approach the subject less decorously. Sex aside, Howells was bold in his choice of subjects: psychological subtlety characterizes his treatment of the problems of professional women in *Dr. Breene's Practice*, of factory workers in *Annie Kilburn*, of self-made men in *The Rise of Silas Lapham*, of blacks crossing the color line in *Shadow of a Dream*, and of divorce in *A Modern Instance*, to name only a few of his characteristic novels.

Howells did not confuse realism with local color, but he saw sympathetic allies in the growing number of regional writers who were finding the stuff of real literature in the banal events of their communities; these creations included the Hoosier schoolmaster of Edward Eggleston, the Kansas town of Ed Howe ("the sage of Potato Hill"), the Creole society of George Washington Cable, Mark Twain's Missourians, Hamlin Garland's middle-border farmers, and Abraham Cahan's lower-east-side Jews.

Howells was not doctrinaire, and he ventured outside realism to write poetry, utopian novels of ideas, and even ghost stories. However, he was generally unsympathetic to romances of Hawthorne and others of his generation, and Howells believed that the age of verse had also passed with the romantic movement. Howells nevertheless established himself as an influential critic of contemporary verse, as a theater critic and author of thirty-three plays, even as an art critic—conceding that he had no special training in the fine arts but pointing out that "There *is* no acknowledged authority on art in this country."[13]

Although literary business kept Howells in New York City for most of the last forty years of his life, he never bought a house there or settled into the community, as he had in Boston, preferring to live in hotels and other temporary accommodations and listing his permanent place of residence in *Who's Who* as Kittery Point, Maine. To Howells, New York remained a commercial center that was not a community and certainly not a literary center in the sense that Boston had been a literary center for a remarkably literate community. Despite its metropolitan pretentions, polyglot New York was definitely not America in the view of this Bostonized New Yorker from Ohio,[14] a view that was shared by others of those Bostonized New Yorkers, who made up a substantial part of the Academy.

The election of John Hay among the first seven members of the academy was not to be explained by Hay's literary accomplishments. As a creative writer Hay was clearly not the equal of Twain, Howells, Stedman, or for that matter two authors whom Hay himself nominated in the second round of Academy selections: Henry James and Henry Adams. Hay's literary reputation rested upon two volumes of verse; a book of Spanish travel sketches; *The Bread-Winners*, a novel; and a ten-volume biography of Lincoln, which he coauthored with John George Nicolay. Hay's forte was not writing, however, but being the American gentleman nonpareil, reputedly unequaled among his countrymen in the art of civilized social intercourse. Literature was an avocation for this statesman and diplomat, who had begun his career as President Lincoln's private secretary (serving in this capacity together with his coauthor, Nicolay) and ended it nearly a half century later as Theodore Roosevelt's secretary of state. Hay possessed a remarkable talent for attracting warm and enduring friendships, a talent that served him well indeed when he applied it to politics, and one that he expended even more lavishly upon the literati, whose company he most valued. "If a man may be judged by the company he keeps," the historian Brooks Adams wrote, "Mr. Hay must be conceded to have always stood high among his contemporaries, for . . . his friends have been more notable than those of any other man of his generation."[15]

The literary form in which Hay was judged to stand first among his notable friends was the art of conversation. He "had at his tongue's end," the historian James Ford Rhodes recalled, "what we used to call belles-lettres and his conversation thereon was a profit and a delight." Rhodes doubted whether "there has ever been any better talker in the country," and the diplomat Elihu Root described him as "the most delightful of companions," capable of expressing "a thought that in substance and per-fection of form left in the mind the sense of having seen a perfectly cut precious stone."[16] A man of wealth by marriage, Hay was a princely figure who represented to the gentlemen of the institute, not one of the four leading writers of the nation, certainly, but nevertheless the nation's first gentleman of letters.

ᴀ IV ᴋ

THERE WERE NO HARVARD graduates among the first seven members of the academy, but among the next eight, Cambridge was represented by six former students. They were Henry James, Henry Adams, Charles Eliot Norton, Theodore Roosevelt, Thomas Bailey Aldrich, and the archi-tect Charles Follen McKim. Thereafter the fifteen-man academy became to a considerable extent the "Adams circle." Hays was Henry Adams's closest friend, the two of them living in adjoining halves of a duplex they had built in Washington, D.C. In the field of the fine arts, La Farge and Saint-Gaudens had been among Adams's closest companions. Among writers, Adams shared especially close ties with Henry James. The vener-able Norton had launched Adams on his writing career by accepting his first article in *North American Review*. Roosevelt had attended Harvard when Adams taught there, though it was only later on that Adams came to know him, chiefly at the homes of Secretary of State Hay and of Sena-tor Henry Cabot Lodge (who gained admission to the academy in the fifth round of selections). McKim, whom Adams admired as one of the nation's best architects, had begun his career under the late Henry Hobson Richardson, one of Adams's closest friends since his Harvard days. The only surviving member of Adams's carefully cultivated inner circle missing from the academy was Alexander Agassiz, who as a zoologist was not eligible for membership but who was currently serving as president of the National Academy of Science.

These men were not simply a group of friends; they belonged to a circle that Adams had consciously set out, early in life, to organize. Henry Adams had been sent to England in 1861 to serve as secretary to his father, the wartime American minister to Great Britain. From the vantage point of literary London, the twenty-four-year-old Henry wrote his brother Charles Francis Jr. in 1862 about the prospects for their generation of Americans, once the war was over.

> What we want is a *school*. We want a national set of young men like ourselves or better to start new influences not only in politics, but in literature, in law, in society, and throughout the whole social organism of the country—a national school of our own generation.[17]

Henry Adams returned from Europe in 1868 determined to develop himself beyond the Bostonian provincialism of his youth and heritage. Following unsuccessful attempts to establish himself in New York and Washington, D.C., Adams reluctantly returned home to accept a teaching position at Harvard, where he remained for six years. Having trained himself as a historian, however, Adams then returned to Washington, D.C., and established his permanent residence there, within close range of Congress and the White House. Meanwhile, he was collecting friends —his national set of men of his own generation—and he sought them consciously beyond the confines of Cambridge, as he pointed out in *The Education of Henry Adams*. One of his closest friends turned out to be the architect Richardson, whom he had met at Harvard. But Richardson

> came from far away New Orleans, [and] certainly the college relation had little to do with the later friendship. . . . Adams would have attached himself to Richardson in any case, as he attached himself to John La Farge or Augustus Saint-Gaudens or [the geologist] Clarence King or John Hay, none of whom were at Harvard College.[18]

Throughout his life Adams remained acutely conscious of the age of his cohorts, and as a representative of the generation that came to maturity in the early 1860s, he had increasing reason to wonder why no subsequent younger intellectuals emerged to supersede his own increasingly antiquated contemporaries. As for children of the twentieth century, he "asked no longer to be teacher or even friend; he asked only to be a pupil, and promised to be docile, for once, even though trodden under foot." This new American "would deal with problems altogether beyond the range of earlier society. To him the nineteenth century would stand on the same plane with the fourth—equally childlike.[19] When the secretary of the Institute of Arts and Letters, Robert Underwood Johnson, asked Adams to present a paper to the institute, Adams declined on grounds that he had been dead for the past fifteen years.[20]

By that time most of Adams's closest friends were literally dead, and Adams had taken their dying hard. The most painful alienation expressed in the *Education* is directed against the turn of the century as a time of dying for Adams's national set of men. The *Education* ends with the death of John Hay, after which "It was time to go" for Adams, who "had no motive —no attraction—to carry it on after the others had gone."[21] Adams completed the *Education* the year he was appointed to the academy and he survived thereafter, self-consciously superannuated yet still, absurdly enough, the undoubted intellectuals' intellectual of the academy.

≈◁ V ▷≈

ADAMS WAS THE FIRST HISTORIAN to be admitted to the academy, but by the time it had rounded itself out to fifty members, history was more substantially represented than any other branch of letters. And in no other area of intellectual activity was the vulnerability of the old-fashioned patrician, liberal arts, moral philosophy orientation of the academy more evident. Poets, who would have dominated Senator Sumner's proposed academy in 1864, were represented in 1908 only by Stedman and Thomas Bailey Aldrich. Prose fiction, which had lacked respectability to a degree in Hawthorne's day, was the chief stock-in-trade of eight academicians, in addition to which two playwrights were included. But historical or biographical studies formed the chief contributions of thirteen of those thirty-four academicians who were associated with letters rather than arts.

Most of these were gentlemen historians and not academic professionals. Among them, Woodrow Wilson and Andrew Dickson White had started out as academic historians, but they were later elected to the academy as university presidents, not history professors. Henry Adams had taught history at Harvard, but he had not trained himself to become a university professor and he did not remain one. Among the academicians, only Professor William Milligan Sloan, a Leipzig Ph.D. and professor at Princeton and later Columbia, represented the type of professional who in fact had by that time come to dominate historical writing in America.

From colonial times, but preeminently from the mid-nineteenth-century era of Motley, Prescott, Parkman, Bancroft, and academician Henry Charles Lea, history had been considered a literary form especially well suited to gentlemen. Beyond being generally learned in ancient languages and history as defined by the traditional classical college curriculum, the historian would ideally be a widely experienced man of affairs. Historical research suited the condition of gentlemen of leisure, who had the time to engage in extended researches, who could afford to travel extensively, and who enjoyed the station in life and the social contacts that were so often necessary to gain access to widely scattered family papers and private collections of documents.

It was not until the post–Civil War rise of the university that history began to make its way into academic curriculums as a distinct subject. In 1880, after Henry Adams had left the teaching profession for good, there were only eleven history professors in all of American higher education. To any young men who entertained ideas of training themselves for such positions, President Eliot of Harvard advised that this "would be the height of imprudence on their part." It was supposed, as history professor Ephraim Emerton of Harvard complained in 1884, that

> Any "cultivated gentleman" could teach European history; and as for America, one might suppose a knowledge of its history to form a part of those innate ideas some philosophers tell us about, for all the efforts visible to compass it by way of education.

However, times were changing, and Henry Adams warned Francis Parkman that same year that "before long a new school of history . . . will leave us antiquated."[22]

In 1876, as Henry Adams edited his last issue of *North American Review* and made plans to retire from teaching, Herbert Baxter Adams of Amherst, Massachusetts, received his doctorate in history with highest honors at Heidelberg and accepted an offer to teach history at the newly founded Johns Hopkins University, which was organizing the first graduate program in any American university leading to the Ph.D. degree. John Franklin Jameson received the first doctorate in history at Johns Hopkins, and H. B. Adams and Jameson directed their energies thereafter to the formation of the university-oriented American historical profession, beginning with the founding of the American Historical Association (AHA) in 1884. Adams remained secretary of the AHA until a year before his death in 1901.

In 1895 a group of academic historians founded the *American Historical Review*, independently of the AHA, under the editorship of Jameson as a professional journal that would maintain professional standards. In the course of the following decade, the *American Historical Review* became the official journal of the AHA without altering its editorial policy to accommodate amateurs. By the time the Academy of Arts and Letters came into being, the new professional school of historians had indeed left the old gentleman's school antiquated, as Henry Adams predicted it would.

For gentlemen of the old school, history remained a branch of literature; for academic professionals it was a science. The division between the schools was not clear-cut, however, since the best literary historians engaged in basic historical research and drew their conclusions from the historical record while scientific historians were not necessarily free of literary aspirations. The leading gentleman historians of the late nineteenth century—James Ford Rhodes, Henry Adams, Henry Cabot Lodge, and Theodore Roosevelt, to name ones who became members of the academy—were certainly more "scientific" in methodology than the generation of historians that had preceded them. At the same time, such professional historians as Edward Channing and Woodrow Wilson sought to write methodologically scientific history as narrative literature. However, the more characteristic product of the professional scientific historian was the monograph and the edited manuscript, addressed to fellow professionals rather than to that intelligent reading public which had bought and read quantities of volumes of Parkman and Bancroft. This reading public demonstrated a continuing interest in the multivolume histories of Henry Adams and especially Theodore Roosevelt's *Winning of the West*, but they largely ignored the historical monographs superintended by Herbert Baxter Adams and others, as it was intended they should be by the nonliterary historical profession.

While academic historians sought to remove their discipline from literature and put it on a scientific basis, professors of the equally new academic field of English literature pursued a conscientiously antiscientific course toward the reconstruction of what one of the more embattled of their number, Irving Babbitt, called *neohumanism*. The old humanism had vanished beyond recall with the general abandonment, following the Civil War, of Greek and Latin college requirements in favor of the elective system. This irrevocable break with the culture of classical languages was reflected in the composition of the Academy of Arts and Letters. While a number of its members may have remained competent classicists, only Gildersleeve of Johns Hopkins was a classical scholar by vocation. If classical culture was to remain the enduring foundation of civilization, it would have to do so in English translation (as Benjamin Franklin had recommended in the eighteenth century). The classics therefore became primarily a branch of English literature, along with the rest of what was coming to be referred to in American universities as *Western civilization*. English professors saw themselves as preeminently the custodians of this civilization within the universities.

These English professors were gentlemen scholars who reflected well the outlook of the Academy of Arts and Letters and who were represented there by Brander Matthews of Columbia, Thomas Raynesford Lounsbury of Yale, and Henry van Dyke of Princeton. Among early replacements to the academy were English professors George Edward Woodberry of Columbia and Bliss Perry and Barrett Wendell of Harvard. Woodberry expressed their position when he wrote President Seth Low of Columbia that he certainly did "not mean to yield my designation as a man of letters to that of a scholar."[23] While history departments were organized by scientific historians, English departments emerged as gentlemen's quarters amid the noisy academic construction of *"parvenu* science," as one of their number complained, "crass, boorish and overbearing, as the *parvenu* generally is." These English professors presented themselves as broadly cultivated witnesses to "the breakup of knowledge into pieces," by academic scientists, social scientists, and scientific historians, resulting in the "dissevering of sympathy and dehumanizing of scholarship . . . the literal 'provincialization' of learning." They identified themselves with a social elite that was in a position to pursue knowledge for its own sake in the spirit of the amateur and the aristocrat. Wrote Yale professor William Lyon Phelps:

> Academic life is delightful to men and women of scholarly tastes; one is removed from the sordid and material side of the struggle, and one's associations and friendships are based on a community of intellectual interest. One does not dwell in a daily atmosphere of cloth and pork.[24]

If all-absorbing worldliness was the characteristic offense against civilization of businessmen, however, unworldliness remained a contrary extreme that men of letters guarded against. The ivory tower scholar who knew and cared little of the world beyond his study was dismissed as a specimen of arrested development and skewed humanity, regardless of the breadth of his humane learning. "At Columbia," wrote Professor Brander Matthews, a founding member of both the Authors Club and the Players Club,

> the professor is not uncommon who is both urban and urbane, who is not only a gentleman and a scholar, in the good old phrase, but is more or less a man of the world, and, on occasion, a man of affairs. . . . So far as I have been able to form an opinion there is no university in the United States where the position of professor is pleasanter than it is at Columbia.[25]

Barrett Wendell would presumably have supposed that the position of professor at Harvard was pleasanter, but he would have agreed that town and gown were both necessary to the complete man of letters. The Academy of Arts and Letters admitted to its company professors who behaved like gentlemen but not those who behaved like academics.

The same criterion would have excluded academic social scientists had they been eligible for admission. The orientation of doctoral training generally was specialized, technical, monographic, nonliterary, and studiously cautious about broad generalizations. In an era when professors could be fired arbitrarily by academic administrations, many social scientists, with the encouragement of their professional organizations, cultivated expertise in limited and noncontroversial areas and pursued the ideal of scientific objectivity to the extent of avoiding those large ideas relating to broad public issues that were the legitimate concern of intellectuals. On the other hand, there were bolder social scientists who risked their academic careers during the progressive era in pursuit of truth and also social justice. The modern university was in the process of developing a new class of professional intellectuals who were undermining the cultural authority of the literary gentlemen of the Saturday Club in Boston and the Century Club in New York. This process was not sufficiently advanced during the opening years of the new century, however, to disturb the literary gentry that formed itself into the Academy of Arts and Letters.

⤙ VI ⤚

BY THE TIME THE ACADEMY was formed, it had long since ceased to be necessary for a well-trained painter or sculptor to be college educated in order to be accepted as a gentleman. As far as men of letters were concerned, however, college training remained as critically important as it had traditionally been since the eighteenth century to membership in the American Republic of Letters. Among the forty initial members of the academy in the field of letters, thirty-four had attended college, eleven at Harvard and seven at Yale. Of the six who had not attended college, two were members of wealthy families who had received exceptional private educations: Julia Ward Howe, whose father had seen to her widely diversified instruction, and Henry Charles Lea of Philadelphia, who had been kept out of college for reasons of health and was privately tutored.

The remaining four—Twain, Howells, George Washington Cable, and Joel Chandler Harris—all hailed from the south and west and had acquired their learning in newspaper offices. Among them Howells, like William Cullen Bryant before him, had mastered classical languages by self-study sufficiently to be able to correct the Latin of Harvard professors in copy submitted to *Atlantic*. Twain educated himself omniverously in his native language but not in the dead ones as well. Consequently he remained inferior to Howells and to his college-educated friends in Hartford and New York in this department, and it was not an inferiority that Twain could laugh off. It remained one of those enduring consequences of his uncultivated Missouri upbringing that prevented him from being as complete an educated gentleman as he would have wished to be.

The charter membership of the Academy of Arts and Letters represented the end of the era, extending back into colonial times, when intellectual society in America had been the product of the liberal arts college and when the prime purpose of a college education had been to provide the classically oriented training that would perpetuate intellectual society in a culturally underdeveloped region of the world. By the same token, the academy marked the end of the era of the American Intellectual as Gentleman, the era when ideals of true civilization were unquestioningly identified with bourgeois American ideals, whether in the minds of Revolutionists and founding fathers in the late eighteenth century, of liberal Republicans and Mugwumps in the late nineteenth, or the aged academicians of 1908, most of whom remained of the Mugwump persuasion. It is true that Howells and Twain sometimes questioned the legitimacy of the capitalist system. Howells supported the Chicago anarchists charged with the Haymarket bombing in 1886, and he was permitted to use his column in *Harper's* as a platform for their defense. Twain employed his wit and fury against racism, especially where it was directed against blacks, Chinese, and Jews in America. Both men endorsed trade unions and argued the moral superiority of socialism over capitalism. Nevertheless both men normally adhered to the liberal Republican-Mugwump policy of respectable reform. As Howells put it in a letter to his father, he and his wife, together with Twain and his wife, were "all of accord in our way of thinking: that is, we are theoretical socialists, and practical aristocrats. But it is a comfort to be right theoretically and to be ashamed of one's self practically."[26]

On moral as opposed to economic issues, Twain and Howells together with other academicians remained uncompromisingly Victorian. Twain might ridicule Christianity, but he remained, despite his private scatalogical writings, a devout believer in the religion of respectability.

When Maxim Gorky came to America in 1906 to raise money for the Russian revolution, Howells and Twain supported him until it was discovered that he was not legally married to the woman who accompanied him to New York. Upon learning of this, the two theoretical socialists would have nothing further to do with Gorky. In defense of this rejection of the man who had been publicized as the Huck Finn of literary Russia, Twain later wrote that Gorky's violation of the moral code had discredited him more seriously than a breach of the law would have done. Law was only sand, Twain wrote, but "custom is custom, it is built of brass, boiler iron, granite; facts, reasonings, arguments have no more effect on it than the idle winds have on Gibraltaer."[27]

As Victorian heirs to the Whig revolution of 1776, the liberal Republican-Mugwump literary intellectuals preserved a traditional Anglo-American culture of humanism and gentlemanly respectability that presumably remained authoritative among most educated Americans at the turn of the century just as those academicians who embodied it remained authoritative in the literary community at the time of their election to the academy. The tradition they embodied proved to be as antiquated as they were, however, and almost as mortal. Ellen Glasgow wrote of them that they had "had their day, those hopeful spirits, and their day, as it happened, was long and sunny," but that presently it "passed away, and the world it made has crumbled around us."

Glasgow later experienced the transition in American intellectual society from the drawing room and the gentleman's club in her youth to the café and the speakeasy in her middle years. From her vantage point, the later, less restrained generations did not appear to "have reached higher levels." Gone with the silly ritual and rubric of the elders was their "finest creation, a code of manners," which had been "ridiculed and discarded" by "modern iconoclasts who are without culture" but who "possess, apparently, all the courage."[28] The Academy of Arts and Letters of 1909 formed an icon of native American respectability—prosaic, prudish, bourgeois, Anglophile—which became an easy target for younger generations of intellectuals beginning a few years later with the Greenwich Village generation, who undertook the task of recasting the image of the intellectual in twentieth-century America.

❧ NOTES ❧

PREFACE

1. Henry Adams, *History of the United States: During the Administrations of Jefferson and Madison*, 9 vols. (1889–1891). One scholar, outside the academic profession, who did write exhaustively on the literary class of the United States was Van Wyck Brooks, whose *Makers and Finders*, 5 vols. (1936–1952) chronicled men and women of letters in *The World of Washington Irving* (1944), *The Flowering of New England, 1815–1865* (1936), *The Times of Melville and Whitman* (1947), *New England Indian Summer, 1865–1915* (1940), and *The Confident Years, 1885–1915* (1952). These volumes advanced no major themes other than that America possessed a literary heritage which Americans would do well to appreciate. Brooks described them as a recording of "the pageant of American genius," which he considered to be a form of literary history. When challenged by critics who asserted that true literary history is the history of literary forms and not literary lives, Brooks concluded that he had evidently invented a scholarly form of his own which he would defend on its own grounds. [Brooks, *The Writer in America* (1953), 44, 13.] The usefulness of these widely popular volumes to other scholars remains limited by the subjective, not to say possessive, style of narration and the lack of documentation. Brooks is not cited anywhere in *Republic of Letters*, but this study as a whole is influenced by his accounts of patterns of literary life in America. Brooks's continued relevance is attested to by two scholarly biographies: James Hoopes, *Van Wyck Brooks: In Search of America* (1977) and Raymond Nelson, *Van Wyck Brooks: A Writer's Life* (1981).

2. *American Historical Review* 56 (1951), 471. Gene Wise, "'Paradigm Dramas' in American Studies: A Cultural and Institutional History of the Movement," *American Quarterly* 31 (1979), 293–337, surveys the common origins of American Studies and American Intellectual History.

3. Adams, *History of the United States*, I, 75.

4. Edmund Wilson, ed., *The Shock of Recognition: The Development of Literature in the United States Recorded by the Men Who Made It* (2 vols., 1943), I, 5.

CHAPTER 1: THE COLLEGIATE ARISTOCRACY

1. Jonathan Elliot, ed., *Debates in the Several Conventions on the Adoption of the Federal Constitution*, 5 vols. (1861), 2:246.

2. Vernon L. Parrington, *Main Currents in American Thought*, 3 vols. (1927–30), 1:284.

3. *Letters from the Federal Farmer*, vol. 2 of Herbert J. Storing's *The Complete Anti-Federalist* (1981), 267.

4. Clinton Rossiter, *1787: Grand Convention* (1966), 144, 147. That the founding fathers comprised the college-educated intellectual elite of the new nation was a commonplace for Mugwump historians of the Federal School such as John Fiske, who presented a pre-Beardian composite portrait of the Constitutional Convention in these terms in *The Critical Period of American History, 1783–1789* (1897), 242ff. Charles Beard's *An Economic Interpretation of the Constitution* (1913) did not dispute the educational attainments of the founders, but it rendered them irrelevant to the issue of the Constitution as Beard defined it in economic terms for political historians. Supporters of Beard continued to define the character of the founders in terms of their holdings in public securities and personalty in land, slaves, mercantile holdings, and money at interest, and so did Beard's leading critics. Robert E. Brown, *Charles Beard and the Constitution* (1956), and Forrest McDonald, *We the People: Economic Origins of the Constitution* (1958), perversely reinforced the Beardian interpretation by meeting Beard upon his terms and attacking his use of evidence rather than the orientation of his argument. Nor did these attacks convince younger Beardian historians such as Jackson Turner Main, who defended the master in "Charles A. Beard and the Constitution: A Critical Review of Forrest McDonald's 'We the People,'" *William and Mary Quarterly*, 3d ser., 17 (1961).

In *The Social Structure of Revolutionary America* (1965), Main himself ventured beyond property and income data to determine cultural as well as economic expressions of class distinctions. But higher education, in his account, remained a luxury of the rich in a society where "the quality of culture" naturally "varied with the economic status of the people" (268). Main cited the word of contemporary newspaper writers that education "fitted one for political leadership and was, together with wealth, essential for achieving the highest social rank" (251), but he himself apparently did not buy this argument. Nor, evidently, did Richard D. Brown when he gathered statistics for "The Founding Fathers of 1776 and 1787: A Collective View," *William and Mary Quarterly*, 3d ser., 33 (1976). Brown omitted education altogether as a detail in his collective portrait.

While Beard's interpretation continues to influence the writing of American political history, it failed from the outset to convince leading legal and consti-

tutional historians such as Max Farrand, Charles Warren, and most of their leading successors, and in the long run it has failed to persuade either the political
scientists or the intellectual historians of Revolution and Constitution. Among
intellectual histories, Parrington's *Main Currents in American Thought* hewed
closely to Beard's economic interpretation; while it remained an underlying assumption of Merle Curti's *Growth of American Thought* (1943) as well. After
World War II, however, intellectual histories of Revolution and Constitution rejected Beard's economic motivation in favor of ideological motivation. This
ideological interpretation received its now-classic statement in three studies:
Carolyn Robbins, *The Eighteenth-Century Commonwealthmen: Studies in the Transmission, Development, and Circumstances of English Liberal Thought from the Restora-
tion of Charles II until the War with the Thirteen Colonies* (1959); Bernard Bailyn, *The
Ideological Origins of the American Revolution* (1967); and Gordon Wood, *Creation
of the American Republic* (1969). Together these studies narrate developments in
radical Whig thought from seventeenth-century Britain through the American
Revolution to the founding of the American federal system.

Ideas not only replaced economic interests in the Bailyn-Wood interpretation; they replaced people as well, except as people contributed collectively to
the large body of literature of controversy surrounding the Revolution and Constitution (a body of literature that was taken to constitute the intellectual history
of these events, as synthesized by Bailyn, Wood, and others of this school). It
was chiefly left to scholars outside the history profession to revive ideological
interpretations of the Constitutional Convention in terms of the men involved,
as with Fred Rodell, *Fifty-Five Men* (1936); Nathan Schachner, *The Founding Fathers*
(1954); John P. Roche, "The Founding Fathers: A Reform Caucus in Action,"
American Political Science Review 55 (1961); Catherine D. Bowen, *Miracle at Philadelphia: The Constitutional Convention* (1966); and Rossiter, *1787*. Rossiter's work
remains the most informative modern account available of the Constitutional
Convention as an historical event played out by a particular group of men motivated by ideology as well as politics and economics.

Robert E. Shalhope, "Toward a Republican Synthesis: The Emergence of an
Understanding of Republicanism in American Historiography," *William and
Mary Quarterly*, 3d ser., 29 (1972): 49–80, described the substantial consensus that
the Robbins-Bailyn-Wood school enjoyed among published scholars in the early
1970s. Shalhope's "Republicanism and Early American Historiography," *William
and Mary Quarterly*, 3d ser., 39 (1982): 334–56, recounted modifications and frag-
mentations of this consensus in subsequent scholarly writings, the most influential
modification being the conception of *civic humanism* developed by J. G. A.
Pocock in *The Machiavellian Moment: Florentine Political Thought and Atlantic
Republican Tradition* (1975). Pocock stressed classical and Renaissance sources of

republican thought, whereas Robbins and Bailyn had stressed Protestant sources. Scholars also attempted in the 1970s to distinguish between *court* and *country* aspects of American republicanism, drawing upon Perez Zagourin, *The Court and the Country: The Beginning of the English Revolution* (1969).

5. Allen Johnson and Dumas Malone, eds., *Dictionary of American Biography*, 20 vols. (1928–44).

6. Evarts B. Greene, *The Revolutionary Generation, 1763–1790* (1943), 123. Many college-educated men fled the country soon after 1776 in the Loyalist exodus.

7. Compiled from *Dictionary of American Biography*; supplemented by *Biographical Directory of the American Congress, 1774–1949* (1950).

8. John Adams and Abigail Adams, *Familiar Letters of John and Abigail Adams*, ed. C. F. Adams (1873), 207.

9. Adams to William Tudor, 5 January 1817, *American Historical Review* 47 (1942): 807.

10. Adams and Adams, *Familiar Letters*, 206.

11. Philip Fithian, *Journal and Letters, 1773–1774*, ed. Hunter D. Farish (1943), 161.

12. David L. Wagner, ed., *The Seven Liberal Arts in the Middle Ages* (1983).

13. Quoted in Carl Van Doren, *Benjamin Franklin* (1938), 770.

14. Edward P. Cheyney, *History of the University of Pennsylvania, 1740–1940* (1940), 186.

15. Ralph Waldo Emerson, "New England Reformers," *Works*, Riverside Ed. (1903), 3:259.

16. Robert A. McCaughey, *Josiah Quincy, 1772–1864: The Last Federalist* (1974), 167–78.

17. Edward W. Emerson, *The Early Years of the Saturday Club, 1855–1870* (1918), 18.

18. Codman Hislop, *Eliphalet Nott* (1971).

19. Francis Wayland, "Report to the Brown Corporation," in *American Higher Education: A Documentary History*, ed. Richard Hofstadter and Wilson Smith, 2 vols. (1961), 2:478.

20. Sears, cited in Walter G. Bronson, *History of Brown University, 1764–1914*, (1914), 321–22.

21. Jeremiah Day, report of 1828, in *American Higher Education*, 1:276–91.

22. Ibid., 1:288–89.

23. Josiah Quincy, *The History of Harvard University*, 2 vols. (1840), 2:123.

24. Colin B. Burke, *American Collegiate Populations* (1982), 54. In colonial America only an inconsiderable fraction of a percent of college-age males attended college.

25. Edmund Morgan, *Gentle Puritan: A Life of Ezra Stiles, 1727–1795* (1962), 20.

26. In its broadest context, the Scottish cultural presence in America is surveyed in Andrew Hook, *Scotland and America: A Study of Cultural Relations* (1975).

In the field of higher education, two excellent studies are available for the colonial and early national periods: George S. Pryde, *The Scottish Universities and the Colleges of Colonial America* (1957) and the more broadly conceived and substantial Douglas Sloan, *The Scottish Enlightenment and the American College Ideal* (1971). The fullest account of Scottish-oriented academic philosophy in the nineteenth century is Daniel W. Howe, *The Unitarian Conscience: Harvard Moral Philosophy, 1805–1861* (1970). In the field of literature, William Charvat, *The Origins of American Critical Thought, 1810–1835* (1936) provides a survey that emphasizes the predominance of Scottish aesthetics in early national literary thought.

The fundamental importance of Scottish learning to American thought from the Revolution to the Civil War needs to be stressed against a persistent tendency on the part of American historians to discount, devalue, or simply ignore it altogether. Herbert Schneider, *A History of American Philosophy* (1946), described the influence of the Scottish Enlightenment as constituting "probably the most potent single tradition in the American Enlightenment" (246). Beginning around 1820, according to Schneider, the texts of Thomas Reid and Dugald Stewart "set the pattern for the new divisions of philosophy into mental and moral. . . . The Scottish texts furnished the models and inspiration for the new American orthodoxy" (238–39). This conclusion is supported by George P. Schmidt, *The Old Time College President* (1930). In the field of literary thought, according to Charvat, *Origins of American Critical Thought*, 29, America "was culturally allied with Scotland" and wholly dependent upon the Scottish aesthetics of Kames, Blair, and Alison together with the literary criticism of the Scottish reviews.

An earlier history that emphasized the importance of Scottish scholarship is I. Woodbridge Riley, *American Thought from Puritanism to Pragmatism and Beyond* (1923). Among more recent studies, Elizabeth Flower and M. O. Murphey, *A History of Philosophy in America*, 2 vols. (1977), emphasizes the importance of Scottish scholarship to American thought from the revolutionary era through the nineteenth century. Flower and Murphey's rediscovery was presented as though it were an entirely novel finding. "Because the theme of our three chapters runs counter to a negative view so deeply entrenched," the authors wrote (1:205), "and because of its importance . . . we have resorted to heroic measures at a considerable sacrifice to chronological order."

Flower and Murphey, *Philosophy in America*, reflected a revival of serious interest in Thomas Reid and his common sense school already well advanced among philosophers. For an indication of the importance of Thomas Reid to modern philosophy, see Stephen F. Barker and Tom L. Beauchamp, eds., *Thomas Reid: Critical Interpretations* (1976). There has been a revival of interest in Lord Kames as well that is manifested in two major works: Ian S. Ross, *Lord Kames and the Scotland of His Day* (1972), and William C. Lehmann, *Henry Home, Lord Kames and the Scottish Enlightenment* (1971), together with a brief study, Arthur E. McGuinness, *Henry Home, Lord Kames* (1970), which examines Kames's Essays on *Morality and Religion, Elements of Criticism,* and *Sketches of the History of Man.* In general, the 1970s saw a renewed appreciation of the whole array of Scottish philosophers who were individually considered in Princeton president James McCosh's *The Scottish Philosophy* (1875), reviving the importance of that study to American intellectual history.

Lord Kames remains perhaps chiefly important to American thought for the influence he exerted upon Jefferson's worldview at the time of the writing of the Declaration of Independence, an influence that has frequently been overlooked in discussions of Jeffersonian thought. Garry Wills, *Inventing America: Jefferson's Declaration of Independence* (1978), argued the Scottish orientation of Jefferson's thought but erred in attributing Jefferson's ideas to the influence of Francis Hutcheson and Thomas Reid, overlooking Kames. The formative influence of Kames is evident from Jefferson's writings and had been indicated by earlier Jefferson scholars, including Gilbert Chinard, Adrienne Koch, and Dumas Malone. According to Chinard, *Thomas Jefferson: The Apostle of Americanism* (1929), 30, 215–16, Kames was, for Jefferson, "a master and a guide" and the source of "all his conception of natural rights," which "neither Locke, nor so far as I know any political thinker" of Locke's period had defined as Kames and Jefferson defined it. See also Chinard, "Jefferson among the Philosophers," *Ethics* 53 (1942–43). Koch, *The Philosophy of Thomas Jefferson* (1957), 17, observed that "Jefferson had an extravagantly high opinion of Kames; he owned nearly all his books"; and that the influence of Kames, "whose works Jefferson knew in detail," was "distinctly visible" in Jefferson's writings. However, Koch, who did not share Jefferson's high opinion of Kames, associated this influence with an "anti-intellectualist" streak in Jefferson that she did not choose to dwell upon.

The Scottish influence upon the thinking of Jefferson's colleague Madison has been more readily accepted by scholars, who have been impressed by one remarkable article: Douglass Adair, "'That Politics May Be Reduced to a Science': David Hume, James Madison, and the Tenth Federalist," *Huntington Library Quarterly* 20 (1957), in which Adair attributed Madison's argument for the workability of a large republic to an essay by Hume on the "Idea of a Perfect Commonwealth." Adair's argument is circumstantial and open to question, but in the course of advancing it, he familiarized readers with the thoroughly Scottish orientation of Madison's academic background. More broadly, the influence of Scottish learning upon Chesapeake culture generally was indicated in Richard B. Davis, *Intellectual Life in Jefferson's Virginia, 1790–1830* (1964).

27. Thomas Jefferson, *Autobiography,* Capricorn ed. (1959), 20–21.

28. Sloan, *Scottish Enlightenment and American College Ideal*, 36–72, 103–45.

29. Martin Kaufman, *American Medical Education: The Formative Years, 1765–1910* (1976), 18–24.

30. Gilman M. Ostrander, "Lord Kames and American Revolutionary Culture," in *Essays in Honor of Russel B. Nye*, ed. Joseph Waldmeir (1978), 168–79.

31. Wendell Glick, "Bishop Paley in America," *New England Quarterly* 27 (1954): 345–54, argued influentially but erroneously that Paley's texts were favored over others in American colleges in the early national period. In asserting that Paley outsold Stewart in the American academic market, Glick failed to include in his reckoning Stewart's most widely used text, *Outlines of Moral Philosophy* (1793), not to mention the large numbers of additional Scottish moral philosophy texts in use in America at the time.

32. Charvat, *Origins of American Critical Thought*, 29.

33. Ibid., 28–29.

34. Lord Kames, *Elements of Criticism*, 4 vols. (1762), 3:265.

35. Robert A. East, *John Quincy Adams, 1785–1794* (1962), 26.

36. Madeleine H. Rice, *Federal Street Pastor: William Ellery Channing* (1961), 27.

37. Sheldon W. Liebman, "The Origins of Emerson's Early Poetics: His Reading in the Scottish Common Sense Critics," *American Literature* 45 (1973–74): 23–33; Merrel R. Davis, "Emerson's 'Reason' and the Scottish Philosophers," *New England Quarterly* 42 (1944): 209–28; Howe, *The Unitarian Conscience*.

38. George P. Schmidt, *The Liberal Arts College* (1957), 274.

39. For extracurricular college activities see Steven J. Novak, *The Rights of Youth: American Colleges and Student Revolt, 1798–1815* (1977); Joseph F. Kett, *Rites of Passage: Adolescence in America* (1977); David Potter, *Debating in the Colonial Chartered Colleges: An Historical Survey, 1642–1900* (1944); Thomas S. Harding, *College Literary Societies, 1815–1876* (1971); and James McLachlan, "The Choice of Hercules: American Student Societies in the Early Nineteenth Century," in *The University in Society*, ed. Lawrence Stone, 2 vols. (1974).

40. Drew G. Faust, *Sacred Circle: The Dilemma of the Intellectual in the Old South, 1840–1860* (1977), 148.

41. Samuel Eliot Morison, "The Great Rebellion in Harvard College and the Resignation of President Kirkland," *Colonial Society of Massachusetts Publications* 27 (1928): 89.

42. McLachlan, "Choice of Hercules," 486–87.

43. John F. Roche, "The Uranian Society: Gentlemen and Scholars in Federal New York," *New York History* 52 (1971): 121–32.

44. Sidney Willard, *Memories of Youth and Manhood*, 2 vols. (1855), 1:313.

45. Ottis C. Skipper, *J. D. B. DeBow: Magazinist of the Old South* (1958), 98.

46. Robert E. Spiller, ed., *The American Literary Revolution, 1783–1837* (1967), 90.

47. Philip Lindsley, writings in *American Higher Education*, ed. Richard Hofstadter and Wilson Smith, 2 vols. (1961) 1:233, 378.

48. Ibid., 1:249–50.

49. Charles Warren, *Jacobin and Junto; or, Early American Politics as Viewed in the Diary of Dr. Nathaniel Ames, 1758–1822* (1931), 309–11.

50. Brooks M. Kelley, *Yale: A History* (1974).

51. Willard, *Memories of Youth and Manhood*, 1:328.

52. Henry Adams, *The Education of Henry Adams*, ed. Sentry (1961), 55.

53. Henry Adams, *Selected Letters* ed. Newton D. Arvin (1951), 239–40.

54. Irving H. Bartlett, *Wendell Phillips: Brahmin Radical* (1961), 114.

55. Oliver Wendell Holmes, *Elsie Venner* (1861), 3–4.

56. Emerson, *Early Years of Saturday Club*, *passim*.

57. Perry Miller, ed., *The Transcendentalists: An Anthology* (1967). Those men whom Miller included as representatives of transcendentalism, aside from Brownson and Alcott, were: Reed, Ripley, Francis, Hedge, Frothingham, Furness, Osgood, Clarke, Cranch, Channing, Emerson, Parker, Thoreau, and Very. Among them, Cranch attended Columbia College but went on to Harvard Divinity School. The rest of the group had been Harvard undergraduates.

58. Thomas Woody, *Women's Education in the United States*, 2 vols. (1929), 2:137; Frederick Rudolph, *The American College and University* (1962), 307; Morgan, *Gentle Puritan*, 432.

59. Woody, *Women's Education*, 2:154–55.

60. See Thomas R. Dew, "On the Characteristic Differences between the Sexes, and on the Position and Influence of Women in Society," *Southern Literary Messenger* 1 (1835): 493–512, 612–32, 672–91, in which a southern gentleman-scholar attributes the subordinate position of women in the world's societies to physical weakness as compared to dominating man, rejecting any assumption of mental or psychological differences between men and women as dubious and unprovable.

61. Nancy F. Cott, *The Bonds of Womanhood: "Woman's Sphere" in New England, 1780–1835* (1977), 104–5.

62. David F. Hawke, *Benjamin Rush: Revolutionary Gadfly* (1971), 390.

63. Carol V. George, ed., *"Remember the Ladies": New Perspectives on Women in American History* (1975), 1.

64. Cott, *Bonds of Womanhood*, 111.

65. Ibid., 15.

66. Linda K. Kerber, *Women of the Republic: Intellect and Ideology in Revolutionary America* (1980), 193; Eleanor Flexner, *Century of Struggle: The Woman's Rights Movement in the United States* (1959), 29–30.

67. Woody, *Women's Education*, 1:204.

68. Paula Blanchard, *Margaret Fuller: From Transcendentalism to Revolution* (1978), 18.

69. Ibid., 342.

70. Wayland, "Report to the Brown Corporation," 2:482.

71. Viewed from the perspective of the twentieth-century multiversity, "the old-time college" came to be viewed by scholars with condescension, if not downright disdain. Particularly influential in the 1950s and afterward was Richard Hofstadter's discussion "The Old-Time College, 1800–1860," in Richard Hofstadter and Walter P. Metzger, *The Development of Academic Freedom in the United States* (1955), chap. 5. For Hofstadter, higher education of the antebellum period reflected fundamentalist and anti-intellectual Jacksonian influences and constituted a "great retrogression" from more enlightened times. Other standard accounts, including Rudolph, *The American College and University*, took much the same view. Christopher Jencks and David Riesman, *The Academic Revolution* (1968), went further dismissing all higher education before the Civil War as ineffectual. Jencks and Riesman asserted that "while the pre-Jacksonian college was almost always a pillar of the establishment, it was by no means a very important pillar," and they added that the religious "special interest colleges" represented separatism rather than social integration and were "probably no more important or effective as bulwarks of traditional values than were their colonial predecessors." (pp. 1, 7). James McLachlan has commented on the tendency of historians "to treat a particular individual's three-or-four-year stay in an American college as little more than a useful status indicator," ignoring its influence in decisively shaping the cultural style of successive generations of American leaders down to the Mugwump generation of the late nineteenth century. See McLachlan, "American Colleges and the Transmission of Culture: The Case of the Mugwumps," in *The Hofstadter Aegis: A Memorial*, ed. Stanley Elkins and Eric McKitrick (1974), 185, 195, 203.

CHAPTER 2: THE PHILADELPHIA ENLIGHTENMENT

1. Boucher, cited in David F. Hawke, *Benjamin Rush: Revolutionary Gadfly* (1971), 40.

2. Carl Bridenbaugh, *Cities in Revolt: Urban Life in America, 1743–1776* (1955), 5, 216.

3. John Adams, *Diary and Autobiography*, ed. Lyman H. Butterfield et al., 4 vols. (1961), 2:101.

4. Ibid., 103–10.

5. Ibid., 114–16.

6. John Adams and Abigail Adams, *Familiar Letters of John and Abigail Adams*, ed. C. F. Adams (1875), 207, 216–17.

7. Ibid., 207; Adams, *Diary*, 2:156.

8. Adams and Adams, *Familiar Letters*, 149.

9. Durand Echeverria, *Mirage in the West: The French Image of American Society to 1815* (1957), 179.

10. E. Digby Baltzell, *Puritan Boston and Quaker Philadelphia: Two Protestant Ethics and the Spirit of Class Authority and Leadership* (1979); Alan M. Zachary, "Social Thought in the Philadelphia Community, 1800–1848" (Ph.D. diss., Northwestern University, 1974).

11. Ethel Rasmusson, "Philadelphia Upper Class in Transition, 1789–1801" (Ph.D. diss., Brown University, 1962), 55.

12. Frederick B. Tolles, *Meeting House and Counting House: Quaker Merchants of Colonial Philadelphia* (1948), 74–80.

13. Ibid., 121.

14. Carl Bridenbaugh, *The Colonial Craftsman* (1950), 155–57.

15. Carl Bridenbaugh and Jessica Bridenbaugh, *Rebels and Gentlemen: Philadelphia in the Age of Franklin* (1942), 30.

16. Sam Bass Warner Jr., *The Private City: Philadelphia* (1968), 5–7.

17. Bridenbaugh and Bridenbaugh, *Rebels and Gentlemen*, 22–24.

18. Franklin, quoted in Carl Van Doren, *Benjamin Franklin* (1938), 141.

19. Edward P. Cheyney, *History of the University of Pennsylvania, 1740–1940* (1940), 17–52.

20. Ibid., 40–44, 72–73, 167–75; Henry F. May, *The Enlightenment in America* (1976), 80–87.

21. Henry A. Pochmann et al., *German Culture in America*, 2 vols. (1961), 1:44–46.

22. Brooke Hindle, *David Rittenhouse* (1964), 8–9.

23. Ramsey, cited in Whitfield J. Bell, "Science and Humanity in Philadelphia, 1775–1790" (Ph.D. diss., University of Pennsylvania, 1947), 189.

24. Barton, cited in Herbert G. Eldridge, "A Study of Literary Ideals and Intentions in Philadelphia, 1783–1827" (Ph.D. diss., University of Pennsylvania, 1961), 163.

25. Richard B. Shryock, *Medicine and Society in America* (1959), 44–81; Martin Kaufman, *American Medical Education: The Formative Years, 1765–1910* (1976), 3–32.

26. Bridenbaugh and Bridenbaugh, *Rebels and Gentlemen*, 264–67.

27. Courtney R. Hall, *A Scientist in the Early Republic: Samuel Latham Mitchill* (1934), 47–48.

28. J. Bennett Nolan, *Benjamin Franklin in Scotland and Ireland, 1759 and 1771* (1938); Bridenbaugh and Bridenbaugh, *Rebels and Gentlemen*, 279, 283.

29. Lester S. King, *The Medical World of the Eighteenth Century* (1958), 139–43, 214–19.

30. Hawke, *Benjamin Rush*, 320–37, 358–80.

31. Bell, "Science and Humanity," 218–20.

32. Bridenbaugh and Bridenbaugh, *Rebels and Gentlemen*, 293–94, 333–38.

33. Cited in Brooke Hindle, *The Pursuit of Science in Revolutionary America, 1735–1789* (1956), 143–45.

34. The account of the Morgan-Shippen-Rush imbroglio is drawn from Hawke, *Benjamin Rush*; Bridenbaugh and Bridenbaugh, *Rebels and Gentlemen*; and Bell, "Science and Humanity."

35. Hosack, cited in Christine C. Robbins, *David Hosack: Citizen of New York* (1964), 150.

36. Eldridge, "Study of Literary Ideals," 166.

37. Kaufman, *American Medical Education*, 166.

38. Benjamin Franklin, *Autobiography*, Pocket Library ed. (1954), 87, 99.

39. Van Doren, *Franklin*, 234.

40. Lewis A. Coser, *Men of Ideas* (1965), discusses French and English salons in relation to American intellectual society.

41. Elizabeth Drinker, *Extracts from the Journal of Elizabeth Drinker, from 1759–1807 A.D.*, ed. Henry D. Biddle (1889), 364.

42. Bridenbaugh and Bridenbaugh, *Rebels and Gentlemen*, 112–13.

43. Rush, cited in Bridenbaugh and Bridenbaugh, *Rebels and Gentlemen*, 112–13.

44. Thomas Jefferson, *Papers*, ed. Julian P. Boyd et al. (1950–), 13:151–52.

45. Adams, cited in Baltzell, *Puritan Boston and Quaker Philadelphia*, 193.

46. Rufus Griswold, *The Republican Court* (1867), 265, 293–302, 308–12.

47. Jefferson, cited in Bell, "Science and Humanity," 2.

48. Griswold, *Republican Court*.

49. Rasmusson, "Philadelphia Upper Class," 105; Hamilton, cited in Zachary, "Social Thought in the Philadelphia Community," 1.

50. Howard Mumford Jones, *American and French Culture, 1750–1848* (1927), 252–66.

51. J. H. Powell, *Bring Out Your Dead: The Great Plague of Yellow Fever in Philadelphia in 1793* (1949), 8–15.

52. James S. Young, *The Washington Community, 1800–1828* (1966), 49.

53. Augustus John Foster, *Jeffersonian America. Notes on the United States . . . 1805–12*, ed. Richard B. Davis (1954), 84–85.

54. Thomas Jefferson, *Jefferson Himself*, ed. Bernard Mayo (1942), 227.

55. Claude G. Bowers, *Jefferson in Power* (1936), 46–49.

56. William Maclay, *The Journal of William Maclay*, ed. E. S. Maclay (1890), 265–66.

57. Constance M. Green, *Washington: Village and Capital, 1800–1878* (1962), 3–55.

58. Fisher Ames, *Works*, ed. Seth Adams, 2 vols. (1854), 2:392.

59. Belknap, cited in Bell, "Science and Humanity," 147.

60. Adams and Adams, *Familiar Letters*, 207.

61. Hall, *Samuel Latham Mitchill*, 129–30; Robbins, *David Hosack*, 155; Alexandra Oleson and Sanborn C. Brown, eds., *The Pursuit of Knowledge in the Early American Republic: Scientific and Learned Societies from Colonial Times to the Civil War* (1976).

62. Hosack, cited in Robbins, *David Hosack*, 155–58.

63. Hugh Henry Brackenridge, *Modern Chivalry*, vol. 1, bk. 2, chap. 1.

64. Van Doren, *Franklin*, 401–2.

65. Jefferson, *Papers*, 8:245.

66. Adams and Adams, *Familiar Letters*, 216; Joseph J. Ellis, *After the Revolution* (1976), 79.

67. Thomas Jefferson, *The Complete Jefferson*, ed. Saul K. Padover (1943), 1085.

68. John Adams and Thomas Jefferson, *The Adams-Jefferson Letters*, ed. Lester J. Cappon, 2 vols. (1959), 2:291, 295.

69. A. L. Ford, *Joel Barlow* (1971), 41.

70. Schoolcraft, cited in Hall, *Samuel Latham Mitchill*, 16.

71. Ibid., 14.

72. Claude-Anne Lopes and Eugenia W. Herbert, *The Private Franklin: The Man and His Family* (1975), 28.

CHAPTER 3: REPUBLIC OF BELLES LETTRES

1. John Quincy Adams, *Memoirs of John Quincy Adams*, ed. C. F. Adams, 12 vols. (1874–77), 1:472–73; 7:423.

2. Josiah Quincy, *The History of Harvard University*, 2 vols. (1840), 2:132–34.

3. Esther Cloudman Dunn, *Shakespeare in America* (1939), 84–107.

4. Philip Hone, *Diary of Philip Hone, 1828–1851*, ed. Allan Nevins, (1927), 778.

5. George H. Daniels, *American Science in the Age of Jackson* (1962), 36.

6. Bruce Sinclair, *Philadelphia's Philosopher Mechanics: A History of the Franklin Institute, 1824–1865* (1974), 136.

7. Howard S. Miller, *Dollars for Research: Science and Patrons in Nineteenth-Century America* (1970), 7.

8. Kenneth Silverman, *A Cultural History of the American Revolution* (1976), 90, 105–6; Carl Bridenbaugh and Jessica Bridenbaugh, *Rebels and Gentlemen: Philadelphia in the Age of Franklin* (1942), 108–11, 126–28.

9. Moses Coit Tyler, *The Literary History of the American Revolution, 1763–1783*, 2 vols. (1963), 1:164.

10. Benjamin West to Charles Willson Peale, 1767, quoted in Silverman, *Cultural History*, 100.

11. Robert C. Alberts, *Benjamin West: A Biography* (1978); Charles C. Sellers, *Charles Willson Peale* (1969).

12. Richard Hofstadter and Wilson Smith, eds., *American Higher Education: A Documentary History*, 2 vols. (1961), 1:137–46.

13. Douglas Sloan, *The Scottish Enlightenment and the American College Ideal* (1971), 133.

14. Joseph J. Ellis, *After the Revolution* (1976), 79.

15. Russel B. Nye, *The Cultural Life of the New Nation, 1776–1830* (1960), 240.

16. Ellis, *After the Revolution*, 80.

17. Robert Spiller, ed., *The American Literary Revolution* (1967), 9.

18. Brooks M. Kelley, *Yale: A History* (1974), 49–90.

19. Leon Howard, *The Connecticut Wits* (1943), passim.

20. Ellis, *After the Revolution*, 162.

21. Silverman, *Cultural History*, 519.

22. Marcia E. Bailey, *A Lesser Hartford Wit: Dr. Elihu Hubbard Smith* (1928); James E. Cronin, "Elihu Hubbard Smith and the New York Friendly Club," *Publications of the Modern Language Association* 64 (1949), 476–78; Eleanor B. Scott, "Early Literary Clubs in New York City," *American Literature* 5 (1933), 724.

23. Robert Canary, *William Dunlap* (1970); Donald A. Ringle, *Charles Brockden Brown* (1966).

24. Charles Warren, *History of the American Bar* (1911), 4.

25. Alexis de Tocqueville, *Democracy in America*, ed. Philips Bradley, 2 vols. (1959), 1:128.

26. Gary B. Nash, "The Philadelphia Bench and Bar, 1800–1861," *Comparative Studies in Society and History* 7 (January 1965): 207–8. All quotations concerning Coke are from Charles Warren, *History of Harvard Law School and of Early Legal Conditions in America*, 2 vols. (1908), 1:136–41.

27. Ibid., 1:139, 150, 124.

28. Perry Miller, *The Life of the Mind in America from the Revolution to the Civil War* (1965), 135.

29. Ibid., 122.

30. Ibid., 184.

31. Barnet Baskerville, *The People's Voice: The Orator in American Society* (1979), 32.

32. Ibid., 45–46.

33. Warren, *History of Harvard Law School*, 1:86.

34. Samuel Eliot Morison, *Harrison Gray Otis* (1969), 238.

35. John T. Queenan, "The *Port Folio*: A Study of the History and Significance of an Early American Magazine" (Ph.D. diss., University of Pennsylvania, 1972), 3.

36. Harold M. Ellis, *Joseph Dennie and His Circle* (1915), 94.

37. Frank L. Mott, *A History of American Magazines*, 5 vols. (1930–68), 1:224.

38. Ellis, *Joseph Dennie*, 170–71.

39. Joseph Dennie, articles in *Port Folio*, 11 April 1801; 16 May 1801; 15 August 1801.

40. Ellis, *Joseph Dennie*, 146–47, 190–91, 195.

41. Lewis P. Simpson, ed., *The Federalist Literary Mind: Selections from the Monthly Anthology and Boston Review, 1803–1811* (1962), 10–29.

42. Ibid., 19.

43. Ibid., 81.

44. Henry David Thoreau, *The Journal of Henry D. Thoreau*, ed. Bradford Torrey and Francis H. Allen, 14 vols. (1906), 5:39.

45. Thomas Jefferson, *Papers*, ed. Julian P. Boyd et al. (1950–), 15:396.

46. David H. Fischer, *Revolution of American Conservatism: The Federalist Party in Jeffersonian Democracy* (1965), 45.

47. Alan M. Zachary, "Social Thought in the Philadelphia Community, 1800–1848" (Ph.D. diss., Northwestern University, 1974), 47.

48. Edward H. Foster, *Catharine Sedgwick* (1974), 28, 29.

49. Fischer, *Revolution of American Conservatism*, 15, 26.

50. Lawrence Buell, "Joseph Stevens Buckminster: The Making of a New England Saint," *Canadian Review of American Studies* 10 (1979), 4.

51. Thomas P. Govan, *Nicholas Biddle* (1959), 5–8.

52. Ibid., 25.

53. Zachary, "Social Thought in Philadelphia," 224.

54. Ibid., 30–31.

55. John B. McMaster, *A History of the People of the United States from the Revolution to the Civil War*, 8 vols. (1883–1913), 5:307–42, is the main source for this account of the battle of the quarterlies.

56. See *Edinburgh Review*, (January–May 1820): 69–80.

57. See *North American Review* 31 (1830): 26–28.

58. Fred Lewis Pattee, *American Writers* (1937), 23.

59. Robert E. Spiller, *Fenimore Cooper* (1931), 127.

60. McMaster, *History of the U.S. People*, 5:336.

CHAPTER 4: KNICKERBOCKER NEW YORK

1. Lillian B. Miller, *Patrons and Patriotism: Fine Arts in the United States, 1790–1860* (1966), 155–58.

2. William Dean Howells, *Literature and Life* (1902), 179–80. Howells likewise

doubted that Philadelphia had been a true literary center in the age of Franklin, and he was certain that it had not been one since.

3. David C. Humphrey, *King's College to Columbia, 1746–1800* (1976), 38.

4. Michael G. Kammen, *Colonial New York: A History* (1975), 242.

5. Humphrey, *King's College to Columbia*, 38.

6. Ibid., 3–100.

7. Stanley T. Williams, *Life of Washington Irving*, 2 vols. (1935), 1:110–12.

8. Ibid., 1:210.

9. Ibid., 1:147; 2:13.

10. Lewis Leary, *That Rascal Freneau* (1941), 360–61.

11. W. G. Wilkins, ed., *Charles Dickens in America* (1911), 123.

12. Williams, *Life of Washington Irving*, 2:204.

13. Ibid., 2:269.

14. John T. Irving Jr., "Quod Correspondence," *Knickerbocker Magazine* (June 1842).

15. Frank L. Mott, *A History of American Magazines*, 5 vols. (1930–68), 1:424.

16. James G. Wilson, *Bryant and His Friends: Some Reminiscences of the Knickerbocker Writers* (1886), 298–99, 303.

17. Ibid., 377.

18. Perry Miller, *The Raven and the Whale: The War of Words and Wits in the Era of Poe and Melville* (1956), 11–35 and *passim*.

19. Williams, *Life of Irving*, 1:110.

20. Miller, *Raven and Whale*, 322.

21. Robert E. Spiller, *Fenimore Cooper* (1931), 190.

22. James Fennimore Cooper, *The American Democrat: A Treatise on Jacksonian Democracy* (1838), chap. 20; *Gleanings in Europe* (1833), letter 27.

23. Nelson Adkins, *Fitz-Greene Halleck: An Early Knickerbocker* (1930), 287.

24. Charles H. Brown, *William Cullen Bryant* (1971), 84–106, 112, 122–30.

25. James T. Callow, *Kindred Spirits: Knickerbocker Writers and Artists, 1807–1855* (1967), *passim*.

26. John Stafford, *The Literary Criticism of Young America* (1952), 132.

27. Miller, *Patrons and Patriotism*, 90–92.

28. Ibid., 99.

29. Neil Harris, *The Artist in American Society, 1790–1860* (1966), 256.

30. Callow, *Kindred Spirits*, 31.

31. David Kaser, *Messrs. Carey & Lea of Philadelphia: A History of the Book Trade* (1957), 138–58.

32. John Durand, *Prehistoric Notes of the Century Club* (1882), 10–11.

33. M. A. DeWolfe Howe, ed., *Later Years of the Saturday Club, 1870–1920* (1927); Francis G. Fairfield, *The Clubs of New York* (1873).

34. Adkins, *Fitz-Greene Halleck*, 277.

35. Philip Hone, *The Diary of Philip Hone, 1828–1851*, Allan Nevins, ed. (1927), 395–96.

36. Adkins, *Fitz-Greene Halleck*, 32.

37. Christine C. Robbins, *David Hosack* (1964), 165–68.

38. Adkins, *Fitz-Greene Halleck*, 200.

39. Mary Alice Wyman, ed., *Selections from the Autobiography of Elizabeth Oakes Smith* (1924), 90.

40. Ibid., 88.

41. Brown, *Bryant*, 135–37.

42. Edgar Allen Poe, *Complete Works*, ed. J. A. Harrison, 17 vols. (1902), 16:1–137.

43. Robert E. Spiller, *Fenimore Cooper* (1931), 209.

44. Wilkins, *Dickens in America*, 7.

45. Ibid., 21–23.

46. Ibid., 87.

47. Adkins, *Fitz-Greene Halleck*, 292.

48. Mott, *History of American Magazines*, 1:376.

49. Loprete, "J. T. Irving, Jr.," 21

50. William Charvat, *Literary Publishing in America, 1790–1850* (1959), 20.

51. Kaser, *Carey & Lea*, 25–41.

52. Charvat, *Literary Publishing*, 42.

53. Eugene Exman, *The House of Harper* (1967), 85.

54. Ibid., 127–30.

55. Spiller, *Fenimore Cooper*, 85.

56. Mott, *History of American Magazines*, 1:544ff.

57. Arthur H. Quinn, *A History of the American Drama: From the Beginning to the Civil War*, 2d ed. (1951), 244–46.

58. Herbert G. Eldridge, "A Study of Literary Ideals and Intentions in Philadelphia, 1783–1827" (Ph.D. diss., University of Pennsylvania, 1961), 217.

59. Quinn, *History of American Drama*, 199–203.

60. Albert Parry, *Garrets and Pretenders: A History of Bohemianism in America* (1933), 43–48.

61. William Winter, *Old Friends* (1914), 57–58, 60.

62. William Dean Howells, *Literary Friends and Acquaintance: A Personal Retrospect of American Authorship* (1900), 70–71.

63. Parry, *Garrets and Pretenders*, 18, 19.

64. Ibid., 26.

65. Mott, *History of American Magazines*, 2:528.

66. Franklin Walker, *San Francisco's Literary Frontier* (1939).

67. Mott, *History of American Magazines*, 1:376–77.

68. Ralph Waldo Emerson, *Works*, 12 vols. Concord ed. (1903–4), 7:31–32.

CHAPTER 5: BRAHMIN BOSTON

1. John Adams and Abigail Adams, *Familiar Letters*, ed. C. F. Adams (1875), 207.

2. Carl Bridenbaugh, *Cities in Revolt: Urban Life in America, 1743–1776* (1955), 5, 216.

3. Josiah Quincy, *The History of Harvard University*, 2 vols. (1840), 2:123.

4. Madeleine H. Rice, *Federal Street Pastor: William Ellery Channing* (1961), 27.

5. Adams and Adams, *Familiar Letters*, 120.

6. Michele de Crèvecoeur, *Letters From an American Farmer*, Everyman ed. (1912), 41.

7. Ibid., vii.

8. Ruth M. Elson, *Guardians of Tradition: American Schoolbooks of the Nineteenth Century* (1964), 66–71.

9. Arthur H. Shaffer, *The Politics of History: Writing the History of the American Revolution, 1783–1815* (1975).

10. E. Digby Baltzell, *Puritan Boston and Quaker Philadelphia* (1979), 270.

11. Adams and Adams, *Familiar Letters*, 206.

12. Benjamin O. Spencer, *The Quest for Nationality* (1957), 264.

13. Samuel Eliot Morison, *The Founding of Harvard College* (1935), 432–33.

14. John W. T. Youngs Jr., *God's Messengers: Religious Leadership in Colonial New England, 1700–1750* (1976); Edmund Morgan, "The American Revolution Considered as an Intellectual Movement," in *Paths of American Thought,* ed. Arthur M. Schlesinger Jr., and Morton White (1963), 15–22.

15. Adams and Adams, *Familiar Letters*, 99.

16. Wallace Brown, *Good Americans: Loyalists in the American Revolution* (1969), 230.

17. Harold Kirker and James Kirker, *Bulfinch's Boston, 1787–1817* (1964), 135.

18. Alexander Hamilton, quoted in Carl Bridenbaugh, ed., *Gentleman's Progress* (1948), 146.

19. Samuel Eliot Morison, *Harrison Gray Otis, 1765–1848. Urbane Federalist* (1969), 42.

20. Kirker and Kirker, *Bulfinch's Boston*, 57–63.

21. Quincy, *History of Harvard*, 2:132–33.

22. Lawrence Buell, "Joseph Stevens Buckminster: The Making of a New England Saint," *The Canadian Review of American Studies* 10 (1979): 1–29; Conrad Wright, *The Beginnings of Unitarianism in America* (1955).

23. Charles Warren, *Jacobin and Junto, or, Early American Politics as Viewed in the Diary of Nathaniel Ames, 1758–1822* (1931), 309.

24. Henry Adams, *The Education of Henry Adams*, Sentry ed. (1961), 32.

25. Robert A. McCaughey, *Josiah Quincy, 1772–1864: The Last Federalist* (1974), 132.

26. Quincy, *History of Harvard*, 2:312–34.

27. David B. Tyack, *George Ticknor and the Boston Brahmins* (1967), 90.

28. Henry A. Pochmann et al., *German Culture in America, 1600–1900*, 2 vols. (1957), 1:44–46.

29. Tyack, *George Ticknor*, 45–50.

30. McCaughey, *Josiah Quincy*, 138.

31. Ibid., 138–40.

32. Carl Diehl, *Americans and German Scholarship, 1770–1870* (1978), 50–100.

33. Samuel Eliot Morison, "The Great Rebellion in Harvard College and the Resignation of President Kirkland," *Colonial Society of Massachusetts Publications* 27 (1928): 54–112.

34. John Adams, quoted in McCaughey, *Josiah Quincy*, 17.

35. Ibid., 178.

36. Ronald Story, *The Forging of an Aristocracy: Harvard and the Boston Upper Class, 1800–1870* (1980), 80.

37. Tyack, *George Ticknor*, 92.

38. Story, *Forging of an Aristocracy*, 80.

39. Ibid., 86–87.

40. Russel B. Nye, *George Bancroft, Brahmin Rebel* (1945), 58.

41. Tyack, *George Ticknor*, 184.

42. Edward L. Pierce, ed., *Memoirs and Letters of Charles Sumner*, 4 vols. (1877–93), 3:8.

43. Tyack, *George Ticknor*, 185.

44. Ibid., 228.

45. Ibid., 151.

46. Morison, *Harrison Gray Otis*, 242.

47. Ibid.

48. Martin Duberman, *James Russell Lowell* (1966), 192.

49. Ibid.

50. Adams, *Education*, 307.

51. David Donald, *Charles Sumner and the Coming of the Civil War* (1960), 39; McCaughey, *Josiah Quincy*, 157.

52. Clinton H. Gardiner, *William Hickling Prescott: A Biography* (1969), 283.

53. Edward W. Emerson, *The Early Years of the Saturday Club, 1855–1870* (1918), 11–20.

54. Warren S. Tryon, *Parnassus Corner: A Life of James T. Fields, Publisher to the Victorians* (1963), 233.

55. Ibid.

56. Gardiner, *William Prescott*, 281.

57. Lewis P. Simpson, ed., *The Federalist Literary Mind: Selections from the Monthly Anthology and Boston Review, 1803–1811* (1962), 112.

58. McCaughey, *Josiah Quincy*, 85.

59. Ibid., 85–86.

60. Thomas Gold Appleton, quoted in Emerson, *Saturday Club*, 218, 220.

61. Irving H. Bartlett, *Wendell Phillips: Brahmin Rebel* (1961), 102.

62. Ralph L. Rusk, *The Life of Ralph Waldo Emerson* (1949), 228, 252; Emerson, *Saturday Club*, 9.

63. Mary Alice Wyman, ed., *Selections from the Autobiography of Elizabeth Oakes Smith* (1924), 136.

64. Lydia M. Child, *Letters from New York*, 2 vols. (1849), 2:289.

65. Rusk, *Emerson*, 256.

66. Emerson, *Saturday Club*, 11–20.

67. Ibid., 13.

68. William Charvat, *The Profession of Authorship in America, 1800–1870* (1968), 298.

69. Wyman, ed., *Autobiography of Elizabeth Oakes Smith*, 143–44.

70. Louis H. Tharp, *The Peabody Sisters of Salem* (1950), 134–35.

71. The most scholarly full biography of Margaret Fuller remains Madeleine B. Stern, *The Life of Margaret Fuller* (1942). Recent works include Belle Gale Chevigny, *The Woman and the Myth: Margaret Fuller's Life and Writings* (1976), and Paula Blanchard, *Margaret Fuller: From Transcendentalism to Revolution* (1978). For the voluminous literature on this subject, see Joel Meyerson, *Margaret Fuller: An Annotated Secodary Bibliography* (1977) and the introduction to Meyerson, ed., *Critical Essays on Margaret Fuller* (1980).

72. Joseph Slater, ed., *Correspondence of Emerson and Carlyle* (1964).

73. Ibid., 462.

74. Ibid., 470.

75. Harriet Beecher Stowe, *Sunny Memories of Foreign Lands* (1854), 240.

76. *Atlantic Monthly* 50 (November 1907) gives a detailed account of the origins of the magazine together with relevant documents.

77. Thomas Higginson, *Cheerful Yesterdays* (1898), 176–80, is the source for the account of the Stowe dinner. There are various versions of this event, but Higginson's is precise and detailed, as though written from a diary account.

78. Julia Ward Howe, *Reminiscences* (1899), 400.

79. Ibid., 80.

80. Grace E. King, *Memories of a Southern Woman of Letters* (1932), 54.

81. Deborah Pickman Clifford, *Mine Eyes Have Seen the Glory: A Biography of Julia Ward Howe* (1978), 84.

82. Harold Schwartz, *Samuel Gridley Howe, Social Reformer* (1956), 328–29.

CHAPTER 6: LITERATI IN DEMOCRATIC-WHIG AMERICA

1. John Quincy Adams, *Memoirs*, ed. C. F. Adams, 12 vols. (1874–77), 9:305–6.

2. Arthur M. Schlesinger Jr. and Fred Israel, eds., *American Presidential Elections*, 4 vols. (1971), 1:304.

3. John Quincy Adams, inaugural address, in *Compilation of the Messages and Papers of the Presidents, 1789–1897*, ed. James D. Richardson, 10 vols. (1969), 2:860–65.

4. Andrew Jackson, first message to Congress, in *Compilation of Messages*, 3:1012.

5. Henry Ammon, *James Monroe: The Quest for Nationality* (1971), 373.

6. Philip Hone, *The Diary of Philip Hone, 1828–1851*, ed. Allan Nevins (1927), 96–97.

7. Adams, *Memoirs*, 8:546–47.

8. James Russell Lowell, *New Letters*, ed. Mark DeW. Howe (1932), 237; Martin Duberman, *James Russell Lowell* (1966), 274.

9. George Bancroft, address at Williams College, in Joseph L. Blau, ed., *Social Theories of Jacksonian Democracy: Representative Writings of the Period 1825–1850* (1954), 263–73.

10. Marvin Meyers, *The Jacksonian Persuasion* (1957); Daniel W. Howe, *The Political Culture of the American Whigs* (1979).

11. *The Correspondence of Emerson and Carlyle*, ed. Joseph Slater (1964), 100.

12. Ralph Waldo Emerson, *Works*, 12 vols., Concord ed. (1903–4), 3:209–10.

13. Ralph Waldo Emerson, *Letters*, ed. Ralph L. Rusk, 6 vols. (1939), 2:357; idem, *Journals and Miscellaneous Notebooks*, ed. William H. Gilman et al., 20 vols. (1960–82), 4:57.

14. Allan M. Zachary, "Social Thought in the Philadelphia Community, 1800–1848," (Ph.D. diss., Northwestern University, 1974), 112.

15. Ibid., 208.

16. Ibid., 166–67, 209.

17. Ellis P. Oberholzer, *Literary History of Philadelphia* (1906), 354–56.

18. Duberman, *Lowell*, 69.

19. Rufus Choate, quoted in Howard S. Miller, *Dollars for Research: Science and Patrons in Nineteenth-Century America* (1970), 15.

20. Ibid., 22.

21. Hone, *Diary*, 40–41; Charles H. Brown, *William Cullen Bryant* (1971), 185–87.

22. Arthur M. Schlesinger Jr., *The Age of Jackson* (1945), 132–43, 177–209.

23. Glyndon G. Van Deusen, *Horace Greeley, Nineteenth-Century Crusader* (1953), 185–87.

24. Frank L. Mott, *A History of American Magazines*, 5 vols. (1930–68), 1:677.

25. John Stafford, *The Literary Criticism of "Young America"* (1952), 20, 1–10.

John Quincy Adams is quoted in Jay B. Hubbell, *Who Are the Major American Writers?* (1972), 63.

26. James G. Wilson, *Bryant and his Friends: Some Reminiscences of the Knickerbocker Writers* (1886), 417–19.

27. Edmund Wilson, ed., *The Shock of Recognition*, 2 vols. (1943), 1:72; Perry Miller, *The Raven and the Whale: The War of Words and Wits in the Era of Poe and Melville* (1956), 322.

28. Stafford, *Literary Criticism of "Young America,"* 62, 107.

29. Ibid., 70.

30. Emerson, *Works*, 3:197.

31. David B. Tyack, *George Ticknor and the Boston Brahmins* (1967), 196.

32. Clifford S. Griffen, *Ferment of Reform, 1830–1850* (1967); John L. Thomas, "Romantic Reform in America, 1815–1865," *American Quarterly* 17 (1965): 656.

33. Edward Beecher, "The Nature, Importance, and Means of Eminent Holiness Throughout the Church," *American National Preacher* 10 (1835), 193–224.

34. Emerson, "New England Reformers," *Works*, 3:251.

35. Henry David Thoreau. *Writings*, 20 vols., Walden ed. (1906), 4:369.

36. *Emerson and Carlyle Correspondence*, 283.

37. Lindsay Swift, *Brook Farm* (1900); Charles Crowe, *George Ripley: Transcendentalist and Utopian Socialist* (1967).

38. Emerson, "New England Reformers," 259.

39. Charles C. Cole Jr., *The Social Ideas of the Northern Evangelists, 1826–1860* (1954); John R. Bodo, *The Protestant Clergy and Public Issues, 1812–1848* (1954).

40. Benjamin Quarles, *Black Abolitionists* (1969); Bertram Wyatt-Brown, "William Lloyd Garrison and Antislavery Unity," *Civil War History* 1 (1967):5.

41. James M. McPherson, *The Abolitionist Legacy, From Reconstruction to the NAACP* (1975), 6–10; David Donald, "Abolitionist Leadership: A Displaced Elite," in *Lincoln Reconsidered* (1962).

42. Russel B. Nye, *William Lloyd Garrison and the Humanitarian Reformers* (1955), 20, Merton L. Dillon, *Benjamin Lundy and the Struggle for Negro Freedom* (1966).

43. Samuel Flagg Bemis, *John Quincy Adams*, 2 vols. (1949 56), 2:256.

44. Nye, *Garrison*, 24.

45. Leonard L. Richards, *"Gentlemen of Property and Standing": Anti-Abolition Mobs in Jacksonian America* (1970).

46. Harold Schwartz, *Samuel Gridley Howe, Social Reformer, 1801–1876* (1956), 5.

47. Maria Chapman, quoted in Irving H. Bartlett, *Wendell Phillips, Brahmin Radical* (1961), 102.

48. Lawrence J. Friedman, *Gregarious Saints: Self and Community in American Abolitionism, 1830–1870* (1982), 43–67, discusses the Boston clique.

49. Robert E. Spiller, *Fenimore Cooper, Critic of His Times* (1969); for American writers' attitudes toward Europe, see Cushing Strout, *The Image of the Old World* (1963).

50. Russel B. Nye, *George Bancroft, Brahmin Rebel* (1944), 163, 184ff.

51. Tyack, *George Ticknor*, 226.

52. Clinton Harvey Gardiner, *William Hickling Prescott: A Biography* (1969), 314.

53. Newton Arvin, *Hawthorne* (1961), 237, 245.

54. Ibid.

55. It had become customary for those going to Europe for no assigned purpose to give health as a reason. Channing went to England for his health, and the robust Cooper gave health as one reason for his trip.

56. Ralph Waldo Emerson, *English Traits*, Concord ed. (1903), 3–4.

57. Ibid., 275.

58. Ibid., 292–93.

59. Martin Duberman, *James Russell Lowell* (1967), 127.

60. Warren S. Tryon, *Parnassus Corner: A Life of James T. Fields, Publisher to the Victorians* (1963), 241; Ralph L. Rusk, *The Life of Ralph Waldo Emerson* (1949), 185.

61. Orie W. Long, *Literary Pioneers: Early American Explorers of European Culture* (1935) deals particularly with Ticknor, Everett, Cogswell, and Bancroft.

62. Hone, *Diary*.

63. Thomas Gold Appleton, quoted in Edward W. Emerson, *The Early Years of the Saturday Club, 1855–1870*, (1918), 225.

64. Paul R. Baker, *The Fortunate Pilgrims: Americans in Italy, 1800–1860* (1964).

65. Kermit Vanderbilt, *Charles Eliot Norton* (1959).

66. Stephen Larrabee, *Hellas Observed: The American Experience of Greece, 1775–1865* (1951), 294.

67. Ibid., 35.

68. Emerson, *Works*, 10:179.

69. Ibid., 1:111.

CHAPTER 7: THE SOUTH IN THE LITERARY REPUBLIC

1. Jay B. Hubbell Jr., *The South in American Literature, 1607–1900* (1954), 369–400.

2. George W. Bogby, quoted in Frank L. Mott, *A History of American Magazines*, 5 vols. (1930–68), 1:655.

3. Agnes M. Bondurant, *Poe's Richmond* (1942), 1, 16.

4. Joseph Le Conte, quoted in Hubbell, *South in American Literature*, 213.

5. E. Brooks Holifield, *The Gentlemen Theologians: American Theology in Southern Culture, 1795–1860* (1978), 24.

6. Ibid., 45.

7. Thomas Jefferson, *Papers*, ed. Julian P. Boyd et al. (1950–), 1:537; idem, *Selected Writings*, ed. Adrienne Koch and William Peden (1944), 697; Robert Healey, *Jefferson and Religion in Public Education* (1962), 233.

8. John Holt Rice, quoted in Hubbell, *South in American Literature*, 174.

9. Ibid., 266.

10. Josiah Quincy, *Memoir of the Life of Josiah Quincy, Jun.* (1825), 103; Frederick P. Bowes, *The Culture of Early Charleston* (1942), 106.

11. Carl Bridenbaugh, *Myths and Realities: Societies of the Colonial South* (1963), 113.

12. Bowes, *Culture of Early Charleston*, 45.

13. Hugh Swinton Legaré, quoted in Hubbell, *South in American Literature*, 266–67.

14. William Gilmore Simms, quoted in ibid., 577.

15. Mott, *History of American Magazines*, 2:491.

16. Paul Hamilton Hayne, quoted in Hubbell, *South in American Literature*, 746.

17. John E. Uhler, "Literary Taste and Culture of Baltimore: A Study of the Periodical Literature in Baltimore from 1815–1833," (Ph.D. diss., John Hopkins University, 1924), 153, 266.

18. John Pendleton Kennedy, quoted in Hubbell, *South in American Literature*, 491.

19. Ibid., 482.

20. Mott, *History of American Magazines*, 1:629–57.

21. John R. Thompson, quoted in Hubbell, *South in American Literature*, 521–22.

22. Drew G. Faust, *A Sacred Circle: The Dilemma of the Intellectual in the Old South, 1840–1860* (1977), 1–6.

23. Ibid., 117.

24. James H. Hammond, quoted in Hubbell, *South in American Literature*, 411.

25. William Harper et al., *The Pro-Slavery Argument* (1853), 5–13.

26. Faust, *Sacred Circle*, 127.

27. Ibid., 53.

28. Ibid., 141.

29. See the *Southern Literary Messenger* I (1835), 499 512, 612 32, 672 91.

30. Ibid., 494.

31. Ibid., 495.

32. Ibid., 690, 691.

33. Wilbur J. Cash, *The Mind of the South* (1941), 97.

34. William S. Jenkins, *Pro-Slavery Thought in the Old South* (1935), 210; Anne Fior Scott, *The Southern Lady: From Pedestal to Politics, 1830–1930* (1970), 16–17, 21.

35. William R. Taylor, *Cavalier and Yankee: The Old South and American National Character* (1961), 143.

36. Ibid.

37. Sarah Moore Grimké, *Letters on the Condition of Women and the Equality of the Sexes* (1838), 46.

38. Clement Eaton, *A History of the Old South* (1949), 452.

39. Grimké, *Letters on the Conditon of Women*, 47.

40. Scott, *Southern Lady*, 19.

41. C. Vann Woodward, *Mary Chesnut's Civil War* (1981), 38.

42. Ibid., xlix.

43. Eleanor Flexner, *Century of Struggle: The Woman's Rights Movement in the United States* (1959), 46.

44. Grimké, *Letters on the Condition of Women*, 122.

45. Louis Filler, *The Crusade Against Slavery, 1830–1860* (1960), 77.

46. Woodward, *Chesnut's Civil War*, 43.

47. William W. Freehling, *Prelude to Civil War: The Nullification Controversy in South Carolina, 1816–1836* (1966); David D. Wallace, *South Carolina: A Short History, 1520–1948* (1951), 408.

48. Hubbell, *South in American Literature*, 365.

49. Ibid.

50. Joseph V. Ridgely, *William Gilmore Simms* (1962), 123.

51. Ibid., 124.

52. Hubbell, *South in American Literature*, 267.

53. Ibid., 745–46.

54. Ibid., 523.

55. Ibid., 517.

56. Ibid., 487.

57. Ibid., 586.

CHAPTER 8: BOSTONIZATION OF THE LITERARY REPUBLIC

1. Ralph Waldo Emerson, *Works*, 12 vols., Concord ed. (1903–04), 9:125.

2. Charles Francis Adams, quoted in David B. Tyack, *George Ticknor and the Boston Brahmins* (1967), 226.

3. Emerson, *Works*, 11:244.

4. On Stowe's commitment, see the *Atlantic Monthly* 50 (November 1907).

5. David Donald, *Charles Sumner and the Coming of the Civil War* (1960), 3–69.

6. Ibid., 286.

7. Ibid., 300.

8. Stephen B. Oates, *To Purge This Land with Blood: John Brown* (1970), 128, 129.

9. Otto J. Scott, *The Secret Six: John Brown and the Abolitionist Movement*

(1980); Jeffery Rossbach, *Ambivalent Conspirators: John Brown, the Secret Six, and a Theory of Slave Violence* (1982).

10. Henry Steele Commager, ed., *Documents of American History*, 2 vols. (1963), 1:361–62.

11. Gerald Sorin, *The New York Abolitionists: A Case Study of Political Radicalism* (1971), xi–xii, 110.

12. Edward K. Spann, *Ideals and Politics: New York Intellectuals and Liberal Democracy* (1972), 39–40, 44–45, 166–71, 178–79.

13. Glyndon G. Van Deusen, *Horace Greeley* (1953), 137.

14. Francis O. Matthiessen, *The American Renaissance* (1941).

15. Frank L. Mott, *A History of American Magazines*, 5 vols. (1930–68), 1:757.

16. Perry Miller, *The Raven and the Whale: The War of Words and Wits in the Era of Poe and Melville* (1956), 315–22.

17. Mott, *History of American Magazines*, 2:419–28.

18. Miller, *Raven and Whale*, 319.

19. See *Putnam's Monthly Magazine* 4 (November 1854), 531.

20. Mott, *History of American Magazines*, 2:494.

21. Mark DeW. Howe, *The Atlantic Monthly and Its Makers* (1919), 13–15.

22. See the *Atlantic Monthly* 50 (November 1907), 579.

23. Ibid., 671.

24. Ibid., 674.

25. Martin Duberman, *James Russell Lowell* (1966), 169–70.

26. See the *Atlantic Monthly* 50 (November 1907), 676.

27. William Dean Howells, *Literary Friends and Acquaintance: A Personal Retrospect of American Authorship* (1900), 70–76.

28. Ibid., 12.

29. For Hawthorne's text, see *Atlantic Monthly* 10 (July 1862), 56.

30. Ralph Waldo Emerson, *Letters*, ed. Ralph L. Rusk, 6 vols. (1939), 5:253.

31. George M. Frederickson, *The Inner Civil War: Northern Intellectuals and the Crisis of the Union* (1965), 113.

32. Ibid.

33. Basil Lee, *Discontent in New York City, 1861–1865* (1944).

34. Albert Parry, *Garrets and Pretenders: A History of Bohemianism in America* (1933), 28–31.

35. Miller, *Raven and Whale*, 329–31, 330, 346.

36. Frederickson, *Inner Civil War*, 56.

37. Gordon Milne, *George William Curtis and the Genteel Tradition* (1956).

38. Spann, *Ideals and Politics*, 192.

39. William M. Armstrong, *E. L. Godkin: A Biography* (1978).

40. Hans L. Trefousse, *Carl Schurz: A Biography* (1982).

41. Howells, *Literary Friends and Acquaintance*, 101.

EPILOGUE: THE ACADEMY OF ARTS AND LETTERS, 1904–1909

1. Ralph Waldo Emerson, *Letters*, ed. Ralph L. Rusk, 6 vols. (1939), 5:392–97.

2. Mary O. Furner, *Advocacy and Objectivity: A Crisis in the Professionalization of American Social Science, 1865–1905* (1975), 21; Thomas L. Haskell, *The Emergence of Professional Social Science: The American Social Science Association and the Nineteenth-Century Crisis of Authority*, (1977); Anne C. Rose, *Transcendentalism as a Social Movement, 1830–1850* (1981).

3. Furner, *Advocacy and Objectivity*, 29–30.

4. Robert Underwood Johnson, *Remembered Yesterdays* (1923), 440.

5. Mark DeW. Howe, *The Later Years of the Saturday Club, 1870–1927* (1927).

6. William Dean Howells, *A Life in Letters*, ed. Mildred Howells, 2 vols. (1928), 2:277.

7. William Dean Howells, *My Mark Twain*, in Edmund Wilson, *The Shock of Recognition*, 2 vols. (1943), 2:695.

8. Jay B. Hubbell Jr., *The South in American Literature, 1607–1900* (1954), 396.

9. Ellen Glasgow, *The Woman Within* (1954), 139.

10. Johnson, *Remembered Yesterdays*, 446.

11. Louise Hall Tharp, *Saint-Gaudens and the Gilded Age* (1969), 250.

12. Wilson, *Shock of Recognition*, 2:1238–41.

13. Clara Marburg Kirk, *W. D. Howells and Art in His Time* (1965), viii.

14. William Dean Howells, *Literature and Life* (1902), 179–80.

15. Kenton Clymer Jr., *John Hay: The Gentleman as Diplomat* (1975), 3.

16. Ibid., 5–6.

17. Henry Adams, *Selected Letters*, ed. Newton Arvin (1951), 37.

18. Henry Adams, *The Education of Henry Adams*, ed. Sentry (1961), 64.

19. Ibid., 496–97.

20. Johnson, *Remembered Yesterdays*, 447.

21. Adams, *Education*, 505.

22. Carol F. Baird, "Albert Bushnell Hart: The Rise of Professional History," in *The Social Sciences at Harvard, 1865–1920*, ed. Paul H. Buck (1965), 135, 136.

23. Laurence R. Veysey, *Emergence of the American University* (1965), 200.

24. Ibid., 216.

25. Horace Coon, *Columbia: Collossus on the Hudson* (1947), 173.

26. Howells, *Life in Letters*, 2:1.

27. Dan Levin, *Stormy Petrel: The Life and Work of Maxim Gorky* (1965), 120–31.

28. Glasgow, *The Woman Within*, 140–42.

❧ INDEX ❧

Index

⊰ ABOUT THE AUTHOR ⊱

GILMAN MARSTON OSTRANDER was author of over a dozen books on American intellectual and cultural history including *A Concise History of the United States; The Rights of Man in America, 1606–1861; Early Colonial Thought; American Civilization in the First Machine Age, 1890–1940; The Prohibition Movement in California, 1848–1933;* and *Nevada: The Great Rotten Borough, 1859–1964.* After earning his doctorate at the University of California at Berkeley in 1952, Ostrander embarked on a teaching career that spanned some thirty-five years, including stints at Reed College, Ohio State University, the University of Missouri, Michigan State University, and the University of Waterloo in Canada. At the University of Waterloo, where he was professor of history from 1971 until his death, he helped found the bilingual journal *Historical Reflections/Reflexions Historiques.*

COLOPHON

Republic of Letters is typeset in Monotype Dante, a digitized version of a typeface originally designed by Giovanni Mardesteig in 1954. Dante is one of the great achievements of twentieth-century typography: a finely tooled and stately neohumanist roman coupled with a lively and lucid italic.

Designed by Gregory M. Britton

Typeset by Kevin Morrissey

Printed by Sheridan Books